Sacred and Ceremonial Textiles

Proceedings of the
Fifth Biennial Symposium
of the Textile Society of America, Inc.

Chicago, Illinois
1996

Textile Society of America, Inc.

SACRED AND CEREMONIAL TEXTILES
PROCEEDINGS OF THE FIFTH BIENNIAL SYMPOSIUM
OF THE TEXTILE SOCIETY OF AMERICA, INC.

ISBN 0-9645106-1-8

This volume contains papers delivered at the Fifth Biennial
Symposium of the Textile Society of America, Inc. held at
The Art Institute of Chicago, Chicago, Illinois, September 19-21, 1996

The Textile Society of America, Inc. provides a forum for the exchange and dissemination of information about the historic, cultural, socio-economic, artistic, and technical aspects of textiles. It was founded in 1987 and is governed by a Board of Directors which includes scholars from museums and universities, as well as fiber artists.

The *Proceedings* of each biennial symposium are distributed as a benefit of membership. The previous titles are:

1988 *Textiles as Primary Sources*
1990 *Textiles in Trade*
1992 *Textiles in Daily Life*
1994 *Contact, Crossover, Continuity*

Titles still in print are available for $35.00 each (US currency only), postage included. Payment may be by check or money order drawn on a US bank or by Visa card. Make checks payable to Textile Society of America, Inc. For Visa orders, include the credit card number, expiration date, and name as it appears on the card. For information about publications, write: Kathleen Epstein, 4502 Poteau Circle, Austin, Texas 78734.

For information about membership, write: Textile Society of America, Inc.
3010 Hennepin Avenue S. #231, Minneapolis, MN 55408.

Cover photo: Detail of a chalice veil, Italy, about 1680.
Linen, plain weave; edged with linen, needle lace with raised details.
Courtesy The Art Institute of Chicago, restricted gift of Louise Lutz, 1991.549.

CONTENTS

Session 5

Panel: Sacred and Ceremonial Textiles and the Constitution of Value in Africa

Session 6

Sessions 7 and 8

PREFACE

The Fifth Biennial Symposium of the Textile Society of America, Inc. was hosted by The Department of Textiles at The Art Institute of Chicago, Chicago, Illinois from September 19-21, 1996. This *Proceedings* contains the thirty-one papers and one abstract of a paper presented at the symposium, plus introductions or abstracts of the five videos presented.

The theme 'Sacred and Ceremonial Textiles' was chosen so that researchers throughout the world, working within a wide range of cultures and time periods, could offer participants the broadest possible exploration of this important universal subject. The resulting papers offer a wide variety of points of view including: glimpses into the structure and use of textiles that are central to ancient traditional ceremonies; speculations about the faraway origins of others; the inspiration and evolution of contemporary sculptural forms based on textile models; along with a review of laundry, a common domestic ritual.

In the course of the sessions some presenters considered the role that textiles have played in private or in public ceremonies, the textiles' types and construction, the visual appearance of ceremonial costumes and the textiles of which they are constructed, and modern adaptations of traditional textiles.

Rita J. Adrosko, Curator Emeritus, Smithsonian Institution

Sacred Textile Banners of Japan

Monica Bethe

Exploratory rather than definitive, this paper summarizes some controlling concepts that inform the sacred banners of Japan, touching particularly on their form, function, and fabrics used in early banners. Interwoven with my ideas are some of the concerns that came up in discussion (small print), reflecting the pan-Asian implications of the topic.

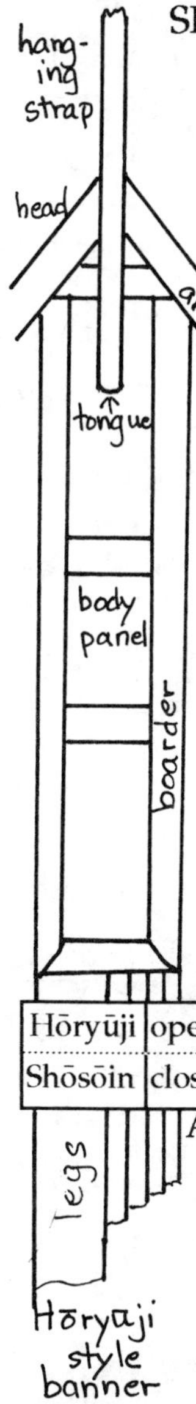

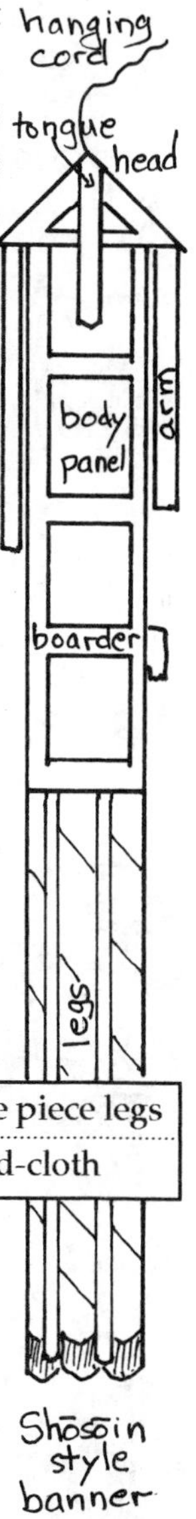

SHORT HISTORY. Banners traveled to Japan with the earliest introduction of Buddhism. The *Chronicles of Japan* record that in 552 the king of Paekché sent the essential trappings of Buddhism to Emperor Kinmei of Japan: a gilt bronze image to worship, sutras (scriptures) to chant, and canopies and banners for adornment and ceremonial functions.[1] Then Prince Shotoku (572-621) made Buddhism the state religion and in 607 founded the monastery of Hōryūji, which preserves till today the oldest banners and the oldest depiction of banners in Japan.[2]

The construction of the seventh century banners parallels that of 6th and 7th c. Chinese banners, as found in Dunhuang and Turfan and as depicted on the walls of the Buddhist caves dotting the Silk Road. All the components of the baner are present: head, tongue, arms, segmented body and multiple legs. Large numbers of such banners were made in the late seventh and the eighth century and many have been preserved both at Hōryūji and at the Shōsōin Repository of the temple of the great Buddha, Tōdaiji. Although the basic elements remain constant, the proportions of the banners and some fabrics change over the years, reflecting changes in Chinese styles.

Hōryūji	open head		extension arms	wide boarders	3 elongated panels	single piece legs
Shōsōin	closed, equilateral	attached		narrow	4 or 5 near-square	joined-cloth

Almost every type of silk weave, surface decoration technique and braid (see Kinoshita essay) found in textiles of the ancient period (7th-8th c.) are represented in the banners. Thus, the possibility of dating banners through tracing the evolution of their form, verified by inscriptions and temple records, has provided scholars with an invaluable key to dating textiles in general.[3]

(Hōryūji style banner diagram labels: hanging strap, head, arms, tongue, body panel, boarder, legs — Hōryūji style banner)

(Shōsōin style banner diagram labels: hanging cord, tongue, head, body panel, arm, boarder, legs — Shōsōin style banner)

❋┼

Whether the anthropomorphic labels used by the Japanese, Chinese (and Tai) for the parts of the banner were symbolic or merely conventional (as the Japanese profess) became a recurrent topic in the discussions after my speech. I suspect the terms to be Chinese. Parallels with the Yogic concepts of centers energy in the body were suggested. These concepts would have traveled east by way of Tibetan Buddhism.

❋┼

Unfortunately essentially no textiles remain from the 9th-12th centuries (Heian period) due to the destruction and the dispersion of court culture connected with the civil wars ending in 1185. Although actual examples Heian banners no longer exist, painted depictions verify a continuation of the same format and extensive use for a variety of purposes. Thirteenth century Japanese banners, of which a number are preserved abroad as well as in Japan, reveal a very fixed, balanced form with three, essentially square segments making up the body.[4] The majority of these banners are embroidered with Buddhist figures and symbols and contain the intriguing element of rendering the hair with actual human hair, possibly from the devotee. Later banners may have arms folded in along the sides. Extant banners from the early sixteenth century and on (see Maruyama essay) are often assembled from scraps of garments dedicated to the temple for the repose of a soul. Similar recycling can be seen in Buddha's injunctions to patch together the mendicant's robe (*kesa*) from various types of cast-off rags.

13th & 14th

arms-in style

16th c. with recycled garments

So far I have not come across scriptures detailing the construction of a banner, naming its parts, or prescribing the materials of its construction. Japanese today do not feel there are set rules, only customs. Recycling may have been operative from early on. There are 8th c. examples of the same fabric being used in banners and for cushion covers, but we also know that new fabric was produced specifically for banners. Left over scraps must have been used.

FUNCTIONS

Banners appear in and around a temple ground, some hung permanently, others hung for special occasions, and still others carried in ceremonies. Materials include cloth, metal, wood, jewels, rope and paper. Easy to store, they impart a grandiose impact when unfurled. Symbolic import based on the scriptures authorizes their use.

Temple adornment

Chikō Mandala 1200

Most commonly, banners are found decorating the holy area hung above, beside and around a Buddhist image. As such they evoke a vision of Buddha's world where celestial beings, Buddhas, bodhisatvas and other enlightened 'souls' reside in perpetual beauty among fragrant flowers, gleaming jewels and sweet music. Banners are described as adoring the holy stupa in the sky, and as offered in homage to the Buddha, incurring merit to the donor. The adornment is perpetually perpetrated through fresh offerings and supplication.

painting on Tamamushi Shrine 7th.

Itsuku-shima Shrine

Garland Sutra 12th c.

> In front of Buddha a Stupa... sprang up... decorated wih precious things ... and countless banners and flags and jewel garlands ... All... paid homage to the stupa with flowers, perfumes, garlands, streamers, canopies, and music... Everywhere jewel-decked awnings were spread, banners and canopies hung ...[5]

The origins for this vision can be found in India in the decoration of the holy stupa with flowers and streamers, both generally offerings. Along the same lines, in Japan for special services a normal room may be converted into a holy area by hanging cloth and flowers in the form of banners and garlands (keman) along the beams.

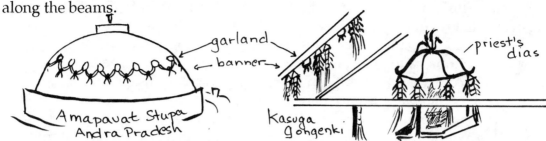

The close connection between the banner and the stupa rises in part from the stupa as a representation of the Buddha, fittingly adorned with signs of Indian royalty, such as canopies, banners and flowers and jewels. Buddha is shown preaching and meditating under canopies hung with banners. In Japanese temples banners (or jewel bells) hang at the corners of canopies set above the Buddhist image, the altar implements (esoteric), and above priest's seat.

The canopy bedecked with banners can be traced also, I believe, to a central story of Buddhism, that of Shakyamuni sitting under the Bodhi tree, fighting off the many temptations of the Mara and finally at dawn defeating them by revealing to them the banner, or the light, of his wisdom. His Enlightenment is synonymous with the unfurling of the banner that dispels Chaos and establishes Order. In Mahayana Buddhism, the Buddha Ratnaketu-- "jewel banner" or "jewel light" (ketu meaning both banner and light) embodies this banner of light appearing with the first rays of the sun (Agni, or fire, in the Vedic world), the revelation of the Dharma, the light of Wisdom that severs and dispels the darkness of ignorance.[6]

As pointed out at the conference, the banner as *ketu* also becomes the central shaft, or *axis mundi*

Representing the sun's rays with strips of cloth might be best effected with long narrow strips, and such streamers can be seen, for instance in the Indian practice of hanging narrow strips of cloth from the sacred bodhi tree to memorialize Shakyamuni's enlightenment.[7] In a Chinese metal repoussé we see the Buddha sitting under a canopy-like tree strung with pendants and tassels. (Here I use "pendant" for dangling decorations, often stones or beads, "streamer" for long strips of cloth straight off the loom, and "tassel" for appendages to larger objects.)[8] In an 8th century embroidery of the Buddha Preaching (Nara National Museum) we see him under a "jewel" tree whose branches are entwined with a canopy and strung with tassels. Dunhuang relics and wall paintings show the Buddha siting under a canopy with banner-like tassels forming a fringe and classic banners (with heads, arms and legs) hung at the corners.

In 12th century Japanese depictions of the Pure Land the canopy is often a roof with tassel-banners hanging along the rim and standard banners (or bells) from the eaves.[9] Banners may appear again in the bottom section of these paintings, particularly of illustrations of the Garland or Lotus Sutras where figures offer banners, gaining merit and opening an avenue for mortals to eventually enter the everlasting world of bliss.

In considering the banner context, a cluster of imagery emerges: tree, stupa, canopy, banner, streamer, jeweled pendants, bells. Telescoping and magnification operate. Microcosms contain macrocosms and a part may not only stand for the whole, but incorporate the whole within it. Just as the stupa signifies the *axis mundi*, the Buddha, the tree of life, and a multiplicity of other things, so also the triangular-headed banner decorating the stupa replicates the pagoda (stupa) form, and might thereby signify it. On some later banners the imagery may be regenerated with the banner containing a depiction of a pagoda, or of yet another banner.[10]

Banner with Bodhisattva holding a banner Dunhuang (Seoul N. Museum)

Stupa (Fresco, Kucha 5th c.

Banners as weapons against evil

The obvious military implications of the banner used to vanquish the evil enemy echoes secular uses of the banner, as a standard to rally forces in battle. Military imagery can be found elsewhere in the sutras. The *Holy Teachings of the Vimalakirti* describe how the Bodhisattvas "raise their standard (banners) on the field of enlightenment."[11] The *Kyōyō shinshō* presents religious endeavor as a metaphorical battle, stating that prayer " is like the banner of the brave warrior because it can disperse the entire army of evil spirits"[12] Various of the guardian deities that inhabit the Buddhist world appear dressed in armor and some carry flags: squares of cloth with appended strips. These flags, attached at two corners to a pole or spear, are the horizontal counterpart to the vertical banner and their prototype can be seen in Chinese war flags. Wielded against evil, the flags hold the enemy at bay as Bishamonten does in the Hekija-e: Painting of the Annihilations of the Demons (12th c., Nara National Museum). The spears of guardians, even when not equipped with square-tailed flags, generally have at least a strip of cloth tied to them and flapping in the wind. The prototype for such simple flags can be seen on the walls of Ajunta, India.

Hekija-e (12th c.)

Chinese tomb fresco (711)

Jap. simple "flag"

Depictions of Shakyamuni and 16 heavenly beings (*Shaka jūroku zenshino*) show him flanked on one side by a figure holding a vertical banner and on the other one holding a horizontal flag. Although there is no absolute correspondence, generally a gentle figure holds the banner, a military figure the flag. (Everywhere bodhisattvas hold vertical banners only)

Ajunta

These paintings were set up for the recitation of the Heart Sutra (*dai hannya kyō*) to avert calamity. The depicted banners here serve two ends: to protect against evil encroachment and to mark the identity of the crowd of figures.

←Banners flanking Shakyamuni→

Hōryūji 14th c.

Banners as ensigns and to lead processions

Held high the banner is a signpost calling all to a gathering. For processions banners are carried like standards and function as an ensign of the presence of the Buddha or Bodhisattva. The Buddhist iconography derives from ancient Indian practice, where the king's entourage usually carried a canopy over the king to keep him in the shade and a banner to announce his presence. A similar function informs the custom in Tang China, recorded by the Japanese monk Ennin, of flying banners from tall temple buildings to advertise the presence of a holy spot, much as a medieval castle flew pendants from its towers.[13] Today for festivals, Japanese fly long strips of five colors stitched into a tubular form at one end (*fuskinagashi*) from high poles.[14]

fukinagashi

The function as an ensign is acted out in ritual processions and depicted in paintings. Particularly beautiful examples can be seen in the Pure Land Buddhist *raigo*, or Descent of Buddha (usually Amida) ceremonies and paintings. Surrounded by a host of 25 Bodhisattvas Amida descends to transport the deceased to his Pure Land. Among the host is always one Bodhisattva who leads carrying a canopy to place over the deceased, and another with a banner waving in the breeze.

stupa fresco Kazil 7th c.

raigo-e

Banners to measure out and mark sacred space

For festivals and rituals banners are set up to mark out sacred space: usually circumscribing the precincts, or at least standing at the cardinal directions, and lining the sides of the approach. They may be hung from long poles set in ground foundations, or from the rafters of buildings. The hundreds of banners made for the inauguration ceremony, or Eye Opening, of the Great Buddha at Tōdaiji in 752 must have been used, in part at least, to establish the sacred area. When recently they celebrated the reroofing of Tōdaiji with gala performances reminiscent of the 752 celebration, they hung large replicas of 8th c. banners on high poles set along the approach and about the precincts as well as from the eaves of the building. The banner poles (both stationary and carried) have intricately modeled heads, the most popular form being in the shape of a dragon. From the dragon's mouth the banner streams downward. Protectors of Buddhism, dragons are creatures

Possible placement of banners

Banner staff (Hoam Art Museum Korea) 12th~13th c

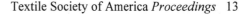

of the clouds and water who control the rainfall. They have been depicted spurting water over the new-born Shakyamuni.[15] The imagery is repeated when large banners (*daikanjōban*) are placed over the head of an initiate during an ordination ceremony, during which his head is sprinkled with water.

Banners as ceremonial tools

Banners may be carried during a ceremony and used symbolically. In some ordinations (*kanjō*) the banner is made to flow over the forehead of the ordained thus transmitting the virtue of the Buddha inherent in the banner to the initiate.[16] The popular use of banners for ordinations in the early Japanese Buddhism is reflected in there being 14 *kanjō* banners dated to 747 at Hōryūji and 12 of the same date at Daianji and many more from 757 in the Shōsōin.

Offeratory banners

Offering banners to gain merit and ensure success gave birth to a variety of specific types of offertory banners (see Takeda essay).[17] The use of an offertory banner constitutes a prayer for the soul of the maker, the person for whom it was made, and any person whose belongings (hair, garment) are incorporated in the banner. At the same time it brings them merit. An obvious and early form of supplication with banners was to pray for health. Already in the 3rd c. BC King Ashoka is said to have had a miraculous recovery from severe sickness by having banners set on the posts of his bed. His life was extended 12 years.[18] Banners for the dead (*semmōia* or *myōkaban*) assure extra merit in after life. A number of banners, one from 688, inscribed with the name of the deceased, date and the word *myōkaban* remain in Hōryūji. They are mostly plain weave, solid color banners with spindly arms and some have filled in heads (unusual for Hōryūji banners). For funerals today, plain strips of inscribed white cloth are slung from poles and carried in the funerary procession, one at each of the four corners of the coffin. Prayers for the dead continue at set intervals. In 757 Japan held a state ritual to memorialize the first anniversary of the death of Emperor Shōmu. For this, records indicate that over 2500 banners were used, most produced in the space of one year. Some remian in the Shōsōin, others were sent as thank you payment to the provinces.

Buddha just born (chinese woodblock)

Votive banner (nobori)

688 banner Hōryūji

TEXTILES BANNERS at Hōryūji and the Shōsōin.

The vast majority of the extant 7th and 8th century textiles of Japan are preserved in Hōryūji and the Shōsōin. While the former include banners possibly from as early as the 650s, most of the banners in the Shōsōin were made in the 750s, many produced for two state-wide gala ceremonies: the Eye Opening of the Great Buddha (752) and the First Anniversary of the Death of Emperor Shōmu (757).[19] Even in the five years between these two ceremonies, dynamic changes can be seen in the textile techniques and patterns.

❀❀❀❀❀❀❀❀❀❀❀❀❀❀❀❀❀❀❀❀❀❀❀❀❀❀❀❀❀❀❀❀❀

TYPES OF FABRIC IN BANNERS[20]

Hōryūji	plain weave :solid color, crepe, ikat	nishiki*	aya**	
Shōsōin	plain weave, solid color, crepe	nishiki	aya	gauze

TYPES OF SURFACE DESIGN

Hōryūji	embroidery, ink
Shōsōin	embroidery, painting, block resist, bind resist, wax resist (hand painted, block printed (stenciling?) , gold painting

*NISHIKI FABRICS WITH MULTICOLORED PATTERN WARP OR WEFT

Hōryūji	warp *nishiki*	geometric links	beaded medallions	
Shōsōin 752	warp & weft	geometric links		*karahana*
Shōsōin 757	mostly weft		a few medallions	*karahana*

**AYA: FIGURED FABRICS

(TWILL PATTERN ON PAIN GROUND, OR AGAINST TWILL IN THE SAME OR THE OPPOSITE DIRECTION)

Hōryūji	plain ground	geometric links	beaded medallions	
Shōsōin 752	mostly plain / some twill	geometric links		*karahana*
Shōsōin 757	mostly twill / some plain	geometric links	beaded medallions	*karahana*

❀❀❀❀❀❀❀❀❀❀❀❀❀❀❀❀❀❀❀❀❀❀❀❀❀❀❀❀❀❀❀❀❀

The implications in the shift from warp to weft patterning, from multicolored to single color weft patterning, from Persian-inspired designs to Chinese and their Japanization, etc. are discussed in detail by Japanese scholars.[21] Topics touched on include imported versus Japanese-produced cloth, technique and weave structure; also sociological implications such as the textile artisans employed by the central court, the dissemination of techniques to the provinces, and the role of tax and tribute paid in cloth.

Rather than repeat this information, I would like to pose a few questions.

◆◆◆◆◆◆◆◆◆◆◆◆◆◆◆◆◆◆◆◆◆◆◆◆◆◆◆◆◆◆◆◆◆◆◆◆◆◆◆

The early *ikat* found in the *kantō* (or *kanton*) banners of Hōryūji (now at Tokyo National Museum) and the few fragments of multicolored *ikat* in the Shōsōin were probably imported. From where? Uemura Rokurō suggests that the argument that the name "Kanton" reflects their origin in Canton, i.e. South China, is simplistic.[22] He points out smilarities in motif to Tai and Indian *ikat*. Similarities to modern Afghan *ikat* were mentioned in the conference.

✳✳✳✳✳✳✳✳✳✳✳✳✳✳✳✳✳✳✳✳✳✳✳✳✳✳✳✳✳✳✳✳✳✳✳✳✳✳✳

Kyōkechi, or block resist, described and illustrated in Ms. Bernard's presentation, is the most frequent form of surface decoration on Shōsōin banners. Introduced from Tang China (only a few, very simple examples remain), it flourished with highly sophisticated results for a short period in the 8th century, but then died out, except for a very simplified process known as *itajime* restricted to decorating linings for aristocratic ladies. Several attempts have been made to reconstruct the old technique. Yamanobe Tomoyuki investigates the Indian origins of block resist.[23] Takada Yoshio describes his reconstruction experiments for the Ise fabrics.[24] A major difference between the Ise pieces and the Shōsōin pieces is that the former uses the cloth flat, while the latter created symmetrical patterns through folds, and possibly used a system of stacking blocks so more fabrics could be dyed at once.

✳✳

What did "Five Color Banners" (*goshiki ban*) look like? Were they five different solid color banners? Or are the many banners with strips of different color legs in the Hōryūji Five Color Banners? What about those with blocks of different plain colors composing the body (Hōryūji and Dunhuang)?

❊❊

Was the diagonal division of banner sections merely aesthetic?

✳✳

Are the single panel gauze banners with fluted diamond lozenges (a pattern found only on the 757 Shōsōin banners) a variation on the diagonal theme, or do they represent a more general flower-in-diamond motif, possibly inspired by the lotus-in-square motif found in Buddhist iconography?

~~~~~~

There is no way of telling whether the 8th c. Japanese understood the original intent of the motifs they were copying. Japanese today tend not to want to read symbolism into motifs, but rather to enjoy their visual interplay. Instinctively they view decorative elements with an emotive response. Patterns evoke poetic allusions, seasonal ambiences. Matsumoto (1984) suggests this native instinct can be seen already in the Japanization of the Persian motifs on the banners made in 757. Yet one wonders whether, for instance, the "arrow " (chevron) pattern used for many of the flat braids was not a protective device to "shoot off" encroaching evil.

✳✳

Banner associations with the five elements are intreguing, but so far unresearched, to my knowledge: Fire (*ketu* :agni), water (dragons), wood (cloth, dyes), metal (decorative elements), earth (marking out areas. And air: wind. See note 14.

✳✳

Were there sewing stipulations for banners? Who did the sewing? How were the materials chosen? How were they given body: we see paper lining reinforcement,bamoo stifeners, metal reinforcement, double thickness for heads, and strengthening through embroidery and patchwork layering. Obviously the choice of stiffer fabrics, like *nishiki* for boarders, heads, and weights at the end of the feet must also be considered.

◆◆

Finally, both in China and Japan textile banners remained abstract patchworks of color and shape until the mid to late in the 8th century.[25] Perhaps the earliest painted representational banner is one in the Shōsōin showing a seated Bodhisattva in each of the four sections of the banner body. Of slightly later date are the many stunning banners of painted figures found in Khocho and Dunhuang including some elaborately articulated banner mandalas.[26] The new emphasis put on painting by the esoteric (Tantric) sects must have contributed to the sudden outburst of these representational banners and presumably to a shift in their use. Extant 13th century Japanese embroidered banners clearly function as a canvas for figures that might be hung in the altar, and not merely as decorations around it.[27] These banners are similar to embroidered hanging scrolls of the period. [28]

▼▼

[1] W.G. Aston, *Nihongi : Chronicles of Japan from the Earliest Times to A.D. 697* (Vermont and Tokyo, Tuttle. 1972) Vol. 2p. 65. Another present, from Silla, sent in 622 included 13 banners (p. 149)

[2] The Tamamushi zushi, a portable shrine of Lady Tachibana with paintings on its sides. One depicts Buddha preaching to the dragon king in a pavillion with banners hanging from its pillars.

[3] This field has been well researched by such Japanese textile historians as Matsumoto Kaneo, [including "Shōsoin no senshokuban, zengohen" (The Textile Banners of the Shōsōin) in *Shosōin nempō* (Annual Report on the Shōsōin) vol. 3&4 (Nara: Office of the Shosōin, Imperial Household Agency, 1981-82). *Shōsōin no nishiki* , no 293 of Nihon no bijutsu, (Tokyo: Shibundo, 1990) and *Shōsōin no senshoku,* no102 of *Nihon no bijutsu* (Tokyo: Shibundo 1964). Aslo Okumura Hideo, "Nihon jōdai no ban ni tsuite" (Japanese Banners of the Ancient Period) in *Hōryōji kennō kōmotsu: senshoku I* (Treasures from the Hōryūji: Textiles I)(Tokyo National Museum, 1986). Sawada Mutsuyo, including "Senshoku: genshi kodai" (Textiles: prehistoric and ancient periods)no. 263 in *Nihon no bijutsu* (Tokyo: Shibundo, 1988) and various reports on restoration of banners in *Museum* (Tokyo National Museum, 1992, 1994,1995). A good English language reference is Matsumoto K., *Jōdaigire* (Kyoto: Shikosha, 1984) and his article "The construction of Ancient Cloth Banners: Hōryūji style and Shosōin style" in *The treasures of the Shōsōin: buddhist and Ritual Implements* , Mitsumori M, ed. (Kyoto: Shikosha) 1993.

[4] Hickman, M. "Notes on Buddhist Banners" *Boston Museum Bulletin* 71 (1973) #363 p 4-20. Kitamura, T. " On the Embroidered Banners in the Henushi Shrine" *Bijutsushi* Vol 7 No. 2 (1957) p. 59-68. *Shubutsu* (Tokyo: Kadokawa shoten 1964).

[5] Katō, B. et al tr. *The Three-fold Lotus Sutra* (Tokyo: Kosei Publishing Co., 1975) p. 195-6, 198.

[6] Snodgrass, A., *The Symbolism of the Stupa* (Ithaca, N.Y.: Cornell U. SEAsia Program 1985) p. 172.

[7] Sekine, S. *Butsu/bosatsu to donai no shōgon, Nihon no bijutsu* #281 (Tokyo: Shibundo, 1989) p. 94, fig. 14.

[8] Sanskrit words for banner include: 1) *ketu,* (J:*bukki* 仏旗) discussed earlier. 2) *hvaja* (J: *dō* 幢), hung from a pillar or pole and symbolizing the virtue of the law that wardsoff evil. 3)*pataka* , (J: *ban* 幡) banners of merit. Numerous variations exist in Japan and according to Sekine(1989:93) even in India they are not strictly distinguished .

[9] Bells or bell pendants are common today. Early banners, particularly metal ones, often had bells for arms and legs.

[10] 9th and 10th c. Chinese banners abound in depictions of figures carrying banners. For interesting Tai parallels see Gittinger,M. & Lefferts, L. *Textiles and the Tai Experience in Southeast Asia* (The Textile Museum, Washington D.C. 1992) p130, pl 3.41.

[11] Thurman,R. tr. *Holy Teachings of the Vimalakirti* (University Park, Pen U. Press, 1976), p. 68

[12] Ishida, M. ed., *Kyōgyō Shinshō* (Kyoto: Ryūkoku U., 1966) p. 73

[13] Reischauer, E.O. *Ennin's diary* (New York: Ronald Press, 1955)

[14] The five colors--blue (often represented as green) yellow, red, white and black (often represented as purple). The Japanese trace these to the Ancient Chinese *gogyo* system of associating the colors with compas directions, virtues, parts of the body, pitches, etc. but the Indians also seem to have had a similar type color association. The *fukinagashi,* or "blown streamer" has secular and non Buddhist ritual parallels , in particular in April and May for the celebration of Boy's day, many households fly carp streamers (*koinobori*) with the top-most streamer being the *fukinagashi.*

[15] Legge M. tr. *A Record of Buddhist Kingdoms: Fa Hsien's Diary.* (N.Y.: Dover Press 1965) p. 66

[16] *Hōbōgirin: Dictionnaire Encyclopédique du Bouddhisme d"après les Sources Chinoises et Japonaises* (LAcademie Impériale du Japon, 1981) p. 49-50. Reischauer 1955, p 302 describes a *kanjō* baptism wehre "5 jars of water were poured on my head. At night I made offerings to the 12 heavens banners...."

[17] The Ordination Sutra (*kanjōkyō* , Ch. 11) lists the benefits incurred by donating banners.

[18] T. 449 stipulates lighting lamps at seven levels and suspending banners of five colors to prolong life and cure illness. Story in Ttt 2040x and 2123x.

[19] Mitsumori, M. ed. *The Treasures of the Shōsōin:: Buddhist and Ritual Implements* (Kyoto: shikosha, 1993)p. 11. As the inscriptions are written in the Chinese cyclical year system, they could be off.

[20] These charts are a simplification of Table III in Matsumoto,1984, p 216.

[21] See note 3. Recently in English: Matsumoto 1984, Mitsumori 1993, Matsumoto *Shosoin Textiles* (Kyoto: Kyoto Shōin, 1993).

[22] Uemura, R. "*Indo no kasuri to sono shūhen* "(Indian *ikat* and its repercussions)*Senshoku to Seikatsu* no. 11, Winter '75:138-142

[23] Yamanobe, T. "*Indo no kyōkechizome*' (Indian block resist dyeing)*Senshoku to Seikatsu* no. 11, Winter '75: 133-137

[24] Takada, Y. "*Kyōkechi fukugen no koro* " (When I recreated *kyōkechi*) *Senshoku to seikats* No. 17, Summer '77 p 50-53.

[25] Hickman 1973, p. 11- 13

[26] Today many of these are in the Musée Guimmet in Paris, the British Museum, London, the Otani coleection in the Seoul National Museum, Korea, and the Tokyo National Museum.

[27] The embroidered banners at Henushi Shrine are believed to be representations of the 32 lesser deities of the Kongōkai, meant to surround the five central figures. See Kitamura Tetsuo, "On the Embroidered Banners in the Henushi Shrine" *Bijutsushi: Journal of the Japan Art History Society,* Ocober 1957.

[28] Indeed the banner and hanging scroll have a related structure. Not only the triangular head and elongated body are similar, but also technical parallels can be seen in the considerations necessary to stabilize the patchwork of different weight cloths and to maintain the shape by strengthening it at the top and weighting it at the bottom. One wonders at the origin of such nonfunctional parts of the hanging scroll as the *futai* decorative strips descending from the spot where the triangular hanging cords are attached. The *fuchin* , or supplementary tassels, function like the feet of the banner to stabilize the hanging scroll.

Braids on Early Japanese Banners

Masako Kinoshita
5 Winthrop Place, Ithaca, NY 14850

INTRODUCTION

The silk braids which adorn some banners in the Hōryūji and Shōsōin collections represent the four basic types of braids from the seventh and eighth centuries in Japan (Fig. 1). Of the four, type I, the square braid, is found primarily as hanging cord. Type II, the four-ridge flat braid with a twill pattern, was used as trimming around design figures.[1] Types III and IV, the oblique ribbed twine braid and the braid with a plain-weave pattern respectively, are flat and generally wider than the first two types. They compose the "head," "tongue," and "arms" of some banners, giving a necessary firmness to the shape of the banners (Fig. 2). Narrow braids of Type III were occasionally used as edge trimmings. To my knowledge, no banner adorned with braids from later era has yet been found.

Some braids in the Hōryūji collection have been attributed to be of Chinese origin.[2] It has been generally understood that braiding techniques were also brought to Japan by Koreans in the sixth century. I have not yet had a chance to trace the Japanese braiding techniques back to their origin.

The construction of these braids has puzzled modern braiders versed in traditional Japanese braiding techniques known as *kumihimo*.[3] Kumihimo braiders felt that the uniformity of the patterns as well as the difficulty of handling the large number of the fine gauge strands of the loose degummed silk in such long lengths as one finds in the ancient braids eliminated the possibility of their having been made with braiding techniques other than kumihimo. On the other hand, it proved difficult for them to replicate the pliancy of the old braids. They also realized that the build-in structural symmetry of ancient square braids does not agree with that of square braids made using kumihimo. I believe such discrepancies have arisen because the ancient braids were not made with kumi- himo techniques using elements with individually separated working ends, but rather with loop-manipulation techniques in which working ends of elements were tied into fixed pairs.[4]

I have reconstructed this method of braiding from three manuscripts written around 1800 AD and labeled it *kute-uchi*, or "hand-strap braiding," borrowing a term used in them.[5] The loops, or paired elements tied to the hand-strap, kute, forming a loop, are supported singly on the fingers or held in the hands. A beater is the only tool required. The adopted name, however, is used in a wider context than was meant in the nineteenth century, when the more elaborate techniques used in the middle ages had already been long lost.

Although similar techniques known collectively as loop-manipulation are found throughout the world, the Japanese methods have proven to be the most developed.[6] The most common world-wide practice is to support the loops singly on the fingers (finger-held method) and transfer each loop through the inside or over the other loops. In Japan, they are also held in the hands (hand-held method) and transferred around the outside of the other loops as well.[7] Because of these two modes of loop transfers and the fact that more loops can be used with the hand-held method, Japanese techniques have developed to a unique height during the twelfth century.

In order to prove my hypothesis that the ancient braids were made with loop-manipulation and not kumihimo, I conducted an extensive analysis of construction methods, and surveyed the ancient braid specimens by existing data from published sources.[8] I also made replicas and compared them with the originals. In each of four types of braids found on the ancient banners, kute-uchi braids proved closer to the original than kumihimo braids.

In *kute-uchi*, the elements are stretched between the fixed head end to working looped ends where they are mounted on the fingers or aligned over the hands (Fig. 3, 4). The braiding elements, even if they are soft non-plied silk such as used in Shōsin braids, do not tangle or wear out because they are transferred by one loop at a time while they are held taut. For braids with a large number of elements, several braiders collaborate sitting side by side.
The number of elements used in the old braids with a solid structure is a multiple of an odd number, such as 28 (=7x4), 56 (=7x8), and 72 (=9x8). To make the kinds of braids found in historical braids using kute-uchi would require either an odd number or a multiple of an odd number of loops, which makes the basis of the number of elements an odd number times two. In contrast, using kumihimo, the number of the loops would more likely be based on an even number, such as 32 (=8x4). Color designs of the majority of old braids are based on an odd number. If braiding starts with an odd number of loops in hand, as kute-uchi does, it is only natural to compose a color design based on an odd number. Moreover, the braids made using kute-uchi turn out to resemble closely the old specimens in pliancy and appearance, while using kumihimo techniques involve complex and contrived procedures yet results are far less satisfactory.

TYPE I: SQUARE BRAID. (Fig. 1 left)
Twenty of the 240 surveyed square braids in the Shōsōin collection are listed as having belonged to banners.[9] Six among them have been identified as hanging cords. Many among the 84 specimens listed as being of unknown origin could have belonged to banners. The majority of the square braids are 1.5 to 3.5 mm (1/16" to 5/32") wide and less than 100 cm (40") long.

Before examining the old specimens, let's discuss the kute-uchi construction procedure for square braids and the structural characteristics of the braid.
The principle for constructing square braids using kute-uchi or loop-manipulation is essentially the same regardless of ethnic origin, the number of the loops used or how the loops are held; An odd number of loops is more often used, and they are distributed initially so that one hand gets the extra one (Figs. 5, 6, left).[10] For an even number of loops, they are allotted equally to each hand (Figs 5, 6, right) While the maximum number of loops that can be used is usually seven for the single-person finger-held method, a larger number of loops can be used with the hand-held method.[11] The loops are transferred one at a time, from one hand to the other in one pick and twisted a half turn before being deposited on the other hand. The procedure is mirror symmetric

and all loops circulate in a serial order. In the structure thus produced, each of the two elements forming a loop is interlaced as an individual element composing two superimposed layers. This makes the number of elements of the square braid the number of loops times two.

A square braid is described more specifically as a four-ridge tubular braid with a twill pattern. The square braids constructed using loop-manipulation always have an irregular twill pattern. While those made with an odd number of loops having a twill pattern, such as 3/4/4/3 or 4/5/5/4 and a trapezoidal cross section, those made using an even number of loops have a twill pattern, which may be 2/3/4/3 or 3/4/5/4, and a cross section of an irregular quadrangle (Fig. 7). They would never have a true square cross section such as those made using the kumihimo technique. Since those made using an odd number of loops are less skewed than those made using an even number of loops, the former predominates in any culture where square braids are made by means of loop-manipulation.

The Shōsōin square braids

According to the statistics published in the survey records of the Shōsōin braids carried out by the Office of Shōsōin, out of 240 registered square braids, including those used for the banners, two thirds had the element number of an odd number x 2 (Tab. 1).[12] Those with elements of an even number x 2 amount to only one third. Actually, it is these statistical facts that prompted me to seek the possible use of loop-manipulation techniques in Japan. We already know that these statistics are not anomalies if the braids were made by means of loop-manipulation. This, however, was a great puzzle to the traditional kumihimo braiders because in the methodology of traditional kumihimo the norm for square braids is to have elements of an even number x 2, and a true square cross section. My examination of a 16-element Shōsōin square braid from a photograph among the Office of Shōsōin survey has shown that it did not have a true square cross section but had exactly the same skewed structure (3/4/5/4) as those made using kute-uchi. The statistics, the reaction of the traditional braiders to them, and the skewed cross section of the Shōsōin 16-element square braid demonstrate that the Shōsōin braids are not consistent with the norm of the methodology of kumihimo. The reason must be that the ancient method could only make skewed structures. Thus kute-uchi is the strongest candidate technique for these braids.

Another piece of evidence as strong as above statistics is the mirror symmetric color pattern of the Shōsōin square braids (Fig. 8). The patterns result from the mirror symmetric nature of the construction procedure, which is characteristic to kute-uchi. Such patterns do not occur if the braids were made using the rotationally symmetric kumihimo procedure with a conventional color arrangement.

TYPE II: FOUR-RIDGE FLAT BRAID WITH A TWILL PATTERN. (Fig. 1 second left)
This type of relatively narrow and thin braid suitable as trimmings can be made using a procedure similar to that of square braids. The loop is twisted only when it is transferred from, say, the left hand to the right and not twisted in the opposite movement (Fig. 9). All type II ancient braids characteristically have an even number of elements and the numbers of the float of the two center ridges

differ from each other by one. These characteristics match exactly those of braids made using kute-uchi. While braids with the same structure can also be made using kumihimo, these features are not characteristic of kumihimo braids of this type. The pliancy of ancient braids also matches kute-uchi in contrast to kumihimo braids, which are generally firmer.

THE CONSTRUCTION TECHNIQUES FOR TYPES III and IV
Whereas the techniques for type I and type II braids have been found among those reconstructed from historical sources, no Japanese bibliographic record has yet been found of those for type III and type IV braids. I, therefore, devised procedures to replicate these two types of braids, which work differently from those for the first two types of braids. Rather than constructing two superimposed layers as do the first two, they construct a single layer.[5] I have chosen loop-manipulation rather than other techniques as more viable techniques for constructuing these braids.

The devised techniques have proven to produce braids that have structural characteristics that agree with those of ancient braids.

TYPE III: THE OBLIQUE RIBBED TWINING BRAID (Fig. 1 second right)
In type III braids, paired elements form an oblique ribbed pattern by twining around the elements in countered courses and covering them entirely There are two varieties of type III braids in the collections; one has the same pattern all the way, the other a periodical pattern inversion. The color pattern used most often for the former is a chevron, and for the latter, double columns of diamonds. Braids composing the "head," "tongue," or "arms" of some Hōryūji banners and two narrower braids listed as a hanging cord and trimming of Shōsōin banners are of the former variety. Those with a pattern inversion exist only in Hōryūji collection. They may have been pendant ornaments to a canopy.

Each element of all Hōryūji type III braids consists of a single end of Z double-ply silk or gold threads. Paired elements are again Z-twisted. In the Shōsōin braids of this type, paired elements are twisted in Z in one half of the width and in S in the other.

My hypothetical procedure has been substantiated by a recently-uncovered fifteenth-century English treatise on finger-held loop-manipulation.[4] The treatise documents instructions that operate on the same construction principle as mine for making both varieties of oblique ribbed twining braids.

From several mis-aligned twining patterns found in some specimens as well as the fact that the smallest number of elements in the specimens is 36, I have proposed a hand-held method rather than finger-held (Fig. 10). The loops are twisted as they are passed one by one from one hand to the other. All loops in the Hōryūji braids are twisted counterclockwise, and are twisted opposite to each other in the right and left halves of the Shōsōin braids. The outermost loops are then transferred inside through the loops to the midpoint. The two transferred loops are then crossed, one passing inside through the other.

My analysis predicted that, in a braid made using this hand-held procedure, the width would tend to increase in the area where the rib pattern is less compact. I confirmed this tendency from the measurements taken of a photograph of Shōsōin braid #32.[5] In kumihimo, there is no such relationship between width and firmness of braids because the width is controlled by the braider and the firmness by bobbin weight. I also anticipated that the working mechanism of the procedure would make it impossible to produce a firm braid, such as those made using kumihimo. The firmness of the braids can be observe in the angle of their chevron pattern. When braids are firmer, the angle gets wider. To compare the firmness of the braids of this type, I measured the ratio of the length of a color pattern cycle to the width at the area where the pattern cycle is measured.[6] The ratios measured proved to be between 1.8 to 2.1 in kute-uchi braids and the Hōryūji and Shōsōin specimens, while the ratios for similar kumihimo run from 1.2 to 1.8 (Table 2). The important fact is that there is no way to change these ratios at the braiders' will for kute-uchi, yet they are remarkably close to that of the original. The wide variation in the kumihimo measurements indicates that various factors of the technique were tampered to make a better replication. As the data suggest, however, they have not quite been successful. The ratio for conventional oblique ribbed twine braids of today runs from 1.2 to 1.4.

TYPE IV: FLAT BRAID WITH A REGULAR INTERLACING PATTERN (Fig. 1 right)

The two variations in type IV braids in the collections are one with a plain-weave pattern and the other with a 2/2 twill pattern. All those used in the Shōsōin banners, forming the "head," "tongue," or "arms," are of the former variety. They were also used as edgings on large banners about 126 cm (50") wide.

Twenty nine braids of this type, listed as having belonged to banners, are 7 to 11 cm (2 3/4" to 4 1/4") wide. Their conspicuous design characteristic is that the oblique plain-weave pattern is formed by paired double-ply yarns twisted in opposite directions. That the paired yarns, not the individual yarn ends, indeed were used as the basic element in constructing these fabrics can be discerned from specimens decorated by beads strung through the paired yarns. The number of elements, ranging from 52 to 68, includes both odd and even numbers.

Of some wide braids of this type, the curvature of the elements that run obliquely in the structure reverses at mid-length, implying that the braids were made from the center towards the ends. The fact makes sense if loop-manipulation were used but not if kumihimo were used.

I have devised a finger-held method capable of producing flat braids with a regular pattern in which loops work as elements (Fig. 11). One of the two shanks of the loops is composed of an S double-ply yarn and the other of a Z double-ply yarn. Loops are held in the palms-up position and the small fingers are used to pick a shed and transfer the loops. This finger position complies with the Japanese folk practice of today[17] as well as those depicted in picture books of the Edo period (Fig. 3).[18] While the folk technique produces type I and type II braids described earlier, my devised technique constructs a flat braid with either a plain-weave or twill pattern, depending on the pick selected. Since each braider can hold only eight loops at most, several braiders, as many as nine, must collaborate to accommodate the required number of elements.

This method produces naturally the paired parallel elements that never cross each other and the uniform twists of the double-ply yarns, characteristic of ancient specimens. My conjecture that an analogous one-person technique must be used today in Peru and Bolivia to make three-strand flat braids that decorate ends of some woven bands, has been confirmed by Elayne Zorn.[19]

CONCLUSION

As a whole, I have found that by using kute-uchi, I could accurately and easily reproduce not only the ancient braids used on seventh and eighth-century banners but also most other braid relics produced throughout the middle ages in Japan. More importantly, with kute-uchi, I could account for the peculiarities of these braids.

My acknowledgement extends not only to those who directly helped me in this research, but also to those who spent countless hours measuring hundreds of specimens, without which my research would not have been possible.

NOTES AND REFERENCES

[1] Ridge: A longitudinal alignment of oblique floats.

[2] Matsumoto, Kaneo, "Kumihimo: sono hassei kara Hōryūji no kumihimo made=Braids: Up to the Hōryūji braids," *Nihon no bijutsu=Japanese Arts*, pp. 17-39, no. 308, 1992.

[3] In this paper the term "kumihimo" is used to refer only to the traditional Japanese stand-and-bobbin techniques or braids made using the technique, not as a generic word for braid or braiding. In kumihimo, the stand supports the component strands and the weighted-bobbins, on each of which an individual strand is wound. Each working end of the strands is free to each other. The strands are transferred in either a rotationally or mirror symmetric fashion forming an oblique interlacing pattern.

[4] Element: a single end or multiple ends of yarn set into the structure as one unit.

[5] Kinoshita, Masako, *Nihon kumihimo ko gihō no Kenkyū = Study of archaic braiding techniques in Japan*, Kyoto: Kyōto Shoin, 1994; "A braiding technique documented in a nineteenth-century Japanese treatise 'Soshun bikō'," *The Textile Museum journal 1986*, pp 47-65, 25, 1997.

[6] For the majority of individual reports on l-m techniques, refer to Speiser, Noemi, *The manual of braiding*, pp 146-147, Basel: privately published, 1991 (1983). Kanomi, Takako, *Shinwa no hitobito = People of myths*, Kyoto: Shikōha: 1991, p. 260 (Eng. p. 321); Kitamura, Noriko, "Dōgu o tsukawazu ni kumu hōhō ni tsuite no kiroku=A record on a no-tool braiding technique," the Master's dissertation, Tama Art College, 1975; Lebedeva, N. I., "Priadenie i tkachestvo vostochnykh slavian v. XIX-nachel xx v. (Spinning and weaving in eastern Slaves in the 19th to early 20th c.)," *Trudy Instituta Etnografii im. N. N. Mikluho-Makalaia* n. s., pp 497-506, 31, 1956. Two braiders in the altar piece, "Historia de la Virgen María (Story of the Virgin Mary)," att. Nicolás Zahortiga, 1465, Church of St. Mary of Tarazona, Spain; Many Japanese illustrations from 17th-19th c.

[7] The Sultanate of Oman is the only country other than Japan where hand-held loop-manipulation has been reported; Crocker G. and Glover B., "An Omani braiding technique fro camel reins," *The Journal of Oman studies*, pp 103-106, v. 5, 1979.

[8] Office of Shōsōin, Nara, Japan, *Shōsōin no kumihimo = Braids in Shōsō-in*, Tokyo: Heibonsha, 1974.

[9] Braids in Shōsō-in (Note 8).

[10] There are basically two ways of holding the loops in the finger-held method: palms-up, and palms-down. To transfer the loops, the index fingers are used in both: in the latter small fingers and occasionally ring fingers are also used.

[11] A one-person 9-loop procedure from Morocco has been reported by F. Soher, "Treatise on the making of laces," (see note 14) has one-person 8-loop procedures.

[12] Note 8, (Braids in Shōsō-in), p. 27 (Eng. p. iv).

[13] Note 5, (Archaic Braiding).

[14] "Treatise on the making of laces," *Tollemache book of secrets*, British Library, MS Harley 2320, Publication of Noemi Speiser's analytical research is forthcoming.

[15] Note 8, plate 71.

[16] This method is more accurate than measuring the angle by a protractor.

[17] Note 6 (No-tool braiding technique). Through my own enquiry, I received three more reports. Note 5 (Archaic braiding, pp.51-52.)

[18] Edo period = 1615-1867 AD.

[19] Personal verbal communication, 1992.

Table 1. Statistics according to number of elements in the Shōsōin square braids.

no. of elements	odd no. x 2	even no. x 2	odd no.	unable to count
no. of specimens	160	78	(0)	2
%	66.7	32.5	0	0.8

The number in parenthesis is added by M. K.

Table 2. The ratios of the lengths (H) of a color-pattern cycle to the width (W) of Hōryūji and Shōsōin braids, their replicas made using the loop-manipulation and those made using stand-and-bobbin techniques.

(Other than K. Kinoshita's and my own samplers, the measurements have been taken from photographs.)

Accuracy of measurement: 0.5 mm

	source of material	H mm	W mm	H/W	H/W mean value
specimen #32	*Braids in the Shōsō-in* plate.71	7.5	4	1.9	
		8.5	4	2.1	
		9.5	4.5	2.1	
		10.5	5.1	2.1	2.1
no. of elements 36	replica made using kumihimo (Dōmyō Exhibit '78)	31	20	1.6	
		31	20	1.6	
		31	20	1.6	1.6
	replica made using kumihimo (Dōmyō Exhibit '82)	51.5	30.5	1.7	
		58.5	33.5	1.8	
		58.5	33.0	1.8	1.8
	replica sampler made using loop-manipulation by Masako Kinoshita	24.4	12.9	1.9	
		26.2	13.0	2.0	
		27.5	13.6	2.1	2.0
specimen #332	*Braids in the Shōsō-in* plate 22.	49.5	28.0	1.8	
		49.0	28.0	1.8	
		49.5	27.0	1.8	1.8
no. of elements 92	sampler made using Kara-kumi stand-and-bobbin technique by Kazuko Kinoshita	37.0	27.5	1.3	
		37.0	27.0	1.4	
		37.0	27.5	1.3	
		36.0	27.5	1.3	1.3
	replica sampler made using loop-manipulation by Masako Kinoshita.	51.5	28.0	1.8	
		53.1	28.0	1.9	
		52.9	28.0	1.9	
		52.5	30.0	1.8	1.9
no. of ele. 116	fragment of Hōryūji ribbed twine braid	9.7	5.6	1.7	
		10.5	5.6	1.9	1.8
no. of ele. 120	fragment of Hōryūji ribbed twine braid	7.5	4.2	1.8	
		7.3	3.9	1.9	1.9
no. of ele. 48	replica of a Hōryūji banner (Dōmyō Exhibit '79)	119/2	48	1.2	
		118/2	49	1.2	1.2

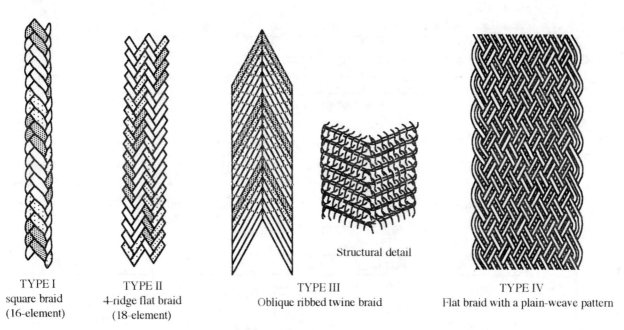

TYPE I
square braid
(16-element)

TYPE II
4-ridge flat braid
(18-element)

TYPE III
Oblique ribbed twine braid

Structural detail

TYPE IV
Flat braid with a plain-weave pattern

Fig. 1 Four basic types of braids in the Horyuji and Shosoin collections

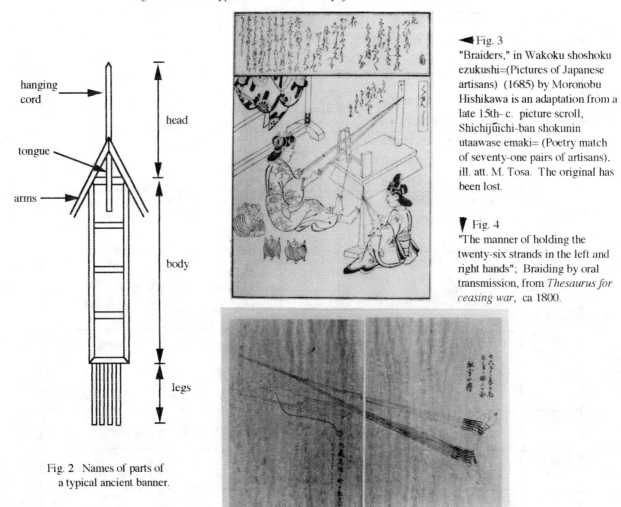

hanging
cord

tongue

arms

head

body

legs

Fig. 2 Names of parts of
a typical ancient banner.

◀ Fig. 3
"Braiders," in Wakoku shoshoku
ezukushi=(Pictures of Japanese
artisans) (1685) by Moronobu
Hishikawa is an adaptation from a
late 15th- c. picture scroll,
Shichijūichi-ban shokunin
utaawase emaki= (Poetry match
of seventy-one pairs of artisans),
ill. att. M. Tosa. The original has
been lost.

▼ Fig. 4
"The manner of holding the
twenty-six strands in the left and
right hands"; Braiding by oral
transmission, from *Thesaurus for
ceasing war*, ca 1800.

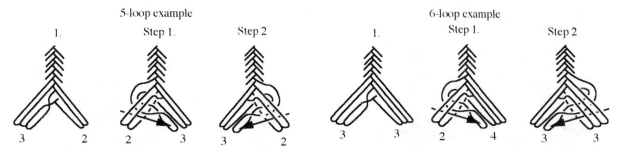

5-loop example

1.   Step 1.   Step 2.

6-loop example

1.   Step 1.   Step 2.

1. Initial allotment of loops.   Step 1: transferred loop is twisted.   Step 2: transferrd loop is twisted.

Fig. 5 Loop-manipulation procedure to make square braids, in which transferred loops go THROUGH the INSIDE of other loops. Used in both FINGER-HELD and HAND-HELD methods.

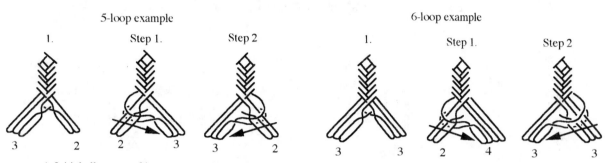

5-loop example

1.   Step 1.   Step 2

6-loop example

1.   Step 1.   Step 2

1. Initial allotment of loops.   Step 1: transferred loop is twisted.   Step 2: transferred loop is not twisted.

Fig. 6 Loop-manipulation procdure to make square braids in which transferred loops go AROUND the OUTSIDE of other loops: An option for HAND-HELD method.

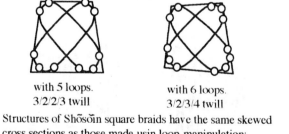

with 5 loops.
3/2/2/3 twill

with 6 loops.
3/2/3/4 twill

Structures of Shōsōin square braids have the same skewed cross sections as those made usin loop-manipulation:

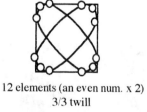

12 elements (an even num. x 2)
3/3 twill

Square braids made using the traditional kumihimo procedure have a true square cross section.

Fig. 7 Diagrammatic side view and cross section views of Shōsōin square braids.

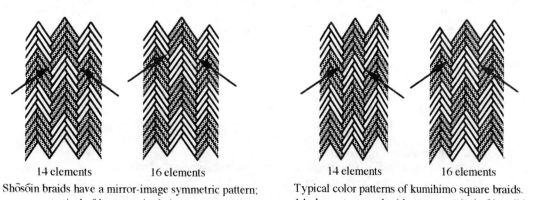

14 elements   16 elements

Shōsōin braids have a mirror-image symmetric pattern; typical of loop-manipulation.

14 elements   16 elements

Typical color patterns of kumihimo square braids. 14-element square braids are not typical of kumihimo.

The outer-most ridges in each diagram has been added to show the connection of the pattern around the braids. Left two ridges and right two ridges are the same ridges.

Fig. 8 Flattened-out patterns of the Shōsōin square braids.

5-loop example

Step 1   Step 2

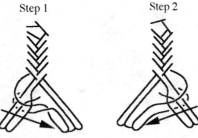

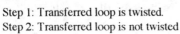

While the braid is being made,
it is folded in two, being
formed in two layers.

When flattend out a
4-ridge flat braid emerges.

Step 1: Transferred loop is twisted.
Step 2: Transferred loop is not twisted

Fig. 9 4-ridge flat braid with a twill pattern

Initial allotment

Step 1

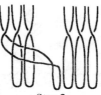

Step 2

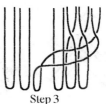

Step 3

Intial allotment: Loops are distributed equally or one more to one hand than the other.

Step 1: Loops are twisted a half turn.

Steps 2 and 3: The outermost loops are transferred through inside of other loops. They are not twisted.

Fig. 10 Procedure to make oblique ribbed twine braids using loop-manipulation.

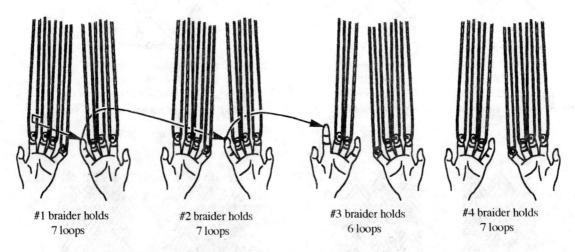

#1 braider holds
7 loops

#2 braider holds
7 loops

#3 braider holds
6 loops

#4 braider holds
7 loops

Step 1: The farthest-left loop is transferred to the left index finger of #3 braider.

Step 2: The loops held by #1 and #2 braiders are shifted back to the left. The right index
finger of #2 braider is left empty and the left index finger of #3 braider is filled.

Step 3: The structure is tightened.

Then #3 and #4 braiders perform the mirror-image processes of steps 1, 2 and 3.

And the steps from the beginning are repeated.

Fig. 11. Loop-manipulation procedure to make flat braids with an oblique over-one-under-one interlacing.
Example: Shōsōin braid #27.   Number of elements: 27

From Secular Garment to Sacred Object:
Kosode Refashioned into Buddhist Altar Cloths and Banners

By Nobuhiko Maruyama
National Museum of Japanese History

Introduction

Altar cloths are rectangular cloths on which Buddhist offerings are placed. Generally, they are made with gorgeous textiles of gold *nishiki*, a multi-colored weft-patterned fabric. In the Momoyama and Edo periods from the sixteenth to nineteenth centuries, however, they were also made from refashioned *kosode*, an early type of *kimono*.

1. Banners and altar cloths remade from kosode

When a person died, his or her *kosode* were often donated to the family temple. The *kosode* were then remade into various religious objects such as altar cloths and banners for Buddhist ceremonies for the deceased. Most of the donated *kosode* were originally created for wealthy women and hence were made with superior materials.

Generally, *kosode* were used until they wore out. That is why few *kosode* remain today. *Kosode* that date to before the late-sixteenth century are especially rare. In contrast, *kosode* refashioned into altar cloths and banners are relatively well preserved in temples. They make up for a shortage of historical examples of *kosode*. Occasionally, an inscription on the altar cloth or banner gives important clues about the *kosode*'s date. This banner [fig. 1] has an inscription indicating that it was made from a *katasuso kosode* in 1530. *Katasuso* is a *kosode* design with motifs only on the shoulders and skirt of the *kimono*. This is the oldest *tsujigahana* textile piece with an inscription that offers a clear date.

fig. 1

Tsujigahana textiles flourished from the sixteenth to early seventeenth centuries. They combine a number of techniques such as the main technique of tie-dyeing by stitch-resist method, drawing and shading in ink, applying red pigment by brush, and impressing *surihaku* gold leaf onto the textile. They also represent one of the earliest steps in the transition from woven decorative patterns to dyed ones.

Before the fourteenth century, plain *kosode* were worn as undergarments by the upper class and worn as outer garments by common people. In the Muromachi period (1392-1573) however, the upper class began to wear *kosode* as outerwear, as well. Tomiko Hino (1440-96), the wife of the eighth samurai general of the Muromachi shogunate, wore *kosode* as an outer garment when she went to a party in 1479 attended by Emperor Gotsuchimikado. This exceptional event provides evidence that *kosode* had taken root as outerwear before the fifteenth century. When *kosode* began to be used as outerwear, the number of decorative techniques increased. *Tsujigahana* is one decorative style that came out of this development.

Another type of *kosode* textile which gradually replaced a style of decorative weaving was a textile made with an embroidery and gold leaf technique known as *nuihaku*. As the importance of *kosode* grew in society, the number donated to temples also increased. Thus *nuihaku kosode* robes have also been preserved in the form of altar cloths and banners, often with inscriptions. An altar cloth at Kodaiji-temple in Kyoto was originally a *nuihaku kosode*. It was donated to the temple in 1601. Shigeki Kawakami, a curator at the Kyoto National Museum, has shown that it is possible to reconstruct almost a whole *kosode* from this altar cloth.

2. The Nomura Collection

When discussing *kosode*, altar cloths, and banners, one must not overlook the *kosode* folding screens of the Nomura Collection (Chiba Prefecture). The Nomura Collection is one of the most well-known and also the largest collection of *kosode*.

Shojiro Nomura (1879-1943) was a pioneer in the collecting of *kosode* and *kosode* fragments. When he began, few people were interested in collecting Japanese fabrics. At the end of the nineteenth century, an anti-Buddhist movement led to the destruction of Buddhist temples and images, and forced temples to dispose of their altar cloths and banners. This tragedy in Japanese history became a splendid opportunity for Nomura to collect the finest fabrics.

To preserve and display the *kosode* fragments, Nomura designed a *kosode* folding screen, which was eventually patented. When he could not reconstruct a whole robe, he pasted the *kosode* fragments onto a two-panel folding screen to give the illusion of a complete garment hanging from a *kimono* stand. Although the *kosode* appear to have been painted, they actually have been made from fabrics that have been attached to the screens.

fig.2   **fig.3**   **fig.4**

One screen [fig.2] uses fragments from a *tsujigahana kosode* that had once formed a banner. The fabric is divided into red and white sections with patterns of camellia and Chinese bellflower created by a stitch-resist technique. There are dark crimson bands which, because they were once covered by the banner frame, retain sometime close to the original color. In the Kyoto National Museum, there is a banner with the exactly same pattern as this *tsujigahana* [fig.3]. The distance between the crimson bands is also the same as that in this example from the Nomura collection. In this connection, a third example of this same fabric can be found in the Toyama Memorial Museum (Saitama Prefecture). These *tsujigahana* fragments were originally all from the same *kosode* [fig.4].

Next, is an example of a Kanbun era (1661-73) *kosode* now remounted on a *kosode* folding screen [fig.5]. This *kosode*, patterned with sedge hat motifs and flowers, had been turned into an altar cloth. A photograph of this altar cloth can be found in the 1985 Asia Society exhibition catalog "*KOSODE* 16th-19th Century Textiles from the Nomura Collection". With the folding screen, Nomura truly recreates a sense of the original *kimono*. The motif of upside-down umbrellas and flowers is not a mistake. The Nomura Collection has another fragment of the same fabric that clearly shows where the shoulder line was and therefore shows which direction was the top of the robe.

A photograph of another altar cloth which Nomura took apart in order to make a *kosode* screen appears in a report by Nomura titled the "The Research of *Yuzen* Dyeing". This cloth is a rare example of an Edo-period *ro*, a type of silk gauze, dyed by *yuzen*, a sort of dyeing technique by rice-paste resist [fig.6].

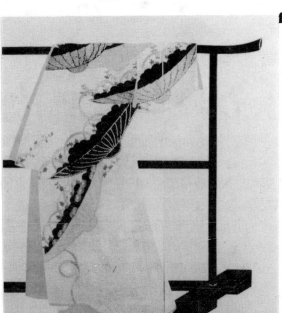

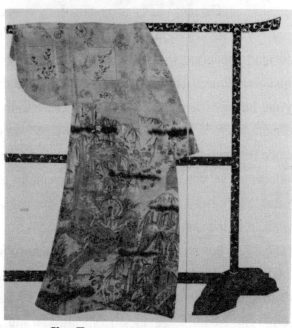

fig.7   fig.6

3. Inscriptions attached to *kosode* folding screens

All the examples have no inscriptions. There are, however, some examples of inscribed *kosode*. One screen from the Nomura Collection has an inscription in ink attached to the back of it that is written on a fragment of what used to be the red lining of the robe [fig.8]. The inscription says that this *kosode* was donated to the temple in 1740. The *kosode* features a typical Korin motif associated with craft designs influenced by the painting style of Ogata Korin of the *Rimpa* school.

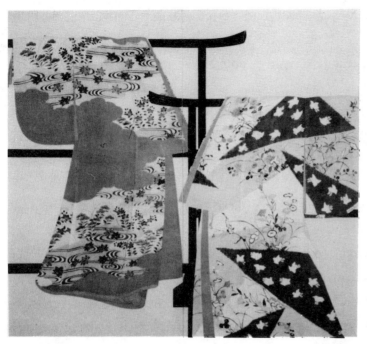

fig.8 (right)

fig.9

fig.10 (right)

fig.11

Korin motifs, which became popular after the seventeenth century, are characterized by a simplicity of expression. The *kosode* has a bird design which is known as the Korin plover. Although many examples of Korin motifs remain, those with inscriptions are rare. Therefore, this *kosode* is an important example of an early Korin motif from the first half of the eighteenth century.

Two *tsujigahana kosode* fragments are featured on another screen [fig.10]. An inscription attached to the back of this screen dates the year of donation to 1663 [fig.11]. This is most likely not form the lining of a robe, but a piece of the same *kosode* fabric as the right *kosode* on the screen.

There are thirty-five other inscriptions besides these two, but these are the only two which are attached to the screens.

It is at times difficult to determine exactly which linings belonged to which *kosode*. Nomura noted the corresponding *kosode* motifs for fifteen of the lining inscriptions.

Unfortunately, not all fifteen linings can be matched to *kosode* fragments on screens. So far, it has been possible to link ten of the linings to *kosode* fragments. Here are three important works from this group of ten inscribed linings:

Koshimaki screen with auspicious motifs [fig.12]

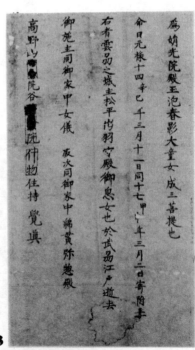

fig.12   **fig.13**

A *Koshimaki* garment was worn over *kosode* in the summer. The upper half was slipped off the shoulders and tied around the waist like a sash. The whole surface of this *koshimaki* is covered with delicate, embroidered patterns of auspicious motifs. It is not clear when such a style of *koshimaki* originated. *Koshimaki* came into fashion after the middle of the eighteenth century, but most of those that have survived belong to the nineteenth century and seldom have inscriptions. This *koshimaki* was donated in 1701, which means it is a not only a rare example from the early eighteenth century, but one of the oldest extant *koshimaki* [fig.13].

Kosode screen with flowering cherry tree and poem slips [fig.14]

fig.14

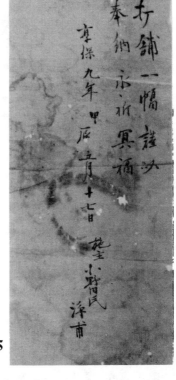

fig.15

This *kosode* was made with the *yuzen* dyeing technique. Like *koshimaki*, extant examples of *yuzen* dyeing rarely have inscriptions. The name "*yuzen*" appears on some inscriptions from the second half of the seventeenth century, but most examples of *yuzen* dyeing belong to the eighteenth century. Therefore, this *yuzen* dyed *kosode* fragment donated in 1724 is one of the earliest examples of *yuzen* dyeing [fig.15].

Kosode screen with cycad palms and earthen bridge [fig.16]

Finally, this *kosode* embroidered with cycad motifs (a kind of Japanese palm tree) deserves special note. Although its design and embroidery technique resemble that of a nineteenth-century *kosode*, the robe was donated in 1760 [fig.17]. Thus, this *kosode* is yet another early example from the first half of the eighteenth century.

fig.16   fig.17

Conclusion

Altar cloths and banners lie on the border between the secular and sacred worlds. The designs of donated *kosode* employed a wide range of motifs from daily life, especially from the world of the upper class. Yet the fact that these *kosode* were chosen for donation confirms their elevation above secular use. Thus, the altar cloths and banners not only mark the historical rise of *kosode* fabrics from undergarments to highly treasured outer garments of the upper class between the fourteenth and sixteenth centuries, but their leap towered sacred use after the sixteenth century.

Although donated *kosode* were refashioned into different form, they stood a better chance of preservation as altar cloths and temple banners than if left in the secular world. Until recently, there was little interest in the history of *kosode* textiles, and many scholars ignored Nomura's work. Yet, Nomura's collection includes superb examples of textiles. The hundred *kosode* folding screens are important because they not only preserve the fine, sacred textiles of altar cloths and banners, but effectively recreate images of the original *kosode* form. The collection is also vital as a standard for dating other surviving *kosode* .

Of course, the date that a *kosode* was made did not necessarily correspond to the date of donation. Donations could be made long after a person's death, and the donated *kosode* did not always belong to the deceased. Even so, the information provided by inscriptions on donated pieces is valuable.

While keeping in mind the historical importance of altar cloths and banners, the National Museum of Japanese History has strived to collect fabrics with inscriptions. Most of these acquisitions belong to the nineteenth century, but there are some rare examples, such as the altar cloth refashioned from a *kosode* of Chinese weave designed for *Noh* performance, which belong to the early-eighteenth century [fig.18-19].

In the summer of 1997, there will be an exhibition of inscribed fabrics at the National Museum of Japanese History in cooperation with the Tokyo National Museum and the Kyoto National Museum. This exhibition will provide an opportunity to further study how Buddhist altar cloths and banners made from *kosode* can advance our knowledge of *kosode* fabrics.

fig.18

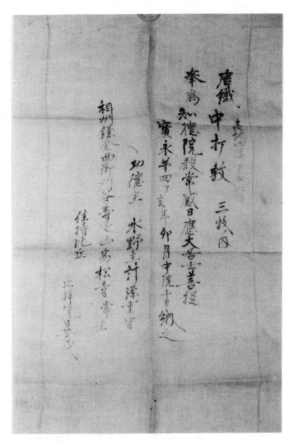

fig.19

OFFERTORY BANNERS FROM RURAL JAPAN: ECHIGO-CHIJIMI WEAVING AND WORSHIP

by

Sharon Sadako Takeda
Los Angeles County Museum of Art

INTRODUCTION

Unlike luxurious silk cloth that was carefully cut and sewn together in a prescribed manner, banners that were offered to rural, syncretic Shintō shrines and Buddhist temples in the Uonuma-gun region of Niigata Prefecture were lengths of locally produced ramie cloth inscribed with *sumi* ink and dedicated primarily by the women weavers who produced them. Whether observed in situ in a neighborhood shrine or temple or viewed in a museum setting, these ramie offertory banners, called *hōgake*, *hōnōbata*, or *hōnō nobori*, are exemplary artifacts. The environmental, social, and economic aspects of the lives of their rural makers are literally woven into an efficient, creative, and whole cloth.

JAPAN'S SNOW COUNTRY

Formally known as Echigo, Niigata Prefecture is a northern province located in Japan's legendary "snow country." In the winter, cold winds from Siberia blow down across the Sea of Japan, pick up moisture, and drop it as snow when they reach the mountains that encroach upon the alluvial plains of Niigata from the east. The mountain valleys of Uonuma-gun can receive as much as six to ten feet of snow within twenty-four hours.[1] Uonuma-gun is one of Japan's snowiest areas and, for its latitude, one of the heaviest snow regions in the world. For nearly eight months of the year, a blanket of snow covers the landscape. Strong wooden barricades are erected around homes to protect windows and walls from violent winds and snowfall. The snow must be shoveled off of rooftops before its weight collapses buildings. Literally buried in snow, inhabitants must carve stairways out of the frozen precipitation in order to exit their homes. In some areas, snow-packed pathways are at rooftop level.

The immense snowfall incapacitated the agrarian society of Uonuma-gun. In olden times, men went off to cities such as Edo (modern-day Tokyo) to look for winter employment. Confined to their dimly lit homes, the villagers who remained behind worked diligently to supplement their incomes by producing subsidiary handicrafts. Rice straw was plied into useful items such as shoes, hats, and household articles, and grass-bast fibers (*asa*) such as ramie were processed into thread and woven into cloth.[2]

The snowy climate of Echigo created an ideal situation for producing asa textiles. Stiff ramie threads, which ordinarily break easily if manipulated in an arid environment, remained soft and pliable in the damp atmosphere of Echigo winters.[3] "Thread is spun and twisted in the snow, the cloth is woven in the snow, it is washed in snow waters and bleached on snow fields. There is [ramie] crepe because there is snow," wrote an Echigo textile wholesaler in the early nineteenth century.[4] In his book entitled *Hokuetsu seppu* (Snow country tales), Suzuki Bokushi (1770-1842) described the life and customs of Echigo inhabitants, including their involvement in ramie thread and cloth production.[5] He credited the development of the exceptionally fine ramie crepe textile known as *chijimi* to the talent, unyielding patience, and perseverance of snowbound craftspeople.[6] "Echigo crepe," he wrote, "owes its fame to the combined powers of man and snow, working hand in hand."[7]

ECHIGO TEXTILES

The origin of asa weaving in Echigo is unclear but assumed to be extremely old. The earliest extant piece of Echigo cloth (Echigo *nuno*) was discovered in the collection of the Shōsōin, an imperial repository for treasures built in Nara over 1,200 years ago. The asa cloth, originally given as tax payment and inscribed with the name of an Echigo village and its leader and dated 731, the third year of the Tenpyō era (729-749), was later made into a storage bag for a folding screen (*byōbu*).[8] The first historical reference to Echigo cloth was made during the Heian period (794-1185) in the *Engi shiki* (Procedures of the Engi era), a code of laws completed in 927. It recorded a decision made in the year 785 about collecting cloth as tribute from producing areas and documented the receipt of one thousand *tan* (bolts) of cloth from the Echigo region.

Echigo cloth became a product of great renown during the Kamakura (1185-1333) and Muromachi (1333-1568) periods, when the military elite favored it as a trading stock and tribute. As recorded in the historical account *Azuma kagami* (Mirror of Eastern Japan) and *Muromachi no kojitsu sho* (Book of Muromachi customs and manners), in the seventh month of 1192 Minamoto Yoritomo, after receiving the title of *sei-i-tai shōgun* (supreme commander), presented representatives sent by the imperial court with a gift of horses, mulberry thread, printed indigo cloth, and one thousand bolts of Echigo cloth.[9] In numerous other Muromachi-period records, Echigo nuno is mentioned either as tribute items or as regulated clothing restricted to certain months unless permission was given by the military government.

The reputation of Echigo textiles was further bolstered early in the Edo period (1600-1868) by advances made in design and production techniques. Up to this point, Echigo weavers produced a plain, coarse asa cloth known as *kojiro nuno*.[10] In the seventeenth century a lordless samurai who had emigrated with his family from Akashi (near present-day Kobe in Hyōgo Prefecture) to Echigo transformed asa weaving there. It is widely believed that it was Hori Jirō Masatoshi (1620-79),[11] his wife, and two daughters who promulgated the idea of weaving with tightly twisted weft threads, which produced the refined crepe fabric known as *chijimi nuno* or, simply, *chijimi*.[12] They also encouraged the production of patterned chijimi nuno, colored with natural dyes and woven into such designs as stripes or ikat (*kasuri*) patterns.

As chijimi production techniques improved, so did its quality and reputation. Chijimi nuno became known to the ruling Tokugawa shōgunate, who began to requisition chijimi in special measurements and designs during the Genroku (1688-1704) and Hōei (1704-11) eras of the Edo period. Chijimi ordered for use in Edo castle was called *honmaru goyō chijimi*.[13] To be chosen to weave for such an order was a great honor for a woman. As it became widely known that Edo castle was ordering chijimi, demand for the celebrated cloth increased. Daimyō and samurai were required to wear ramie garments for certain formal and ceremonial occasions, and aristocrats ordered chijimi to make summer clothing. (Ironically, ramie fibers processed and woven by women during the coldest winter months were used primarily for clothing worn on the warmest summer days.) Production surged, and according to one village's records, 5,062 bolts of chijimi were made in 1682, more than twice as many as the previous year.[14] Production peaked during the Tenmei era (1781-89), when 200 thousand bolts were woven annually.[15]

ECHIGO WEAVERS

Skillful weavers were highly valued in Echigo, where textiles were an important commodity and the source of great revenue. Weaving knowledge was passed down from generation to generation. As women earnestly worked at their looms during the winter, their young children played at their sides with spinning and weaving equipment. When girls reached the age of seven or eight, they performed simple weaving tasks; by the age of twelve or thirteen, they wove simple coarse cloth.[16] Prior to sitting at a loom to begin weaving cloth for the very first time, young girls made a pilgrimage to a shrine to pray to a weaving deity. This practice was called *joji no ju-san mairi* (shrine visits by thirteen-year-old girls).[17] As they reached their mid-teens and twenties, their weaving skills were expected to improve and reach maturity, coinciding with their arrival into womanhood. Traditionally, the finest chijimi was woven by young women in this age group. Cloth woven by older women was considered to lack luster and therefore be of inferior quality.[18]

Bolts of fabric sold at yearly chijimi markets bore tags that identified the weaver and the price she agreed upon for her work.[19] Women competed with each other and vied for the privilege of being chosen to weave the highest quality cloth or textiles ordered by elite clientele. Excellent weaving skills not only brought individual fame within the community but also were considered more important than appearance when it came to acquiring a husband (an accomplished weaver's output added a cash income to a household). Parents, therefore, paid close attention to their daughters' weaving education, and young women placed great pressure upon themselves, working tirelessly at their looms. Extremely high technical standards were maintained, which made both Echigo weavers and cloth legendary.

OFFERTORY BANNERS

With stories of the incredible struggles of Uonuma-gun craftswomen documented in literature and local folk tales, it is not difficult to understand why the practice of worshiping at both the start and finish of each weaving season would continue throughout a woman's creative life.[20] Weavers would cut a narrow strip of their fabric (*kogire*) or the last woven part of a warp, with warp ends intact (*kirisen*), and offer it along with prayers of thanksgiving. These cloth fragments were often tied to the shrine or the shrine bell cord. Longer lengths of cloth were made into banners by attaching them to wooden hangers and inscribing them with the word *hōnō* (offering) or *hōgake* (offertory banner), the date of its dedication, and the name, address, and age of the donor(s). These banners were offered by weavers who hung them on the walls of shrines and temples, often several layers deep, and prayed for good health during the winter season, the improvement of their weaving skills, and the safety of their households.[21] The banners also indirectly advertised the weaving talents of their makers.[22] Recognized now as objects of great historical importance, a number of banners have been designated important cultural properties, by either the Japanese government or Niigata Prefecture, and are kept in museums, textile cooperatives, and private collections.[23] The survival of these banners is remarkable given that they were exposed to the elements while hanging in open shrines and temples. Many were rescued by chijimi wholesalers. These offertory banners, the earliest dating to 1806, the third year of the Bunka era (1804-18), together with dated chijimi swatch books (*mihon-chō*) and pattern books (*hinagata-chō*) are invaluable resources for scholars.[24]

THE DECLINE OF ECHIGO CHIJIMI

The widespread use of cotton, which had been introduced to Japan during the fifteenth century and came into widespread use during the mid-eighteenth century, contributed to a decline in chijimi production during the late Edo period. This was further aggravated by the eventual dissolution of the Tokugawa shōgunate. From 1854 to 1867, chijimi output dropped by 50 percent. During the Meiji period (1868-1912), machine-made thread began replacing handmade thread, and in the mid-Taishō period (1912-25), power looms were introduced. The textile industry began switching from a cottage industry (*kanai kōgyō*) to a factory-based economy. Echigo weavers put their looms away and went to work in local small textile factories.

On the brink of virtual extinction, the traditional hand techniques of Echigo chijimi might have been lost forever had it not been for the combined efforts of concerned Echigo citizens and the Japanese government. A revival of the traditional techniques took place in 1948, and in 1953 the Japanese government placed Echigo chijimi under the authority of the Law for the Protection of Cultural Properties. Recognizing the historical and artistic merits of Echigo chijimi and its specific local attributes, the government designated it as an important intangible cultural property in 1955. At that time, two new official names were given in order to clearly distinguish between ramie cloth with highly twisted wefts (*Ojiya-chijimifu*) and cloth with untwisted wefts (*Echigo-jōfu*). Every bolt of certified Ojiya-chijimifu and Echigo-jōfu must be made within strict production guidelines and meet high standards of workmanship.

KARAMUSHI CULTIVATION

Karamushi or *choma* (*Boehmeria nivea*), commonly known in the West as China grass or ramie, is the raw material used to make Ojiya-chijimifu and Echigo-jōfu. In 1598, as Echigo became famous for both its karamushi cultivation and cloth, Uesugi Kagekatsu (1555-1623), the feudal lord who controlled the area, was transferred to a larger domain at Wakamatsu in neighboring Mutsu (present-day Aizu Wakamatsu in Fukushima Prefecture).[25] He introduced karamushi cultivation to the region, which flourished as it became responsible for supplying all the necessary karamushi to the escalating chijimi trade. Records of tolls taken along the roads between Wakamatsu and Echigo indicate that they were heavily trafficked by merchants who transported the karamushi on their backs to threadmakers in Echigo. Today, a few scattered karamushi fields in the small mountain hamlet of Showa-mura in Fukushima Prefecture are the only reminders of the centuries-old ramie trade relationship between these two areas.

The cultivation of karamushi begins dramatically in mid-May, when fields of sprouting two-year old karamushi plants are covered with dry miscanthus reeds and set on fire. As the fiery ring engulfs a field, uneven karamushi growth is reduced to the ground, leaving hearty roots intact underground. While the blackened field is still warm, it is doused with a natural fertilizer of human feces mixed with water and then covered with straw. From the burnt, alkali-rich soil new growth emerges. To ensure the uniform growth of straight stalks, the new karamushi is protected from the wind by a miscanthus fence built around the perimeter of the field. A soft buffer of hemp keeps the karamushi from adhering to the fence.

By late July or early August, karamushi stalks have reached a height of two meters, and a timely harvest must occur before the skin of the stalks matures and thickens. With a sickle, each stalk is cut on a slant about forty centimeters from ground level and stripped of its leaves.[26] Then, bundled together, the stalks are weighted down in either dammed streams or man-made tanks filled with clear mountain water.

After five to seven hours of soaking, the skin of the stalks is soft enough for decortication.[27] Starting at a point about one-third the length, the stalk is pierced by fingernail and bent open. A thumb is inserted into the break between the outer bark and core and, with one quick and agile longitudinal movement, the core is extracted. The outer skins are retied, washed, and returned to the water to soak for twenty or thirty minutes.

Next comes the tedious but important chore of scraping the karamushi skins away from their inner woody tissue. For several weeks after harvest, women busily work before wooden troughs that are set up in the entryway of their homes. Each wet skin is placed individually between a flexible wooden board sitting in the wooden trough and a hand-held metal blade. As the skin is pulled with one hand, the blade is pushed with the other, scraping off the green surface and revealing a lustrous fiber called *aoso*.[28] Both sides of the aoso are repeatedly scraped in order to even out the surface and give it a polished sheen. Because the fiber cannot be dried in direct sunlight (it will harden and discolor), small bundles are hung indoors, with care being taken to avoid mold. The dried fibers are stored until autumn, when buyers from Uonuma-gun arrive to inspect and carefully select the best aoso for the production of Ojiya-chijimifu and Echigo-jōfu.

THREADMAKING

The traditional threadmaking process, known as *oumi*, is the most time-consuming task in the production of chijimi. Every year, after the autumn harvest is finished, women prepare to make enough thread for one kimono length before spring. A skilled woman can prepare enough thread for three kimono.[29] Like the weavers, threadmakers also visit shrines and temples to pray for the improvement of their oumi technique and product, offering aoso fiber and/or thread.[30]

The process begins by boiling and/or soaking the aoso in lukewarm water to make it soft and pliable. It is further manipulated and moistened by the hands and mouths of the threadmakers. The strands, rather flat like tape, are systematically split by fingernail and shredded into very fine threads. The ends of each strand are then twisted together to form a continuous thread. The intended use of the thread as the warp or weft determines how the ends are patched together. As the thread is made, it is collected into a bucket called an *oboke*.

To put this painstaking labor into perspective, one day of diligent oumi work produces only about six or seven *momme* (nearly one ounce) of top-quality thread.[31] It can take one hundred days to produce enough thread for one kimono.[32]

An additional tight twisting of the weft threads gives Ojiya-chijimifu its characteristic crepe texture. The thread is twisted by a hand spindle that is whirled between two pieces of wood. It is critical to the finished product that all the thread is evenly twisted.

CHIJIMI WEAVING

A weaver begins her work by measuring out the warp using a floor-seated warping board (*hedai*). She stands next to the hedai holding a pair of long, hollow, bamboo sticks (*hebashi*) that have been threaded with one thin ramie thread each. The hebashi, resembling a pair of oversized chopsticks, are swiftly and deftly maneuvered to measure the thread and order the correct sequence of warp threads on the hedai.

Roughly 1,300 threads make up the 36-40-centimeter-wide warp for top-quality chijimi. Special high-quality chijimi can have over 1,800 warp ends.[33] Each thread is drawn through the dents in a reed (*osa*) prior to the warp being wound on the beam and before a unique split-bamboo measuring device is used to create consistently-sized string heddles for every other thread.

Traditional Ojiya-chijimifu and Echigo-jōfu are plain woven in solids, stripes, checks, and ikat patterns on a body-tension loom called an *izaribata*. The weaver sits on a wooden plank raised just inches off the floor with legs outstretched underneath the loom. Her right big toe or entire right foot is slipped into a sling that manipulates a bent, wood lever attached to the string heddles. A cloth beam (*chimaki*) is then placed against the weaver's abdomen and secured by a strap that is brought around the small of the back. In this position the loom becomes an integrated extension of the weaver's body. She can achieve subtle adjustments to warp tension by simply shifting her weight.

A unique oversized wooden shuttle (*hi*) shaped like a large blade carries a moistened bobbin of thread through the shed and also doubles as a beater. The weft is further compressed with the osa, which acts as both a warp spacer and weft beater. Approximately 920 hand and body movements are necessary to weave one foot of chijimi cloth.[34]

After the finished cloth is removed from the loom, it is cleaned, softened, and given its characteristic surface texture through several stages of soaking, washing, and manipulation. The cloth is further conditioned in the unique process called *ashibumi*, where the fabric is massaged and washed with the feet. With the aid of two rope slings suspended from the ceiling, a man stands over a trough of water and dances on the cloth, creating rhythmic sloshing sounds as the cloth is rotated and stomped on. The fabric is then rinsed thoroughly with water and tightly twisted to remove excess water.

SNOW BLEACHING

In late February/early March the dark gray winter sky begins to lighten up over Uonuma-gun. Snowfall turns into sleet and then intermittent rain. Finally, blue skies with billowy white clouds prevail, and it is time for the long winter's yield of thread and fabric to be carried outdoors and bleached. One by one, the wet lengths of cloth, which have been soaked in a weak lye solution, are placed out on top of glistening snow-covered fields. Two people unfurl and carefully stretch kimono lengths of fabric out in neat parallel rows that resemble planted furrows. For ten to twenty days this surreal crop of cloth is exposed to the bleaching properties of the spring sunlight, which is intensified by the white snow. The cloth is further lightened by the penetration of ozone ions from the melting snow.

The sight of length after length of beautiful cloth set against the backdrop of snow, mountains, and blue sky is stunning and magical. All memories of the long, dark, cold winter and the painstaking toil of producing ramie thread and cloth are cleansed from the mind. With the warmth of the spring sun upon their faces, threadmakers and weavers march through the receding snow carrying thread, cloth fragments, and banners to their neighborhood shrines and temples. Offering these samples of their winter labor, they give thanks and pray for continued good health and the improvement of their textile skills.

The author gratefully acknowledges the Japanese Ministry of Education (*Monbushō*) for funding her field research. Generous assistance was also provided by the textile cooperatives, museums, and people of Uonuma-gun, especially Shinoda Shirō, Horizawa Tatsuji, Watanabe Sansei, the late Suzuki Chobōan, and her chijimi weaving teacher, Kobayashi Teru.

NOTES

1. Suzuki Bokushi, p. 11.

2. The Japanese word *asa* is a generic term for bast fibers. The most common Japanese bast fibers used at the time were hemp (*taima* or *honasa*; *Cannabis sativa*) and ramie (*karamushi* or *choma*; *Boehmeria nivea*).

3. The average annual humidity in this region is 79 percent. See Diamond, Inc., p. 120.

4. Suzuki Bokushi, p. 66.

5. *Hokuetsu seppu* was published in Edo in 1835. It is Japan's oldest scientific essay. See Hikida, p. 540.

6. A common demonstration of extremely fine Echigo cloth is to pull a standard cloth width through the seven-millimeter square hole of a Japanese Tenpō-era (1830-44) coin. See Tairyūsha, pp. 18-19, and Watanabe, p. 74.

7. Suzuki Bokushi, p. 66.

8. The Echigo bast-fiber cloth made into a storage bag was discovered by Ōga Ichirō in 1953 (Shōwa 28) while the scholar was reorganizing the Shōsōin collection. See Suzuki Torajurō, pp. 34, 38; Kitamura, p. 32; and Takizawa, p. 39.

9. Watanabe, p. 20.

10. Ibid., p. 110. During the Heian period Echigo paid its tribute with kojiro nuno. See also *Genshoku senshoku daijiten* (Illustrated textile dictionary), s.v. "kojiro nuno."

11. There are conflicting birth and death dates for Hori Jirō Masatoshi (also known as Akashi Jirō). See Watanabe, pp. 109-12, and *Genshoku senshoku daijiten*, s.v. "Akashi Jirō."

12. It is thought that the name *chijimi nuno* is derived from *shijimi nuno* (crimped cloth) and that over time *shijimi nuno* was abbreviated and slurred to *chijimi*. See Suzuki Bokushi, p. 63. The term *chijimi* was used to refer to all ramie cloth produced in the region, whether it had crinkles or not. It is also possible that the term *chijimi* is from the verb *chijimu* (to shrink).

13. Also known as *omeshi chijimi* and *goyō chijimi*. See *Genshoku senshoku daijiten*, s.v. "goyō chijimi."

14. Diamond, Inc., p. 112.

15. Watanabe, p. 110.

16. Suzuki Bokushi, p. 67.

17. Tōkamachi-shi hakubutsukan 1987, p. 146.

18. Suzuki Bokushi, p. 67.

19. Ibid., p. 77; Yamazaki, p. 168.

20. Suzuki Chobōan, p. 40.

21. Bunka-chō bunka-zai hogo-bu, p. 104; Tōkamachi-shi hakubutsukan 1987, p. 146.

22. Hauge and Hauge, p. 250.

23. The largest collection of chijimi offertory banners designated as important tangible cultural properties by the Japanese government (*jūyō yūkei minzoku bunka-zai*) and Niigata Prefecture (*Niigata-ken shitei yūkei bunka-zai*) are in the collection of the Tōkamachi City Museum (Tōkamachi-shi hakubutsukan).

24. A sample book dated 1782 and containing swatches of ramie ikat produced in the Uonuma region is the earliest proof of Uonuma kasuri. See Diamond, Inc., p. 120.

25. See *Kodansha Encyclopedia of Japan*, s.v. "Uesugi Kagekatsu."

26. Watanabe, pp. 143-44. The best-quality fiber comes from stalks that are 6 millimeters in diameter and 1.5 meters in length. If the plant has not grown to a sufficient height to harvest a stalk 1.5 meters in length when cut 40 centimeters above ground level, it can be cut at ground level, but the quality of the fiber is not as good.

27. Ibid., p. 144.

28. During the skinning process a green juice emerges that seems to tint the fiber a faint green. The Chinese character for *green* (青; *ao*) was combined with the character for *karamushi* (苧; *[s]o*), thereby distinguishing the fiber (aoso) from the plant (karamushi). The plant, however, is also occasionally referred to as aoso. See Watanabe, pp. 15-16, 144-45.

29. Ibid., p. 146.

30. Tōkamachi-shi hakubutsukan 1987, p. 146.

31. Watanabe, p. 150. One momme equals .1325 ounce or 3.75 grams.

32. Horiuchi, p. 89; Watanabe, p. 182.

33. Warp thread counts are calculated by *yomi*. One yomi equals eighty warp threads. Special high-quality chijimi is 20-23 yomi; top-quality chijimi is 16-17 yomi; mid-quality chijimi is 10 yomi; and low-quality chijimi is 6-7 yomi. These counts are based on a standard kimono-cloth width measuring approximately 36-40 centimeters. See Nishiwaki, p. 236; Watanabe, p. 173; and Tōkamachi-shi hakubutsukan 1983, p. 20.

34. Watanabe, p. 175.

BIBLIOGRAPHY

Bunka-chō bunka-zai hogo-bu, ed. *Minzoku shiryō senshū 3: Bōshoku shūzoku I* (An anthology of folk customs data 3: Manners and customs of spinning and weaving I). Tokyo: Zaidan-hōjin kokudo chiri kyōkai, 1975.

Diamond, Inc. *The Traditional Crafts of Japan.* Vol. 1, *Textiles.* Tokyo: Diamond, Inc., 1992.

Hauge, Victor, and Takako Hauge. *Folk Traditions in Japanese Art.* New York: International Exhibitions Foundation, 1978-79.

Hikida Keiichirō. "Snow and 'Ramie Crepe.'" *Japan Quarterly* 26, no. 4 (1979): 539-48.

Horiuchi Kazuko. "Echigo jōfu: Choma tsukuri kara seihin made" (Fine ramie cloth of Echigo: From the making of ramie to final product). *Senshoku no bi* (Textile arts), no. 25 (early autumn 1983): 81-96.

Kitamura Tetsurō. *Senshoku: Dentō kōgei* (Textiles: Traditional crafts). *Nihon no bijutsu* (Arts of Japan), no. 307. Tokyo: Shibundō, 1991.

Nishiwaki, Shinjirō. *Echigo no chijimi* (Ramie crepe from Echigo). Ojiya: Ryōgensha, 1953.

Suzuki Bokushi. *Snow Country Tales: Life in the Other Japan.* Translated by Jeffrey Hunter with Rose Lesser. New York and Tokyo: Weatherhill, 1986.

Suzuki Chobōan [Suzuki Torajurō]. *Echigo chijimi no kōtei* (The process of Echigo crepe). Tōkamachi: Chuō Shuppan, 1953.

Suzuki Torajurō. "Echigo jōfu Ojiya chijimifu no rekishi to genkyō" (The history and present situation of fine ramie cloth of Echigo/Ojiya crepe). In *Echigo jōfu/Ojiya chijimi* (Fine ramie cloth of Echigo/Ojiya crepe), 34-40. Ningen kokuhō shiriizu 42 (Living national treasure series no. 42), edited by Okada Yuzuru. Tokyo: Kōdansha, 1978.

Takizawa Eisuke. "Echigo chijimi" (Ramie crepe from Echigo). In *Some to ori* (Dyeing and weaving), 39-42. Kokoro no furusato o motomete Nihon hakken 19 (Japan discovery: In pursuit of one's spiritual home, no. 19). Tokyo: Akatsuki kyoku tosho kabushikigaisha, 1981.

Tairyūsha. *Chijimi to jōfu: Kokoro de oru soboku na nuno* (Ramie crepe and fine ramie cloth: Simple cloth woven from the heart). Tokyo: Tairyūsha, 1981.

Tōkamachi-shi hakubutsukan, ed. *Orimono seisan kōtei: Tōkamachi-shi hakubutsukan jōsetsu tenji kaisetsu sho/3* (Weaving production process: Commentary on the permanent collection of Tōkamachi City Museum/3). Tōkamachi: Tōkamachi-shi hakubutsukan tomo no kai, 1983.

Tōkamachi-shi hakubutsukan, ed. *Saiyū no joshu to chijimi ori: Echigo chijimi no bōshoku yōgu oyobi kanren shiryō* (Married women's groups and ramie crepe weaving: Spinning and weaving tools of Echigo ramie crepe and related documentation). Exh. cat. Tōkamachi: Tōkamachi-shi hakubutsukan tomo no kai, 1987.

Watanabe Sansei. *Echigo chijimifu no rekishi to gijutsu* (History and techniques of Echigo crepe cloth). Tokyo: Komiyama, 1971.

Yamazaki Mitsuko. "'Echigo chijimi' hatten no yōin--Ori nuno bi e no ori me no ishiki--" (The primary factor in the development of 'Echigo ramie crepe'--The awareness of women weavers toward the beauty of woven cloth--). *Kenritsu Niigata Joshi Tanki Daigaku kenkyū kiyō* (Study bulletin of Niigata Prefecture Women's Junior College) 10 (1973): 160-68.

The Tenjukoku Shūchō and the Asuka Period Funerary Practices

Maria del Rosario Pradel
University of California, Los Angeles

Introduction

A square support fabric measuring 90 centimeters on each side holds the arbitrarily mounted fragments of an embroidered textile known as the Tenjukoku Shūchō 天寿国繍帳 or Tenjukoku Mandara 天寿国曼荼羅.[1] The artifact belongs to Chūgūji 中宮寺, a Buddhist temple in Nara prefecture, but it is now housed in the Nara National Museum for preservation purposes.[2] Despite their fragmentary condition, it is possible to reconstruct the history of the fragments because of the abundance of documents associated with them. An inscription recorded in an eleventh century document indicates that a shūchō (繍帳, "embroidered curtain") depicting Tenjukoku was made sometime in the Asuka period (538 or 552-645 C.E.).[3] The history of the Tenjukoku "embroidered curtains," however, is not limited to the Asuka period. Documents of the Kamakura period (1185-1333 C.E.) mention the discovery of the artifact in 1274, where it is called Tenjukoku Mandara.[4] Furthermore, there is reference to the manufacture of a replica of the so-called Tenjukoku Mandara, which was finished in 1275, and consecrated by the Buddhist ritual of the "eye-opening."[5] A record shows that both artifacts were in Chūgūji,[6] and consequently both the original artifact, and its

---

[1]   The most comprehensive study on the fragments of the Tenjukoku Shūchō/Mandara is the book published by Ōhashi Katsuaki, *Tenjukoku Shūchō no kenkyū* (Tokyo: Yoshikawa Kōbunkan, 1995). Hereafter: Ōhashi, *Tenjukoku Shūchō no kenkyū*.

[2]   There are other fragments in the Tokyo National Museum, Hōryūji, and Shōsōin.

[3]   The inscription is recorded in the *Jōgū Shōtoku taishi hōō teisetsu* 『 上宮聖徳太子法王帝説 』 (*Imperial View of the King of the Law Prince Saintly Virtue of the Upper Palace*). The document is a compilation of documents related to Shōtoku Taishi (Prince Saintly Virtue, hereafter Prince Shōtoku) and consists of five sections. The inscription of the Tenjukoku Shūchō is recorded in the third section, which also includes the text of the inscriptions on the mandorlas of Hōryūji Kondō Shaka triad, and the Yakushi image. See: Ienaga Saburō, *Jōgū hōō teisetsu no kenkyū* (Tokyo: Sanseidō, 1972), and for an annotated version, Ienaga Saburō et al., *Shōtoku Taishi shū* (Tokyo: Iwanami Shoten, 1975).

[4]   The Sanskrit term *mandala* is usually used to designate the diagrams depicting the Esoteric Buddhist deities, but in the Kamakura period, *mandara* referred to all types of illustrations that explained something religious. The use of the term *mandara* in the Kamakura period is discussed by: James H. Foard, "In Search of the Lost Reformation," *Japanese Journal of Religious Studies* 7.4 (1980): 261-291.

[5]   For a detailed account of the Kamakura history see: Ōhashi, *Tenjukoku Shūchō no kenkyū*, 63-84.

[6]   See: *Shōtoku Taishi denki* 『 聖徳太子伝記 』, a Kamakura period document reproduced in: *Yamato koji taikan: Hōkkiji, Hōrinji, Chūgūji*, vol. 1 (Tokyo: Iwanami Shoten, 1977): 89. Hereafter *Yamato koji taikan*.

replica were damaged in the fires of 1309 and 1311, that partially destroyed the temple complex.[7]

The information regarding the size of the original artifact, and its replica varies from source to source. Some documents state that it was almost five meters, others state that it was six meters, but it is not clear if this information refers to the width or to the length. Another source says: "it was a big mandala, and it stretched between three bays." Since it is known that the "old mandara" and the "new mandara" were in Chūgūji, it is assumed that the bays mentioned in the sources refer to the spaces between the pillars of that temple. Excavations at the old temple site reveal that the space between the pillars was 2.8 meters, therefore, the "mandara" must have been almost eight meters wide.[8] Thus, in its present state the so called Tenjukoku "embroidered curtains" or Tenjukoku Mandara is made up of fragments of two embroidered artifacts that were manufactured 650 years apart, and that were subsequently randomly mounted on a support fabric, some time in the nineteenth century.

This paper will focus on the Asuka period original artifact, and on the basis of technical aspects and textual interpretation attempt to establish the context of manufacture and the function of the "embroidered curtains" in the seventh century. The analysis of motifs and the reconstruction of the subject matter are crucial for the interpretation of the fragments, but they will not be addressed at this time.

Before continuing with the subject of this paper, it is important to give some information regarding the time period when the panels of "embroidered curtains" were made. The Asuka period is considered to be the beginnings of Japan's historical era, when the Chinese culture of the Northern and Southern dynasties (386-589 C.E.) was transmitted to the Japanese archipelago through a natural geographical bridge: the Korean peninsula. The time frame for that period is 538 or 552 to 645 C.E., and its starting date is marked by the date of the official introduction of Buddhism to Japan from the Korean peninsula, specifically from the kingdom of Paekche (18 B.C.E.-660 C.E.). After long internal disputes, Buddhism became the State Religion. The religion, however, was part of a larger cultural complex from the continent which also included a writing system, the compilation of histories, and technology. Records show that the kingdom of Paekche dispatched not only Buddhist monks, but also temple architects, sculptors, tile makers, painters, etc. Temples, Buddhist icons, tiles, and other manifestations of material culture dated to the Asuka period show strong continental influence, particularly that of the Three Kingdoms period of the Korean peninsula. Therefore, the "embroidered curtains" as a product of a period of intense cultural

---

[7]   For a short history of the temple, see: Nishikawa Kyōtarō, "Chūgūji no rekishi, " in: *Yamato koji taikan*: 55-59.

[8]   Ōhashi, *Tenjukoku Shūchō no kenkyū*: 89-92.

interchange, will be better understood if they are considered as part of the pan-East Asian culture of the sixth and seventh centuries.

Technical aspects

Analysis of the fabric structures and embroidery techniques support the information given by the documentary evidence.[9] Research has determined that the fragments with bright colors, and well preserved embroidery threads, are part of the Asuka period embroidered curtains, whereas the deteriorated sections with faded colors are fragments of the Kamakura period replica. The ground fabric of the fragments dated to the Asuka period is a complex alternating gauze (羅, ra) forming a diamond motif, in purple silk. Some issues are raised regarding the gauze fabric used in the "embroidered curtains." Ōta points out that it is not clearly established when the gauze technique began to be utilized in Japan. He suggests that the technique was probably known before the Asuka period but that it is difficult to determine if the fragments of the Shūchō were made in Japan or that they might be regarded as an import. He presumes that the gauze technique was surely known in the Nara period (646-710 C.E.), since there are some fragments in the Shōsōin.[10] Mōri Noboru suggests that the gauze weaving technique was unknown in Asuka Japan.[11] Furthermore, Nishimura argues that the fabric was an import from the continent.[12] The fragments of the Kamakura period, are of two different types: some woven in purple twill (綾, aya), and others in white plain silk (平絹, heiken).

In the same way, the embroidery threads and embroidery stitches clearly differentiate the fragments of the original artifact from those of its replica. The threads used to embroider in the Asuka period are of a very tight Z-twist, and the patterns are filled with contiguous rows of overlapping stem stitch. In the Kamakura fragments, the embroidery threads are of a loose S-twist, this low degree of twisting being the reason for their deterioration, because in silk threads, a high twist is more satisfactory for abrasion resistance and retention of shininess. There are also a variety of embroidery stitches: flat satin stitch (used on the people's clothing and turtle shells), false satin stitch (used on the people's clothing, metamorphosis motif and lotus flower), long stem stitch

---

[9]   The first study of the fabric structure was made by Nakagawa Tadayori, "Tenjukoku Mandara ni tsuite," Shisō 20 (1923): 333-341. This study was followed by Ōta Eizo, "Tenjukoku Mandara no shugi to Kenji shūri ni tsuite," Shiseki to bijutsu 188 (1948): 161-176, who concentrated on the embroidery threads, and the different types of stitches. Other studies dealing with technical aspects are: Mōri Noboru, "Tenjukoku Shūchō ni tsuite - Shūchō no genpon to Kenji saikō no Shūchō ni tsuite," Kobijutsu 11 (1965): 27-38, and Nishimura Hyōbu, "Zuhan kaisetsu - Tenjukoku Shūchō," in Shūbutsu, edited by Nara Kokuritsu Hakubutsukan (Tokyo: Kadokawa Shoten, 1964): 12-18. The most recent study, which concentrates on the support fabric and the lining: Sawada Mutsuyo, "Tenjukoku Shūchō no genjō," Museum 495 (1992): 4-25.

[10]   Ōta, Op. cit., p. 169.

[11]   Mōri, Op. cit., p. 31.

[12]   Nishimura, Op. cit., p. 16.

(used as the outline stitch), and also composite stitches, using various forms of couching.[13]

Other technical aspects are revealed by the research of the fabric structures. For instance, a lining paper was found underneath the Kamakura period fragments, therefore, it was concluded that a paper with the pattern diagram and the ground fabric was put together in order to embroider the different motifs. For the longest time, textile specialists wondered how the motifs were embroidered on to the Asuka period thin gauze fabric, since they could not find any lining paper among the fragments. In a recent study, Sawada Mutsuyo of the Tokyo National Museum discovered a very small portion, where there is a thin light purple plain woven silk underneath the gauze fabric. She concluded that the plain woven silk played the same role as the lining paper used in the Kamakura period. This discovery was particularly important because it corroborated the dating of the fragments to the Asuka period.[14]

The turtle shells and the inscription

The turtle shells with four characters each, are particularly important because they carried the inscription. Among the extant fragments there are four turtle motifs (only one belonging to the original artifact), and there is another turtle shell, and five small fragments in the Shōsōin, a repository in the grounds of Tōdaiji. In all, there is a total of twenty-five extant characters. Records show that there were one hundred turtle shell motifs embroidered on the original artifact, and thus the inscription consisted of four hundred characters.[15] The first part of the inscription is a detailed genealogy of a couple, Prince Toyotomimi, and one of his four consorts, Princess Tachibana. The second part of the inscription indicates that the mother of the prince, Empress Anahobe no Hashihito, died in the year corresponding to 621 C.E., and that the following year,622 C.E., Prince Toyotomimi passed away. Princess Tachibana was devastated by the loss of her husband and her mother-in-law in such a short period of time, and she went to see her grandmother, Empress Suiko, and expressed her grief. The princess mentioned that her husband used to say: "This world is empty, the only truth is the Buddha," and because he was a believer, he must be in Tenjukoku. She, however, could not visualize that land, and expressed her wish to depict him in that afterlife world in order to cherish his memory. Moved by her grandchild's suffering the empress ordered the manufacture of two panels of embroidered curtains (*shuchō nichō* 繡帳二張), which were designed by Yamato Aya no Maken 東漢末賢 , Koma no Kasei 高麗加西溢, and Aya no

---

[13]   See: Sawada, *Op. cit.,*pp. 13-15, for an explanation of the embroidery techniques, illustrated with detailed photographs.

[14]   *Ibid.*, p. 15-16.

[15]   The text is written in Classical Chinese. For a rendering in Classical Japanese see Iida Mizuho, "Tenjukoku Shūchō mei o megutte," *Kobijutsu* 11 (1965) 1965): 46-47. Also: Nishimura Hyōbu, *Op. Cit.* An English translation , and a dicussion of the inscription is available in J.H. Kamstra, *Encounter or Syncretism. The Initial Growth of Japanese Buddhism* (Leiden: E. J. Brill, 1967): 379-381. There are, however, some serious mistakes in the translation, particularly the dates.

Nukakori 漢奴加己利, and embroidered by the ladies in waiting, under the supervision of Kurabe no Hata no Kuma 椋部秦久麻 .

Although many issues regarding seventh century Japan can be discussed in relation to this inscription, only those relevant for the purpose of this paper will be addressed.

1. The "embroidered curtains" are associated with prince Toyotomimi, which is another name for prince Shōtoku (574-622 C.E.).[16] He is an important figure of Asuka history, according to orthodox Japanese historiography, because he is given credit for the diffusion of Buddhism in Japan. He is also believed to have played an important political role as regent during the reign of Empress Suiko (r. 592-628 C.E.).

2. The inscription gives an indication on the date of manufacture, since it states that the "embroidered curtains" were made sometime after the death of prince Shōtoku in 622 C.E.

3. Princess Tachibana, in her grieving, wanted to see the prince in the afterlife world she did not know, named Tenjukoku.[17] According to the characters, Tenjukoku means: 天 *ten*, heaven; 寿 *ju*, long life, and 国 *koku*, land, which can be translated as the "Land of Heavenly Life."

4. The inscription also explains the specific function of the artifact as curtains, and also that they consisted of two panels (二張 *nichō*, two panels). Since the inscription suggests that the "embroidered curtains" were made as a memorial, one should consider the function of curtains within a funerary context.

5. As mentioned before, the Asuka period is characterized by the strong continental connections. The names of the designers, and the supervisor are associated with influential immigrant clans. For instance, the Koma were people from the kingdom of Koguryo in the Korean peninsula; the Aya, which uses the character of the Chinese Han dynasty (206 B.C.E.-220 C.E.) were descendants of Chinese who had earlier settled in the Korean peninsula. Particularly important in relation to the "embroidered curtains" is the name of the supervisor. It is known that the Hata were associated in early history

---

[16] For other names of prince Shōtoku, see: Mayuzumi Hiromichi and Takemitsu Makoto, eds., *Shōtoku Taishi jiten* (Tokyo: Shinjinbutsu Ōraisha, 1991): 286.

[17] Tenjukoku is a very controversial term. Most of the studies attempt to explain the term in a Buddhist context. Tenjukoku, however, does not apparently appear in any of the Buddhist sutras. For the various interpretation of Tenjukoku, see: Ōhashi, *Tenjukoku Shūchō no kenkyū*: 125-131.

with sericulture, weaving, and metallurgy, techniques that they might have helped to introduce to Japan. Significantly, *hata* means loom. [18]

6. Particularly relevant is the information regarding the activities of women in Asuka Japan. Women were patrons of the arts, since it is known that the embroidered panels were manufactured upon request of Princess Tachibana and ordered by Empress Suiko, and, moreover, it shows that women actively participated in the manufacture of the curtains by embroidering.

A major issue regarding the fragments is the reconstruction of the arrangement of the turtles shells. Scholars have proposed a variety of explanations based on the information given by the sources, and some argue that the turtles were placed around the borders, whereas others suggests that the turtles were at the botton. [19] Most of the arrangements are proposed on the basis of textual interpretation; however, Ōhashi carefully observed the fragments, and realized that on the only large extant fragment (right side of the upper left fragment) there was a red bird, a lotus flower, a cloud, a turtle, a bud-like motif and part of a garment. This fragment is particularly important because it reveals the relationship between the motifs in the composition and we know that the motifs did not cover the whole surface of the ground fabric, but that they were scattered on it. On the basis of the analysis of this fragment, Ōhashi concluded that the turtles were placed among the other motifs, being elements of the whole composition, and having the function of carrying the inscription. [20]

Function of the Tenjukoku Shūchō

Because the fragments are now housed in a Buddhist temple, the present artifact was classified as an embroidered Buddhist icon (繡仏, *shūbutsu*), and believed to have served as an object of worship, or as a wall hanging to decorate a temple. [21] The inscription, however, clearly states the function of the original artifact. It explains that they were make as a pair of curtains with embroidered motifs representing prince Shōtoku in the "Land of Heavenly Life." The facts that the ground fabric from the original artifact is of a very thin gauze with translucent quality and that the embroidered

---

[18] For a discussion of the immigrant lineage of the designers, and the supervisor, see: William Carter, "Aya family" and "Hata family," *Kodansha Encyclopedia of Japan*, vol. 1 and vol. 3, respectively (Tokyo & New York: Kodansha, 1983): 125 and 11. See also: Wontack Hong, *Relationship between Korea and Japan in Early Period: Paekche and Yamato Wa* (Seoul: Ilsimsa, 1988), and *Paekche of Korea and the Origin of Yamato Japan* (Seoul: Kudara International, 1994).

[19] Ōhashi, *Tenjukoku Shūchō no kenkyū*: 92-95.

[20] *Ibid.*, 105-110.

[21] This interpretation has its basis on the Kamakura period events, and especially on the fact that, at that time, the "embroidered curtains" and its replica are called mandara.

patterns are not fully covering the ground fabric which allows light through, further supports the theory that they functioned as curtains.

Ōhashi investigated the use of curtains in ancient Japan, and pointed out that they had two main functions: first, they were used around beds, as seen in this painting by Ku K'ai-chih (ca. 344-406), from the "Admonitions Scrolls" entitled "Uncertain Bedfellows," (British Museum, London), and second, they protect Buddhist images, as seen nowadays in Buddhist temples.[22] Since the inscription suggests a funerary context, I searched for the use of curtains within that context. An entry from *Nihon shoki* 日本書記, or *Chronicles of Japan*, corresponding to 646 C.E., refers to the reform of funerary practices when issues related to the tomb size, offerings, use of hearses, etc., were established. Interestingly, regarding curtains the edict says: "At the time of the interment white cloth shall be used for the curtains of the bier," which is the frame upon which a coffin or corpse is taken to its burial.[23] It is difficult to establish if embroidered curtains were used before the reform, but this entry in *Nihon shoki* confirms the role of curtains in the funerary rituals.

Conclusion

To conclude, the reconstruction of the history of the fragments is particularly interesting because it allows one to trace back the variety of roles played by textiles in Japanese ritual or sacred contexts. Firstly, we have a pair of embroidered curtains made sometime after 622 C.E., which were probably used for the funerary rituals, or as a memorial for an important figure of the Asuka period. These curtains were carefully kept in the repository of a Buddhist temple, and rediscovered in 1274. The following year the panels were replicated, and consecrated with the Buddhist ceremony of the "eye-opening," and both the "old mandara" and the "new mandara" were kept in the Buddhist nunnery of Chūgūji. When the temple was partially destroyed in the fires of 1309 and 1311, the fragments were badly damaged, but they were carefully kept, and pasted together sometime in the nineteenth century. Since then, the fragments have been worshiped as a sacred object related to prince Shōtoku.

Nowadays, people go the modern concrete building that is Chūgūji, and worship the fragments. Only a few notice that the object being worshiped is a replica of the fragments, made in 1982, in order to preserve the ancient fragments of a Japanese National Treasure, which are carefully kept in the Nara National Museum.

---

[22] Ōhashi, *Tenjukoku Shūchō no kenkyū*: 95-101.

[23] *Nihon shoki*, vol. 68 of *Nihon koten bungaku taikei* (Tokyo: Iwanami Shoten, 1965): 292-294, and W.G. Aston., trans. *Nihongi. Chronicles of Japan from the Earliest Times to A.D. 697* (Rutland, Vermont & Tokyo: Charles E. Tuttle Co., 1988): II, 218.

Bibliography

Aston, W.G., trans. *Nihongi. Chronicles of Japan from the Earliest Times to A.D. 697.* Rutland, Vermont & Tokyo: Charles E. Tuttle Co., 1988.

Carter, William. "Aya family." *Kodansha Encyclopedia of Japan*, vol. 1. Tokyo & New York: Kodansha, 1983.

-----. "Hata family." *Kodansha Encyclopedia of Japan*, vol. 3. Tokyo & New York: Kodansha, 1983.

Foard, James H. "In Search of the Lost Reformation." *Japanese Journal of Religious Studies* 7.4 (1980): 261-291.

Hong, Wontack. *Relationship between Korea and Japan in Early Period: Paekche, and Yamato Wa.* Seoul: Ilsimsa, 1988.

----- *Paekche of Korea and the Origin of Yamato Japan.* Seoul: Kudara International, 1994.

Ienaga Saburō 家永三郎. *Jōgū hoo teisetsu no kenkyū*『上宮聖徳法王帝説の研究』(*Research on the Jōgū hoo teisetsu*). Tokyo: Sanseidō, 1972.

----- et al. *Shōtoku Taishi shū*『聖徳太子集』(*Prince Shōtoku Collection*). Tokyo: Iwanami Shoten, 1975.

Iida Mizuho 飯田瑞穂. "Tenjukoku Shūchō mei o megutte"「天寿国繡帳銘をめぐって」("On the Inscription of the Tenjukoku Embroidered Curtains"). *Kobijutsu*『古美術』11 (1965): 39-49.

Kamstra, J.H. *Encounter or Syncretism. The Initial Growth of Japanese Buddhism.* Leiden: E.J.Brill, 1967.

Mayuzumi Hiromichi 黛弘道 and Takemitsu Makoto 武光誠, eds. *Shōtoku Taishi jiten*『聖徳太子事典』(*Prince Shōtoku Dictionary*). Tokyo: Shinjinbutsu Ōraisha, 1991.

Mōri Noboru 毛利登. "Tenjukoku Shūchō ni tsuite - Shūchō no genpon to Kenji saikō no Shūchō ni tsuite"「天寿国繡帳について‐繡帳の原本と建治再興の繡帳について」("Tenjukoku Shūchō: About the Original Embroidered Curtains and the Revival of the Kenji era). *Kobijutsu*『古美術』11 (1965): 27-38.

Nakagawa Tadayori 中川忠順."Tenjukoku Mandara ni tsuite" 「天壽國曼荼羅に就いて」("About the Tenjukoku Mandara"). *Shisō*『思想』20 (1923): 333-341.

Nihon shoki『日本書紀』(*Chronicles of Japan*). Vol. 68 of *Nihon koten bungaku taikei* 日本古典文学大系(*Compendium of Japanese Classical Literature*). Tokyo: Iwanami Shoten, 1965.

Nishikawa Kyōtarō 西川杏太郎. "Chūgūji no rekishi"「中宮寺の歴史」("The History of the Chūgūji"). In: *Yamato koji taikan: Hōkkiji, Hōrinji, Chūgūji*『大和古寺大観: 法起寺、法輪寺、中宮寺』(*General View of the Old Temples of the Yamato Region*), vol. 1. Tokyo: Iwanami Shoten, 1977, pp. 55-59.

Nishimura Hyōbu 西村兵部. "Zuhan kaisetsu - Tenjukoku Shūchō"「図版解説 - 天寿国繍帳」("Plate explanation - Tenjukoku Shūchō") In: *Shūbutsu*『繍仏』(*Embroidered Buddhist Icons*). Edited by Nara Kokuritsu Hakubutsukan 奈良国立博物館監修. Tokyo: Kadokawa Shoten, 1964.

Ōhashi Katsuaki 大橋一章. *Tenjukoku Shūchō no kenkyū*『天寿国繍帳の研究』(*Study about the Tenjukoku Shūchō*). Tokyo: Yoshikawa Kōbunkan, 1995.

Ōta Eizō 太田英藏. "Tenjukoku Mandara no shūgi to Kenji shūri ni tsuite"「天寿国曼荼羅の繍技と建治修理について」("The Tenjukoku Mandara's Embroidery Techniques and Repairs of the Kenji era"). *Shiseki to bijutsu*『史迹と美術』188 (1948): 161-176.

Sawada Mutsuyo 沢田むつ代. "Tenjukoku Shūchō no genjō"「天寿国繍帳の現状」("The Present Condition of the Tenjukoku Shūchō"). *Museum* 495 (1992): 4-25.

Acknowledgments

I wish to thank professor Ōhashi Katsuaki from Waseda University and Ms. Sawada Mutsuyo from the Tokyo National Museum for their insightful first hand information. Research trips to Japan were made possible by the generous support of the Sasakawa Foundation and the Dickson Travel Fellowship (UCLA). I would like to particularly thank my advisor, professor Donald McCallum for his patience and wise advice in this research project.

The Reproduction and Ceremonial Offering of Sacred Textiles and Apparel in Ise Jingû's Shikinen Sengû

by
Rosemarie Bernard

This paper addresses the reproduction and ceremonial offering of sacred textiles and apparel on the occasion of the vicennial transfer rituals (Shikinen Sengû), which take place once in twenty years in Ise Jingû. The most recent performance of the 1300-year old ritual tradition took place in 1993. The ritual climax of the Shikinen Sengû consists of the ceremonial transfer of the "body" of the deity Amaterasu Omikami (a sacred mirror) from the 20-year old sanctum to an identical structure constructed in an adjacent area. Along with the body of the deity, thousands of magnificent treasures, textiles and apparel are ceremonially carried to the new sanctuary, where they remain alongside the deity for twenty years.

There is a total of 1085 textiles and apparel, in 525 categories, which are offered to the deities on the occasion of the Shikinen Sengû. Their production is characterized by the effort to reproduce exactly the objects produced twenty years before. This paper examines the production of some of the most important textiles and apparel offered in the Sengû, notably the *ake no nishiki no mizo* (scarlet brocade), and *aokôkechiwata no mizo* (blue cotton wool clothing dyed according to the binding technique called *kyôkechizome*. Attention is drawn to the importance of historical continuity in the production and the ceremonial offering of these and other textiles and apparel, as well as to change and innovative recreations of ancient production techniques.

Rosemarie Bernard is a Ph.D. Candidate in Social Anthropology at Harvard University. She conducted field research in Ise, Japan from April 1991 to September 1994, on the topic of the vicennial rites of the Shikinen Sengû (transfer rites) in Ise Jingû. While in Ise, she was affiliated with a Shinto divinity school, Kôgakkan University, and was an employee of the Office of Information and Public Relations of Ise Jingû, in which capacity she was involved in the preparations towards the performance of the 1993 performance of the Sengû. The rituals of the Sengû are the focus of her dissertation. She is also writing about the architectural and artistic traditions which are important aspects of the Shikinen Sengû.

Haitian Drapo Vodou: Imagery, Ritual and Perception

Susan Elizabeth Tselos

During the last decade, boutiques and galleries from New York to Los Angeles have been displaying sparkling works of art depicting images of Catholic Saints and mystical symbols created with thousands of tiny sequins and beads.[1] These textiles, made in Haiti as part of a cottage industry of "art flags" are a widely celebrated derivation of the traditional ritual flags known as drapo *Vodou* which have been used by the Haitian people during their religious ceremonies since they were brought to the new world as slaves.

Perhaps more than any other of the ritual objects used by Haitians to honor the spirits of Ginen, known to them as "*lwa*", the consecrated drapo document the deeply syncretized cultural elements which are the foundation of this misunderstood religion.

The shapes, colors, materials, and symbols incorporated into these drapo reflect many fragmented origins, including Fon, Yoruba and Kongo religious beliefs and asthetics, 18th Century European mysticism, French Catholicism, Freemasonery, French military regimental colors, Rosiancrucianism, and Muslim influences.[2] They are not only witness to

Fig. 1. Image of St. James Major representing Sen Jak, on the wall of a Vodou temple in Port-au-Prince.

Haiti's tortuous past, they are living mediations; shimmering, visual boundaries between the old world and the new, the spiritual world, and the world of mortals. Each drapo has one meaning projected onto its surface, while a second meaning lies in shadow below, simultaneously concealing and unveiling the spiritual power held within their borders.

The roots of Haitian Vodou lie in Africa primarily among the Fon and Yoruba, where the pantheon of spirits who oversee the well being of humans are honored and appeased through ceremony and sacrifice; and who manifest themselves through spirit possession of chosen devotees.[3] Music, dance, visual images and sacred objects work together in unison to create an environment in which the spirit will arrive on earth to give advice and heal ills.

These religious elements made their voyage to the New World by way of the brutal migration of the slave trade. Forced onto the sugar plantations of San Domingue, the slaves sought to reassemble their traditional beliefs and methods of worship.

By the time of their arrival, many of the Africans, especially those from Dahomey and Kongo were already familiar with Catholicism, due to the presence of Portuguese explorers who had established outposts along the west coast of Africa as early as the 14th Century. For those Africans not already familiar with Catholicism, French priests were ready with images and instruction in the lives of the saints in preparation for converting the slaves' souls for eternal salvation.

However, religious instruction in Catholicism proved to be a intermittent affair, since the Africans had been brought to San Domingue to work, not savor the lives of the saints. In fact, the slaves were worked so brutally, that they died within several years of arriving. As a result, there was a constant supply of new slaves, each bringing their religious beliefs with them.[4]

The consequence of this was that the European Catholic saints proved to be fertile ground for identification of these African dieties. Many of the Africans, especially the Fon, were already used to assimilating spiritual imagery and beliefs from neighboring groups in their homelands, and they found in the images of the Catholic saints, familiar visual icons with which they could identify their own *lwa*. .

It is most likely that the first Catholic saint to be syncretized with an African *lwa* was St. James Major, the patron saint of Spain; and it has been documented that this syncretization commenced in Africa. In 1491, the year before Columbus landed in the Americas, the Portuguese gave the king of Kongo a banner embroidered with the image of St. James Major, who then went on to become the patron saint of Kongo.[5]

To the Haitian Vodouisants, the image of St. James Major, whom they call Sen Jak, symbolizes the head figure of the group of warrior *lwa* known as Ogou. (Fig.1) In Dahomey and western Nigeria, Ogun is the patron of warriors, iron smiths and other metal workers. The symbols in the image of St.James Major which have come to represent Ogou

Fig.2. Image of Danbala Wedo as represented by the image of St. Patrick on the wall of a Vodou temple in Carrefour - du-Fort, Haiti

in Haiti are the central image of a triumphant warrior, and the iron sword held in his hand. As a warrior, he is believed to have played a major role in the successful slave rebellion in which the slaves won their independence in 1804. Today, he represents power, not only military, but in politics as well. And as the patron of metal, he is honored by taxi drivers, who hang a strip of cloth in his traditional color red on their rear view mirrors.

The Catholic image of St. Patrick was adopted as the visual representation of the Vodou *lwa* Danbala. (Fig.2) St. Patrick, as he drives the snakes out of Ireland, appears as a venerable elder, standing at the edge of a watery abyss with snakes writhing at his feet. These symbols became creolized representations of DanWedo, the benevolent serpent spirit of the Fon. Danbala is one of the most ancient, venerable of the Haitian *lwa*, and he is believed to inhabit streams and pools. The watery abyss in the picture of St. Patrick is identified as Ginen, the home of the ancestral Vodou spirits, and is simultaneously believed to be the place where the souls of the deceased go for a year and a day before they are reclaimed in a ceremony in preparation for their union with other ancestors.

The Virgin Mary, in her incarnation as the suffering Madonna syncretized with Ezili Freda Dahomey, who, as her name suggests, was a Vodou *lwa* from Ouidah, Dahomey. (Fig.3) She is the *lwa* of love, the Vodou Aphrodite, who demands perfumes and riches, but who also weeps for the suffering of the world. She is syncretized with the image of the Madonna through the image of a beautiful woman who is surrounded by riches and jewels, but whose heart is pierced by a sword. The colors which represent her are pale colors, pink, blue, and white. During ceremonies honoring her, cakes iced in pink and blue will be offered, along with large amounts of champagne. During colonial times she represented the luxury and grandeur of the privileged, European woman. Today, every Haitian woman identifies with Ezili, as the personification of love and beauty.

Fig.3. Ezili Freda Dahomey as represented by Mater Dolorosa on the wall of a Vodou temple in Martissant, Haiti.

Early Drapo

The drapo have undergone a metamorphoses throughout their history. Unfortunately, there are virtually no drapo remaining which existed prior to the late 1930's, due in part to Haiti's hot, humid climate, but primarily due to several anti superstition campaigns waged by the Catholic church in which almost all Vodou artifacts were destroyed. Although there is written documentation of drapo being used in Vodou ceremonies during the colonial period, visual documentation dates only to the early decades of the 20th century.[6]

Photographs from that period show drapo which are basically unembellished,but if the color codes which exist today have remained constant, one can speculate that the fabric from which the drapo were made contained the colors appropriate to the *lwa* being served. There is evidence remaining that some of the older drapo had metal sequins sewn onto them. And it is possible that these may have been more common than thought, although the heaviness of the metal, and the fact that the threads that held them would fray easily, was possibly a deterrent to using them in great numbers. By the 1940's, plastic sequins had become readily available, and their lightweight quality made it easier to more highly embellish the drapo.

The early drapo show the images of the *lwa* in subtle polychrome sequins on background fabric of appropriate colors. (Fig.4) The images from this period appear delicate, and not as well defined as the later drapo. The images are executed in the style of "*simen grenn*" which translates to "scattering seeds", in which the sequins are used sparingly, and great amounts of background fabric is unadorned. Robert Farris Thompson believes that the pattern of dotting that this type of sequin design produces is related to the Kongo concept of ritual dotting as a mediation of the secrets and power of the dead.[7]

Fig. 4. Vodou flag for Ogou, circa 1940. Note the image of St. James who represents Ogou. The early iconography is monochromatic in Appearance.

In the early drapo, the iconography is done entirely in sequins using "*veve*" symbols. *Veve* are lacy, symbolic lines drawn on the floor of the temple by the Vodou priest (*oungan*) during the ceremonies to honor the *lwa*. Each *lwa* has specific symbols with which they are identified. The *veve's* purpose is to help summon the *lwa* into the temple. By simply creating the lines of the *veve* on the ground in flour or cornmeal within the ritual context, the *lwa* is pressured to make an appearance.

Like the pictorial representations of the *lwa*, much of the *veve* iconography originates in the imagery of the Catholic Saints as well. The *veve* for Sen Jak is adapted from his pictorial representation. The sword and flags are removed from their background and placed together as a spiritual unit. Danbala's snake has been lifted from the the feet of St. Patrick and entwines himself in heavenly rapture with his wife Aida Wedo. Together they encircle the palm tree representing Aizan, the venerable Dahomean spirit who oversees initiation. (Fig.5)

Often, the *veve* for Danbala and Aida Wedo share space with the *veve* for Ezili Freda Dahomey, whose symbolic heart with the letter "M" has been borrowed from the Catholic imagery of Mater Dolorosa. Often the heart of Ezili is divided in to squares, and sometimes it is pierced with the sword which is also borrowed from her pictorial imagery. (Fig.6)

In addition to the iconography just discussed, often there are other symbols depicted in sequins as well. The Masonic crossed compasses are used frequently, especially for Ogou and Danbala, who are both considered to be Masons, like many of the *oungans* who serve them, and there are star like motifs called *pwe* which are points in which potent spiritual power may be caught within the drapo.

The drapo have traditionally been made directly within the Vodou temples, often by the *oungan* himself who receives a request from the *lwa* he serves. If he is not adept at fabricating the drapo himself, he may purchase it from another *oungan* who has more artistic talent. When the drapo are completed, they are consecrated on the day of the week reserved for honoring the *lwa* for whom the drapo has been made.

Each temple has at least two drapo which are essential elements for the ceremonies honoring the cool, benevolent, branch of *lwa*. Almost without exception, these drapo usually represent Ogou, and Danbala. If additional drapo are owned by the temple, they will represent other *lwa* important within the specific societie. For example, there are many drapo for Baron Samedi, head of the graveyard *lwa* known as Guede, who are honored November 1st & 2nd. (Fig.7) Temples near the sea may have a drapo for Agoue, the patron of sailors and fishermen; and those in the countryside may own drapo dedicated to Azaka, *lwa* of agriculture.

Fig. 5. Vodou drapo for Danbala Wedo, circa 1940. The snake representing Danbala is entwined with his wife Aida Wedo around the palm tree which represents Aizan.

Vodou Drapo in Ceremony

The following description is of an initiation ceremony (canzo) which was performed near Port-au-Prince in September of 1992. Most Vodou ceremonies begin with the *oungan* drawing a *veve* near the base of the *poteau mitan*, the centerpost of the temple, (the pathway for the spirits to enter from their watery home in Guinen). Taking a pinch of flour or cornmeal, the *oungan* will let it slip from between his fingers onto the ground, creating the thin, lacy, geometric motifs. Once the lines and symbols of the *veve* are complete they are consecrated by placing small plates of grilled maise, peanuts and other dried foods on them. They may also be sprinkled with rum. Finally, a lit candle is placed on top of the *veve*.

The *oungan* then begins his invocation to the *lwa*. As he sings, a choir of initiates, called *hounsis* begin to accompany him, clapping their hands in unison.

The first *lwa* to be called in any Vodou ceremony is *Legba*, guardian of the threshold to the world of the invisibles. *Legba* must open the gates before any mortals can enter the world of the *lwa*.

> *Papa Legba remove the barrier for me*
> *Open the gate, Papa Legba*
> *To let me pass through*

As *Legba* is being invoked, the *hounsis* approach the *oungan* with paquet Kongo, the charms which act as mediating material between the two worlds. With his *rattle* and a pitcher of water, the *oungan* salutes the paquet, then salutes the four cardinal points: north, south, east and west. He then turns to salute the drums with libations, and then salutes the visiting *oungans* and other dignitaries by shaking his rattle (*asson*) and pouring rum at their feet.

Fig.6. Vodou drapo for Danbala Wedo, circa 1970. Here, Danbala is paired with heart which represents Ezili Freda Dahomey.

During these salutations the temple is a cacophony of singing, handclapping and drumming. Suddenly the drums interrupt the noise with bursts of staccato which raises the level of energy even more, and, finally, the incessant rhythm of the drums gives order to the chaos. At this point the *hounsis* bring out the sacred *govi* pots from the altar room. The *govi* are the resting place for the spiritual essence of the ancestors. They are paraded into the temple, and to the four cardinal points. As the *hounsis* walk with them, the power of the spirits can be felt as the *hounsis* stagger with spiritual energy.

The singing continues with a song to the *lwa Sogbo*, protector of the flags.

> *Papa Sobo who is in the oumfo*
> *he asks for the flags.*
> *Papa Sobo who is in the oumfo*
> *he asks for the flags of the lwa.*

The *La Place*, assistant to *oungan*, picks up a machete from the base of the *poteau mitan* and begins to circle it. He is entrusted with the care of the sacred machete, which is associated with the warrior *Ogou*.. It symbolizes the combat through which spiritual authority is expressed. As he circles the *poteau mitan*, two female *hounsis* step forward to escort him into one of the altar rooms at the far side of the ceremonial area. As they come from the altar room, the two *hounsis* are wrapped in the breathtakingly beautiful drapo . They enter the ceremonial area with the drapo standards clutched in their right hands.

The arrival of the drapo into the *peristyle* (temple) is an essential mediation between the worlds of spirits and mortals. The brilliant, shimmering beauty of the drapo reinforces the symbols created in the *veve*, and their arrival indicates that an appearance by the desired *lwa* is imminent.

The trio proceeds to the four cardinal points at the edges of the *peristyle*. The *La Place* follows them, pitcher of water in one hand, candles in the other. Here they perform more ritual salutations which are concluded by kneeling and kissing the ground three times.

The trio charges back to the *poteau mitan*, and circles it in a mock battle of flag waving and sword flashing.The salutations are repeated, and they quickly move on to the drums, and then approach the guests. As they do so, they join the tips of the flag standards and present them to the dignitaries in a sign of respect. The dignitaries return the respect by kissing the guard of the machete and the staff of the drapo.

After this mutual recognition, the trio retreats and circles the *poteau mitan* once again with numerous quick changes in direction. Finally the two *hounsis* lower the drapo, roll them loosely around the standards and lean them against the *poteau mitan* for the duration of the ceremony.

Within the frenzy of the drapo presentation, the *lwa* arrives and takes possession of of the *oungan's* body. By this time the *veve*, which was so carefully drawn on the ground of the *peristyle* is obliterated by the feet of the dancing initiates. The spirit has arrived, the salutations have been a success.[8]

The function of the *veve* as well as the function of the drapo is now over.   After the ceremony is complete, they will be carried back to the altar room where they will lean against the altar for the *lwa* to whom they are dedicated. Through this they will renew their spiritual strength in preparation for the next ceremony.

DESIGN METAMORPHOSES

Although the *veves* have been used throughout the decades as symbolic designs on the drapo, attention to the visual design of the drapo grew as the decades of this century progressed. In the 1940's the designs of the drapo were fairly simple; the image of the *lwa* centerfield, and there are usually no encompassing borders. Occasionally simple, partial, diagonal borders appear on the corners of the flags. Although the outer layer of fabric on the drapo is usually of expensive satin or velvet, generally a layer of recycled cotton lies below. This layer acts to stabilize the weight of the sequins so that the fabric does not sag when the flags are in use. The

Fig.7. Vodou drapo for Baron Samedi, head of the Graveyard *lwa* known as the Guede. Circa 1970.

stabilizing layer of fabric generally was taken from cloth bags previously used for rice.

By the 1950's there was more attention to full color areas, which began to appear in more defined shapes. Color was used to fill the images, and by this time paper chromolithographs of the saints which represent the *lwa* began to be used in the designs as well. The paper images were laid down over the silk or velvet, and the sequin work was done over them. However, in a practice which is still honored today, the face and sometimes the hands of the *lwa were* left uncovered.

Simple borders had become popular by the early 1960's, but the borders themselves, as well as the central field remained sprinkled with sequins in the "*semin grenn*" style. By this time the muslin fabric backing the fancy outer fabric had been replaced by burlap.This was a heavier material,but it enabled the sequins to begin to be used in greater numbers without concern for sagging.

Fig.8. Vodou drapo for Ezili Freda, circa 1970. By this time the paper image of Mater Dolorsa is being used in the center filed , and the borders are fairly sophisticated.

Fig. 9. Vodou drapo for St.Jak/Ogou, circa 1980. By this time the attentionto multiple borders is well established, and the drapo is fully covered with sequins.

By the late 1960's and early 1970's burlap was used regularly to back the satin and velvet face fabric. (Fig.8) Sequins had become more plentiful in Haiti due to the presence of American owned companies which had their garment piecework assembly done at Haitian factories. By this time the attention to borders and imagery of the symbols had become sophisticated. The colors reflected not only those appropriate to the *lwa*, but the borders had become very important, possibly a reflection of the "op art' and graphic textile designs so popular in the United States and Europe at the time. (Fig.9) Although the heavy burlap backing had enabled the drapo to carry the weight of more sequins, the combined weight made this style of drapo extremely heavy for ceremonial use.

Sophisticated designs and borders remained consistent elements of the drapo until the trade embargo of the mid 1990's, at which time the remaining factories left Haiti, and the supply of sequins ran out. The support fabric had changed again in the early 1990's to a lightweight, plastic burlap, resulting from a change in the fabric used for bags of imported rice.[9] This was successful in reversing the problem of excessive weight, however, as the sequins became less available, the flagmakers, reverted to the "old style' of "*simen grenn*" designs, thereby decreasing the weight of the flags even more.[10] Today, a few of the more successful artists who fabricate drapo for the art market are able to continue their art at increased prices. For the drapo fabricated to serve the *lwa*, the "*simen grenn*" style is an unexpected return to the traditional designs of the earlier decades of this century.

NOTES

[1] See Maggie Steber's article "Voodoo Flags" in Connoisseur , February, 1988, and Victoria Lautman's article "Into the Mystic: The New Folk Art" in Metropolitian Home, June 1989. pp. 78-79.

[2] See Donald J. Cosentino's chapter "Imagine Heaven" in The Sacred Arts of Haitian Vodou, Fowler Museum of Natural History, UCLA, 1995. pp. 25-55.

[3] Ibid.

[4] See Alfred Metraux's Voodoo in Haiti. Oxford University Press, New York, 1959. pp. 32- 34.

[5] See Patrick Polk's chapter "Sacred Banners and the Divine Cavalry Charge" in The Sacred Arts of Haitian Vodou, Fowler Museum of Cultural History, UCLA, 1995. pp332.

[6] See photographs following the text in William Seabrook's The Magic Island, Harcourt, Brace and Co., New York, 1929.

7 See Robert Farris Thompson's article "From the Isle Beneath the Sea: Haiti's Africanizing Vodou Art" in The Sacred Arts of Haitian Vodou, Fowler Museum of Natural History, UCLA, 1995. pp107.

[8] The description of the Vodou ceremony is based on a *canzo* initiation ceremony I witnessed at Societie De Real in September, 1992.

[9] Newfield Partners Ltd. of Miami, Florida started using these bags in 1991 to import their U.S. Long Grain rice into Haiti, Their name and phone number is printed on the plastic burlap bags recycled to line the Vodou flags.

[10] Interview with *oungan* and flagmaker Pierrot Barra, April 1994.

PHOTOGRAPHY CREDITS

Figures 1,2,3, by Susan Elizabeth Tselos
Figures 4-9 by Sibila Savage

BIBLIOGRAPHY

Cosentino, Donald J. ed. *The Sacred Arts of Haitian Vodou.* The Fowler Museum of Cultural History, UCLA, 1995.

Courlander, Harold. *The Drum and the Hoe.* Berkeley: University of California Press, 1960.

Deren, Maya. *Divine Horsemen: The Living Gods of Haiti.* London: Thames and Hudson, 1953.

Metraux, Alfred. *Voodoo in Haiti.* New York: Oxford University Press, 1959.

Thompson, Robert Farrris. *Flash of the Spirit.* New York:Random House,1983.

Yonker, Dolores. *"Invitation to the Spirits."* A Report, S.F. Craft & Folk Art Museum, Spring, 1985.

Some Breton and Muslim Antecedents of Voudou Drapo

by

LeGrace Benson

The drapo that appears in every Haitian Voudou *houmfo* is *drapo nasiyonal*, the flag of Haiti. Historians dispute the actual events that brought the red and blue drapo and its device of palm tree, cannons, anchor and drums into being, but the legends and esoterica move along in a deep current of real meaning.

When Aristide became President of Haiti, hundreds of murals appeared on street walls all over the country. A great number of them included the re-instituted red and blue national flag of liberation Dessalines had dramatically produced in 1803. With the stitching help of Catherine Flon, mambo of the Mérote Voudou *houmfo*, he ripped the white from the French tricolor and joined the red band for the slaves and the blue for the freedmen in equality at the hampe. Under this banner the warriors expelled the French and proclaimed an independent Haiti, January 1, 1804. *Drapo nasiyonal* appears in every houmfo not so much for political insurance, as is sometimes claimed, but as an assertion of identity as free Haitians. Even under the most repressive conditions, the mythos of the successful slave uprising remains present and potential.

Beyond this chief drapo are all the others, created to some extent in its aura, and even two hundred years later echoing its call to arms. It is true, as Patrick Polk and others have pointed out, the flags bear many resemblances to French military banners and to European flags implanted in Africa during the era of slave trade.[1] It is true also that the drapo function in the ceremony with certain military protocols, including mock battles, that appear to derive from the same sources. But there is more than the armies of Napoleon at work on these drapo and in their ritual deployment.

The Matter of Islamic Africa

The two proto-heroes of the slave revolution, Mackandal and Boukman, both leaders of momentarily thwarted uprisings, were, according to contemporaneous witness, literate and knowledgeable Muslims.[2] General Jean-Jacques Dessalines, under whose leadership the revolution finally succeeded, if not Muslim, nevertheless evidenced influence from Muslim mysticism and magic. These were present in Haitian slave life just as Muslim mysteries and magic pervaded every West African locality where Muslims traded or had political hegemony. Dessalines created the flag in February 1803, months before its dramatic apparition in Archahaie on the eighteenth of May, reportedly after a ceremony in the houmfo he frequented.[3] Eighteen May is the day for honoring the African lwa (spirit), Aloumandia (or Allahmandia). The name is thought to be a form of "Allah."

Some scholars say that another hero, General Alexandre Pétion, put the palm tree, which for the insurgents was the tree of liberty, on the drapo.[4] His lwa was Ayizan, whose symbol was the palm. Ayizan, become a divinity, has historical root as a West African dowager queen whose strength and cleverness allowed her progeny to take over an older kingdom. The palm appears on the national flag and on a great many Voudou drapo not only for Ayizan but for other lwa as well. Whether or not it was Pétion who caused the palm to be placed on the national flag, the act was one that synthesized African and French militancies. A thoughtful reading of reports on the style and their actions of Haiti's liberation leaders suggests that their conception of the conflict into which they entered was not necessarily or simply a following of the notions of the rights of man articulated in the French Revolution and spread to Haiti: more personally and deeply it was a holy war—a *jihad.*

The drapo that appear next most frequently in houmfo are those of Sin Jak, St.-Jacques Majeur, the Santiago of Iberia and Spanish America, the Santiago whose chapel the Portuguese built in Elmina in Old Ghana in 1480. At that time, the peoples of the coastal districts were resisting the Muslims, and Santiago was conflated to Ogun, the powerful old deity of the Edo, the Yoruba, and the Fon. Ogun's beginnings are lost in antiquity and his endings are not in sight; he now assists car mechanics, soldiers and computer experts. The assimilated Santiago/Ogun as an emblem of resistance among the Yoruba who became Islamized at about the time of European colonization of Africa in the late eighteenth and through the nineteenth century is ironic but comprehensible: he is a figure of armed opposition rather than of religious dogma. Santiago/St.-Jacques/Ogun arrived on Hispaniola early, perhaps even as early as the Colombian landfall in 1492. As Sin Jak-Ogun he is the lwa who enables the oppressed to overcome; his great popularity will last until the revolution is fully implemented, they say.

To review quickly the several ways Muslim influence came to St.-Domingue and Haiti:

1. The first Muslims in the New World were the Malinke who arrived in Brazil in 1312 under the leadership of Abubakri of the royal house of Mali. There has been a continuous presence in Brazil to the present as well as influences radiating out to the coasts of central America, northern South America and the Caribbean.[5]
2. Ship's manifests and inventories of plantations show heavy importation of Islamic Mande peoples to Hispaniola, especially in the early eighteenth century.
3. Muslim influence pervaded West Africa as a result of trade networks and political or cultural hegemony reaching as far back as 900 C.E., with Muslim amulets and divinations actively used by peoples not otherwise Islamic.
4. Muslim immigrants came in large numbers into the Caribbean, including Haiti, during the nineteenth century. Mostly from India, the Hindus of that migration spoke disparagingly of the Muslims among them as "Madingas, " thus implying a West African continuity not in India, but in the Caribbean.

Although the number of Muslims among the slave population was small, and although it was nearly impossible to set up the *ulama* system of education under plantation conditions, there is much evidence from the eighteenth century forward of efforts made to preserve Muslim heritage.[6] Slaves made ink from citrus and mimosa and used dried palm leaves for pages to create copies of the Qur'an. It is reported that such books were so highly prized that people would rescue them from burning cabins. It is documented that during the revolution, some insurgents wore amulets thought to protect them from bullets, or were they to be killed anyway, assured their return to Lan Giné, the African homeland. Islamic imams made and distributed such amulets for exactly this purpose throughout West Africa.[7] It seems reasonable to presume that the repository of so much else of African heritage, the Voudou houmfo, would likewise preserve the valued Islamic remnants. A look at certain drapo seems to confirm this possibility.

Photo by Dr. Halvor Jaeger. Courtesy Jaeger Collection
Drapo by Clotaire Bazile, Port-au-Prince, circa 1977.

The drapo motifs that show the strongest visual congruencies with Islamic designs are the repeated squares, often diagonally divided, as borders, especially for Sin Jak drapo. It is true that repeated squares and lozenges are a motif found all over the world, and certainly on French military banners; but there remains the density and elaboration of the motif. The resemblance of some of the earlier drapos to number squares on Qur'an boards is striking.[8] When we recall that such mystical square diagrams were on battle amulets, furthermore that the *imams* used the washings from the boards as healing potions for animals and humans, appearance of the squares on the drapo, at the site of a religion focused on winning freedom and curing sickness should almost be expected.

The mystical quadrille appears on flags and vèvè (symbols drawn on the ground at the beginning of a Voudou service) for Ogun Badagris and Papa Zaka. It appears as well on the vèvè for the lwa (spirit) Boussou Sinbi, a lwa of the "Fanmi Senigal," again from Islamic territory, and on the costume for this lwa both in Haiti and in the Islamicised Senufo district of Côte d'Ivoire, where it is known as *Kâgba*. Motifs other than the magic squares also appear; for example, exact replicas of Islamic divination symbols appear on drapo for Sin Jak.

Most scholars of Voudou regard the Islamic contribution as marginal, and this is clearly the case for cosmology and theology. However, some of the valued symbols, especially those tied to healing and *jihad*, tenaciously hold their place in the vèvè and on the drapo.

The Matter of Brittany

To the drapo of *jihad* coupled with French military design, add the third factor of Roman Catholic church banners conceived of in those times as the battle oriflammes of the Church Militant. Christians of the era of exploration and domination show abundant evidence in their tracts, sermons, prayers, hymns and mission activities of a pervading conception of militancy –the church at war against the Devil and all his works in "heathen" cultures.

Priests and religious were among the first arrivals from Europe. In what became St.-Domingue as France dominated the western half of Hispaniola, more and more of them arrived from the Breton ports of Nantes and Brest. In the so-called "tunnel period" of Haiti between her declaration of independence and the Concordat signed in 1860 with the Papal See, some seventy percent of all missionaries came from Brittany. In colonial times, the religious were accompanied by sailors, colporteurs, adventurers, managers for absentee landlords and small entrepreneurs seeking their fortunes in the richest colony of the world. Missals and crucifixes arrived in the same ships as books of magic and alchemy, full of magic number squares, owing something to Arabic influence. Such books have a continuous presence on the island from 1700 to the present –the same versions are sold on the streets of Port-au-Prince to this day, and have a place on many a Voudou pè. So the Bretons, high and low brought their efficacies high and low: whatever would win or cure from the Kingdom of Heaven or the Kingdom of this world.

The priests also brought special objects and ceremonies peculiar to Brittany, among them the Maypole, which until very recently was a feature of Karneval, joining as easily to old Taino ways as it had to old Celtic, Druid ways. They set up the same kind of *calvaires* (sculptural representations of the Crucifixion) that appear all over Brittany all over Haiti, most frequently at crossroads, as they had in Brittany. They held special observances for the saints, especially for St. Anne, the patron of Brittany, often coupled by Haitians with Ayizan,; and for St. John Baptist. Such special occasions took on the characteristics of the Breton observance of the so-called "Pardons," with services, prayers, and processions out into the fields or to the shore, accompanied always by banners splendidly embroidered with gold and silver threads, beads and sequins on fine velvets and satins, gadrooned in gold braid, a depiction of a saint usually at the center.

At these services in Brittany, the first ritual takes place inside the church, with a visiting priest serving in an honored function, just as a visiting mambo or houngan fulfills a special role in a Voudou ceremony. Subsequently, there is a procession of banners and crucifixes into a large *parvis* outside the church, the emblems are oriented to compass points –so too in a Voudou service--, followed by the "kissing" of the banners, gestures seen in Voudou ceremonies as well. In great probability the Breton actions mirror a Druidic ceremony of earlier times. After a time, the procession recommences to parade throughout the countryside, stopping at certain special locations for hymns and prayers of rogation and benediction, the banners marking out the sacred space. Eventually all return to the church for concluding vespers. In the seventeenth and eighteenth centuries, the procession path was marked with designs made of flour, charcoal and flower petals, like vèvè. The *via sacra* thus created under the banners is once again similar to certain Voudou ceremonies. The splendid *drapeaux* from many churches would be returned to their homes later and remain either on display or in special cabinets and closets, as do the Voudou drapo. The banners of Brittany and those of Voudou have not only their devotional splendor in common, but also the saint displayed in the center. Military banners are more apt to carry simple, quickly identifiable emblems.

The Voudou drapo that does carry a simple emblem in the center is usually that of the lwa Ezuli represented by a heart. The Breton priests and religious taught veneration of the Sacred Heart to their Haitian flocks.

Photo by Dr. Halvor Jaeger. Courtesy Jaeger Collection

Anonymous drapo in so-called "old-style," date unknown.

Anne Sauvy[9] tells how the sacred heart became a primary teaching aid in Brittany. Michel Nobletz in the sixteenth century promulgated the images throughout Brittany, and even now they appear in every mission where there are Breton priests and religious. The Breton missionary who eventually became the Archbishop of Haiti at the time of the Concordat was among those who tried to have Nobletz canonized for his work with the image of the Sacred Heart.[10] Louis Maximilien, writing on Voudou, tells how the emblem, of Hermetic origin during the Middle Ages, became venerated in the Roman Church, and from thence came into Voudou.[11] It is, like Sin Jak-Ogun, the sign of an essential of human character rather than a sign for religious dogma. Where Sin Jak-Ogun is the emblem of resistance and war, the Heart of Ezuli is the emblem of all forms of human love. We have on drapo what the Greeks and Romans understood as *eros* and *thanatos*, love and war, Venus and Mars, Sin Jak-Ogun and Sin Mari-Ezuli. (Perhaps it is not beside the point to remark that Miryam, the Virgin Mother of Jesus is honored in the Qur'an, Surah 19.)

The Breton hearts were sometimes banded to indicate stages in the ethical progress of a Christian soul toward the pure love of God. Sometimes the entire poster was quadrilled with hearts centered in each square. In Haiti, Ezuli's heart is sometimes quadrilled, sometimes pierced with swords, sometimes surrounded with reduplicated squares like those of Islamic hatumere (amulets) and Qur'an boards. It is an adding up of emblems of power and might: the magic squares of the *grimoire* books brought in by the sailors and adventurers unaware of the Arabic esoterica embedded in them; the sacred heart of Jesus and Mary brought in by Breton religious; the Islamic amulets brought in by enslaved Africans: drapo emblems to carry the whole freight of power from Africa and Europe, mystical religions and efficacious magic.

Other drapo may also echo Brittany. Small votive ships hang from the ceiling near the sanctuary of many a Breton chapel and from many a Haitian houmfo. In Haiti, such ships are emblems of the sea lwa, Agwe. The emblem appears in vèvè and on drapo[12]. What is different from the Breton votives is the word "imamou," clearly a survival from Islamic heritage. For Breton sailors and for those brought to Haiti in the ships they manned, such an emblem would carry a complex emotional cargo.

Certain colors on drapo that may owe something to Breton liturgical practices include white for the marriage of Ezuli with her devotees; black for the gède/Baron spirits of death; and violet or purple for Gran Brigit, another lwa of the gède family, wearing the penitential color for Advent and Lent, seasons of special observance for Christians and Voudouisants simultaneously. *Toukolé* (all colors) on drapo, some garments, apparently continue a tradition found in many West African locales, and by some accounts seem to be related to keeping evil at bay.

The Matter of Haiti

Drapo, their associated vèvè and ritual actions richly skein back into European and African ancestral homes of today's Haitians. They emerge from ineffably complex systems people devise for coming to terms with the human condition: entraining a procession to alter the physical space; undergoing a possession to alter the perception of self; meditating, dancing, praying. Breton and Muslim survivals on the Voudou drapo have taken on different meanings from those in the original settings, yet they preserve some of the same poetry of splendor, of the powers of color and scintillations, of a thing that constantly changes and stays the same; a piece of cloth that marks out a sacred space to deal with the timeless and formless invariants of the human plight. Parading the drapo at a certain time a certain place *rive nan baye ent syel ak té*—arrives to where the gates of heaven open on an aperçu from the ordinary into the extraordinary.

*****

[1] Polk, Patrick, "Sacred Banners and the Divine Cavalry Charge," in Sacred Arts of Haitian Vodou, Donald J. Cosentino, ed. Los Angeles:UCLA Fowler Museum of Cultural History, 1995. Pp. 325-347.

[2] See especially, Madiou, Thomas, Histoire d'Haiti. Port-au-Prince:Editions Henri Deschamps, 1989(1847). Tome I, p. 35.

[3] Fombrun, Odette Roy, Le Drapeau & Les Armes de la République d'Haïti. Port-au-Prince:Editions Henri Deschamps, 1987. P.34ff.

[4] Desquiron, Lilas, Racines du Vodou. Port-au-Prince:Editions Henri Deschamps, 1990. P.141.

[5] Celebration of this event took place in Mali in 1992 as an alternative to the excitement about the Colombian quincentenary, reported by Robert Lacville, "Sail of the Centuries to America, " Manchester Guardian Weekly, 28 February, 1993. Abdullah Hakim Quick discusses the historic evidence for this early and continued presence in Deeper Roots: Muslims in the Caribbean Before Colombus to the Present. Nassau:AICCLA, 1990. See also Bastide, Roger(trs. Helen Sebba), The Black Religions of Brazil. Baltimore and London:The Johns Hopkins University Press, 1978(1960). See especially Chapter 7, "Black Islam in Brazil."

[6] LeFrau, G., "Le Noir d'Afrique," a nineteenth century essay cited by Jean Fouchard in Les Marrons du Syllabaire. Port-au-Prince:Editions Henri Deschamps, 1988. P.20.

[7] Bravman, René A., Islam and Tribal Art in Africa. Cambridge:Cambridge University Press, 1974. Bravmann provides substantiation for the pervasion and endurance of Islamic traditions throughout the region, describing situations that seem to support a parallel supposition that such influence could be sustained in Brazil or Haiti, or elsewhere.

[8] Prussin, Labelle, Hatumere: Islamic Design in West Africa. Berkeley and Los Angeles, London:University of California Press, 1986. Prussin includes a great many illustrations of Islamic design relevant to the topic of Islamic preservations in Haiti, as well as extended discussions of use and meaning.

[9] Sauvy, Anne, Le Miroir du Coeur, Quatre siècles d'images savantes et populaires. Paris:Les Editions du Cerf, 1989.

[10] Cabon, Père A., Mgr. Alexis-Jean-Marie Guilloux, Deuxième Archevêque de Port-au-Prince. Port-au-Prince:Archevêveque de Port-au-Prince, 1929.

[11] Maximilien, Louis, Le Vodou Haïtien . Port-au-Prince:Imprimerie Henri Deschamps, 1982. P. 51.

[12] Concerning a specific drapo for Agwe as well as those for several other lwa, I have benefited from discussions with Clotaire Bazile, houngan and drapo-maker of Haiti. Harvard doctoral candidate, Anna Wexler, very generously provided this opportunity for me. I am grateful to her also for the knowledge and insights she has shared, based upon her extensive work with drapo and drapo makers.

FOR THE FLOWER OF GINEN: THE ARTISTRY OF CLOTAIRE BAZILE,
A HAITIAN VODOU FLAGMAKER[1]

Anna Wexler

As the only objects in significant numbers to cross over from the ritual space of the <u>perisil</u> (Vodou temple) into international art markets[2], the sequinned surfaces of Haitian Vodou flags now reflect tracklights in North American galleries as well as candles burning in darkened sanctuaries. Clotaire Bazile is one of the great contemporary flagmakers and the pivotal artist in the relatively recent metamorphosis of the flag from a primarily ritual form into a commercial art object.[3] He is also a working <u>oungan</u> (Vodou priest) who has conducted services for the <u>lwa</u> (spirits) and private healing consultations for close to thirty years. My doctoral research has focused on the interface between his work as a <u>oungan</u> and his career as a flagmaker, including his transposition of modes of contact with the spirits - and the standards which shape his expression of this privileged access - to the sphere of artistic/commercial production.

In 1973 two French travellers who had come to Bazile in Port-au-Prince, Haiti for a card reading (divination) asked him to unroll the flags they could see resting on top of a cabinet in his altar room. Here is his account of the interaction:

> A tourist guide leads two French people for a card reading. While I am reading the cards for them they look up - (I think it is) because of the roof, it is so crude. At that time gas lamps (discolored it with smoke). The roof was made with tin from an oil drum. When I notice that I tell the guide, look how they're staring like that, they're too nosey, don't bring them again. But they don't hear that. And the woman continues to examine something and talks to her husband and then she asks me (in French), do you want to show me that object, it interests me. I ask which thing. She says it's the thing with fringe which interests me. I say O.K. I open it. I show them - a beautiful Sen Jak, a beautiful Danbala. She goes crazy! She says to her husband she wants to buy it. I say it's not to sell, I made it, it's for the beautiful <u>lwa</u>, to signal the <u>lwa</u> when I conduct services. She asks how much money I would ask for it. I repeat it's not for sale. The guide says if you sell it, the same way you made these you can make others. I'll send other people to buy them.[4]

As a result of the ensuing transaction, Bazile began to produce flags for the French customers and others they sent his way. His younger brother, Jean Benjamin, an <u>ebenis</u> (cabinetmaker), helped him to build the frames on which the satin surface and burlap backing were stretched for sewing. There were already boxes of sequins and beads around which his older sister, Charlotte, had brought home from the American owned garment factory in Port-au-Prince where she worked as a supervisor. The "flash of the spirit" (Thompson, 1983) in the glittering, sequin saturated contemporary flag travelled via such factories where crocheted and embroidered clothes were ornamented with sequins and beads which workers (earning approximately $.14 an hour (Ridgeway, 1994)) swept up after an order was finished and their colors were no longer needed.[5] They brought them home or sold them cheaply in the Mache Fè, the central marketplace of Port-au-Prince. Bazile attributes the proliferation of sequins on the commercial flags beginning in the late 1960's/early 70's to the operation of these garment factories, a consequence of the economic policy first articulated by François Duvalier in the late 1960's and initiated around the time of his death when his son Jean Claude assumed the presidency. A principle goal was increasing U.S. investment in light assembly, re-export industries based on the allure of an ostensibly docile, cheap labor force (Trouillot, 1990).

I came to Bazile seeking an ideal of religiously motivated artistic activity which I envisioned as flowing seemlessly from the inspiration of the lwa and only incidentally resulting in monetary rewards. I sought an image of his creativity cordoned of from economic motives, projecting the split between inspiration and remuneration in the European Romantic figure of the artist. I wanted to see Bazile as almost accidentally producing flags (with and for the spirits) close to their religious prototype rather than consciously transforming them into art objects to appeal to tourist markets. As such, they would retain their aura of ritual sanctity while crossing into the domain of "pure" art.

Unconditioned by what Bourdieu (1993) describes as the "charismatic" image of the artist whose commercial motives are transposed to the dealer, Bazile presented his marketing activities as integral to his creative production. Shortly after we were introduced by an American collector of Haitian art in 1991, he showed me a business card which he had designed in the initial phase of his career, presenting it to me as a sign of his accomplishment as an artist/flagmaker. Under his name it read "Expert on Voodoo Decoration, Wholesale and Retail" with small drawings of a radiating sun and candle to the left of the words. He explained that these images identified him as a oungan who could "balanse tout bagay" (make everything go forward) with the light of the sun and the burning candle. When I asked him if he felt any conflicts about making Vodou flags for sale as "art" - until the late 1940's or early 1950's a strictly ritual form - he matter-of-factly answered no. He explained that he turned all the proceeds back into his temple, into serving the lwa and supporting his family and sosyete (members of his temple society). "Se menm bagay" (it's the same thing), he told me. It wasn't until our later discussions of his dreams that I began to comprehend the interconnections between worlds encapsulated in that brief remark.

From the beginning flagmaking has been an expression of Bazile's gift for communication with the spirits. A year or so following his formal initiation as a _oungan_, he made his first pair of flags after dreaming that the _lwa_ wanted two for his temple and receiving instruction on how to design them, just as he had learned to draw the _vèvè_ (figural and abstract emblems for the _lwa_) and make remedies in dreams during the early stages of working as a healer. Transmission of vocation in Haitian oral traditions, especially those which involve transformative activities and objects (Brown, 1991; Tessonneau, 1983), is often experienced initially in dreams involving the _lwa_ or other spiritual agents. In his dreams, Bazile saw the flags he was to make for his temple -one for Sen Jak with the warrior from the chromolithograph of St. James the Elder, commonly used to represent this chief of the Haitian Ogou, and one for Danbala Wèdo, the benevolent serpent spirit, with a heart for Ezili Freda between two uncoiled snakes representing the spirit and his wife, Ayida Wèdo. Together the flags for these two spirits would represent all the _lwa_ of the major Rada pantheon, known as the flower of Ginen, for ritual purposes.

Associating dream transmission with preparation for ritual vocation, I later asked Bazile if dreams played a more significant role in his creative process in the initial (not yet commercial) phase of his career as a flagmaker. "No", he replied, "the _lwa_ continue to come to tell me what to do, who is going to buy, what kind of flag to make for people to buy." It was primarily the peasant _lwa_ Kouzen Zaka who began to help him during the commercial phase of his development as a flagmaker because, as he explained, this spirit is "_nan biznis_" (in business). Discussing his ability to innovate in his artistic work, Bazile described the pragmatic thrust of Zaka's guidance in dreams:

> Yes, it is the spirit who guides you to change the work. For example, he says you shouldn't do the work that way today, don't divide the squares into eight triangles (for the border), just divide them into two triangles, cut it like that, using two colors, it's another idea. (See Figure 1) A person may appear, he or she likes that style, now I say good. If too many people like (copy) that style, I use another one, I do something different. I make it bigger, I make it smaller, it's your ideas which direct you. If you don't have ideas, things won't work out.

In addition to generating artistic, and commercially viable, ideas, dreams may also serve as a medium for the needs of a _lwa_ when they are not being adequately met through ritual obligations. Ordinarily, in order to sustain his relationships with the spirits and to benefit from their advice, inspiration, and forewarnings, Bazile performs a cycle of annual ceremonies to honor and feed them according to their ritual requirements. When he first started to make flags systematically for sale, however, Bazile was told in a dream that he must escalate his ritual commitments now that he was beginning to reap substantial profits from his business. It was Zaka, already actively helping him in the development of his flagmaking enterprise, who insisted that a large service be organized in his honor in 1975. Bazile acted on the dream communication immediately and began to organize a big ceremony for Zaka in his temple where he eventually brought three truckloads of poor people to be fed from the large ritual meal prepared for the spirit.

Dreams, in Bazile's accounts, are not just gratuitous, spontaneous events in the life of an artist predisposed toward mystical sources of inspiration but serve as

Figure 1: Flag for the military spirit, Sobo, one of the patrons of the flags, with squares divided into two triangles in the border design. Photo: Virgil Young.

conduits of transmission and exchange in a creative process which must be nourished by ongoing reciprocal acts towards the lwa with whom he is allied. What was initially given in dreams by the lwa, the vision and impetus to create a pair of flags for his temple in order to serve them properly, led eventually to Bazile's development as a commercial artist, his systematic transformation of the ritual flag into a marketable art object. Although spirit mediated dream in this phase of his artistic career were directed toward helping him to change and perfect the flag aesthetically for art markets, they also served to remind him to integrate his commercial project into the ritual cycle by which he sustains his relationships with the lwa in order to receive their support in his other, more ostensibly "sacred" activities as a oungan, such as healing and creating spirit invoking objects for ceremonies and for private treatments. In the course of our discussions of this dimension of his creativity as a commercial flagmaker, I began to understand why he told me when we first met that he had no conflicts about making Vodou flags for profit - profit which goes back into serving the lwa who guide and inspire Bazile in the business which generates the money to feed them, his family and members of his sosyete and maintain the temple where the spirits dance after the tables on which the flags are sewn are cleared away.

While Bazile honors the contribution of the lwa to his artistic development, he also insists on the importance of "aksyon" or action, his ability to act on what he receives, to give tangible form and elaboration to his vision. His penchant for geometry in school, for example, was an important resource for designing and developing the borders for his flags after the initial impulse to use precise geometric patterns was given in dreams. When I asked him for his definition of an artist, he gave the most emphasis to implementation:

> What kind of activity is art ... it's action, action which shows you what you like, what is possible, what you can produce. If you don't have production, you don't have art.

The capacity for generative action is also fundamental to his conception of the role of the oungan, a major principle which shapes the practice of his spiritual vocation and which he carried over into the construction of his artistic career and the aesthetic development of the Vodou flag. In terms of his work as a oungan, he links the importance of action to the demands which he faces as a healer who must invoke and materialize the spiritual energies necessary for dealing with frequently critical situations. When ill people come to his house for healing, he explained, he has to perform a "gwo aksyon" (big action) - sometimes involving intense, dramatic elements like fire associated with the fast acting Petwo spirits - so that his clients will not die and the lwa, whose reputations also depend on the effectiveness of his treatments, will not desert him.

Bazile's emphasis on akson as effective response to the intense demands which he faces as a healer is closely linked to his conception of konsantrasyon or concentration. Remembering and executing ritual detail correctly is critical to summoning and controlling the lwa whose energies he must channel constructively for his healing work. The consequences of negligence are grave. To be careless about rendering a vèvè, he explained, is to potentially disrupt a ceremony because the spirit being called may not recognize the pattern and other less welcome lwa may arrive. People may die as a result of failure to concentrate or "mete tèt ou anplas" (put your head in place) to carry out a ritual service according to the requirements of tradition. Forgetting a single, apparently insignificant detail can invite serious problems:

> To serve the spirits, it's like an egg, it's like an egg you hold, if you forget it's an egg in your hand, you let it drop to the ground ... but if you do everything with honor, respect, you are not going to have difficulty.

During the course of my fieldwork in Miami and Port-au-Prince, I observed Bazile's flair for detail in the myriad ritual preparations and domestic labors involved in his healing practice. Cooking and cleaning, whether connected to a specific ritual occasion or the general well-being of the house, were carried out with the same concentration brought to other more dramatic ritual work. Whether serving coffee to clients waiting to see him, sweeping the yard, or washing the enamelled tin cups and bowls with which the lwa are served, Bazile worked with a meticulous attention which was never precious or rigid; it energized those around him and lent each task a visible aura of finesse.

The same focus on executing detail correctly is also reflected in the technical excellence of his flags. According to the Vodou flag collector, the late Virgil Young, he was the first flagmaker to achieve a consistently high level of craftsmanship in his work.[6] After Bazile designs the flag and designates its colors on pieces of satin stretched on a frame, each sequin is sewn on with a tiny seed bead in an extremely labor intensive process. Bazile insists that every sequin be sewn down tightly, evenly overlapping the one before it, that all lines in his pieces are straight, and that the vèvè or image of the saint be perfectly centered within the geometric borders that usually enclose the sacred form.

When he taught me his sewing techniques in Miami, Bazile emphasized that each time I added another sequin, I must bring the needle up through the fabric right against the edge of the tiny 5mm sequin preceding it so that they overlapped evenly in straight lines and there was no space between them. He pointed out any sign of carelessness in my sewing immediately as well as in my treatment of materials. The area outdoors where we were working was always swept clear of leaves and other debris, and if he found stray sequins on the ground, he would pick them up one by one and place them deliberately on the fabric to remind me of my negligence.

"Jis kenbe lin dwat" (just keep the line straight), he explained, is the central standard he maintains in flagmaking. This seemingly technical standard, one which could be seen simply as a pragmatic response to consumer demand for uniform craftsmanship, also expresses another major principle which guides his activities as a oungan - direction or orientation:

> ... if your line isn't straight you don't have direction. In whatever you do, if you don't have

direction, it isn't good ... If, for example, you are working as a oungan, you don't act with respect, if someone brings you money to do work, you take the money to resolve a personal problem, the <u>lwa</u> are angry also, because if it is the <u>lwa</u> who are working with you, you must do everything ... the spirit collaborates with you ... you don't see him or her, they stand near you to guide you, to make everything straight ...

Ritual orientation in Vodou is performed by saluting the four cardinal points with all the offerings, flags, and other objects used in the cremony. The four points or directions are indicated by lines that intersect in the Vodou cross which represents the point of contact between the physical world and the domain of the <u>lwa</u>. Bazile insists that the basic cross of the <u>vèvè</u> be drawn on flat ground so that the lines provide the correct directions for ritual orientation; the lines on the flags must be drawn and sewn straight for the same reason. Directionality is not only a structural principle, but one which activates contact between human and spiritual beings, and also delineates the moral quality of that contact, as the above remarks by Bazile suggest.

Figure 2: Perfectly executed flag for the <u>lwa</u> Bossou, a militant spirit Bazile describes as aggressive but not destructive. Photo: Virgil Young.

Bazile describes his flags as "classical" referring to his sense of their continuity with the sacred form from which they evolved. This can be seen in his mastery and elaboration of certain design elements and techniques from embellished ritual flags, such as what Bazile and his entourage refer to as <u>simen grenn</u> (literally scattering seeds or dotting the background fabric with sequins or beads), borders with geometric patterning, a central <u>vèvè</u>, and the insertion of figures of saints from the Catholic chromolithographs used to

represent the _lwa_.[7]
Though developed for
commercial markets, his
flags exemplify an ethos
of creativity which Maya
Deren (1953) has described
as committed to enhancing
collective participation
in ritual expressions
directed toward the _lwa_
rather than toward
individualistic displays
of genius, improvisation
which serves tradition
rather than virtuoso
performance. In this
sense, the aesthetic
developments in Bazile's
flags both recapitulate
and transfigure the
history of the form,
moving the past into the
present through
improvisation which
heightens the beauty and
vitality of the ritual
flag, still serving the
flower of Ginen, the great
lwa.

Figure 3: A portrait of the
artist in front of his altar for
the Rada spirits in Port-au-
Prince. Photo: Susan Tselos.

NOTES

1. Portions of this paper are drawn from my essay, "I am going to see where my <u>oungan</u> is", forthcoming in *Sacred Possessions: Vodoun, Santería and Obeah in the Literatures and Cultures of the Caribbean* (Olmos, M. and Paravisini-Gebert, L., Eds.), Rutgers University Press. Many thanks to the late Virgil Young and Susan Tselos for visual contributions.

2. See the exhibit catalogue, *Sacred Arts of Haitian Vodou* (Cosentino, 1995), for multiple examples of ritual and commercial flags.

3. According to the late Virgil Young, a well known collector of Vodou flags, Bazile was the first flagmaker to produce systematically for tourist markets in the early 1970's. Personal communication, 10/12/93.

4. Translated from the Kreyòl by author and Lionel Hogu. I gratefully acknowledge his help in translating this passage and the other quotations from Bazile which appear in the text.

5. The piles of leftover, glittering sequins which factory workers collected take on a bitterly ironic sheen when juxtaposed to the criminally low wages paid for their labor. The fact that the word sequin derives from the Arabic <u>sikkah</u> for coin further heightens the unintentionally instructive irony of their status as trash in the garment factories. (Thanks to LeGrace Benson for pointing out this derivation.)

6. Personal communication from Virgil Young, 10/12/93.

7. Of these features, only <u>simen grenn</u> appears to be a general characteristic of decorated ritual flags which predate commercialization (see *Sacred Arts of Haitian Vodou* (Cosentino, 1995) for many examples). The other elements noted may or may not be present. For example, the collector and expert on the ritual flag, Susan Tselos, has indicated to me that on some of the embellished flags from the 1930's and 40's the <u>vèvè</u> is not framed and highlighted by distinct borders, color contrasts, and central positioning. A documented history of the evolution of the textile form has yet to be written.

BIBLIOGRAPHY

Bourdieu, Pierre.
   (1993). The Field of Cultural Production: Essays on Art and Literature (Ed. Randal Johnson). New York: Columbia University Press.

Brown, Karen.
   (1991). Mama Lola: A Vodou Priestess in Brooklyn. Berkeley, CA: University of California Press.

Cosentino, Donald (Ed.).
   (1995). Sacred Arts of Haitian Vodou. Los Angeles, CA: UCLA Fowler Museum of Cultural History.

Deren, Maya.
   (1953). Divine Horsemen. New Paltz, NY: McPherson.

Ridgeway, James (Ed.).
   (1994). The Haiti Files: Decoding the Crisis. Washington D.C.: Essential Books.

Tessonneau, Alex Louise.
   (1983). Le Don Reçu en Songe. L'Ethnographie, 79(1):69-82.

Thompson, Robert Farris.
   (1983). The Flash of the Spirit. New York: Random House.

Trouillot, Michel-Rolph.
   (1990). Haiti: State Against Nation. New York: Monthly Review Press.

Laundry as Ritual

Whenever I mention I am going to give a talk on laundry, almost every listener responds with a personal recollection. Susie Brandt, an artist whose work attends to the details and obsessions of daily life, was reminded of her laundromat days in Chicago when she was a graduate student in the Fiber Department at The School of the Art Institute. In her neighborhood were many recent immigrants from Mexico. She noticed that they washed their clothes with the washers' lids open, swishing their hands in tandem with the agitators' motion. Was it disbelief in the power of the machine to do a thorough cleaning? Or was it desire for a manual task to authenticate the cleaning process? Susie's story suggests that the physical task remains the essence in the ritual of laundry.

Laundry has the power to elevate one's spirit. Kathleen Norris wrote "Laundry has an almost religious importance for many women. We groan about the drudgery but seldom talk about the way it saves us, the secret pleasure we feel at being able to make dirty things clean, especially the clothes of our loved ones, which possess an intimacy all their own. Laundry is one of the very few tasks in life that offers instant, gratifying results."[1]

This is one view of laundry, but ritual encompasses demeaning repetition as well as celebratory renewal. Laundry, and especially the occupation of laundress, is seen as one of the great subjugators of women. Praising laundry for its ritual component may result from the ease with which it is completed today. What was in the past an onerous task becomes pleasant activity because the drudgery is removed. Whatever the reasons, finding delight in the ritual acknowledges the ceremonial significance. The sacredness that laundry implies is cleanliness; *to launder* is prized because both the activity and the result sanctifies. Cleanliness is next to godliness, and a goodly amount of power rides on that.

Spanking clean clothes draw power from the visual, but it is the appearance of cleanliness more than the actuality. Mark Wigley, in his recent book, *White Walls, Designer Dresses*, equates white walls, promulgated by LeCorbusier in his early writings, with whiteness in clothes, particularly white shirts. Wigley observes: "In the extended history of the concept of cleanliness, architecture joins the doctor's white coat, the white tiles of the bathroom, and the white walls of the hospital. Yet the argument is not about hygiene but a certain look of cleanliness, a hygiene of vision itself. Whitewash purifies the eye rather than the building. Indeed, it reveals the central role of vision in hygiene."[2]

He goes on to say: "the white surfaces that traditionally mark cleanliness do just that, they mark rather than effect it...Putting on a new white shirt was equivalent to taking a bath. Cleanliness was the visual effect that marked social class rather than the state of one's body. To mention linen, then, and associate it with whiteness, was to associate it with a certain condition... The whole economy of hygiene remains fundamentally visual rather than sensual."[3]

Wigley points out the primacy of the visual. But it is doing laundry that connects the physical to the sensual, and that experience, gained through repeated body knowledge, gives the ritual of laundry its appeal. In the power of whiteness as the embodier of cleanliness, this correlation between architecture and the ritual of laundry is significant. While the visual carries certain social information, it the *act*, doing the laundry, that sanctifies. The ritual of laundry satisfies through repetition and through sensual pleasures of touch and smell. With ritual it is the process more than the product that matters. *To launder* appeals in the intersection of the physical— labor—and the constructed— appearance.

Laundry is rich subject matter for contemporary artists because of its duality; it satisfies a human need for cleanliness (as well as Wigley's statement—the look of cleanliness) and it has historically fallen on the poor and the oppressed.

In the September 1996 in the inspirational magazine, *Guideposts*, the cover story makes the most of the virtuous power of laundry. "Miss McCarty: The Laundress Who Gives Scholarships" depicts a smiling older woman seated in an old-fashioned metal lawn chair, an equally beaming young woman kneeling with her arm on the chairback, and bright, colored laundry pegged with wooden clothespins in the background.

While watching her mother wash clothes in a big, black pot, boiling them clean, young Osceola McCarty learned to wash and iron her school clothes. Her teacher asked her to do her ironing and paid her a quarter instead of the requested dime. Miss McCarty put the money under the pink lining of her doll buggy and added her accumulating laundry earnings. In the sixth grade she dropped out of school due to her aunt's illness. She writes: "I was sad to miss out on learning, but felt good about helping my aunt. The next year my classmates had moved on, I felt so far behind I never went back to school."

This life is portrayed as one of great satisfaction not sacrifice. She expresses no desires for herself. Her only material acquisition is "one cedar chifforobe." She opens a bank account and is helped by the bank officers to move her deposits from a checking account, to savings, to CD's. At age 86 she retires because of creeping arthritis. She writes: "At the bank one day they asked me where I wanted my money to go when I passed on.

'I want to help some child go to college,' I said. 'I'm going to give my money to the University of Southern Mississippi, so deserving children can get a good education. I want to help African-American children who are eager for learning like I was, but whose families can't afford to send them to school.'

The bank officer looked at me funny and said," 'Miss Osceola, that means you'll be giving the school a hundred and fifty thousand dollars.'"

Osceola McCarty's magnanimous gift does not go unnoticed. President Clinton honors her with a Presidential Medal. She is invited to the United Nations. While it is her selflessness that garners her fame, we can not neglect that the instrument of her faith is the power to do a good job through doing other people's laundry. Nor can we ignore the fact that Miss McCarty is African-American. It has been the role of black folks to do white folks laundry. [4]

Lynn Yamamoto is an artist raised in Hawaii now living in New York. Her installations, *Ten in One Hour, How I Remember Her,* and *I hang up my hat after work* offer an opposite reflection on the effects of a lifetime of doing other people's laundry. As a picture bride Yamamoto's grandmother immigrated to Hawaii where she was a washerwoman for most of her life. There are no direct references to the ritual of laundry in Yamamoto's work but rather she presents bodily evidence that takes on the attitude of limp laundry drying on the line. Long hanks of hair dangle like garroted heads. Slivers of soap appear as specimens, worn down nubs from which every possible ounce of use has been wrung. The artist draws a parallel between her grandmother's suicide and the force of performing a service for others.

The performance of any ritual is accompanied by the instruments which make the ceremony possible. Yamamoto's installation connects soap and the performance of laundry, that is, the ritual not the result. Yamamoto's cast glass resemblances to human legs, live grass, hair, and shredded soap connect the body and laundry, the cycle of growth, death, and decay.

Soap manufacture, the tools, the process, and the distribution are a prominent part of the text on the cultural history of laundry. The importance given to soap making suggests that rituals attached to cleanliness are carried in the making of the tool as they are in the performance of the tool's function. In Philip Levine's poem "Growth", soap is the metaphor for growth in the adolescence of the city as well as the boy. Levine's scene is overhung with an edge of grime and decay. There is strong disillusionment, like that in Yamamoto's installations, that effaces the satisfaction of ritual cleansing as described in the McCarty story or the Norris quote.

Growth

In the soap factory where I worked
when I was fourteen, I spoke to
no one and only one man spoke
to me and then to command me
to wheel the little cars of damp chips
into the ovens. While the chips dried
I made more racks, nailing together
wood lath and ordinary screening
you'd use to keep flies out, racks
and more racks each long afternoon,
for this was a growing business
in a year of growth. The oil drums
of fat would arrive each morning,
too huge for me to tussle with,
reeking of the dark, cavernous
kitchens of the Greek and Rumanian
restaurants, of cheap hamburger joints,
White Towers and worse. They would
sulk in the battered yard behind
the plant until my boss, Leo,
the squat Ukrainian dollied them in
to become, somehow, through the magic

of chemistry, pure soap. My job
was always the racks and the ovens—
two low ceilinged metal rooms
the color of sick skin. When I
slid open the heavy doors my eyes
started open, the pores
of my skull shriveled, and sweat
smelling of scared animal burst from
me everywhere. Head down I entered,
first to remove what had dried
and then to wheel in the damp, raw
yellow curls of new soap, grained
like iris petals or unseamed quartz.
Then out to the open weedy yard
among the waiting and emptied drums
where I hammered and sawed, singing
my new life of working and earning,
outside in the fresh air of Detroit
in 1942, a year of growth.[5]

The collusion between the soap ovens in Detroit and the gas ovens in concentration camps is clear. The narrator's youth, his growth is pitted against another actuality, one that he and the world is unaware of in 1942. Like war, this world of manufacturing and commerce is sinister. It is only outside the factory, when the poet is making the tools to make the soap that he feels alive and clean.

Before bleach, before dryers, the sun was the route to the prized whiteness that clean laundry offers. Nor was the clothesline even necessary. Both newly woven linen yardage and laundry were stretched in the sun to dry. Clothes dried outside smell differently, and, many would say, better than clothes from the dryer. Jane Kenyon's poem associates the intimacy of sweet smelling laundry and the loved one:

Wash Day

How it rained while you slept! Wakeful,
I wandered around feeling the sills,
followed closely by the dog and cat.
We conferred, and left a few windows
open a crack.   Now the morning is clear
and bright, the wooden clothespins
swollen after the wet night. The monkshood has slipped its   stakes
and the blue cloaks drag in the mud.
Even the daisies—goodhearted
simpletons—seem cast down.

We have reached and passed the zenith.

The irises, poppies, and peonies, and the old
shrub roses with their romantic names
and profound attars have gone by
like young men and women of promise
who end up living indifferent lives.

How is it that every object in this basket
got to be inside out? There must be
a trickster in the hamper, a backward,
unclean spirit.
                    The clothes—the thicker
things—may not dry by dusk.
The days are getting shorter......
You'll laugh, but I feel it—
some power has gone from the sun.[6]

There is a terror afoot in the laundry, laundry performed by the speaker
takes on its own life. It operates outside the poet's safe knowledge, that is, the
domestic world. It is the sign of natural world, "a trickster in the hamper, a
backward,/unclean spirit." We usually see laundry only as extension of human
effort and so Kenyon's inversion, her naming the laundry as the agent and the
poet as the recipient, delineates this power zone, this place where cleanliness
may be more than godliness. It may become godliness.

In Emily Severance's installation, which she constructed during her post
baccalaureate studies in Ceramics at The School of the Art Institute, laundry
lines fill the whole room, gray and stiff. There is a basement air of clothes drying
when it is raining outside; clothes turning sour. Severance dipped hundreds of
cloth fragments in slip, hung them in crisscrossing lines at eye level.

The artist extended the conjunction between home and laundry by
including her classmates, asking each for a dreamed destination. The answers
ranged from Philippines to Las Vegas. Severance wrote those names in lint.
She placed the lint mats in the bottom of plastic laundry tubs and filled the tubs
with water. Tellingly, the answer HOME was the one to which her classmates
most responded. In doing laundry lies daydreams. Whereas the physical
evidence, the slip-dipped cloths, suggest tedium and bedraggledment, the lint
words remind that the tedium of ritual is also the opportunity to daydream.

Historically, the place to do the laundry was at the river. The laundromat
is like the age-old gathering site where people came to talk as well as wash
their clothes. The laundromat is site of suspended time, a place where one is
captive. It is a hiatus in the rushed schedule and, for many, a time of forced
frittering.

But the laundromat is different from the river, it is a polyglot mix of
strangers—an opportunity to observe others without necessarily socializing.
The confusion, the noise make it difficult to concentrate so it is a place to simply
be quiet, to reflect. There is a similarity to the house of worship in the enforced
stilling of the hands and the mind.

Greg Vendena made and bound a book of photographs and text meant to be kept and read at the laundromat. His interest in laundromat as site grew from his architectural studies that later moved to art. In Vendena's *Laundry Book* the text of the Jorge Borges's parable, *The Lottery in Babylon,* is superimposed on photographs of the interior of the laundromat while the responses of the customers are superimposed on photographs of their hands. Vendena asks questions, such as, "How long have you been coming here?" or "What do you think of gentrification?" or "What do you think about prejudice and racism?"

By definition a lottery is democratic, anyone can buy a chance and all chances are equal. But Borges inverts the rules of the lottery. The narrator begins: "Like all men in Babylon, I have been proconsul; like all, a slave." Losing is more than not winning. The ticket holders could win a sum or they could be forced to pay a fine. In the end the terror of chance spreads to all actions, assuring the absolute power of the Company, the government.

The residents in Babylon seemingly make choices but are controlled in this autocratic game of chance. The Borges story is initially organized around coins but the lottery soon permeates every decision. In reading Vendena's book the equal placement of the two texts makes them appear equal, but gradually the Borges dominates. The survey questions pale beside the terror of *The Lottery in Babylon.*[7]

Laundry, apparently so democratic, undertaken by all classes and walks of life in this laundromat, is perhaps not such a leveling activity after all. For in reality only a certain stratum of society uses the laundromat. Wealth frees one to buy appliances and/or drop it off at the local laundry and dry cleaners.

The laundromat is usually viewed through the eyes of the customer. In the film, *My Beautiful Laundrette* , the perspective is from the entrepreneur. The film indicates how economic power changes political power. Set in London in the mid-1980s the immigrant population of Pakistanis economically threatens the existing class structure. The hero, Omar, is an outsider both because he is Pakistani and gay. The story revolves around his success in converting a laundromat from dingy to designed. He makes it into *the* place to do one's laundry. In an early scene Omar hangs out his laundry on the balcony of the tenement flat where he lives with his father, a displaced intellectual subsisting on vodka and the past. Unable to help his son, the father advises Omar to go to his brother, the uncle who has successfully "squeezed the tits of the system" as he puts it. The uncle sets up his nephew with a rundown laundrette ("There is money in muck").

The nephew relies on the physical strength of his lover, a bloke, to establish the business, to keep away the riffraff, the bloke's former gang. The two young men remodel the laundrette, originally named CHURCHILL'S LAUNDRETTE, and open it as POWDERS. The uncle and his mistress, Rachel, waltz on the new linoleum floor while the lovers make love in the back and the crowds wait to enter. Life is not this wonderful for long.

Omar's father finally confronts himself, his disillusionment, his son's success. The uncle loses Rachel. And perhaps most significantly the power structure is undone by the disenfranchised, the first neighborhood occupants who, in fact, were never in power but exert power through violence.

Laundry and power flow through the film in an undercurrent which crystallizes the complexities of women's historical, societal role in doing the laundry viz a viz the pleasures that the ritual may deliver. The uncle's mistress demonstrates what it means to be ostracized from the world of women. She is present in the male world of the garage and the laundrette, which in this instance *is* a place of power, because we see it from an economic perspective. Rachel is powerless in the domestic world. The uncle's daughter says to this rival who undermines her mother, "I don't like women who live off men." The mistress replies, "You must understand, we are of different generations, different classes. Everything is waiting for you. The only one who has ever waited for me is your father." Rachel's constructed appearance entitles her to another kind of power, one which is divorced from menial labor and domesticity.

Today laundry is divorced from menial labor. Historically laundry has separated one class from another, either you could afford to have someone do your laundry or you must do your own. It was complicated and required skill to do correctly. Today almost every one does her or his own and It involves practically no know-how. The economic barometer is whether or not one's living conditions and income permit the luxury of owning machines. Even if a visit to a coin laundry is necessary, the relatively small cost of operating automatic washing machines and dryers enables doing effortless laundry at little expense of time or money.

As the labor of laundry lessened, the task and the implements attached to the procedure were romanticized. The early machines for home use are often seen with nostalgia. The 1930s and 1940s are pivotal because women were freed from drudgery but not from their traditional role. Nostalgia ties laundry to washboards, enormous irons heated on wood stoves, clothes blowing on clotheslines, wringer washers and mangles. There is an ambivalence in the memory of the physical labor and the subjection that laundry evokes. The ritual endeavor carries the dark side as well as the invigorating side that often slips into nostalgia. The intersection of these two memories come together in remembering and reenacting a ritual that has lost much of the deliberate, repetitious steps of ritual. It combines both the communal and the private. Laundry is silence as much as it is the conversation of a community gathering.

At Haystack Mountain School of Crafts in the summer of 1996, Sheri Simons's fiber students spontaneously struck up a performance staged at the entrance to the dining hall. Dressed alike and muzzled with latex mouthguards, they called to each other, "hello, hello," while they ironed with irons or tea kettles. The viewers, especially the women watching, were disturbed. They wanted to remove the women's muzzles but the performers wouldn't let them. The outsiders were not allowed into this closed community. Though their actions and their constructed appearance represented the subservient, in fact a definite power clung to them.

[1] Kathleen Norris, "It All Comes Out in the Wash," (*The New York Times Magazine*, August 18, 1993), p. 16.

[2] Mark Wigley, *White Walls, Designer Dresses*, (Cambridge, MA: The MIT Press, 1995), p. 5.

[3] *ibid.*

[4] Osceola MaCarty, "Set Aside a Portion," *Guideposts Magazine*, September 1996, p. 1-5.

[5] Philip Levine, "Growth," *What Work Is*, (New York: Alfred A. Knopf, 1992), p. 10.

[6] Jane Kenyon, "Wash Day," *Let Evening Come*, (St Paul, MN: Greywolf Press, 1990), p. 59.

[7] Greg Vendena's *Laundry Book* resides in the Able Fabric Care Coin Op Laundry Dry Cleaning, San Francisco, CA. All quotes from a conversation with the artist, August 1996.

Ceremonial Textiles of the Mardi Gras Indians

Dr. Ann M. DuPont
Specialist, Textiles & Apparel
The University of Texas at Austin
Austin, Texas 78712

The appliquéd, beaded, and pieced textile sections or "patches" that are combined to form the ceremonial costumes of the Mardi Gras Indians of New Orleans, Louisiana are widely considered to be one of the best examples of African-American folk art in North America. Created in secret by black male gang members, these works of indigenous art are rarely seen outside the culturally isolated black neighborhoods.

The black Indian masking tradition sprang from a myriad of African-American heritage and nineteenth century experience in creole Louisiana. The ritualistic combination of dance, music, chanting, and use of ceremonial textiles is still relatively mysterious to the white community. The purpose of this study was to interview masking members of the leading Mardi Gras Indian organizations. With the permission and cooperation of the Indian Council interviews were conducted and actual construction, practices, and presentations were observed. Tribe members were questioned regarding their design inspiration, sewing techniques, work habits, and training related to the actual production of the individual patches, fabric, and suits. It is impossible to understand or truly appreciate the folk art of the Mardi Gras Indians without an informed awareness of the complicated factors that have helped shape, transmute, and inspire them.

In Colonial America the foundations forged in the early Afro-American experience evoked distinctive expressions of a transposed heritage that have remained remarkably consistent and intact. One of the more obscure African -American phenomena to emerge is the Mardi Gras Indian tradition of New Orleans, Louisiana. The Indians have been trivialized by the uninitiated as a colorful costume element of Pre-Lenten celebrations in the city. The "Indian" however, by situation and choice is not easily deciphered. He is not of Native American ancestry; not a part of the official, public, or elite Carnival; not satirical in nature; not part of a rural folk tradition or mainstream religious expression. The Mardi Gras Indian tribes are wrapped in enclosure and yet preeminent in influence within the working-class black neighborhoods in which they exist.

Colonial and Early Creole Culture

The first person of Afro-American descent to arrive in the Americas accompanied Columbus in 1492, and at least two other blacks settled in 1494 in the Spanish colony at Hispañola. Originally, the plan was to coerce the existing native population to meet the labor demands in the Caribbean, but this approach failed. The native Indian population declined rapidly as a result of mistreatment and exposure to European disease (Palmer, 1992: 66), and the remaining segment was not adaptable to slave labor. A solution long familiar to the Spanish, African slavery, was the next solution as Ferdinand and Isabella granted permission in 1501 for the importation of African slaves to Hispañola.

Prior to the eighteenth century, the West Indies was the point of sale for legions of African slaves as it served as a transfer point at the end of the Middle Passage. A new, intermediate social group, the Castas, with combined white, black, and Indian blood emerged creating a unique cultural milieu. African slaves in transit to North America were often "seasoned" in the culturally diverse environment of the Caribbean Basin.

As African slaves came into French Louisiana they entered a blended culture in which they were only one of several forcibly immigrated groups. These varying ethnicities were allied by circumstance and common situation. "Desperation transcended race and status, and cooperation existed among diverse peoples in their efforts to escape the colony. Indian and African slaves, deportees from France, including women sent against their will, Swiss as well as French soldiers, indentured workers(engages) fled in all directions" (Midlo-Hall, 1992: 131). Marginalized groups turned to each other repeatedly for support and safe harbor.

In 1729 the Natchez Indians opposed the French appropriation of their sacred burial grounds. It was the 280 African slaves that had been imported to work by the Company of the Indies in the tobacco colony that joined the Indians in their revolt. Although inevitably put down by the French with the aid of the Natchez' arch enemy the Choctaws, the warrior image of the Black/Indian union gained enough repute to lead Perrier to write in 1731, "The greatest misfortune which could befall the colony and which would inevitably lead to its total loss would be a union between the Indian and the black slaves... " (Midlo-Hall, 1992: 183). Fear of such uprisings resulted in the early 1730's of cessation of the slave trade under French rule. The mystique of the mighty Indian/African prowess in warfare, however, was forged.

Labor requirements of the plantation economies accelerated the slave trade; between 1740 and 1810 an annual average of about 60,000 slaves were sent to the Americas. The majority of the Africans sent to colonial Louisiana were Senegalese. Adept tradesmen and artisans they were encouraged to participate in the diverse market economy. The relatively tolerant French view of the parameters of slavery in and around New Orleans endured later Spanish and American rule.

By 1800 the African creole culture was one of six ethnic groups with a sizable creole population. The resulting cosmopolitan atmosphere of New Orleans was far more European than American, more permissive than austere. "African slaves as well as Native American slaves were highly valued in New Orleans and allowed considerable autonomy" (Smith, 1992: 23). In addition to the opportunity for enslaved persons to participate in the marketplace and social gatherings, a large group of free persons of color played a notable role in the economy and society of the city. In 1791 of 2,751 blacks in New Orleans, 41.7% were free, by 1800 of 4,950 blacks, 45.5% were free (Kinser, 1990: 23). Sunday gatherings in the Place des Negres or Congo Square could number 500-600. In 1819 Benjamin Latrobe described hundreds of people performing a circular form of dance, the calinda, to the beat of bambouli drums (Kinser, 1990: 30).

As Anglo-Americans became the majority and controlling sect in New Orleans by the mid-nineteenth century the city became increasingly polarized between the downtown old creole city and the uptown American city with Canal Street the line of demarcation. The median of that wide boulevard is still called the neutral ground. The increasingly discriminatory laws were often compromised by the fact that most black creoles (free and enslaved) lived in the autonomous creole municipal districts created in 1816 where "enforcement of almost all laws was notoriously lax" (Logsdon and Bell, 1992: 207).

During federal occupation of New Orleans after 1862, whole new parameters of economic and social opportunity were opened to the African creole population, but when the troops withdrew in 1877 the Reconstruction backlash and Jim Crow laws had a militantly racist caste.

Benevolent Societies

Ironically, it was not politics in the mid-nineteenth century that posed the greatest threat to the African-Americans of New Orleans – it was disease. To some observers, death appeared to be so common among African-Americans following emancipation that their very ability to survive as free men was seriously debated. The Louisiana Board of Health of New Orleans reported high mortality rates for both blacks and whites, however, the black death rate from 1864 to 1880 fluctuated between 32/1000 and 82/1000 compared to a white mortality rate in the period that ranged from 5/1000 to 32/1000. Life expectancy for a black male was 36 as compared to 46 for white males (Blassingame, 1973: 163). Although charity hospitals and social agencies were in existence , the benevolent societies with roots in the Second Great Awakening at the end of the eighteenth century became mainstream health care systems in late nineteenth century New Orleans. Almost 4/5ths of the local population, both black and white, belonged to such groups in 1888 (Jacobs, 1985: 22). Dues were paid and the members received medical care from society-retained doctors, access to pharmaceuticals, ministrations from the membership. and death benefits. While white benevolent societies organized along ethnic lines; social status, family associations, and religion were more important in the black societies (Jacobs, 1985: 23). Blassingame notes the black benevolent societies also were "the most important agencies involved in efforts to solve community social problems, aid to the sick, a sense of belonging, organizing social life and impressive burials" (Blassingame, 1973: 167). In most groups adult males were regular members while women and children were "passive" members who also received benefits. One expression common to all the black benevolent societies is the ritual parade format. In the funeral parade, the immediate family of the deceased constitutes the first line of mourners, and the sympathetic community and society members form the second line, often thematically costumed. While the funeral celebrates the "true freedom" of death, the parade format is a cultural expression of liberty. Michael P. Smith explains, "Jazz funerals merge church life with street life. They are rites of passage with profound spiritual resonance: more than just burying the dead and celebrating eternal freedom, they serve as a ritual of community affirmation" (Smith, 1994: 30). He also notes, "The Mardi Gras Indians are more than a part of the mutual-aid tradition, they are the prototype" (Smith, 1994: 51).

Religion

Christianity was imposed on African slaves by law via the French Code Noir and the American Slave Code. French Catholicism was superimposed on the patterns and traditions of African (Spirit) religion. It incorporated the aspects of dance, music, magic, medicine, and functionaries, and thus became a medium for African belief systems that in effect "masked Catholic." During the peak of the Caribbean infusion into New Orleans (1809-10), voodism, the indigenous religion of Haiti, provided many New Orleans slaves with an expression of their heritage and an avenue to power (Williams, 1972: 45). The Spiritual churches of New Orleans, founded by Leafy Anderson have connections to various older religions including Mainline Protestant, folk Catholicism, the Pentecostal Movement, Nineteenth Century American Spiritualism, and Voodoo (Jacobs, 1989: 46). Spirit guides and possession are important elements of the Church. These are symbols of protest and empowerment. A primary Spirit Guide is Black Hawk. He is the spirit of a Native American Chieftain in the Upper Mississippi Valley in the late nineteenth century. Altars are dedicated to Black Hawk and special services honor him. Black Hawk, the "Watchman on the Wall," is closely aligned in the religion to Biblical references of Saint Michael and secular references to Martin Luther King – "the three communicate a clear message of militancy" (Jacobs, 1989: 55). Spiritual possession is a part of masking Indian - a ritual involving prayers for spiritual guidance. "They (Mardi Gras Indians) do not exist to put on a show, but to follow a ritual involving power and pride" (Williams, 1972: 29).

Most individual accounts of a "successful" Indian masking include a sensation of being possessed.

Early Development of Mardi Gras in New Orleans

Carnival societies have paraded in the Gulf Coast Region since 1857. The Mistick Krewe of Comus and the men's social club that supports it, The Pickwick Club, set the elitist mode for the white or "first carnival". It is coded in secret ceremony, but expressed in public display. As civic values related to tourism surfaced, a public role for Mardi Gras emerged. Kinser writes, "Official-culture support for Carnival, the backing of city officials, and even of church groups and welfare organizations are complimentary to elite-culture enthusiasm... it is as clear to the city's politicians as it is to most citizens that Mardi Gras is an unbelievably good commercial investment" (Kinser, 1990: 294). The silent partnership between elite and official sub-groups was cemented in 1872 when Rex was introduced and police and military escort added to the procession" (Kinser, 1990: 295).

Concurrently, the "second carnival" or inversion of white carnival's royal ceremonies surfaced when the Louisiana State Legislature made it legal to mask on Mardi Gras Day "from Sunrise to Sunset." The satirical black Zulu tribe dressed as a parody of white stereotypes of the black "savage." Carnival activity is the sole, seasonal activity of the group. "Zulus make conscious, grotesque use of the white man's racial clichés...but they were never violent, only satirical" (Kinser, 1990: 235). Today they parade along the officially approved parade routes of the first carnival krewes and act as escort to Rex.

Two distinctive neighborhood expressions of the second carnival genre also appeared in the 1880's: the Baby Dolls and The Mardi Gras Indians. Neither have ever been a part of white, official carnival, nor particularly influenced by white society or its conventions. Groups of black prostitutes chose to "strut" on Mardi Gras Day in frilly baby dress costumes and bonnets. Williams notes "Baby Dolls appeared almost a generation before white women began marching in parades" (Williams, 1972: 48).

The Mardi Gras Indians

The Indian masking tradition is used by the black working-class males of the tribes to metaphorically express the "exotically marginalized" position of the Native American Indian and the African American by using mediums of expression deeply rooted in African heritage. Williams explains, "Masking Indian allows the African-American to "safely" call attention to his likeness to the Indian, at the same time veiling from the dominant white culture what he is actually doing – flamboyantly expressing his African ancestry" (Williams, 1972: 87). Tootie Montana, Chief of the Yellow Pocahontas explains," It was simply a separate thing – Black folks always did different things – the supper, parades, dancing and drumming competitions originated purely out of the black culture – going all the way back to Africa" (Smith, 1992: 74).

In recent years scholars have proposed cultural links to the medieval "wildman", Indian bands in Haiti, and John Canoes (Kinser, 1990: 229). Some have drawn parallels in the challenges, chants, and musicology with rebel groups in Trinidad (Draper, 1973: 11). The same elements certainly existed in the black experience throughout the Pan-American region indicating commonalities would emerge, yet there are few clear examples. In New Orleans creolization of African traditions combined in the late nineteenth century with the realities of Reconstruction, the Native American expulsion , and white supremist messages encoded in the stories of the American frontier experience and the Wild West Show. In this context, allegiance and affinity of the Blacks and Native American Indians rekindled, drawing on intermixed family associations, mutual opposition to the white establishment, and collaborative activities in militant stances and covert activities such as the Underground Railroad.

In the 1880's when the oral history of the Mardi Gras Indian begins the first gang "Creole Wild West" was founded by Becate Batiste, a Seventh Ward creole of African, French, and Choctaw descent (Berry, Jason, Foose, and Jones, 1986: 211). The tribes were established as benevolent societies, not social and pleasure clubs, or carnival krewes, and that remains their primary ascription. Traditionally, their only public (neighborhood) appearances are made on Mardi Gras Day and Saint Joseph's Night. The tribes are stabilizing and powerful groups in the black community. The Mardi Gras or Black Indian label is meaningless to gang members. It is the tribe affiliation they affirm – The Yellow Pocohontas, Golden Star Hunters, White Cloud, Wild Magnolias, White Eagles, Black Eagles, Wild Tchoupitoulas, etc. The newly formed Indian Council estimates there are about 32 gangs with an average membership of 10-12 members and additional female and children associates. Basically defined by neighborhoods, cultural and aesthetic preferences vary with the territory.

Challenge and competition in drumming, chanting, dancing, oral-poetry, and costume are the venues through which tribes test each other and gain supremacy. During the fall, Indians practice in local bars and clubs. Each tribe has a hierarchy of assignments for gang members. These include: Wild Man, Medicine Man, Spy Boy, First Flag, Second Flag, Gang Flag, Council Chief, Second Chief, Big Chief, and Witch Doctor. There are also prescribed auxiliary roles for women (Queens) and children that mask with the gang. A complicated, well rehearsed ritual is developed to prepare the gang to meet other gangs in confrontations designed to intimidate and subligate. Tribe signals and street directions are directed by the charismatic chiefs using a pidgin version of Creole French, English, and African dialect. Prior to World War II , gang confrontations took place largely in an area cleared to build the Superdome called the Indian battlefield or "Bucket of Blood". Tootie Montana recalls, "In my Daddy's day you got your name, not by your costume, but by how bad you were, how violent" (Smith, 1992: 58). Today the rivalry has become one essentially of aesthetics and performance, but the possibility of violence is ever- present. Two of the chiefs interviewed had been shot at practice or on parade and every Indian with which I spoke told me "My Mother didn't want me to mask Indian." Chief Larry Bannock advised, a few individuals still, at the slightest excuse, "spread a tablecloth of blood". The Indians still parade without permit or designated route reminiscent of marron tribes. M. Smith notes "Nothing white is inviolable - unmoved cars are used as dance floors, busses and trolleys must give way. The Indians are coming still is a street cry which sends chills down the back of most downtown people and smiles on the face of those who know" (Smith, 1992: 97).

Costuming

No element is more critical , time consuming, or competitive than the design and construction of a suit for the Indian planning to mask. Basically a three piece ensemble consisting of pantaloons or leggings, an apron or tunic with an elaborate belt, and an enormous headdress. It may also include gloves, foot coverings, a separate mask and hand held accessories. The complicated suit weighs well over 100 pounds and costs several thousand dollars. Each masker designs and sews his own costume in relative secrecy until the finishing phase in which as many as twenty helpers may help with the last minute touches. There are no "professional" designers or craftsmen of Mardi Gras Indian costumes nor would they have a clientele. The emphasis is on personal creation and commitment. Several months are spent turning design ideas or visions into brown paper patterns and cloth. Chief Montana, who has masked for forty years, describes his creative process, " My designs come straight from my head. I sit down and create and sometimes it takes weeks , cutting up cardboard, doing designs, trying creations, and getting different ideas" (Smith, 1992: 42).

Sewing can occupy four to five hours a day for six months. Integrity and pride are closely related to personal involvement in the design and construction of the suit. Chief Bannock of the Golden Star Hunters advises, "You know what Indians are sewing and what Indians are playing." My own introduction to Chief Bannock was prefaced by his proud display of calloused, needle -pierced fingertips as evidence of his constant beading and sewing.

The cost of the suit is a source of frustration; many cannot afford to mask each year. Johnny "Kool" Stephenson of the Wild Magnolias reveals certain suits may contain $2,500 of materials with a completed value of $6,000 to $10,000. Suits are not repeated or reused. Depending on the tribe location, aspects of the costume or beaded patches may be re-arranged and enhanced in subsequent suits. In other areas no feature of the costume can be repeated. Traditionally the suits are worn only twice, Mardi Gras Day and St. Joseph's Night. With media "discovery" of the Indians in the 1970's, some Indians have the opportunity to participate in shows, exhibits, or Jazz Fest and other suits are used for these "performances". These appearances and costumes lack the significance to the wearer of his Carnival suit, but these new venues have provided a way to help finance masking. Especially significant suits are fashioned into home altars as reminders of a spiritual reawakening.

Distinctive differences in aesthetic expression exist by neighborhood. Uptown, downtown, back of town, and mid-town costume genres have evolved. Smith proposed the source of these differences is rooted in the origins of the various communities: Downtown extractions from the Senegambian colonial importations; Mid-town and Uptown styles affecting the influence of Haitian, American (English-speaking slaves), and Louisiana plantation (creole speaking slaves) immigrations.

Design concepts also follow sectional preferences. Uptown pictorial motifs often feature Western "Cowboy and Indian" scenes depicted in beaded patches arranged in an allegorical manner. The viewer "reads" the "story" from top to bottom. Uptown Indians usually have two suits. Downtown designs are more abstract and three dimensional. M. Senette of the Yellow Pocahontos describes the Downtown suits as sculptural. His goal is to extend and incorporate his person into a larger presence or space (Senette, 1996).

Materials and fabrications also distinguish territorial preferences. Uptown suits are noted for elaborate beadwork "patches" made of thousands of colored beads and small rhinestones. The time-consuming beading process takes months as small denier beads are necessary to the detailed pictorial effects. Three dimensional beadwork in which layers of beading create a raised effect is highly prized. When the suits are dismantled in late Spring, significant patches are used in subsequent years in different arrangements. Wild Magnolias Johnny "Kool" explains, "You reuse your patches every year. You may tear down certain patches and rearrange them. They are supposed to tell a story" (Smith, 1994: 87). Chief Bannock recalls, "When I first started in 1972 all you needed was four patches and now you need twenty-some patches to make a costume" (Smith, 1994: 140). Ribbon and velvet are also commonly featured elements uptown. In all Indian tribes the feathered headdresses or crown with trails is the ultimate expression of both flight and freedom. Uptown crowns are made with ostrich plumes and maribou.

Downtown, the Africanesque tribes use more sequins, mirrors, pearls, and large glass stones. They glue rather than sew the ornamentation. In earlier times, salvaged throw beads, foil from gum wrappers, and dyed egg shells might have been found in the creole costumes.   Downtown Indians prefer feather trims for their elaborate headdresses; Feathers, turkey or other types, are sewn to the crown with a specialized loop stitch that locks the feather but allows flexibility and motion.   Cardboard and wire mesh are base materials for the more sculptural forms of the Downtown suits.. Differences in application techniques, sewing conventions, production sequencing, and aesthetic priorities vary by tribe and area.

The twenty four hours prior to Mardi Gras Day for an Indian are often a marathon of frenetic activity as suits are completed under exhausting pressure. Each person interviewed, however, indicated that as he walked into the streets of his neighborhood on Mardi Gras Day in his new suit , the spiritual power felt as others admired his creation took him beyond reality into the spirit world. To be the prettiest or most beautiful is to achieve the highest level of power or self-esteem.

Conclusion

The Mardi Gras Indian history is oral and closely held by choice. Recent interest in the Indians has brought mixed response from the members.   While opportunities have expanded to have their creations seen and appreciated by a larger audience, that was never their goal. They have felt exploited by exposure of their culture with no apparent reward to their community. The attempts to explain masking Indian to the world beyond the enclosed neighborhoods have often trivialized concepts at the core of their spiritual being. The Indian Council has made plans but very little progress on a written history of the tribes and the concept of masking Indian.

ACKNOWLEDGMENTS

I have gained insight, entree, and exposure to sensitive imagery related to the Mardi Gras Indian culture from the work and generous assistance of Michael P. Smith. His soul is connected to the "cultural wetlands" of New Orleans as an enthusiastic champion and an empathetic interpreter.

BIBLIOGRAPHY

Bergan, Mary Brooke. (1989) *Storyville: Plate, Discourse, Argument, Extrapolation, Voice*. Unpublished doctoral dissertation, University of Illinois at Chicago.

Berry, Jason, Foose, and Jones. (1986) *Up from the Cradle of Jazz: New Orleans Music since World War II*. Athens: University of Georgia Press.

Blassingame, John. (1973) *Black New Orleans 1860-1880*. Chicago.

Draper, David Elliott. (1973) *Mardi Gras Indians: the Ethnomusicality of Black Associations in New Orleans*. Unpublished doctoral dissertation, Tulane University.

Jacobs, Claude F. (1988) "Benevolent Societies of New Orleans During the Late 19th and Early 20th Century," *Louisiana History* (pp. 29-22).

Jacobs, Claude F. (1989) "Spirit Guides and Possessions in the New Orleans Black Spiritual Churches," *Journal of American Folklore*, 102 (pp. 45-67).

Kinser, Samuel. (1990) *Carnival, American Style*. Chicago: University of Chicago Press.

Logsdon, Joseph and Karyn Bell. (1992) "The Americanization of Black New Orleans." In (Logsdon and Hirsch, eds.), *Creole New Orleans: Race and Americanization*. Baton Rouge and London: Louisiana State University Press.

Midlo-Hall, Gwendolyn. (1992) *Africans in Colonial Louisiana: The Development of Afro-Creole Culture in the Eighteenth Century*. Baton Rouge: Louisiana State University Press.

Palmer, Colin. (1992) "The Cruelest Commerce," *National Geographic*, Vol. 1822, (pp. 64-91).

Reid, Mitchell. (1995) *All on a Mardi Gras Day, Episodes in the History of New Orleans Carnival*. Boston: Harvard University Press.

Sennette, Marlon. (1996) Personal interview, New Orleans, Louisiana.

Smith, Michael P. (1992) *A Joyful Noise*. Dallas: Taylor Publishing Co.

Smith, Michael P. (1994) *Mardi Gras Indians*. Gretna: Pelican Publishing Co.

Smith, Michael P. (1992) *Spirit World*. Gretna: Pelican Publishing Co.

Spitzer, Nicholas R. (1987) *Zydeco and Mardi Gras: Creole Identity and Performance Genres in Rural French Louisiana*. Unpublished doctoral dissertation, The University of Texas at Austin.

Williams, Karen Luane. (1972) *Images of Uneasy Hybrids: Carnival and New Orleans*. Unpublished doctoral dissertation, Emory University.

Vesilind, Priit. (1995) "Upbeat, Downbeat, Offbeat New Orleans," *National Geographic*, Vol. 187, No. 1 (pp. 90-119).

Between Light and Shadow

Video: 27 min. VHS color, 1996
Producer: Kathryn Lypke Vigesaa
Co-director: Kathryn L. Vigesaa and John McKay

Using a complex style of personal interviews and ethnographic documentary, visually rich in intimacy, lyricism, metaphor and sometimes startling images drawn from her subjects daily lives, the filmmaker looks at the role that textiles play in the lives of the Maya in Guatemala. Cloth is the first material that touches a child's body, it appears in every important event in a persons life and is the last to touch a person at their death. In Quiché cosmology there are strong connections between house (milpa) and the huipile, both have 4 corners and 4 sides, all are reflections of the "skyearth"; the four corners and sides a boundary of earth and sky with the weaver/wearer at the center. To the Maya, cloth represents place, status and culture. Today some of these same Maya women are using images of their weaving patterns and textiles in paintings to express their hopes and dreams and to remember their culture, others wear *traje* from many different villages to identify themselves as part of the Maya Nation at the same time that they are studying to become experts in marketing, health care or teaching. Focusing on these changes to their life style, weaving, and textiles the filmmaker considers the impact on the Maya and their culture.

***

Professor Kathryn Lypke Vigesaa has been teaching in the Department of Sculpture, Ceramics and Fibres at Concordia University in Montreal since 1977. In 1988 she first visited Guatemala as a consultant to CAUSE CANADA, a non-governmental relief and development organization, to aid in the establishment of weaving cooperatives. She returned in early 1991 with John McKay to begin the filming for the video, *Daughters of Ixchel, Maya Thread of Change*, which has won numerous awards, including the Society for Visual Anthropology Award, American Anthropological Assoc. selection, Intl. Film & TV Festival of NY Award and the Canadian Intl. Film Festival honoree. She has served as a visiting artist and professor for numerous Universities and Art Institutions in the US, Canada, and Europe. Her art works have been shown in numerous solo and group exhibitions in the US, Canada, Europe and South America. She received her M.A. from the University of California at Berkeley.

Introduction

The term "sacred" in our symposium title implies the existence of "secular" and thus conceptually divides the world into a dualism which is characteristic of Western thought. Perhaps though, that is <u>not</u> the way the ancient Andeans, whose textiles we are to briefly examine, saw their world. They did not divide the world into animate and inanimate, into flora and fauna, or neatly into secular and sacred. Every <u>thing</u> was a living, interactive part of their cosmos and every textile, regardless of its rank, was considered to be spirited. With last year's discovery of a fully clothed 13 year old Inka girl who had been sacrificed in Inka ritual on a mountaintop and then frozen, to be found five hundred years later, we can glimpse the end of this three thousand year Andean textile story.

Geography

In 1500, the approximate year of the sacrifice and just before the Spanish meltdown, the Inka ruled the western face of South America from their capital at Cusco. The sacrifices and the textile offerings with which we are concerned were the result of an Inka ritual called <u>Khapak Hucha</u>[i]. which[ii] involved the empire's best looking teenagers, who were nominated by their parents or selected by the Inka, sent to Cusco and feted. They were then carried in a processional, which moved only in straight lines, across the country to the selected mountaintop where they were sacrificed to serve as propitiation to a mountain, lightning or other deity.

Ampato is the name of the site of Johan Reinhard's frozen mummy discoveries.[iii] It is a volcanic peak amongst a chain of peaks in Southern Peru[iv], is ice covered and is 21,000 feet high. The sacrificed girl was found inside the volcanic crater, having tumbled with her associated offerings from her disintegrating mountaintop platform. Also Reinhard, with Jose Antonio Chavez of the Universidad Catolica in Arequipa, discovered on a lower plateau a grouping of associated buried ritual offerings. Each set of offerings was marked by a circle of stones and two of the offering pits contained fully clothed burials.

Offering containing Mummy #2

One of the offering pits, when excavated, proved to contain a fully-clothed, frozen young female who had been surrounded by some 40 Inka ceramics. X-rays of the body have revealed the presence of <u>tupus</u> which are Inka women's clothing pins, indicating that the burial was undoubtedly a female. The sacrificed girl was wearing an elaborate feather headdress which had been rudely crushed. Johan Reinhard reports there was a big rock in the bottom of the pit limiting the Inka excavation, with the digger's solution to the problem being the crunching down of the headdress which otherwise would have projected above the ground level. In the burial process, the attached feathered cap was shoved forward over the face.

Headdress of Mummy #2

The headdress feathers which are Macaw tail feathers, probably from the jungle below Cusco, had formed an approximately 18 inch high semi-circle above the head. This type of headdress though <u>not</u> represented by Huaman Poma[v], does appear on Inka figurines. The creation of the headdress involved the construction of a semi-circular ridge of plaiting which went over the head from ear to ear. It was attached to the base cap which was feather-covered with small feathers pre-assembled on strings which were then sewn onto the base textile. The upright Macaw feathers had been individually inserted and fastened into the fiber ridge so that when the headdress was crunched down during burial, some of the fibers of the ridge structure were also broken.

Outer wrapping of Mummy #2
This sacrificed child before burial, had been placed in the middle of a large rectangular textile, which had been spread out on the ground. This enormous ground cloth and mummy wrapper, probably an Aksu, had simple warp striping. The four corners had been brought up and tied, enclosing all of the mummy except for the head and the headdress. Her orientation was such that when the wrapping textile would have been untied, presumably in the next world, it would have unfolded to be square with that world also, suggesting that the next world was modeled on this one. The warp of the textile was placed north/south with her facing orientation toward the south, sometimes considered the direction of death in the Inca world. It also tells us that the people engaged in the ritual, her handlers, were probably deeply concerned with establishing the correct resonance between the textiles and the Inka cosmos.

She was then put into the burial pit where she was surrounded by Inka ceramics which were primarily sets of paired vessels, perhaps for her and a male next-world counterpart. The textiles worn by the mummy were similar to the outer wrapping and quite intact, but astonishingly, the burial had been struck by lightning and the body tissues destroyed. A quarter-sized hole in the head marked the entrance and path of the lightning through the body which can be traced by examination of the bones.

Tunic of Mummy #2
When the outer wrapping of mummy #2 had been untied and removed, and the headdress lifted off for conservation, the textiles actually worn by the sacrificed girl could be studied. Like the outer wrappings, they were brown, warp-faced, with simple striping and seemingly stylistically unrelated to the elaborate headdress.

Additional Tunic of Mummy #2
One textile, though, was clearly not being worn by the mummy, nor was it being used as a wrapper. It was a separate textile which had been folded and placed by her side during the burial. Because a neck slot was present, it appeared to be a male garment although in a female grave. The folded condition of the textile and its placement indicated that it had been placed there as an offering - with the sacrificed girl, his neck slot at her side, the bottom of the tunic near her feet. It was apparently for her husband in the next world. The tunic appeared to be weft patterned with the warps running horizontally as in other Inka men's tunics, but it had been constructed in two pieces with a center seam like much earlier Wari tunics. The bottom selvage had an attached elaborate tie-dyed fringe. As to interpretation, there is a reference in the chronicler Molina [vi](1) to Inka men at a Cusco festival wearing a long red unku with a red and white fringe. Possibly, someday enough such textile interpretations can be found, to enable an understanding of the whole sacrifice.

The offering also contained, placed above the body, a golden spatula-like object which was probably a golden feather. Noting that vertical feathers are associated with Inka male headgear, perhaps it was associated with the red male tunic buried below. It may have, perhaps intentionally, functioned as a lightning rod, since it shows evidence of having been struck by lightning .

Offering containing Mummy #3
Another of the stone offering circles on that same plaza, when excavated, revealed the burial of a probable male, which had also been struck by lightning. The textiles had disintegrated and the body had been reduced to carbonized bones.

Though disturbed by the excavation process, a large group of tan reed-like vegetable fiber elements were associated with the skull and were believed by the excavators to have formed a fringe around the head. Each of these reed-like elements had been pre-formed --- doubled and then bent with a hooked top --- and strung together in the manner of the feather work. A possible reconstruction of this headband/fringe produces a wearable item but not one like any of the Spanish illustrations.

Male figurine associated with Mummy #3
A miniature silver male figurine some four inches high, found amongst the leg bones of the carbonized mummy, had been struck by the lightning. Melted silver appears around the entrance and exit holes created by the lightning as it ripped diagonally through the casting of his body. The resultant heat severely darkened the finish of the silver. He has the solemn face of a mature and deeply reverent male but his tumescence speaks of youth and fertility. His ear lobes have deep loops which were used by the Inkas to to hold decorated ear spools. This standing male may be resonant with the standing deities of the earlier pre-Inka Andean cultures such as Tiwanaku.

Because of the lack of oxygen in the frozen ground, the clothing of the figurine, though severely toasted by the heat of the lightning, did not seem to actually burn. It is possible that the whole human offering and its associated artifacts was intended for the God of lightning and thunder whose Inka name was Illapa.

Figurines associated with Mummy #1
Johan Reinhard on his initial trip to the top of Ampato which resulted in the retrieval of the frozen mummy #1, saw emerging from the slope just below the collapsed Inka platform at some 21,000 feet, the feathers of three sets of miniature figurines. Such figurines, found primarily with the Khapak Hucha ritual sacrifices. are of gold, silver or spondylus shell, and wear replicas of Inka clothes.[viiviii] Their clothes, however, were seemingly always oversized, perhaps because the Inkas believed that the figurines would, like seeds, grow after being placed underground. Miniatures, had a high status in Andean society and, no doubt, the sacrificed teen-agers may also have been considered to be a form of miniature.

One of the figurine is of gold, is female and is constructed largely of sheet metal though her face may be a casting. Gold is associated with the sun in Inka mythology. The chroniclers have many references to full-size realistic Inka sculptures representing deities, but none have survived. Such carefully constructed miniatures thus provide for us a keyhole view into that tradition.. The figurine wears an outer mantle or llyclla, an inner wrap-around dress called an aksu, and a cord which connects two of her three tupu pins. The llyclla worn by the golden figurine is about 1/12 the size of an adult llyclla. From the figurine's Tupu connecting cord, hang four suspended spondylus shell fragments attached with the same half-hitch knot used by the Inkas in the construction of their quipus. Prior to the Ampato discovery, this necklace-like arrangement was considered normal for Inka women's wear, however differences now emerge in the arrangements used in the miniatures, in burial, and in real life.

The second figurine of the group of three found by Johan Reinhard is also female but is made of cast silver which is associated with the moon in Inka cosmology. She has a fan-shaped white feather headdress, and her clothing is predominantly of natural undyed material with no linear patterning. Her tupu and connecting cord are constructed like those of the first figurine but she carries only two spondylus fragments. This "snow" woman's cap and train are constructed of white alpaca except for the final fringe which is bright blue. Her white cap of single element looping, forms the structural basis for her feather headdress. A miniature version of the plaited semicircular feather-base ridge similar to that of the big headdress of Mummy #2 is visible. She also wears a very fine inner Aksu probably of tan vicuna. The significance of these pristine clothes on this silver girl is unknown.

The third figurine of the group is also female with clothing similar to those of number one, but she is carved of spondylus shell, a material which is associated with the sea and was imported from the coast of Ecuador. She has not yet been disassembled so the construction of her connecting cord is not yet known. Her headdress is fan-shaped but of coral and yellow feathers. Yellow feathers on a white base textile form the train which extends down her back from the cap and coral red top feathers of her headdress. Her tupus are of bronze.

Possible Chimu featherwork associations
The feather headdresses on the miniatures and on the mummy may well have been derived from the clothing styles of the Chimu. Several full-size Chimu feather headdresses exist in museum collections --- headdresses which have both an upright array and a feathered train. The chroniclers report that the Chimu empire was conquered by the Inka, their feather workers were taken to Cusco and made to work for the Inka.

Mummy #1
The first full-sized frozen mummy discovered by Johan Reinhard on his initial assent up Mount Ampato was the mummy bundle which had rolled down the inner side of the extinct crater after the collapse of the Inka burial platform. She is called Juanita after the name of her discoverer.

Outer wrapping of Mummy #1
Her outer wrapping was a gray-with-white-striped warp-patterned alpaca textile, probably a mantle, which was damaged in her rolling descent.   Associated with these outer wrappings were a belt and an awayo (carrying cloth) containing her personal possessions, a coca bag, some small balls of human hair, some string, and a fragment of spondylus. The awayo had been darned and repaired. These textiles, probably her own sacred textiles, as distinct from her offering garments, may be able to be related to local clothing of the 16th century.

Mummy #1 Headcovering
Over her head was a rectangular cloth used as a head covering which had disintegrated exposing her face to the weather. This head covering was the first of the special ceremonial textiles to be removed from the frozen bundle. It had been pulled down over her head for burial, (presumably after her death) and was held down by a tupu pinned in front. This tupu was probably the central, third tupu, used in life to hold together the left and right sides of her llyclla or shoulder mantle. This action by her handlers, presumably after her death, of pulling her head covering down over her head and pinning it in place so that the striping and the warps of the textile were carefully aligned with her body, seems intentional. Because she was not found in a buried position, her burial orientation is not known, but this careful alignment of headcovering with her body seems resonant with the more extensive evidence of the cosmic alignment of textiles and body found in the case of mummy #2. Though a simple two color design, this head covering had beautifully

constructed and patterned two color warp and weft selvages. Its colors and quality of construction suggest that it is a part of her ceremonial clothing rather than the outer set of clothing used as wrappers.

Ceremonial clothing of Mummy #1

When the outer gray wrapping and her head covering were removed, her elaborate Inka textiles began to be revealed. Having been in the deep freeze for 500 years, and protected by the wrapping set, they were in like-new condition. Apparent were her <u>llyclla</u> and her <u>aksu</u>, though the folds, convolutions, fading etc. made them very difficult to identify. She was a young girl, perhaps 13 or 14, but the clothes are fully adult.

<u>Llyclla</u>

Her shoulder-wrap or <u>llyclla</u> is a predominantly red, finely woven textile with characteristic and easily recognizable classic Inka designs and edging details. The llyclla has upper and lower broad red bands and a central white band band separated by design bands. Selvages are bound with a simple wrapping stitch in a red, yellow, and black repetitive pattern except around the corners where the wrapping is given a crossed loop stitch finish, presumably for reinforcement. The design bands have patterns in red, yellow and near-black, with the patterns consisting of variations on a drawing of the cross section of a textile showing the under-and-over characteristic of weaving. This patterning in these woven lines contains the memories of more than a millennium of Andean textile history. The diagonal color reversals and the symbolic weaving structure pattern recall designs from their predecessor cultures - Pucara and Tiwanaku.

Belt

Her belt, still firmly frozen, is probably a complementary-warp patterned weave with three-span floats in alternating alignment. and would properly be called a <u>mamachumpi</u> [ix]. The edge pattern of waves and dots no doubt also represents textile structure. The patterning on her belt does not resemble the _tokapu_ patterns portrayed on women's belts by Human Poma.[x] Inka clothing is always symmetrical with the body and not asymmetrical like togas or saris.

<u>Aksu</u>

The most basic element of Inka women's clothing was the <u>aksu,</u> which was a large folded rectangular cloth used as a wrap-around dress. The cloth was folded horizontally so that the fold came under the arm pits and the bottom edge reached foot level. It seems likely that <u>aksu</u> were not sized in accordance with the wearer but in accordance with the occasion.. Perhaps the fold made possible adjustments in accordance with the height of the woman. The upper corners of this folded rectangle were crossed in back and then came generously over the shoulders. These corners were then held in place in front with pins called <u>tupus</u>.

The design of the <u>aksu</u> contains no detailed patterning but consists exclusively of color bands. The edge binding is of a single color. By measuring along visible selvages, a reconstruction of the <u>aksu</u> was developed. The <u>aksu</u> was constructed in three pieces with two almost invisible seams occurring within color areas and not along points of color change. The top and bottom color bands and the central color band is a bluish-red or plum, an unprecedented color for Inka textiles but one which continued into colonial times Additional color bands are in brilliant red, yellow and orange. The rainbow of colors which characterize the <u>aksu</u> were a shock to those who have previously seen the Inka world only through the colonial black and white ink line drawings

Tupus

Two silver <u>tupus</u> which had four inch fan-shaped heads and 3/16th inch shanks, held up her <u>aksu</u> were inserted upward. In the process the tupus had to penetrate through many layers - seemingly eight - of tightly woven heavy cloth --- no easy task . Inka women's garment construction should probably be considered as relatively permanent. Bathing for cleanliness reasons did not occur, clothing removal for toileting was unnecessary and no undergarments were worn. These relatively permanent <u>tupu</u> constructions on either side were then covered by a shawl. In addition to the two <u>tupus</u> used to hold her <u>aksu</u> together, a third <u>tupu,</u> normally used to hold her <u>llyclla</u> together, had been used by her handlers to hold her head covering as well as her <u>llyclla</u> in place.

Supplemental offerings

Her paired tupus were joined together by a beautifully plaited cord with diamond patterning. This cord went through holes in the metal tupus and was knotted - all in a manner like that found on the miniatures. On the miniatures, supplemental offerings were hung from this cord like amulets from a necklace. However the supplemental offerings in this burial were not attached to the cord, but were instead attached directly to the stem of the <u>tupus</u> with half hitch knots. Attached to her <u>tupus</u> in this fashion, were a wide variety of miniature offerings including a pair of miniature carved wooden <u>keros</u> or cups the size of thimbles, a needle made from a cactus spine, and a carved four-footed miniature animal figure. One small object was filled with what appeared to be llama fat suggesting that they were all indeed offerings and not simply "charms." These miniature offerings were of meticulous quality construction.

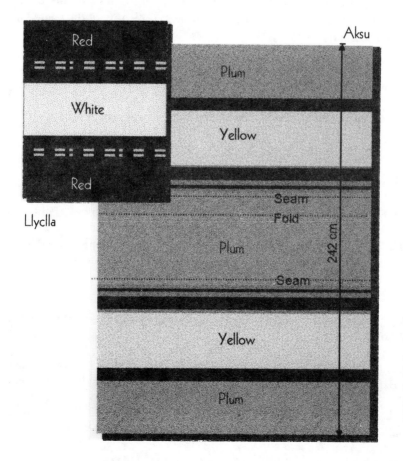

Wardrobe of ceremonial textiles worn by Mummy #1 found by Johan Reinhard and the team from Universidad Catolica on Mount Ampato, near Arequipa, Peru, 1995 Reconstruction dwgs. by WJC

Mummy #1 garment set (Fig. 1)

Mummy #1 garment set

With the aid of reconstruction drawings, see Fig.1, since some of the clothing is still frozen around the body, it is possible to compare the sizes and patterns of her clothing set. The aksu has no detailed patterning and the colors (plum, orange etc.) seem to bear little relation to the classic Inka colors of her llyclla (red, gold and black). The vertical dimension of her aksu when it is unfolded will be about 8 feet.

Conclusions:

The moccasins on her feet are the type which Huaman Poma illustrates for this quarter of the Inka empire (Colla) and were tucked in very tightly, suggesting that she was huddled against the cold at the moment of death. The soft leather soles were finished with a stretch weave binding. Her right hand has a firm grip on her aksu also suggesting huddling. Cat scans performed by Johns Hopkins Medical School have discovered that her scull was cracked probably by a sharp blow to the right side of her head which caused her death.

Although we don't know who this Ampato maiden was, we do have from one of the chroniclers the final words of another such sacrificed girl, as follows: "You can finish with me now because I could not be honored more than I have been already by the feast that they celebrated for me in Cuzco."[x]

In the scientific sense, the forty or so textiles from the Ampato discoveries help us in the technical definition of Inka textiles, but more importantly help to understand the sacred role of textiles in Inka religion as evident in their design and construction, but most critically, in the sacred nature of their placement in relation to the Inka cosmos.

---

[i] McEwan, Colin and Vande Guchte, Martin "Ancestral Time and Sacred Space in the ritual Inka State" Ancient America, Art Institute of Chicago, 1992

[ii] Besom, Tom, "Notes on Khapak Chucha,"personal communication provided to WJC, 1996

[iii] Reinhard, Johan, "Peru's Ice Maidens" National Geographic, June 1996

[iv] Chavez Chavez, Jose Antonio, La Erupcion del Volcan Misti, Zenit, Arequipa, Peru, 1993.

[v] Poma de Ayala, Huaman Felipe, Nueva Coronica y Buen Gobierno, Inst. D"Ethnologie, Paris, 1936

[vi] de Molina,Cristobal, see *Narratives of The Rites and Laws of the Yncas* - Clements Markham, Editor .The Hakluyt Society, London 1873 Molina p.45 in relation to the November festival, sometime after 14th day, "Those who had to take part in the *taqui* (musical event?) wore red skirts, with red and white fringes, reaching to the feet. They called these shirts puca-caychu-uncu. The *taqui* was called *coyo*."

[vii] Dransart, Penny, Elemental Meanings: Symbolic Expression in Inka Miniature Figurines - Institute of Latin American Studies, London. 1995

[viii] Desrosiers, Sophie, "An Interpretation of Technical Weaving Data Found in an Early 17th-Century Chronicle," The Junius B. Bird Conference on Andean Textiles, The Textile Museum, Washington DC. 1986

[ix] Huaman Poma de Ayala, Felipe, op cit

[x] Principe, Hernandez R. "Mitologia Andina," Inca Vol.1, pp25-68, 1923 [1621]

The Great Cloth Burial at Cahuachi, Nasca Valley, Peru
Elena Phipps

Introduction

William Duncan Strong's excavation team, working at the base of the major ceremonial mound at Cahuachi, in the Nasca Valley, on the South Coast of Peru, encountered evidence of a thickly woven plain white cloth (fig.1). His journal entry for September 1, 1952 reads:

> " 'The Carpet Site'. To dig.
> Opened up the cloth 'tomb' at Cahuachi-proved to be a layer of cloth—several centimeters thick, 30 ? meters long – 140 cm broad and 120 (*mas o menos*) deep. The damnedest thing I have yet seen... Dug below it a meter or so and hit solid *caliche* (maritime clay) no tomb—no necropolis. Damn."[1]

Strong was disappointed at the findings of the cut, subsequently referred to as the "'Rag Carpet' site." What he had hoped to find, were richly endowed burials, on the scale of the Paracas Necropolis. What he had actually found was probably the largest single piece of cloth ever woven in the Western Hemisphere, buried at the base of the largest ceremonial architectural mound in the South Coast of Peru[2].

Figure 1 1952 excavation of the "Great Cloth". Photo: Anthropology Department, Columbia University Archives.

In the spirit of the progressive, systematic archaeology of the 1950s, Strong's workmen dug four test holes directly through the cloth[3]. The resulting cloth fragments were shipped to Columbia University, along with other artifacts and documents from the excavation, where they currently reside in the William Duncan Strong Collection Study Room, in the Department of Anthropology[4].

The Cloth:

At present, the remains of the Great Cloth (fig.2) consist of four large fragments.[5] Two appear to be previously untouched, since excavation, and all are full of fine, powdery dirt. Their current, ragged and fragmentary state is due, for the most part, to the excavation methods, and not to natural deterioration of the cloth itself—which had been generally well-preserved in the dry desert climate. Some sections are intact and sturdy.

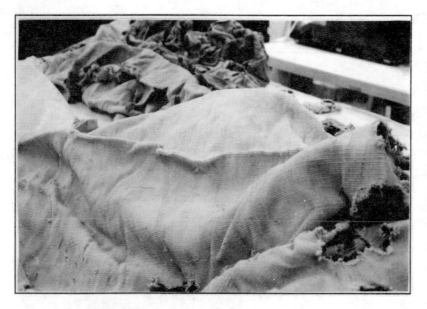

Figure 2 Detail, section of "Great Cloth". Photo: author

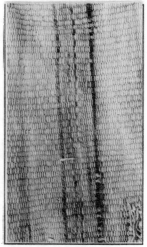

Figure 3 Detail: Warp faced plain weave with brown warp stripes. Photo: author

One section was of better condition, and whiter in appearance[6]; two have traces of brown warp stripes, (fig. 3) which disappear along its length. While some coloration differences can be noted, all appear to be the same type of cloth. The three main sections (fig.4) are basically short and wide: a forth is so ragged that it is difficult to open up to measure[7]. All have at least parts of one weft selvage preserved. In one piece, I have identified a complete loom width, selvage to selvage, of 220 inches—or over 18 feet. Sewn to this is a second fragmentary piece of cloth, which also has part of one selvage.

The extant textile remains representing approximately 20½ feet of length and 18 ½ feet of width of cloth. We cannot know the actual original size of the complete cloth. Strong, at the time of the excavation, estimated the length of the cloth to be at least 50-60 meters or between 164-200 feet.

This extraordinary textile, by its monumental size and related archaeological context, raises many questions including how it was made, why it was made, and why it was buried. Although these questions cannot be answered

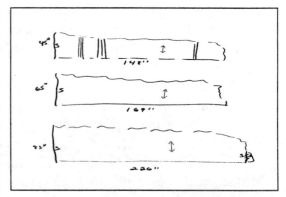

Figure 4 Schematic drawing of the three main sections of the Cloth. Drawing by author.

directly, I would like to explore these issues in relation to the physical characteristics of the textile, and the archaeological record, and in general, about the meaning of such a cloth in the Nasca region.

Archaeological Context

Cahuachi, the largest and most important archaeological site in the South Coast of Peru, is located along a tributary of the Rio Grande river, approximately 500 kilometers south of Lima (fig.5). The site extends for many kilometers, consisting of multiple mounds and open plazas, some of which are delineated by three-sided wall enclosures. Today, the mounds blend into the desert, making it difficult to distinguish between man-made architecture and the natural hills. To the North and South, lie the great pampas.

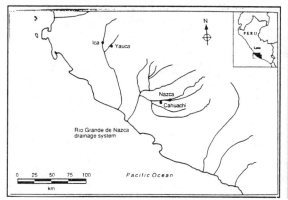

Figure 5 Map of South Coast showing Nasca Drainage.   After Silverman, 1993 fig. 22.3

Figure 6 Nasca Lines photographed in 1926 by A.L. Kroeber. Photo: Courtesy of The Field Museum, Chicago

Water is scarce in the Valley, where the current average rainfall is between 0 and approx. 25 millimeters per year[8]. In other words, it never rains. The water of the Rio Grande originates in the highland watershed which flows towards the sea. When it reaches the Nasca area, it flows underground for kilometers at a time, resurfacing lower down valley. At Cahuachi, however, there are several fresh water springs, in which 'sweet' underground water surfaces,[9] only several hundred meters from the main ceremonial precinct. The presence of this precious water no doubt contributed to the siting of Cahuachi, and to its tremendous ceremonial meaning-- as a place in the desert which always has water. Across the vast pampas -- immediately adjacent to the site-- are the enigmatic Nasca line drawings, (fig.6) some of which are in direct orientation to the main ceremonial complex[10].

Cahuachi has been of interest to archaeologists since the beginning of this century and several major excavations have been conducted. Because of the rich burials associated with the site, -- which has undergone extensive looting--we know that Cahuachi was a place of privilege and ceremony. A. L. Kroeber in an expedition for the Field Museum in 1926 excavated a series of burials yielding many richly embroidered textiles, and other ceramic remains. William Duncan Strong, in his 1952-1953 field season, applied a stratigraphic approach to the excavation of Cahuachi, (fig.7) establishing a chronology of the Nasca culture[11].

The Nasca culture flourished on the South Coast between 0-700 AD and evidence of occupation for all cultural phases are found at Cahuachi. The time of its greatest occupation is considered to be during the Nasca 3 phase of the culture sequence, roughly between 200-400AD[12].

Strong published his excavation report in 1957, in which he described the burial of the Cloth as:

> " ... a simple, plainweave cloth which occupied a trench ...The cloth itself, from selvage to selvage, proved to be 7 m. in width and appeared to be one single piece.   It was complexly folded in from side to side in rough accordion pleats, and then folded end over end at least three times" (Strong 1957:16).

Figure 7 Map of Cahuachi. After Strong 1957, fig. 4. The cloth burial is reported to be West of the Great Temple.

The Making of the Cloth

The weave configuration of the Cahuachi Great Cloth is a warp-faced plain weave with 60 warps and 14 wefts per inch. The warp yarns are composed of 3 Z-spun strands plied into S. The weft is generally a thicker and heavier yarn, composed of 5 Z-spun strands plied into S[13]. (fig. 8). The Z to S is typical of the yarn configuration of the South Coast. What is unusual, is the warp-faced surface of the fabric.[14]

For the area of cloth represented by the extant fragments, we can estimate that over 1 million feet of cotton yarn would have been used.   If the fabric was truly the 50 meters or approx. 164 feet which Strong estimated, that would mean well over 9 million feet or over 1,704 miles of yarn would have been spun for creating this textile. If we apply Goddell's calculations for yarn production rates—knowing that it is rather inappropriate for various reasons—it can be roughly estimated that approx. 44,000 hours-- the equivalent of 5 years time—would be required to spin this amount[15]. From this it is obvious that the yarn would most likely have come from various artisans, in what could have been a type of *m'ita* labor contribution-- an Andean principle of participation in communal rotational work obligations[16].

Figure 8 Detail: Macro photo, 10x. Photo: author

Yarns once produced, must be laid out and measured, for the preparation of the warp. Warp preparation in Andean culture where textiles are produced for pre-defined purposes, is a very important part of the weaving process. Generally, it involves the passing of a continuous yarn around a series of measuring rods set in a pre-defined position calculated for the intended size of the finished textile. The handling of the enormous warp length for the Great Cloth would certainly have required several people, as either the yarn for the warp is walked back and forth across a pathway created with markers, or passed, from person to person[17].

The loom

The Andean loom type varies geographically, regionally, and culturally, depending on available fiber types, cloth requirements, and local traditions. The weaving of the Great Cloth, due to its enormous size, could only have been accomplished on a specialized loom. The warp selvage from the fabric itself, would have been one of the best indicators of loom type: unfortunately, none were preserved.

The body tension loom, typically associated with South Coast weaving, would have been impractical to produce the extra-wide fabric, due to the weight of over 300 pounds of yarn which would have to be maintained by the weavers throughout the process. Fabric widths produced on this type of loom generally do not exceed the span of the weaver's arm reach.

Wide loom weaving, used by the later Huari and Inca cultures for their short and wide tapestries, is considered to have been accomplished on vertical, upright looms. During the Spanish Colonial period, Andean weavers used this type of looms to produce extra-wide tapestries and rugs. The vertical loom, associated with these highland weavers, was generally used for producing weft-faced, and weft-oriented fabrics. With its taught warp in fixed tension, it would most likely not have been used to produce the warp-faced fabric of the Great Cloth.

I believe the horizontal extension of the warp, would have been the most practical mode of weaving a fabric of this dimension[18], on some type of staked-out ground loom or possibly a modified body tension loom[19]. Stretched out horizontally, the weavers could sit and weave the cloth, following its progress, as a journey across the desert. In the persistence of this tradition, it is possible to see contemporary examples of Andean weavers using a Spanish-style treadle loom-- in which the warp would normally be rolled up onto a backbeam—with the warp extended out horizontally.

The weaving of the Great Cloth must have been accomplished by multiple weavers, working together. A detail from the Cloth (fig.9) shows that occasionally, the weft yarn skips a row at the selvage edge. This is evidence that two separate weft yarns were interlaced, an indication that multiple weavers could have been involved. We know that this occurs ethnographically.

The selvage on the cloth which is preserved is clearly a weft selvage. The selvage edge is extremely straight, and does not curve from variable tension, indicating expertise and control during the weaving process. While most wefts transverse the entire width of the cloth, occasional wefts turn around in mid-pass, forming a slight wedge. These were probably intentionally woven-in in order to compensate for uneven tension in the warps, and confirms the warp direction of the fabric. Some few weaving mistakes, consisting of a weft apparently missing occasional single warps in the shed-- probably due to a loose heddle-- can be seen. Throughout all fragments, the plainweave cloth is remarkably even and uniform. The accomplishment of the weaving of this oversized cloth required expertise and planning: its extraordinary size, though, is what stands out.

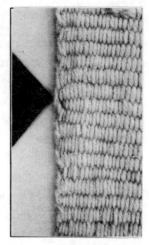

Figure 9 Macro photo10x Selvage with wefts skipping rows.   Photo: author

Comparative Oversized Cloths

If we look for a pan- Andean tradition which produced oversized cloth, the Cahuachi textile shares some features with the outer wrappings of funereal bundles, from other areas. Tello, who excavated the Paracas Necropolis—located North of the Nasca Valley, where over 490 mummies were found wrapped in layer upon layer of richly decorated cloth-- reported a Paracas Mummy #49 (fig.10) as having an outer wrapping composed of two lengths- each approx. 65 feet long x 6 feet wide[20]. Three Necropolis mummies in the collection of the American Museum of Natural History, were unwrapped in the 1930s. The outer wrappings of these mummies were plainweave cotton cloth sewn into bags. These bags were constructed of long strips of cloth, folded across their width, and sewn up along one length. Each were composed of strips approximately 45 inches wide x 20 feet long.[21] During a salvage operation of a pyramid located in downtown Lima, a mummy bundle dated to ca. 1250 A.D. was found, with a large amount (nearly 200 kilograms) of cotton wrapping cloth. One cloth from the bundle was reported to be over 40 meters long, composed of a single web of cloth, woven with thick 'roving-like' cotton weft yarns[22]. While these exceptional burial cloths

Figure 10 Paracas Mummy 49, Museo Nacional, Lima. After Tello, 1921 fig. 87

come, perhaps as close to the loom products, as any other comparable known examples, functionally, the Great Cloth, is not associated with a human burial.

The Folding of the Cloth

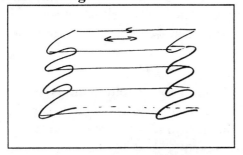 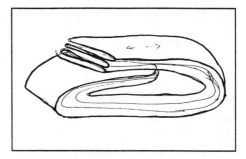

Figure 11a, b Drawings by author following descriptions in archival documents from "RLS"

The description from the excavators working at Cahuachi, was that the Great Cloth appeared to be one piece, accordion-folded, and then folded, end over end, upon itself (fig. 11 a and b). My interpretation from excavation notes, and upon examining the record photography, is that the warp direction of the cloth must have followed the length of the trench[23] I still have some trouble, however, reconstructing the method of folding.

Fold marks are still visible on some of the Cloth sections, particularly in one piece, where indication of three fold lines can be seen. The folds occur between 14" - 20" apart, and follow the same positive direction, across the width of the fabric. This means that the fabric at that section was not accordion-pleated-- which would have alternated positive and negative folding marks-- rather, it must have been folded layer over layer in the same

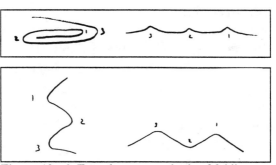

Figure 12 a,b Two alternate methods of folding. Drawings by the author.

direction (fig. 12a and b)—probably folded in half, first. How these folds were then oriented into the trench is unclear.

Although the burial of significant textiles and textile caches can be seen from the earliest manifestation of ritual life in the Andes, the ritualized folding of cloth not associated with human burial, is not well documented. Folding for burial in some cases seems to enable the textile offering to fit inside a particular vessel or container. For the Cahuachi cloth burial, the elaborate folding and the size of the trench which it occupied would seem to indicate that the cloth had some other purpose prior to its ritual interment.

The Function of the Cloth

Strong and others on the excavation team were hesitant to speculate as to the possible function of this cloth. Two proposals—one, that it had been a cloth wall to make a palace, and two, that it had been a carpet to walk on—were both volunteered by the local workmen during the excavation. While matting and other hard fiber constructions have been preserved, we have no archaeological documentation of Andean people walking on textile carpets prior to the Spanish introduction of the idea. There is no evidence that such a function was associated with textiles[24]. There are, however, many ethnographic examples of textiles used as ritual surfaces, in the form of "mesa's" or ritual tables, such as those used by regional curanderos, for curing and other sacred ceremonies, throughout the Andes.

None of these address the unique characteristics of our Great Cloth, and its burial circumstances, located in sterile soil-- indicating no other activity was conducted in the area. Amongst the other archaeological cuts which Strong excavated, no other comparable sterile burial conditions had been encountered. Most of the mound and architectural structures—and even human burials-- contained refuse and other architectural fill. The space, then, was preserved. It could be interpreted as a sacred space. In its interment in the largest open plaza, the Great Cloth most likely served in public ritual, and warrants its consideration of having a public ceremonial component, in both its use as an object, and in the process of its burial. This should be examined in the context of Cahuachi's sacred and ceremonial function.

Interpretation

In the past, archaeologists have interpreted the site of Cahuachi as the major political center of the Nasca culture. Recently, this interpretation of the site has been modified to our understanding of Cahuachi as a ceremonial center. Helaine Silverman, who excavated at Cahuachi in 1984-85, further emphasizes the concept of the site as a pilgrimage center, finding parallels with a contemporary event at the sanctuary of Yauca, in the nearby Ica Valley, where she observed the stages of a

Figure 13: Pilgrimage in 1986 across the desert to shrine of Yauca. After H. Silverman, 1990

once-yearly pilgrimage (fig. 13) to the shrine[25]. This involved the crossing of the desert by the local people, on foot and by bus, arriving at the empty ceremonial site, filling to capacity the once-empty plaza, then once again, leaving --after the festivities-- a deserted, wind-swept city.

Movement across the desert through pilgrimage and the active use of the Lines, by the Nasca people, by walking, running, dancing etc. has been further discussed in Gary Urton's study of the ritual sweeping of the Lines[26]. He argues that the *pampa* was an area of social interaction and the act of making and maintaining the lines was a social construction. This is based on ethnographic – and archaeological analogy -- of the *chhiutas* or defined strips of community- held land-- sacred and ceremonial spaces-- whose responsibility for maintenance was divided among the *alluys* --the socio-political groups composing Andean communities.

This concept of social construction and ritual obligation involving the lines and sacred spaces can be applied to the making of the Cahuachi Great Cloth, where the amassing and preparation of the raw materials, the spinning of the quantity of yarn, the measuring out and preparation of the warp, the construction of the special loom, and the process of weaving, all were a part of some larger community goal. That a relationship exists between the making of sacred lines and textiles can be seen in a group of geoglyphs nearby in Cantayoc, where a series of the Nasca lines form what is now called the needle and ball of yarn. Another is called the loom (fig. 14) .

Conclusion

That the enormous cloth was produced at all, can be seen, perhaps, as a tribute to the weavers of the region, but more discretely, provides evidence of the integration of the act of weaving into the sacred life of the Nasca people. The Great cloth burial was a ritual interment of a remarkable object. In the context of the largest ceremonial center of the South Coast of Peru, adjacent to the line-marked pampas of the desert, and near the life-giving sweet-water springs nearby, it was in good company. From production, use and interment, it marks an extraordinary moment of Andean conceptualism.

Figure 14 "The Loom" Photo: after M. Bridges *Markings (*New York: Aperture,1986 p.21)

Endnotes

[1] W. D. Strong *Journal* 1952-1953 vol 1 p. 65. All excavation documents are stored with Professor Terrance D'Altroy, the Anthropology Department, in the W. D. Strong archive, Columbia University.

[2] The actual location of the trench is in question: Strong notes that it was found to the West of the Great Temple. A drawing by R. Stigler in his Journal Vol. II in the Archives shows a map with Cut 2, a "little mound", and then the carpet site. Silverman believes it to be located at Strong's 'Cut 8' on his map. See Silverman, *Cahuachi in the Ancient Nasca World* (Iowa City :University of Iowa Press, 1993) p..53.

[3] Below the textile: "..found two skull fragments under [test pit] #4 (below textile); a post-fired sherd was found under [test pit] #1. Several lumps of adobe and large river boulders in hole [test pit] #3 below textile." RLS Artifact Data Sheet, 26 Aug [1952?] in the W. D. Strong Archive, (NY: Columbia Univ.) .

[4] The boxes had been sent to Jane Dwyer, in the early 1970s. They were returned virtually untouched, in 1983, at the commencement of the preservation project, funded by the National Science Foundation, supervised by Professor Terrence D'Altroy. The cloth was not incorporated into the NSF project, and rather, has been only thoroughly examined recently in conjunction with this presentation..

[5] The technical examination of the Cloth was conducted by the author at the Textile Conservation Department, MMA.. Travel for this study was funded, in part, by an MMA/CINOA Travel Grant. Photos used for this publication were digitially printed thanks to Barbara Bridgers, MMA Photo Studio.

[6] One puzzling comment on box #3 written in pencil says "the number was lost at the cleaners." There is in fact one remnant of a paper tag stapled to one edge of the fragment. There are no records as to whether these had been given to a cleaners (Chinese laundry?) The pieces remain covered with a fine powdery soil, which seems to indicates that they have not, in fact, been cleaned.

[7] The fragments measure respectively: **Piece #1**   (Box 1) 48 " H x 148" wide: 1 partial loom width with one weft selvage. White with some brown stripes near edge. brown staining. **Piece #2** : ca. 48" x 48"

extremely fragmentary similar to Piece #1 brownish color. **Piece #3:** (Box 3) 83" H x 224" wide, 1 loom width with two weft selvages seamed to second fragment with one weft selvage. Complete loom width 220". White, intact. A seam stitched with white cotton thread, with ca. 6" extant second fabric attached. **Piece #4** 68" H x 169" wide, (Box 4) White cotton, fragmentary, with some large area intact.

[8] Silverman, *Cahuachi* 1993, p.3

[9] I was shown the area in 1983 by the current owner of the Hacienda Cahuachi. He indicated that the water was different "sweeter" than the saline water of the river.

[10] Anthony Aveni "Order in the Nazca Lines?" In ed. A. Aveni, *The Nazca Lines* (Philadelphia: American Philosophical Society, 1990) pp 43-113. Also H. Silverman, *Cahuachi* 1993, pp 305-309.

[11] W. D. Strong, *Paracas, Nazca and Tiahuanacoid Cultural Relationships in South Coastal Peru.* Memoirs of the Society for American Archaeology 13, New York, 1957.

[12] Dating of the culture is based primarily on Strong's ceramic sequence derived from his stratigraphic excavations. See Silverman *Cahuachi* 1993 :pp.30-42 for in-depth discussion.

[13] In some areas, a 3-strand weft yarn, identical to the warp yarn was used.

[14] See E. Phipps *Cahuachi Textiles in the William Duncan Strong Collection: Cultural transition in the Nasca Valley, Peru.* (Ann Arbor: University Microfilm) 1989.

[15] J. Bird, "Fibers and Spinning Procedures in the Andean Area" A. Rowe, E. Benson and A. Schaffer eds. *J. Bird Pre-Columbian Textile Conference* (Washington, D.C.: The Textile Museum,1979) pp. 13-17.

[16] See J. Murra "Economic Organization of the Inca State" Suppl.1 to *Research Economic Anthropology* Greenwich,1980.

[17] Henri Stierlin, in his study of the Nasca Lines in *Nazca: La Cle du Mystere* (Paris: Albin Michel, 1983), makes a comparison to the action of warping of a fabric, in which a set of warp lengths are created by continuous back and forth movement of the yarns to the construction of the zigzag and geomorphic lines in the desert. He further argues that the lines are constituted within the framework of textile production.

[18] A problem however, would have been what to do with the finished weaving, as it progresses. It would normally be rolled onto the loom bars. The roll would eventually get too large and interfere with the weavers. One solution would be to use a circular warp, however, this is not a traditional Andean method.

[19] We cannot know exactly what type of loom would have been used, we do know that at least one pair of straight of loom bars spanning the width of the 18' wide fabric would be required. When we look at the Nasca landscape, the presence of high, hardwood trees is limited. *Cana* –or type of cane-- however, grows in the marshlands. Silverman, during her 1984 excavation at Cahuachi, (Silverman, *Cahuachi* 1993, p. 181) found several bundles of long, thin canes, which she interprets as loom parts. While these probably are, I believe that cane loom bars could not have held the tension of the warps that our Cloth would require. It is likely that the wood could have come from the highlands-- or at least 'up valley' such as used for making rug looms, documented in the 19th century (J. Vreeland , "Vertical Loom in the Andes Past and Present" *Irene Emery Roundtable 1977 Proceedings*, Washington, D.C.: Textile Museum, 1979, pp 188-211). This import of wood for the loom could have been the contribution of communities of the 'upper moieties'—in the Andean division of intra-regional community interaction.

[20] Julio C. Tello *Antiguo Peru: Primera Epoca* Lima: Editado por la Comision Organizadora del Segundo Congreso Sudamericano de Turismo, 1929) pg. 137. Two other wrapping cloths in the Museo Nacional of Lima, are reported to be between 7 and 8 feet wide by Lila O'Neale in "Wide Loom Textiles of the Early Nazca Period" in R. Lowie, ed. *Essays in Anthropology in Honor of A.L. Kroeber* Chicago,1936.

[21] Mummy B: outer bag 20'8" long x 50" wide (two strips).Mummy C outer bag:19' long x 45" wide. (author's measurements taken in June, 1996 at AMNH, thanks to Vuka Roussakis).

[22] J. Vreeland "Ancient Andean Textiles: Clothes for the Dead" *Archaeology* 1977 vol.30 no.3. p.175.

[23] Somewhat contradictory excavation notations are found in the archives at Columbia University.

[24] There are also some colonial documents which refer to 'tents' built by the Inca armies. However, with our Great Cloth, there are no indications of any stretching, or hanging devices or cords which would have been needed for vertical suspension. . See J. Vreeland "Vertical Loom in the Andes." 1979, p.195.

[25] See H. Silverman "The Early Nasca Pilgrimage Center of Cahuachi and the Nazca Lines: Anthropological and Archaeological Perspectives" in A. Aveni, ed. *Nasca Lines* 1990. Pp. 207-244.

[25] Gary Urton "The Ritual Sweeping of the Nasca Lines" in A. Aveni, ed,, *Nasca Lines* 1990 pp.173-206.

Syncretic Cloth, Virgins and Colonization in the Peruvian Andes*
by Karen Michelsen

The current cult of the Andean Virgin of Snow, patron of seamstresses in Cuzco, is a paradigm for the syncretic processes that Andean religious rituals have undergone. The exploration of how this Virgin became associated with textile production mirrors a parallel process whereby an Andean understanding of cloth intermingles with Catholic religious practice.

The Virgin of Snow appears in western history in the fifth century a.D., when in 435 Sixtus III consecrated the church of St. Mary Major under the title of the Virgin Mary. This church was named St. Mary ad Nives, or at the Snow, after a purportedly miraculous apparition by the Virgin Mary in Rome. Upon her invocation snow fell, in the middle of the summer, on Mount Esquilin, the designated area for her church.

This particular dedication of the Virgin Mary thereafter gained popularity in Spain as Saint Mary the White (*Santa María La Blanca*). Exalted was the aspect of purity inherent to snow, the Virgin becoming the most celebrated embodiment of the Catholic Church. It is noteworthy that the temple dedicated to her in Seville in 1665 was constructed over an old synagogue. If Spanish Catholicism sought to depict a triumphant Church over Judaism, pagan priests, medieval heretics, and reformers (Angulo Iñíguez 1981 : 338), so colonial representations of the Virgin are adamant about her participation in the conquest of Peru. Hence the Church virtually transplanted methods of assimilation to the New World.

The chronicler Guamán Poma de Ayala's drawing of the battle of Sunturhuasi, in which Spaniards are about to perish in the fire set by the surrounding Inca army, shows the Virgin Mary saving the Christians from the heathen by virtue of throwing sand into the eyes of the natives. Her vestment, according to Guamán Poma, was "whiter than snow" and her face "resplendent" (1987: 410). Therefore the presence of snow mirrors Mary's own purity as she extinguishes the hellish fire of pagan religion. [1]

The Virgin the chronicler mentions is the Virgin of the French Rock (*Virgen de la Peña de Francia*). His choice of this particular dedication of the Virgin Mary was certainly influenced by the wide circulation of religious images at that time, each admonishing the faithful on the particular powers of a given

---

* I wish to thank the Canada Council for the Explorations grant that allowed me to conduct fieldwork and research in Peru.
[1] Calderón de la Barca in his comedy *La Aurora en Copacabana* creates yet another image of the Sunturhuasi battle, where the Virgin appears dressed in white over a cloud that is snowing (Miró Quesada 1982:184).

saint (Miro Quesada 1982:191), and indispensable to religious colonization (Murra et al. 1987:XXXIII). Guamán Poma's version exhorts both "natives and Spanish" to honor not only the aforementioned Virgin in gratitude for the performed miracles, but also the **Virgin of Copacabana.**

Guaman Poma's inclusion of this latter Virgin within the same rank of the European-introduced Virgin of the French Rock is revealing as a sign of religious syncretism. This Virgin was enthroned by the Jesuits over a mountain in the formerly pagan ceremonial center of Copacabana at Lake Titicaca, and the chronicler relates the mountain element to the cult of the Virgin of the French Rock (Murra et al. 1987:1335).

The example of the Virgin of Copacabana illustrates how Christian deities will be adopted in response to elements found in Andean rituals existent before the conquest. The Spanish Catholicism of the counter reformation developed its particular character in Latin America by adopting elements of the Precolumbian past that would help establish a link between Andean and Catholic tradition (Urbano 1993:266).

What is retained in Andean Catholic religious expression is therefore not the individual history pertaining to each Marian devotion, but interpretations of Christianity that will work when coupled with the Andean belief system. In the cults of the Virgin Mary in the Cuzco area that this paper will introduce their original Catholic provenance is changed, if not disregarded, in favour of an association with a ritual use of textiles.

Christianity *per se* has a syncretic tradition of its own, in that the religious experience is tinted by the cultural expressions on which orthodox Catholicism sought to impose itself . Catholic iconography is not devoid of such pliant character. In the west, medieval representations of the Virgin engaging in textile activities, whose origins derive from the apocryphal gospels, were adapted to the textile and pictorial traditions of the region (Wyss : 155). Hence a chosen passage from the life of the Virgin Mary portrayed her either spinning, embroidering or weaving on different looms, the particularity of the textile technique a product of regional preference (ibid).

As a variety of interpretations of the Virgin's textile iconography existed in the West, so a Marian "taxonomy" proliferated in the Andes. Urbano explains how the successive waves of missionaries and the conflicts that aroused between the different religious groups did not allow for the primacy of a single figure of the Virgin Mary, the religious geography of the Andes remaining as diversified as the interests of each branch of Catholicism (1993:292). It is within this context that the diverse dedications of the Virgin in the Andes can be understood, and how a Marian cult will be adopted in relation to local needs.

The festivity of the Virgin of Snow is celebrated in some towns of the department of Cuzco, on the fifth of August of every year, according to the Christian calendar that commemorates the dedication of the first church to the Virgin Mary, as described earlier. In the city of Cuzco, the Virgin of Snow is the patron saint of seamstresses, their devotion present in the silver basket with sewing tools which the Virgin holds during the procession.

Seamstresses wear and sew *mestiza* attire, a gesture that effaces reference to indigenous identity, which is directly connected to weaving and agriculture. *Mestizo* women therefore include, among others, those who have renounced ethnic dress. Oral tradition has recovered accounts of apparitions of the Virgin of Snow wearing regional *mestiza* garb (Morote Best 1988:32). Hence her costume connotes the position of the saint's devotees towards their own cultural identity.

When asked about their devotion for the Virgin of Snow, seamstresses at the San Pedro market credited both their sewing skills and improvement of living conditions to her. The most important of her qualities was by far her ability to teach them how to sew. This very aspect explains why Mrs. Felipa Alvarez, a seamstress, holds a painting depicting the Virgin Mary embroidering as a treasured representation of the Virgin of Snow. This may not be an art historically correct assertion, but reflects again how Christian iconography undergoes transformation in order to suit cultural contexts in state of flux.

The seamstresses' reverence towards their patron has to be demonstrated in prayer, burning of candles and participation in her procession. Older seamstresses were very critical of the current *mayordomo*, in that he had not adequately organized the *jurka* (whereby obligations are delegated) nor ensured the Virgin a new vestment. The Virgin was a generous yet dangerously powerful deity if not tended to properly, and accounts of her miracles mingle with stories of the deaths of unprepared *mayordomos*.

The importance accorded to the costume of the Virgin of Snow has its origins no doubt in the Spanish baroque tradition (García and Santamaría 1979: 17). Catholicism likewise accorded the clothing of saints with the power to invest sculptural representations of the Virgin with her miracle performing abilities (Calancha 1974:1351).

While the mingling of Catholic and Precolumbian divinities has to be carefully deconstructed, textiles are a measure of how rituals were reinvented to incorporate elements of western and Andean culture. Although differing greatly in world view, both medieval Catholicism (Brading 1992:172) and Andean religion required their spiritual truths to be expressed in a material way. The power with which Catholicism invested sculptures of the Virgin reverberates the belief at the beginning of the middle ages whereby saint's relics, or their corpses, were seen as the preferred medium through which the Christian God acted (Geary 1986:176).

The humanization of deities and their need for symbolic clothing appears also as an element of Andean religion. Nature is seen as a living entity and is tangible evidence of the gods that pervade it. Within the hierarchy of mountain deities or *Apus*, snow peaked mountains have ranked among the most venerated since Precolumbian times (Murúa 1987:428; Albornoz 1989:170). The mountain at the former ceremonial center at Lake Titicaca, later to be converted through the imposition of the cult of the Virgin of Copacabana, was "covered (...) with a curtain of *cumbi*[2] the most delicate and subtle ever seen in the Indies" (Ramos Gavilán 1976:60).

Mountains were also part of the repertory of *huacas* (holy sites) that had an elaborate system of veneration in which cloth figures as an important sacrificial offering. The chronicler Cristóbal de Albornoz , noted for his inventory of *huacas* in an effort to "extirpate idolatry", explains that "all [*huacas*] have their own services, land and cattle, and **clothing** and particular sacrifices (...)" (1989:170). Furthermore, he relates that "all [*huacas*] (..) have *cumbe* clothing which they call *capaccochas*, of the very size of the [*huacas*]. And what needs to be done first is to procure these *capaccochas* , because if they remain in their possession, they will turn to dress whichever stone they want (...) " (196).

Huacas were also associated with landmarks of origin: "(...) they came out of such places and began to multiply from there, so they made [*huacas*]and temples of those places, in memory of the first of their lineage that proceeded from there and this is how each nation wears the clothing **with which they dressed their [*huaca*]** " (Molina 1989:5).

A strong relationship between rock or mountain deities and cloth emerges. Rocks appear often as naturally endowed goods, their properties related to that of skillfully crafted goods - such as textiles - in that they are *tangible*, "composed of and exemplative of particular values or qualities, rather than as merely material things, characterized by physical properties alone" (Helms 1993:150).

The value laid upon the powerful materiality of rock and cloth was evidenced in their use to personify precolumbian deities. The statue of the god Viracocha, housed in the temple of Coricancha, "was made of woolen blankets" (Cobo 1964:156), and there were also "three statues of the Sun, which were made of thick and tightly woven cloth, so that they stood without artifice" (157).

In addition, rocks were often adored in their own raw state. The chronicler Bernabé Cobo describes a rock "idol" at the *huaca* of the Huanacauri mountain, one of the most important temples of the Inca empire. The rock kept at the temple purportedly embodied one of the brothers of the first Inca.

---

[2] *Cumbi* refers to finely woven, silk-like cloth used for highly regarded clothing and ritual purposes.

The rugged, medium sized stone was in the eyes of the Spaniards of such "ordinary" nature that it was spared and overlooked when the temple was looted of all its gold and silver (Cobo 1964:181).

The correlation of cloth and stone acquires a contemporary dimension in the cult of the Virgin Mary in the Andes. The researcher Gertrude Solari, in an effort to explain the Andean metamorphosis of the Virgin of Snow, provided the statement of an Ayacucho peasant: "the snow clothes the sacred mountain, which is in turn covered in a black cloth that melts the snow, providing in that way abundant water for the valleys" (19?:2).

The mountain appearing in the original Roman Catholic legend of the Virgin of Snow transmutes in the Andean context where gods are embodied by mountains. In the town of Cora Cora, department of Ayacucho, where this Virgin is also venerated, a rock "whose appearance resembled that of the Virgin" was discovered among the **snow**, in the mountain facing the village (Ruiz de Castilla 1970:74). I found that in other towns of the Cuzco area her role as textile patron saint, although with different interpretations, appears connected to a mountain. A seamstress in the city of Cuzco explained that the virgin "appeared on a snow peak", while a peasant in the town of Sangarará explained how the Virgin of Snow, patron of seamstresses, had performed a miracle in the mountain that faces the town. In addition, the mountain had a woman's name: Juana Susoyac Accoyac. The men interviewed explained that she was "dangerous","not allowing people to work in the mines".

Colonial representations of the Virgin Mary, such as the painting of The Virgin of Potosí, show the iconic, triangular gestalt of the Virgin being related to mount Potosí, which becomes part of her vestment (De Mesa and Gisbert 1982:301).   Hieratic gestures, along with a triangular-shaped robe, richly decorated in a painting style which aimed to represent sculpture (302), contextualized the image of the Virgin as celestial queen within the Andean religious perception, relating her gender to the fecundity role ascribed to mountain deities and the *Pachamama*, or Earth Mother.

The Virgin does not, however, substitute in any way the cult of the *Apus* (mountain gods) or the *Pachamama*. Rather, she is "added" to the Andean cosmological pantheon. In the community of Q'ero, department of Cuzco, the Virgin Mary is considered to be the "sister" of *Pachamama* (Müller 1984:167). This places the Virgin Mary, regardless of the particular dedication, within a feminine realm.

Although textile production in the Andes is by no means limited to women, the chroniclers explain that a woman "made most of the cloth in which she dressed herself and her family and took the spindle into her grave as a symbol of womanly activity" (Murra 1962:711). In contemporary Andean society, men weave cloth in treddle looms and only occasionally on backstrap looms. Women, on the contrary, mostly specialize in intricately patterned backstrap-woven textiles.

During the month of August, special rituals are performed both for the *Apus* and the *Pachamama*, coinciding with the festivity of the Virgin of Snow. The Spanish-imposed Catholic calendar is adapted to the Andean life cycle that celebrates each period of the year according to its agricultural character. The first days of August, therefore, are considered the beginning of the new year, as the new agricultural cycle starts and the connection between the Andean population and the supernatural is renewed (Müller 1984:169). In addition, the first days of August are among those in which the life of the *Pachamama* is believed to become that of a woman (Condori and Gow 1982:5).

Weaving occurs mostly during those months in which the agricultural demands decrease, therefore August appears to be explicitly related to weaving (Urton 1981:30; Zorn 1978:18). In the community of Q'ero, it is mostly men who, in representation of their families, perform the *despacho*, or ritual offerings, to the *Apus* and the *Pachamama*. However. the women separately enact personal rituals by offering a small *despacho* of coca leaves to the "Star of the Weavers" (Müller 1984:169).

Different *Apus* "rule" throughout the Andes. The cult to the same mountain deities can overlap over geographically close communities. Once an Andean native identifies an *Apu* as its protector and provider, he or she chooses a "star", to which offerings are given to secure protection. A sign whereby the believer understands that his petitions have been recognized by the *Apu* is finding a small sacred stone, or *inkaychu*, whose shape resembles, for example, the animals of his herds in need of protection (Condori and Gow 1982:40).

One of those *inkaychus* was found in the ritual bundle of a weaver in the town of Marcapata. She purportedly found it as she walked through the *puna* (highest altitude level in the Andes, cold and believed to be inhabited by deities), and understood it as a sign of good fortune to have encountered it during the month of August, symbolically dedicated to weaving. The sacred stone in question resembled the shape of a weaver's amulet: a carved stone representing a hand holding a *wichuña* (weaving tool). This "amulet" was referred to as *Mamacha Qapachiqa*.

In analogy to the women weavers in the Q'ero community, weavers in Marcapata offer a set of three coca leaves or *coca k'intu* to the *Mamacha Qapachiqa*, as the sacred stone and the amulet in the ritual bundle were named after. Elayne Zorn describes a weaver's ritual in Puno, before warping, where after offering the required *coca k'intu* she whispered: "Santa Tierra Pachamama, **Apu Qapachiqa** q'aytuta qataypaq qellaqa chumpi puchu, puchu qellapaq (Saint Earth Mother. Lord (spirit) Strengthener, (make) this thread for warping the leftover loose belt, left over for the lazy to redo)" (1978:4).

The weaver in Puno mentions the *Qapachiqa* as "Strengthener". The Marcapata weavers also explained that such stone helped them "to weave faster". *Inkaychus* being produced either by a mountain deity or the

Pachamama herself, this *Mamacha Qapachiqa* appears to possess a female supernatural power which aids the weavers in their laborious textile creation.

Before colonization, the androgynous deity Cuniraya Viracocha was identified by weavers as their protector, "(...) and when they started difficult work, they adored him, throwing coca leaves to the ground [and saying]:"make me remember this, that I may divine it, Cuniraya Viracocha (...) the ancestors talked to him and adored him. And even more so the master weavers who had such difficult work, adored him and pleaded" (Avila 1966:25).

In the contemporary Andes, therefore, the female weavers' belief in the power of the *Mamacha Qapachiqa* to aid them in the weaving process manifests the continuity of Precolumbian cosmology. At the same time, the powers of a female deity are also transferred to the Virgin Mary .

Another Marcapata weaver's ritual bundle contained a triangular stone which she referred to as *Mamacha Santa Barbara*. As observed earlier concerning the flexibility in switching loyalties to different Marian cults, naming a sacred stone after Saint Barbara underlines the pivotal role of gender in determining the relationship between Andean women, textile production and the Virgin Mary. In addition,the woman's choice of Saint Barbara over, for example, the Virgin of Snow, reflects both a personal and community based definition of identity (Urton: 1981:28), analogous to the way an Andean peasant chooses to live under the jurisdiction of a specific *Apu*.

Silverblatt has pointed out to the fact that most informants on whose information the chroniclers based the reconstruction of precolumbian and Inca history were male. This is crucial to the understanding of the Andean belief system, where parallel religious organizations based on gender featured separate rituals for female and male deities (Silverblatt 1990: 30).

The rituals involving the Virgin of Fátima at the Qoyllor Rit'i pilgrimage show another instance where the Virgin Mary's role as patron of female weavers resurfaces regardless of the particular dedication. Certainly the history of the cult of the Fátima Virgin is of relevance only to the Jesuit priests who imposed the small altar of this Virgin on top of a rock that was revered as sacred.

As the Virgin of Snow teaches *mestiza* seamstresses to sew, indigenous weavers believe that the Virgin Mary, or *la Mamacha* , teaches them to weave. The rock beneath the small altar housing the Virgin of Fátima is a repository for the weaver's offerings. These consist of small woven *pallay* (patterns), small drop spindles, unfinished[3] woven bands and little scraps of fiber. Some weavers actually create the weavings beside the Virgin's rock,

---

[3] Among ritual offerings of great importance, the chronicler Martín de Murúa mentions fine clothing, including some that had **not been finished** (1987:420).

others hurriedly leave their community camps to subtly deposit the small objects.

The practice of leaving offerings among rock's openings is a ritual gesture for reaching the *Apus* (Urbano 1976:124). The *Pachamama* as well had holy fields to which small female clothing was offered (Cobo 1964:1978). In fact the small size of textile objects characterizes them as ritual gestures directed at the veneration of the *Apus* (Urbano 1976:136).

As the central Christian image of the pilgrimage, the Lord of Qoyllor Rit'i, appears painted (purportedly a miraculous apparition) on a formerly sacred stone, so the Virgin of Fatima's altar crowns a stone allegedly related to a female mountain deity. The sacred stone of the Christ of Qoyllor Rit'i manifests the importance the *Apu* Ausangate holds for the indigenous communities, who come as pilgrims to revere the rock situated close to the Sinacara snow peak (at 4,500 m.a.s.).

The rock of the Virgin appears related to the daughters of the *Apu* Ausangate, namely María Huamanctilla, Juana Sakapana and Tomasa Quinchu, who lived close to the Ausangate (Condori and Gow 1982:51). An oral account from the village of Pinchimuro explains that "María Huamactilla lives forever. She is an *Apu*. It is the **star** of weavers and spinners, **the star of women**" (53). Analogous to the female mountain Juana Susoyac connected to the Virgin of Snow in Sangarará mentioned earlier, the Virgin Mary at the Qoyllor Rit'i (meaning "Star of Snow" in Quechua) festivity adopts powers of a female mountain in helping weavers to perform textile activities.

While gender is the definitive thread that holds the acculturation of a female Apu in the cult of the Virgin Mary together, earlier observations on how Andean cultures received Spanish catholicism explain how the Virgin Mary acquires powers similar to the ones attributed to natural deities. The chronicler Arriaga dennounced that natives had used the same cloth to dress a *huaca* **and** an image of the Virgin Mary (qtd. in Morote Best 1988:36). Christian religious images, to whom miracles were continuously atributted, "were themselves cult objects, a fact which gave rise to the Indian observation that (...) [they] were the *huacas* of the Spaniards " (Mc Cormack 1984:13).

The Virgin Mary served as tool of colonization in that the Andean people became "her children". However, Andean women appropriated her image in order to reenact female Precolumbian rituals. Before colonization, it was believed that the mythic heroe Tocapo protected all those who made or used textiles. Given the importance that textiles continue to hold in Andean culture, the Virgin Mary could enact the role of a culture heroe who protects weavers.

With the campaign to "extirpate idolatry", weavers in posession of ritual bundles had been branded as "witches". The contents observed in contemporary weaving bundles in Marcapata, namely weaving amulets, coca leaves and a dissecated bird, along with the fibre offerings at the Qoyllor Rit'i's Virgin Rock resound in the case of the Catholic Church against a woman in Cajatambo, in 1662. Juana de los Reyes was accused of witchcraft for possession of ritual bundles in which a three-colour bird's head and a white stone (García Cabrera 1994:406) were found. Another woman confessed that she had received from this Juana de los Reyes a small bundle containing, among other things, birds' feathers of different colours, and some bits of wool and earth. Juana had promised that, if she kept the bundle secretely, the woman would **have many clothes and would be helped in spinning** (ibid).

The colonial witchhunt pushed women to the forefront as representants of traditional Andean culture (Silverblatt 1990:143); many women refused to conform to the impositions of Catholicism. The Virgin Mary, as female deity, was appropriated and its acculturating role subverted, as She became the deity that allowed for a continuity in textile ritual practices.

WORKS CITED

- Albornoz, Cristóbal de. "Instrucción para descubrir todas las guacas del Pirú y sus camayos y haziendas". Fábulas y mitos de los incas. ed. Henrique Urbano y Pierre Duviols. Madrid: Historia 16, 1988.

- Angulo Iñíguez, Diego. Murillo (Tomo I). Madrid: Espasa- Calpe, 1981.

- Avila, Francisco de. Dioses y hombres de Huarochirí. México, D.F.: Siglo Veintiuno, 1966.

-Brading, David A. "Imágenes y milagros: El mundo barroco de Antonio de La Calancha (1584 - 1654)". Europa e Iberoamérica: Cinco Siglos de Intercambios. iX Congreso Internacional de Historia de América, Vol. II. Sevilla, 1992: 169-180.

- Calancha, Antonio de la. Crónica Moralizada. Lima: Ignacio Prado Pastor, 1974 [1638].

-Cobo, Bernabé. Historia del Nuevo Mundo. Madrid: Biblioteca de Autores Españoles/Ediciones Atlas, 1964 [1653].

- Condori, Bernabé y Rosalind Gow. Kay Pacha. Cusco: CBC, 1982.

-De Mesa, José y Teresa Gisbert. Historia de la Pintura Cuzqueña. Lima: Banco Wiese, 1982.

- García Cabrera, Juan Carlos. Ofensas a Dios. Cusco: CBC[*], 1994

- García-Sauco Belendez, Luis G. y Alfonso Santamaría Conde. La Virgen de las Nieves de Chinchilla y su ermita en los llanos de Albacete. Albacete: Instituto de Estudios Albacetences, 1979

- Geary, Patrick. "Sacred commodities: the circulation of medieval relics". The social life of things. ed. Arjun Appadurai. Cambridge/NY: Cambridge University Press, 1986: 169-191.

- Guamán Poma de Ayala, Felipe. Nueva Crónica y Buen Gobierno. eds. John Murra, Rolena Adorno y Jorge L. Urioste. Madrid: Historia 16, 1987

-Helms, Mary W. Craft and the kingly ideal: art, trade and power. Austin: University of Texas Press, 1993.

---

[*] CBC: Centro de Estudios Regionales Andinos "Bartolomé de Las Casas".

-Mc Cormack, Sabine. "From the Sun of the Incas to the Virgin of Copacabana". Representations 8, Fall 1984.

-Miro Quesada, Aurelio. "Calderón de la Barca y el Perú: La Aurora en Copacabana". Nuevos Temas Peruanos. Lima, Perú, 1982: 181-211.

-Molina, Cristóbal de. Relación de las Fábulas y Ritos de los Incas. eds. Henrique Urbano y Pierre Duviols. Madrid: Historia 16, 1989.

-Morote Best, Efraín. Aldeas Sumergidas. Cusco: CBC, 1988.

-Müller, Thomas y Helga. "Cosmovisión y celebraciones del mundo andino: a través del ejemplo de la comunidad de Q'ero (Paucartambo)". Allpanchis No.23, Año XIV, Vol. XX. Cusco, 1984: 161-176.

-Murra, John. "Cloth and its functions in the Inca State". American Anthropologist 64, 1962: 710-728

-Murúa, Martín de. Historia General del Perú. ed. Manuel Ballesteros. Madrid: Historia 16, 1987.

-Ramos Gavilán, Fray Alonso. Historia de Nuestra Señora de Copacabana. La Paz: Academia Boliviana de la Historia, 1976 [1621].

-Ruiz de Castilla Escuza, Emilio. Una fiesta tradicional como medio de sociabilización. Tesis para optar al título de antropología, Universidad Nacional de San Antonio Abad del Cuzco. Cuzco, 1970.

-Silverblatt, Irene. Luna, sol y brujas. Cusco: CBC, 1990.

-Solari, Gertrudis B. La Virgen de las Nieves: patrona de las tejedoras. Unpublished manuscript, Lima, Perú.

-Urbano, Henrique. "Lenguaje y gesto ritual en el sur andino". Allpanchis vol.IX, No.9. Cuzco, 1976: 121-150.

"Sincretismo y sentimiento religioso en los Andes. Apuntes sobre sus orígenes y desarrollo." Etica y Teología ante el Nuevo Mundo:Valencia y América. Valencia, 1993.

-Urton, Gary. At the Crossroads of the Earth and the Sky: An Andean Cosmology. Austin: University of Texas Press, 1981.

-Wyss,Robert. "Die Handarbeiten der Maria". Artes Minores: Dank an Werner Abegg. ed. Michael Settler und Mechthild Lemberg. Bern: Stämpflie; 113-188.

-Zorn, Elayne. Before Beginning Warping: A Ritual in the Peruvian Andes. Unpublished manuscript. Institute of Latinamerican Studies, November 1978.

TEXTILES OF SACRIFICE: AZTEC RITUAL CAPES
Patricia Rieff Anawalt, Center for the Study of Regional Dress,
Fowler Museum of Cultural History, UCLA

This presentation analyzes three long-gone prehispanic textiles, a feat made possible due to the peculiarities of the Aztec language, Nahuatl, and the sixteenth-century Spaniards' dedication to detailed recordkeeping. From Columbus' first voyage in 1492 to Spain's final expulsion from the Americas in the nineteenth century, the Spaniards were exemplary recorders. Fortunately, this trait was particularly evident in the decades following the 1519-1521 conquest of Mexico, a period that yielded invaluable conquistador eye-witness accounts, administrative records and missionary chronicles. It is to the latter genre that we owe the data presented in this paper.

Of all the newly-discovered peoples in the Age of Discovery, the Aztecs of Central Mexico were the most fully documented, thanks in good part to the dedicated work of a remarkable Franciscan friar, Bernardino de Sahagún (1499-1590), the Aztec's most encyclopedic chronicler. In order to convert the Indians, the early Spanish missionaries had to preach in the indigenous tongues. Fray Sahagún not only mastered Nahuatl, the Aztec language, but went on to compile an extensive account of their culture. When Sahagún died at age 91, his *magnum opus* was contained in twelve books that we now know as the *Florentine Codex,* named for the city where the sixteenth-century manuscript presently resides. This Sahagúntine corpus encompasses detailed information on a kaleidoscope of topics covering natural history, religion, secular life, and the stratified levels of Aztec society. Scattered throughout these books are long lists of names of Aztec apparel for various social classes and occasions, all presented in parallel columns of Spanish and Nahuatl.

Sahagún collected his Nahuatl data between 1559-1568, forty years after the Spanish Conquest. To do this, the friar sought out and interviewed aging natives who had lived the best years of their lives under Aztec rule. The responses to Sahagún's questions were, of course, in Nahuatl, which was carefully recorded by the friar's specially-trained assistants. The early missionaries taught the sons of Aztec nobles Latin script so they could use the characters to write phonetically in Nahuatl, an agglutinative language that combines basic terms with various appendages: prefixes, infixes, or affixes. As a result, Nahuatl's compound words are often the equivalent of a short English sentence. Thanks to a Spanish-Nahuatl/Nahuatl-Spanish dictionary compiled by Fray Francisco Molina (1977) in 1555-1571, and a grammar written by El Padre Horatio Carochi (1983) in 1645, it is possible to directly translate most of the Sahagúntine corpus.

With the support of a 1988 John Simon Guggenheim Memorial Fellowship, I have compiled a database that makes it possible to correlate Sahagún's lists of the Nahuatl names for Aztec clothing with the social context in which these garments were worn. Based on my ethnohistorical research with sixteenth-century texts and my ethnographic work among present-day Nahuatl-speaking textile artisans, I have discovered that certain prehispanic and modern textile motifs describe the technology used to create the surface designs that decorate a garment. This phenomenon of naming a textile motif by describing its means of production was not unusual in prehispanic Mesoamerica. An example of technology naming appears in a gloss--a brief explanatory statement--that identifies a richly-decorated cape, the *ixnextlacuilolli tilmatli* (*Matricula de Tributos* 1980:folio 7v) (Figure 1). Rather than referring to the textile's distinctive pattern, this compound Nahuatl word describes the technological process used to produce the cloth's design: *ix(co)* ("on the face or surface [Molina 1977:45r]") + *nex(tli)* ("ash [used for ink] [*ibid*:71v]") + *tlacuilolli* ("writing or painting [*ibid*:120r]"). The *ixnextlacuilolli* was a painted cloak (personal communication: Frances Berdan, 1990).

Multiple examples of technology naming also occur in a group of Aztec cape names that all contain the word *tlalpilli*: "a thing tied or knotted or a prisoner of another (Molina 1977:159v)." In the context of these capes, this term refers to resist-dye techniques, both *plangi*--portions of already-woven cloth are tied-off so these reserved sections will resist the dye--and *ikat*: unwoven yarn is knotted off to reserve it from the dye bath (Anawalt 1996:Tables 1, 4).

The hallmark of the *plangi* technique is the distinctive design left on cloth after it has been dyed. The Japanese call the motif *yokobiki kanoko*, "square ring dot (Wada, Rice, Barton 1983:62-63, 142-143)." This is the repeating design that appears on a *xiuhtlalpilli* cape (Sahagún 1950-1982 Bk.1:44), worn only by rulers or deity impersonators (Figure 2). The *xiuh* element translates blue (Molina 1977:159v) and refers to the type of dye used, indigo (*Indigofera suffruticosa*), the most prominent prehispanic source for the esteemed blue color. Textile fragments bearing *plangi*-created designs have been found archaeologically (Mastache de Escobar 1975).

Evidence for the *ikat* resist-dye technique appears in the Aztec cloak name *netlalpilli ixtlapaltilmatli* (Sahagún 1950-1982 Bk.10:75): *netlalpilli*, a reflexive verb form, ("to be tied [Molina 1977:124v]") + (*ix[co]*, "on the surface [*ibid*:45r]") + (*tlapal[ia]* "to dye something for someone [Karttunen 1992:289]") + *tilmatli* ("cape [Molina 1977:113r]"): cape with an *ikat*-created design. Fray Sahagún, in the Spanish paraphrase (1979 Bk. 8:16r-16v) of his earlier Nahuatl text, describes the weaving of an *ikat* textile (Anawalt 1996:7). Examples of cloaks with *ikat*-created designs (Figure 3) appear in the sixteenth-century Aztec pictorial, *Codex Mendoza* (1992 III:folios 33r, 34r, 35r).

In addition to painted and resist-dyed textile motif names, the process of producing netting also is described in the Nahuatl term for a net cloak worn by warriors (Figure 4) to honor their patron god, Tezcatlipoca (Anawalt 1996:Tables 2, 3). The word *cuechintli* (Sahagún 1950-1982 Bk.12:53), the most prominent translation for net cape, is a term that appears in no Nahuatl dictionary but may derive from the verb *cuechinia* found both in Molina (1977:25v) and in the Nahuatl dictionary of the nineteenth-century French lexicographer, Rémi Siméon (1963:116). *Cuechinia* means to stir or to move in a particular manner, as one swirls sugar into coffee with a spoon, or manipulates a needle to loop a single strand of yarn into netting. Examples of knotted netting have been found archaeologically (Johnson 1967 Vol.2:197).

Having briefly discussed Fray Sahagún's lists of cape terms--as well as the compound nature of Nahuatl words and the language's penchant for bestowing production-technique names on prestigious cloaks--I now would like to consider a pair of particularly intriguing capes worn in connection with ceremonies held on the election of a ruler. Both the new emperor (Figure 5) and his principal lords (Figure 6) wore these cloaks while doing penance in specific temples. Anderson and Dibble (1982-1990), translators of the magnificent English edition of the *Florentine Codex*, render the cape of the ruler, the *neçaoalquachtli xoxoctic omicallo tilmatli*, as "green fasting cape designed with bones (Sahagún 1952-1980 Bk. 8:62)" and the lords' cape, *neçoalquachtli tliltic omicallo tilmatli*, as "black fasting cape designed with bones (*ibid*:63).". Since, in many cases, Nahuatl cape names incorporate technological details, a further analysis may be revealing. We will begin with the textile reference.

The word *quachtli* refers to a large, undecorated, white cotton mantle (Molina 1977:84r) that *Codex Mendoza* (1992:II:35), a sixteenth century document, describes as *tela torcida*, "twisted cloth." The ethnohistorian Frederic Hicks (1994:105n5) suggests that Aztec *quachtli* were made of heavy, tent-like material. Given this clue, "twisted cloth" most likely refers to fabric woven with tight, firmly-twisted cotton yarn that was worked in a plain weave to produce a dense, firm, slightly stiff, weighty textile, much like present-day canvas or sailcloth.

Next, let us analyze the Nahuatl words for the capes' green and black colors: *xoxoctic* is a combining of the terms *xoxo(uilia)*, ("to make something green [Molina 1977:161v]") and *(quil)tic*, ("a green-colored thing [*ibid*:117r]"). Although no one specific prehispanic dye is known that produced green, that color can be created by combining blue dye made of indigo with yellow dye produced from *zacatlaxcalli* (*Cusuta americana L.*), a parasitic plant that appears throughout central Mexico during the rainy season (personal communication: Irmgard W. Johnson, August, 1996). The Nahuatl term *tliltic,* that appears in the name of the lords' fasting cape, translates "to make something black (Molina 1977:148r)."

Having considered the capes' thread, weave, texture and colors, let us now turn to the cloaks' repeating motif, the bones. The word *omicallo* is made up of *omi(tl)*, ("bone [Molina 1977:76v]") and *callo(tia)*, ("to make something fit into a setting [*ibid*:11v]"). Although Anderson and Dibble translate *omicallo* as "designed with bones," their work was done prior to documentation of the textile technology-naming phenomenon (Anawalt, 1990, 1992, 1993, 1996). As already noted in the cases of painted, resist-dyed and netted capes, the Nahuatl language sometimes describes technological processes in cloak names. Given this propensity, let us take Molina's (1977:76r) definition of the word *omicalli* at face value: "to place bones." I do not mean to imply that actual bones were attached to these capes, but rather to suggest that impressions of bones were being "placed" on the cloth by wood, bone or ceramic stamps incised with bone designs. There is a further cape description and depiction that supports this hypothesis.

Sahagún (1950-1982 Bk. 12:52) lists the name of a third cloak with a bone motif (Figure 7), the *tzotzotecomayo oomicallo tilmatli: tzontecomatl* ("head cut and separated from the body [Molina 1977:153v]"); *omicalli*: ("to place bones [*ibid*:76f]"). The duplication of the *tzo* and *o* elements equate to plurals, hence: "cape with severed heads and bones;" note that the cape name does not include clues to the cloak's fiber, weave or dye. The colonial pictorial *Codex Tovar* (Figure 7) contains a picture of a cloak that meets Sahagún's description of the "cape with severed heads and bones." This cloak also appears to be a stamped textile. Although it is possible that the cape's designs, like the bones on the green and black capes, were painted on the cloth, it seems likely--given the subtleties of the Nahuatl language and the uniformity of the images on all three capes--that these motifs were created by repeatedly placing textile-stamp impressions on the cloth to form regular, over-all patterns. Many ceramic stamps have been found archaeologically, although none that have the exact designs shown on these capes. Nonetheless, the common use of prehispanic stamps to decorate bodies, paper and cloth has been clearly demonstrated by the number of these clay objects that have found their way into museums and archaeological collections.

Let us now turn back to the initial Nahuatl term in both the green and black capes' names, *neçaoal*, "fasting," and the implications of this word in relation to the cloaks' motif of bones. From Sahagún's accounts, we know the Aztecs did indeed fast, abstaining from eating altogether during certain ceremonial periods, at other times giving up such favorite condiments as chili and salt as well as their staff of life, maize. But note that it is not images of salt blocks, chili peppers or toasted tortillas that decorate the green and black fasting capes; it is bones, big bones (see Figures 5,6). What kind of bones could these be? What is certain is that they did not come from such big creatures as horses or cows because there were no large domesticated animals in Mesoamerica prior to the Spaniards' arrival. Perhaps the proper question is not What bones? but rather Whose? To answer that disconcerting query we must turn to Aztec ideology.

The Aztecs believed that they, as the chosen people of the sun, bore the heavy responsibility of sustaining the universe. This necessitated providing sustenance to the gods of the natural world: for the sun to rise, the winds to blow, the rain to fall and the earth to be fruitful, the deities responsible for those forces had to be fed. But gods cannot subsist on chili and tortillas; they can only be given the most sacred of foods, the blood and hearts of humans. In the course of continually meeting their sacred obligations, the Aztecs became masters of large-scale human sacrifice.

In recent years, the Aztecs all too often have been associated in the press with wholesale rites of blood lust, sadistic torture and insatiable cannibalism. The reality was quite different: human sacrifice was actually the most holy of Aztec sacred religious acts, one that entailed ritualized, ceremonial behavior from its outset, which usually began with the taking of a warrior in battle. The purpose of Aztec warfare was not the killing of an enemy but rather his capture; the great majority of Aztec sacrificial victims were prisoners of war (Figure 8). Many of these captives were sacrificed during the dramatic ceremonies connected with each of the monthly festivals. Most prisoners died on the sacrificial stone, chests cut open and pulsating hearts immediately extracted to offer to the gods. It was believed that at the moment of sacrifice the victim was transformed into the deity to whom he was offered, thus forging the necessary bond between those on earth and the life-sustaining gods beyond. The sacrificial warriors thus were believed to play a vital role in the maintenance of the culture: theirs were noble deaths. This attitude of reverence was reflected in every aspect of the ritualized behavior between captor and captive.

Of the 18 annual ceremonies where particularly important captives were sacrificed, the one that sheds light on the mystery of the fasting capes' bones was the harvest festival, *Tlacaxipehualiztli*, "the Flaying of Men," which honored the fertility god *Xipe Totec*, Our Lord the Flayed One. During this celebration, the sacrificed body of the captive warrior was flayed and his skin was set aside, to be worn subsequently by a priest or the victorious captor. Following the captive's flaying, his corpse was carried to the captor's courtyard by the old men of his kin group. Once in the courtyard, the body was cut up. After one thigh had been sent by the captor to the emperor (Sahagún 1950-1982 Bk.2:54), the remaining one was prepared as part of the captor's ritual feast featuring *tlacatlaolli*, "dried maize kernels with man," (Molina 1977:115v), a dish of dried maize to which were added strips of the dead captive's flesh. Only the immediate relatives of the captor were invited to partake of this sacred meal, an act Sahagún (1950-1982 Bk.2:54) reports caused the participants themselves to be considered gods during the feast. The captor, however, did not consume his captive's flesh saying, "Shall I perchance eat my very self?"

Following the sacred ritual, the captor had the right to set up a "Pole of the Flaying of Men" in his courtyard, indicating that he had flayed a captive (*ibid* Bk.8:66). From this pole the captor suspended the captive's thigh bone, after he had removed all of its remaining flesh. But before attaching the bone to the pole, the captor first wrapped his sacred trophy thoroughly in paper, thus providing it with a mask; Sahagún (*ibid*) states that the embellished thigh bone was called the god captive (Figure 9). In the sixteenth-century colonial period, a cache of paper-wrapped thigh bones was recovered from the rafters of a prehispanic house, implying that such trophies continued to be valued in the culture long after their courtyard display (personal communication: Susan Schroeder, August, 1996).

Returning to the question of what or whose bones are represented by the designs on the green and black fasting capes--as well as the long bones on the severed-heads-and-bones cloak (see Figures 5, 6,7)--I suggest that these images depict human femurs, sacred trophies honoring valiant, sacrificed warriors (see Figure 9). This is certainly a sobering--nay, even shocking--choice of design motifs to us, living as we do in the "civilized" Western world at the end of the 20th century. Yet this ancient Mexican tradition of depicting human bones in artistic expressions has continued into modern times. Nowhere is this genre better exemplified than in the well-known workshop of the Linares family, located in Mexico City.

The Linares father, Don Pedro, and his sons, Enrique, Felipe and Miguel, are famous for their production of papier mâché *calaveras*, skeletal figures engaged in a variety of activities, but these animated, often-dressed creatures are quite unlike their medieval European counterparts, who were viewed as threatening or penitent. The Mexican *calaveras* often appear in humorous contexts: enjoying lively sports (Figure 10), eating tacos (Masuoka 1994:65) or playing cards (*ibid:*66). What are we to make of these macabre Mexican skeletons whose cheerful behavior belies their deathly visage? Since the mood of their activities does not indicate a European heritage, from whence could this disquieting tradition have come? Is there a distant echo of prehispanic times reflected here?

It must be remembered that in the Aztec world--where existence continued on in one of many forms after death--the sacrificial victim became a god at the time of his sacrifice and his remains--exemplified by the venerated thigh bone (see Figure 9)--continued to have a cultural involvement in its deified guise. The *calaveras* figures also are sometimes depicted playing a socially-supportive modern role. In the aftermath of the devastating 8.1 Mexico City earthquake in 1985, the Linares made a pointed political statement regarding the government's lack of immediate response to the catastrophe by creating a scene of *calaveras* figures providing neighborhood aid to the afflicted (Masuoka 1994:Fig. 81).

In summary, through pictorial, linguistic, technological and ethnographic analyses, this paper has interpreted three sixteenth-century drawings of Aztec ritual capes displaying designs of bones (see Figures 5, 6, 7). As a result of using a multiple approach, it has been possible to come to plausible conclusions about the green and black capes' yarn, weave, dyes and, particularly, a strong suggestion that the repeating-bones motif on all three of the cloaks was applied through the use of textile stamps.

The ritual implication of these sacred capes' design of human thigh bones also has been traced to its prehispanic source. Obviously, the Aztecs had an acceptance of death as a natural part of life (Figure 11), a view still reflected in present-day folk art that conveys an unflinching, albeit humorous, treatment of the final judgment. Octavia Paz (1961:58), the Nobel-winning historian, has noted that Mexican death is a mirror of Mexican life. Death is present in their fiestas, games, loves and thoughts.. Indeed, when one considers the parallel existence that the *calaveras* bones carry on from beyond the grave--a vital "life of their own"--it would appear that the Aztec's descendants continue to hold an accepting, sanguine view of mortal man's demise (Figure 12).

BIBLIOGRAPHY

Anawalt, Patricia

   1990 "The Emperors' Cloak: Aztec Pomp, Toltec Circumstances." *American Antiquity* 55(2):291-307.

   1992 "A Comparative Analysis of the Costumes and Accoutrements of the *Codex Mendoza*," Vol. 1:103-150. In *Codex Mendoza* , Frances F. Berdan and Patricia Rieff Anawalt, eds., (4 vols.) University of California Press, Berkeley.

   1993 "Riddle of the Aztec Royal Robe." *Archaeology* 46(3):30-36.

   1996 "Aztec Knotted and Netted Capes: Colonial Interpretations vs. Indigenous Primary Data," *Ancient Mesoamerica*, Vol. 7, No. 2. In Press.

Boone, Elizabeth Hill

   1994 *The Aztec World*, Jeremy A. Sabloff, ed., Smithsonian Exploring the Ancient World, Smithsonian Books, Washington, D. C.

Carochi, Horacio

   1983 *Arte de la lengua mexicana con la declaración de los adverbios della*. Facsimile of 1645 edition, with introduction by Miguel León-Portilla. Instituto de Investigaciones Filológicas, Instituto de Investigaciones Históricas, Universidad Nacional Autónoma de México, Mexico.

Codex Ixtilxochitl

   1976 *Codex Ixtlilxochitl: Bibliothéque Nationale Paris (M.S. Mex. 65-71), Reproduction des Manuskriptes im Original-format*. Commentary by Jacqueline de Durand-Forest. Akademische druck-u. Verlagsanstalt. Graz, Austria (Origially compiled sixteenth century.)

Codex Mendoza

   1992 *The Codex Mendoza*, Frances F. Berdan and Patricia R. Anawalt eds. (4 vols) University of California Press, Berkeley (Originally compiled ca. 1541).

Duran, Fray Diego

   1967 *Historia de las Indias de Nueva España e islas de la tierra firme*. Angel Maria Garibaya K., ed. (2 vols.) Editorial Porrúa, Mexico. (Originally written 1581).

Hicks, Frederic

   1994 "Cloth in the Political Economy of the Aztec State," In *Economies and Polities in the Aztec Realm*, Mary G. Hodge and Michael E. Smith, eds., Studies on Culture and Society Vol.6:89-111, Mesoamerican Studies, State University of New York, Albany, distributed by University of Texas Press.

Johnson, Irmgard W.

1967 "Textiles." In *The Non-Ceramic Artifacts*, edited by Richard S. MacNeish, Antoinette Nelken-Terner and Irmgard W. Johnson, Vol. 1:189-226. *The Prehistory of the Tehuacan Valley*, Douglas S. Byers, ed. (5 vols.), University of Texas Press, Austin.

Karttunan, Frances

1992 *An Analytical Dictionary of Nahuatl.* University of Oklahoma Press, Norman.

Mastache de Escobar, Alba Guadalupe

1975 "Dos fragmentos de tejido decorados con la técnica de plangi." In *Anales* 1972-1973 IV:251-262. Instituto Nacional de Antropología e Historia, Mexico.

Masuoka, Susan

1994 *En Calavera: The Papier-Mâché Art of the Linares Family.* UCLA Fowler Museum of Cultural History, Los Angeles.

Matrícula de Tributos

1980 *Matrícula de Tributos,* Museo de Antropología, México (Col. 35-52): Vollstandige Farbreproduckton de Codex in Verkleinertem Format. Commentary by Frances F. Berdan and Jacqueline de Durand-Forest. Akademische Druck-u. Verlagsanstalt, Graz, Austria. (Originally compiled sixteenth century.)

Molina, Fray Alonso de

1977 *Vocabulario en lengua castellana y mexicana, y mexicana y castellana.* Editorial Porrúa, Mexico. (Originally written 1555-1571)

Paz, Octavio

1961 *The Labyrinth of Solitude: Life and Thought in Mexico.* Lysander Kemp (trans.), Grove Press, New York.

Sahagun, Fray Bernardino de

1950-1982 *Florentine Codex: General History of the Things of New Spain,* translated and edited by Arthur J. O. Anderson and Charles E. Dibble. Monographs of The School of American Research 14, pts., 1-13. The School of American Research and The Univeristy of Utah Press, Santa Fe (Originally compiled 1575-1577 or 1578-1580).

1979 *Códice Florentine: El manuscrito 218-20 de la Colección Palatina de la Biblioteca Medicea Laurenziana, edita en facsimil.* (3 vols.) Guinti Barbera, Florence (Originally compiled 1575-1577 or 1578-1580).

Siméon, Rémi

1963 *Dictionnaire de la langue nahuatl ou mexicaine.* Akademische Druck -u. Verlagsanstalt, Graz. Austria. (Originally published 1885).

Tovar, Fray Juan de

1972 *Manuscrit Tovar: Origines et Croyances des Indiens du Mexique,* Jacques Lafaye, ed., Akademische Druck- u. Verlagsanstalt, Graz, Austria. (Originally compiled ca. 1585)

Wada, Yoshiko, Mary Kellogg Rice and Jane Barton

1983 *Shibori: The Inventive Art of Japanese Shaped Resist Dyeing.* Kodansha International, Ltd., Tokoyo.

Figure 1: The notation *ixnextlacuilloli* written above this sixteenth-century depiction of an Aztec tribute textile describes the technology used to create the cloth's surface design: it is a painted textile (*Matrícula de Tributos* 1980:folio 7v).

Figure 2: A sixteenth-century depiction of King Nezahualpilli wearing the official blue cape restricted to Aztec rulers and deities. The cloak's surface design was created through the use of resist-dye techniques, as its name implies: *xiuhtlalpilli tilmatli*, "blue-knotted cape" (*Codex Ixtlilxochitl* 1976:folio 108r).

Figure 3: An example of an Aztec tribute textile whose surface design was created through the use of the *ikat* resist-dye technique, as is implied by the technologically-descriptive term *netlalpilli ixtlapaltilmatli* "something knotted and dyed on the surface" (*Codex Mendoza* 1992 III:folio 35r).

Figure 4: An Aztec warrior arrayed in his net cape, the *cuechintli*, a technologically-descriptive term; the Nahuatl verb *cuechinia* means to move the hand in a particular manner (e.g.manipulating a needle to loop a single strand of yarn into netting [*Codex Mendoza* 1992 III:folio 57r]).

Figure 5: The *neçoalquachtli xoxoctic omicallo tilmatli*, "the green fasting cape stamped with of bones." This penitential cloak was worn during ceremonies held on the election of a ruler (Sahagún 1979: Bk.8:folio 46r).

Figure 7: The *tzotzotecomayo oomicallo tilmatli*, "the cape with severed heads and bones" was worn by an idol of the Aztec sun god, Huitzilopochtli. Like the green and black fasting capes, this cloak also displays stamped surface designs (Tovar 1972: Pl.XXII).

Figure 6: The *neçoalquachtli tliltic omicallo tilmatli*, "the black fasting cape stamped with bones." This penitential cloak was worn by principal lords during ceremonies held on the election of a ruler (Sahagún 1979 Bk.8:folio 46v).

Figure 8: A victorious Aztec warrior holds his subjugated battlefield captive, who is destined for the sacrificial stone. The majority of Aztec sacrificial victims were prisoners of war (*Codex Mendoza* 1992 III:64r).

Figure 9: A sacrificial victim's thigh bone wrapped in paper prior to being displayed as a sacred trophy atop the Pole of the Flaying of Men (Sahagún 1979 Bk.2:folio 26v).

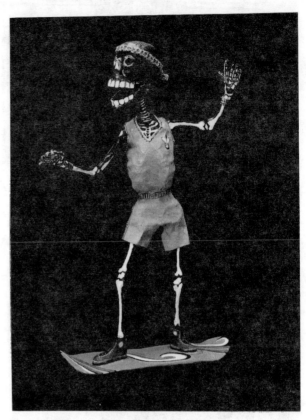

Figure 10: A papier mâché *calaveras* figure from the Mexico City workshop of the Linares family (Masuoka 1994:fig.160).

Figure 11: A prehispanic stone sculpture depicting a *tzompantli*, "skull rack," commemorating departed sacrificial victims (Boone 1994:131).

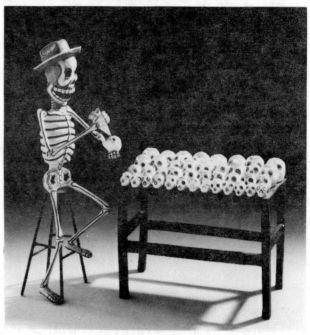

Figure 12: A papier mâché *calaveras* figure ornamenting a group of skulls arranged in a manner reminiscent of a prehispanic skull rack (photo S. Einstein).

MANIFEST INSIGNIFICANCE - THE CONSECRATED VEIL OF MEDIEVAL RELIGIOUS WOMEN

DÉSIRÉE KOSLIN
Adjunct Assistant Professor, Graduate Studies: Costume and Textiles, Fashion Institute of Technology, Seventh Avenue at 27th Street, New York, NY 10001

(I regret that the visual material used when reading this paper cannot be included in these Proceedings, as many of the collections from which they come have severe restrictions in regard to reproduction. I have also excluded shelfmark references for individual manuscripts as some of them are previously unpublished.)

The theme of this paper is part of my dissertation in medieval art history entitled "The Dress of Monastic and Religious Women as Seen in Art from the Early Middle Ages to the Reformation". I would like to introduce some basic concepts relating to female monasticism before I focus on the nun's black veil and the white one of other religious women and how they are represented in the visual arts. This humble textile, solemnly blessed at the nun's consecration, functions in several ways: as textile object, social signifier and symbol.

My richest primary sources are in the medieval illuminations of liturgical and secular manuscripts, in texts such as the Rules of the various Orders, the records from bishops' visits to female convents, and in monastic documents such as wills and administrative records. In the later period, panel painting also offers valuable information. Other medieval art media, including textiles, funeral brasses, stone and wood sculpture and stained glass also contain details for interpretation. Until recently, and with exception for the important contributions by Lina Eckenstein (1895) and Eileen Power (1922),[1] the secondary literature on women's monasticism has been scant. But from the 1970's with the emergence of Women's Studies as an academic discipline, a number of works on medieval women religious have been published by scholars in various disciplines although none has focused on their textiles, dress and visual representations.

Women were early, perhaps the first participants in the monastic ideal of leading communal lives in imitation of Christ, the *vita apostolica*, by observing the tenets of poverty, chastity and obedience. During the first centuries of Christianity the role of women in the Church was in flux; some are known to have been central figures, even preachers in the congregations, a practice soon stopped by the Church Fathers and Councils. If a single factor must be separated out to explain why women's cloistered lives throughout western religious history have been so precarious, it is the (until very recently) strict prohibition against women performing sacerdotal functions, especially that of celebrating mass. As these rituals took place on a daily basis in medieval life, cloistered nuns had to hire male secular or monastic clerics to say masses, hear confessions and perform any other religious ceremonies for the nuns' communities and their parishioners. This created a dependency on visiting or residing male clergy that caused economic, administrative and social problems.

Both men's and women's institutions could also become, paradoxically, victims of their own success. To strictly follow the monastic vows is extremely difficult, and the series of monastic reforms which punctuate the history of Christianity are proof of this. These religious movements often resulted in the founding of new, more stringent orders, or

---

[1] Eckenstein, Lina, *Women under Monasticism*, New York 1963 reprint, and Power, Eileen, *Medieval English Nunneries c.1275 to 1535*, Cambridge 1922.

in the suppression of other communities, deemed heretical. A newly reformed order observing most rigorously the vow of poverty may have found itself so successful in acquiring members that it had to expand, manage endowments and lands on which it depended for its survival; it therefore often became lax and luxury-loving. Conversely, a convent in strict observance without sufficient secular support might have been forced to abandon its common life and dissolve the monastery. Monastic history offers examples of both, but the nunneries' double dependency cited above explain their particular vulnerability.

Scholars have noted the many medieval voices of misogyny of Church Fathers, supervisors and reformers who railed against bothersome and undisciplined nuns. Such 'presentist issues', to borrow a phrase from Carolyn Walker Bynum,[2] are justifiable and necessary, but they also need to be seen against the many manifestations of profound concern and solicitous activities of many clerics who provided for women's spiritual advancement within the confines of medieval society. They had women's welfare foremost; Robert of Arbrissel (1045-1116) and Gilbert of Sempringham (c.1083-1189) established their orders specifically to include poor women, and the first foundation of St. Dominic (1170-1221) was to provide a women's house to combat the heretical Cathar movement in the south of France. Mainstream clerics frequently founded nunneries for female relatives, and important secular families gave lands for their kinswomen's convents.

The long period we call the Middle Ages also shows great diversity in the social origin of religious women. With a broad brush one could depict the early period's nunneries as having members who came exclusively from royal families and the upper aristocracy. By the late eleventh century women from the lower and middle classes were gaining entry; and Marilyn Oliva has convincingly shown that in East Anglia of the later period, thirteenth to sixteenth century, the great majority of nuns came from these lower social strata.[3] In this respect the indices in the visual arts are fascinating and challenging - was the artist following a patron's dictates, stylistic conventions or implying a social commentary? As to the implication and significance of luxury textiles and dress over time, would it have been harder for the early, royal monastics to give up the rare, fine textiles to which their family rank entitled them, than it was for the later period's mainly middleclass women to abandon theirs for a humbler dress? The texts seem to support this. In the seventh century, bishop Aldhelm of Wessex addressed the nuns at the royal Barking Abbey, condemning them for dressing 'in fine linen shirts, in scarlet and blue tunics, in necklines and sleeves embroidered with silk'.[4] In the mid-twelfth century Abbess Tenxwind of the recently reformed Andernach nunnery reproached her colleague Hildegard of Bingen for letting her nuns with loosened hair sing the psalms in church on feastdays 'wearing white silk veils so long that they touch the ground'.[5] By contrast, and whether living cloistered under a rule or not, religious women in the thirteenth century's reform fervor with enthusiasm rejected rich clothes for hairshirts and harsh rags, finding simple dress a sure way to establish a social identity in a rapidly changing society. The Rule of St.

---

[2] Bynum accounts for the many current approaches within medieval studies in 'Why All the Fuss about the Body? A Medievalist's Perspective', *Critical Inquiry* 22 (Autumn 1995), 1-33.
[3] Gilchrist, Roberta and Marilyn Oliva, *Religious Women in Medieval East Anglia*, University of East Anglia, 1993.
[4] Aldhelm, Saint, *Aldhelm The Prose Works*, Michael Lapidge and Michael Herren trs., Ipswich and Cambridge 1979, 128.
[5] Boockmann, Hartmut, 'Gelöstes Haar und seidene Schleier: Zwei Äbtissinnen im Dialog' in Beck, Reiner, ed. *Streifzüge durch das Mittelalter: Ein historisches Lesebuch*, Munich 1995, 213.

Clare of 1253 allows each nun only three tunics and a mantle as she states, 'I plead and exhort my sisters to always wear plain and inexpensive garments'.[6]

Monastic dress was meant to set the spirituals apart from the worldly. As the religious renounced possessions as well as sexual relations, their dress represented denial and self-effacement, its material signalled insignificance. In contrast to the gendered and ever-accelerating fashion changes in secular society, monks and nuns wore identical garments, a plain, sleeved woollen tunic, usually belted to separate the upper and lower body zones, and often accompanied by a scapular, originally a protective apron. Some orders allowed linen undergarments, but the original Rule of St. Benedict specifically forbids it as too comfortable. Wide-sleeved overtunics were worn during service in the choir, and mantles were to be used for the rare ventures outside the convent walls. The colors seen in the tunics, mantles and scapulars which later would so clearly distinguish the various orders were not yet uniform in the central medieval period. While 'black nuns' refer to Benedictines and 'white nuns' the Cistercians, the term 'grey sisters', for instance, for the Franciscan tertiaries belongs in the post-reformation era. Only one early rule, that of bishop Cesarius of Arles (d.542), gets specific as to color; it should be 'simple and dignified, never black, never all white, but always of a natural color'.[7]

It is in the headress that nuns and monks differ. While men would show their tonsured pates and wear a hood attached to their cowls or tunics, women's heads were covered with a veil to hide their hair. The veil had been a marker of marital status of ancient standing for women in the Mediterranean region; Helen, abducted to Troy as a bride, is seen veiling herself in archaic Greek art. The much disputed statement by Paul in I Corinthians, 11:2-16, on the covering of women's heads has been lucidly summarized and applied to the late antique context by Ross Kraemer.[8] In medieval practice it meant that unmarried young women could expose their hair, while married women and widows must cover theirs.

The nun's veil also carried a profound, metaphorical significance beyond acting as a social marker and carrying on traditions established in classical Rome. During the *velatio*, the veiling consecration ritual for the fully professed nun, she became *sponsa Christi*, Bride of the Heavenly Bridegroom. The medieval *pontifical*, a liturgical manual for bishops, contains details of the veiling ceremony; and although the great majority of pontificals preserved are not illustrated, several examples of the later period contain depictions of the rites which the bishop/archbishop was required to perform. Among these illuminated, costly pontificals only a few include complete cycles of images of all episcopal duties. 'Historiated initials' in the pontificals frequently show the initiation of young women to the novitiate, the consecration and veiling of virgins as professed nuns, and the benediction of an abbess. More rarely is the ordination of a deaconess seen, or the blessing by the bishop for a recluse or anchoress, a woman living singly in seclusion.

The *velatio* took place only on designated days of the liturgical year, the Feast of the Ascension foremost among them, a day when the Heavenly Bridegroom would surely be

---

[6] Sources Chrétiennes No 325: *Claire d'Assise Écrits: Introduction, texte latin, traduction, notes et index*, Becker, Marie-France et al., trs. and eds. Paris 1985, 131.

[7] Sources Chrétiennes No 345: *Césaire d'Arles Œuvres Monastiques, Tome1, œvres pour les moniales, Introduction, texte critique, traduction et notes*, Adalbert de Vogüé and Joël Courreau, trs. and eds., Paris 1988, 229.

[8] Kraemer, Ross Shepard. *Her Share of the Blessings: Women's Religions among Pagans, Jews and Christians in the Greco-Roman World*, New York 1992, 146-7. Kraemer's application of Mary Douglas's grid/group theory can equally well be assigned to the medieval secular and religious women expressed in terms of headdress as a guide to social changes in medieval society.

available. The length of the novitiate or probation period preceding the veiling varies over the medieval period, but a year's span of reflection was standard. The mature age of twenty-five for the *velatio* and taking of full vows had been established already in the fifth century, but it is not clear how strictly this was adhered to later and elsewhere. The nun's consecration ritual took much effort to standardize and incorporate into the Church's hierarchy because many important, spiritual women during the early period had proclaimed their rights to declare themselves ordained to a chaste life, a body of evidence which Donald Hochstetler has surveyed carefully.[9] In the prescribed ritual, which underwent many smaller changes during the Middle Ages, the bishop conducts Mass to the end of the Collect, at which point he sits down in front of the high altar. The white-dressed novices approach the bishop carrying their tunics, holding unlit candles in their left hands. The bishop questions them, and the women announce their willingness to enter the Order. Their garments are blessed, sprinkled with holy water and given to the virgins who leave to put them on. They then return to the altar with the candles lit, a clear allusion to the parable of the wise and foolish virgins, the triumph of chastity, as well as to the torches carried in the nuptial procession in antiquity. The veils are then brought before the bishop who blesses them as each of the novices go up singly to the altar to be veiled, kneeling by the bishop who intones, 'Accipe virgo Christi velamen virginitatis...' (Receive, virgin of Christ, this veil of virginity..), as he places the veil on the nun's head. A ring is similarly blessed and given to the nun, after which Mass is concluded with Communion.

For the three following days the new nun must observe complete silence and fasting, her veil drawn around her chin. At the Mass of the Resurrection on the third day the veil is lifted, she can again speak, and a solemn banquet follows at which the now consecrated nuns are treated as brides. The elaboration of this ritual involving the outer and inner person relies heavily on the symbolism vested in the change of garments and the posing of the veil by the Vicar of Christ, symbolizing the passage from the secular life to the religious - or from the temporal to the everlasting.

The pontificals also illustrate the benediction of an abbess, whose headveil color would be black if she had previously been a nun, or white if she had come to the monastery as a widow, which was not uncommon. A previously married woman could not be consecrated as a nun since she presumably was no longer a virgin. In the visual arts, however, this aspect was often overlooked. The Swedish fourteenth-century St. Birgitta, was founder of the Order of St. Savior and a mother of eight children, several of whom joined her Order. She should be seen in only in a widow's white veil, but she will sometimes be given the nun's black one. Tertiaries also had white veils; this term derives from a division of the relígous into three groups: monks being the first, cloistered nuns the second, and lay religious the third, tertiary order. This is an attempt to classify the many faithful who aspired to the *vita apostolica* outside the convent walls. These religious men and women, who form a bewildering and poorly surveyed group, often lived communal lives, sometimes under a Rule or the guidance of a local cleric. They generally led working lives in secular society, frequently in the textile manufactures. The Beguines of northern Europe depended on it as did the Humiliati of northern Italy. In an illustration, the Humiliati sisters are seen working wool, spinning, warping and weaving. A panel painting of the mid-fifteenth century Roman school displays Sa Francesca Romana clothed by the Virgin, while the angel miraculously carries on the warping undisturbed by the dogs and cats, another cloth enveloping Francesca's community of sisters.

In a series of illuminations from a manual belonging to a Florentine Franciscan tertiary house of the late fifteenth century, a veiling ceremony of a somewhat different

---

[9] Hochstetler, Donald, *A Conflict of Traditions: Women in Religion in the Early Middle Ages 500-840*, New York 1992, for instance 99-104.

character is portrayed. A priest officiates here, first giving the postulant a tonsure *in rotondum* as St. Clare's 1253 Rule prescribes. All of her worldly goods and secular garments are divested with the help of the abbess and given to the poor. The postulant kneels to receive her novice garments, and at joining her order she is given three tunics and a mantle. She is next seen being veiled by the priest, with a white veil as the other sisters.

In male-authored texts throughout the medieval period the nuns are instructed to view these humble garments, especially the simple black veil, in their metaphorical significance. John Alcock in the late fifteenth century 'quotes' the early martyr St. Agnes as saying, 'Christ has covered my soul inward and my head with a veil, and if I will love any man better than him I shall go to the color of my veil and that is everlasting death'.[10] The previously cited Aldhelm also vents his ire on those nuns who corrupt the 'decrees of canon law and the norm of the regular life', and who have 'the hair of their forelocks and the curls at their temples crimped with a curling iron; darkgrey veils for the head give way to bright and colored headdresses, which are sewn with interlacings of ribbons and hang down as far as the ankles.'[11] Similar sentiments of clerics, secular authors and social critics continue to appear in the texts during the next several hundred years.

The medieval visual arts allow us to see evidence of these attempts at subversion on the part of the women religious. It is in the veil's material, apparent costliness, and visible decorative additions that we find some of the reasons for the quoted expressions of clerical sumptuary censure. The role of the artist in this process is a thorny issue - if he or she were monastics, was the interpretation rendered by convention or observation? If unfamiliar with the cloistered life, was the artist instructed by his/her patron as to monastic dress details, or was license taken with whatever information was available? In the images a range of interpretations seem possible: when the early eleventh-century abbess Hitda offers her evangilary to her patron St. Walburg there appears to be no question that the very long, elaborately frilled and pleated veil underscores the abbess's status and authority. In a mid-twelfth century martyrology illustration (in which, highly unusually, both the scribe, nun Guta, and the artist, monk Sintram, are named); does her blue veil signal a forbidden exception to nun's black or is it an arbitrary choice from the artist's pallet?[12]

The nun's black veil was made of wool or precious silk, while the wimple and underveil[13] usually were made of linen, sometimes silk. In depictions the differences between the fabric qualities are made very clear - a veil's very deep black could refer only to wool, as it, unlike linen, could be dyed into saturated shades. When the black veil is rendered as transparent, expressed through hatching, and with elegant draping quality, silk seems to be indicated. Both kinds of representation are frequently seen in illuminations and panel paintings. Since works of art were costly to produce and commission, it stands to reason that the patrons would be interested in seeing themselves depicted in their finest, even if forbidden. The fourteenth-century image of Franciscan sisters' transparent white wimples seem then to signal a breach in their humble dresscode, and in a depiction of Augustinian hermit nuns, the beaded appearance of their underveils' edging implies a precious silk or finest linen with perhaps an early form of lace trim.

---

[10] Alcock, John, *(Spousage of a Virgin to Christ) An Exhortacyon made to Relygyous Systers* (Westmynstre (Wynken de Worde) n.d.), facsimile Amsterdam 1974, unpag. 7-8.

[11] Op. cit., 128.

[12] Alexander, J.J.G., *Medieval Illuminators and Their Methods of Work*, New Haven 1992, 18-19. Here is addressed, from a great many perspectives, the act, meaning and intent of medieval representation.

[13] A term I use to indicate the cloth frequently seen with the black veil, and distinct from the wimple (some other languages have words for this: French 'couvrechef', Swedish 'dok' and German 'Gebende').

Where groundplans of the medieval nunneries can be reconstructed, they frequently included spaces reserved for spinning and other textile occupations, but unlike the large male monasteris which had extensive manufactures and export, nuns seem to have performed their textile production and sewing primarily for in-house consumption and their fine needlework for ritual needs. When records do survive, account rolls frequently mention payments made to professionals who spun, wove and fulled the cloth for the nunneries. Surviving documents do not allow us to estimate the extent of nuns' textiles made for secular use as this was at variance with their vow of poverty, although various sources reveal that medieval women obtained their finely worked silk purses and other 'nun's work' from convents.

In 1222 the Council of Oxford decreed, '..nuns and other women dedicated to divine worship shall not wear a silken wimple, nor dare to carry silver or golden tiring pins in their veil.'[14] Such pins can be seen rendered in white and red respectively throughout two English midthirteenth-century prayerbooks. They were made by the same artist for two different nunneries, belonging to different subgroups of the benedictine order. Their dress is, nevertheless, rendered in identical fashion and includes the headveil's pins; this seems to confirm the continuance of this form of abuse addressed by the Council, perhaps even a conceit of the artist's. Augustinian canonesses, an order allowing private property to cloistered women, had early introduced a sign of the cross at center front of their underveil, stitched in red silk on white fabric. As their dress usually is depicted as solid black, like the benedictines, and as they would have been more visible in the secular medieval landscape, this cross may have served a purpose of identification. This custom was adopted by the Cistercian nuns, for whom the red cross was to symbolize the blood of Christ, but they added it to a white cloth 'crown' over their black veils. In a similar striving for a uniform marker, the Brigittines in the late-fourteenth century adopted this Cistercian crown, altering it by introducing five red dots to signify the wounds of Christ.

This brief sampling is intended as an introduction to the rich variety seen in the much-neglected images of medieval nuns and religious women and the textiles they made and wore. Their history was imperfectly recorded, and the depictions in the visual arts are therefore especially useful to aid in a fuller understanding of their society. Although I have not had time here to include the making of artworks in the nunneries, including book production, tapestries and embroideries, such objects offer further clues and will round out my investigation.

REFERENCES

Alcock, John. *(Spousage of a Virgin to Christ) An Exhortacyon made to Relygyous Systers* (Westmynstre (Wynken de Worde) n.d.). Facsimile, Amsterdam 1974.

Alexander, J.J.G. *Medieval Illuminators and Their Methods of Work*. New Haven 1992.

Aldhelm, Saint. *Aldhelm The Prose Works*. Michael Lapidge and Michael Herren trs. Ipswich and Cambridge 1979.

Baker, Derek, ed. *Medieval Women*. Oxford 1978.

Becker, Marie-France et al., trs. and eds. *Sources Chrétiennes No 325: Claire d'Assise Écrits: Introduction, texte latin, traduction, notes et index*, Paris 1985.

---

[14] Power (1922) 585.

Clark, Elizabeth A. *Women in the Early Church*. Collegeville, MN 1983.

Boockmann, Hartmut. 'Gelöstes Haar und seidene Schleier: Zwei Äbtissinnen im Dialog' in Beck, Reiner, ed. *Streifzüge durch das Mittelalter: Ein historisches Lesebuch*, Munich 1995, 213-16.

Bynum, Carolyn Walker. 'Why All the Fuss about the Body? A Medievalist's Perspective', *Critical Inquiry* 22 (Autumn 1995), 1-33.

Eckenstein, Lina. *Women under Monasticism*. Reprint, New York 1963.

Elkins, Sharon. *Holy Women of Twelfth-Century England*. Chapel Hill 1988.

de Fontette, Micheline. *Les Religieuses a l' âge classique du droit canon: Recherches sur les structures juridiques des branches féminines des ordres*. Paris 1967.

Gilchrist, Roberta and Marilyn Oliva. *Religious Women in Medieval East Anglia*. University of East Anglia 1993.

Gutarp, Else Marie. *Hurusom man sig klädde: En bok om medeltida dräkt*. Visby 1994.

Hélyot, Hippolyte. *Histoire des ordres monastiques, religieux et militaires*. 8 vols. Paris 1714-18.

Hochstetler, Donald. *A Conflict of Traditions: Women in Religion in the Early Middle Ages 500-840*. New York 1992.

Kieckhefer, Richard. *Unquiet Souls: Fourteenth-Century Saints and Their Religious Milieu*. Chicago 1984.

Kraemer, Ross Shepard. *Her Share of the Blessings: Women's Religions among Pagans, Jews and Christians in the Greco-Roman World*. New York 1992.

Kroos, Renate. 'Der Codex Gisle' in: *Niederdeutsche Beiträge zur Kunstwissenschaft*, 12 (1973), 117-34.

Kühnel, Harry. *Bildwörterbuch der Kleidung und Rüstung*. Stuttgart 1992.

Piponnier, Francoise and Perrine Mane. *Se vêtir au Moyen Âge*. Paris 1995.

Power, Eileen. *Medieval English Nunneries c.1275 to 1535*. Cambridge 1922.

Ranft, Patricia. *Women and the Religious Life in Premodern Europe*. New York 1996.

de Vogüé, Adalbert and Joël Courreau, trs. and eds. *Sources Chrétiennes No 345: Césaire d'Arles Œuvres Monastiques, Tome1, œvres pour les moniales: Introduction, texte critique, traduction et notes*. Paris 1988.

Wemple, Susan. *Women in Frankish Society: Marriage and the Cloister, 500 to 900*. Philadelphia 1985.

Traditional Textiles in Transylvanian and Danubian Mourning Rituals

by
Joyce Corbett

The role of textiles in the folklife in the regions of Eastern Europe known as Transylvania, Transdanubia, and Eastern Slovakia is vividly present in the rituals of human life passages. This portion of Eastern Europe, comprising a part of the former Austro-Hungarian empire, is bounded by Russia and Poland on the north, former Yugoslavia and Bulgaria on the south, Austria on the west, and the Black Sea on the east. These mountainous regions multicultural, multilingual, and multiethnic, are both buffers and viaducts for ancient and recent cross-cultural influences. The continued presence of archaic historical elements of costume provides a living textile history rewarding close examination.

The connection that links the village community of the living with the village community of the dead is mysterious, magical and fraught with danger to the uninitiated. The uses of material objects in rituals specific to the occasion include textiles and costumes and are essential to guarantee two requirements. The first is that the deceased obtains safe passage from earthly life into the afterlife where he/she will remain, happy and content. The second requirement is that those left behind be secure from haunting and consequent actions of an unhappy spirit, who may return bent on mischief and destruction. It is these two requirements which keep funeral rituals in place and embedded in their social context.

Only special and significant textiles and dress are used in traditional death rituals. These include household textiles used for the vigil and the funeral, the coffin pall and the deceased's shroud, as well as the proper form of dress for the mourners. The clothing that the body is dressed in for burial is also of great importance.

A notable example of mourning dress was found in Somogy County, Hungary, as late as the 1970's. This was the "white mourning" worn by elderly village women who formed a kind of lay women's group whose duties included the funeral vigil and procession, as well as maintenance and decoration of the graveyard. The long white linen costume worn by these women is identical to that found in Renaissance costume books in Germany and Italy labeled as "widow's dress." Its exact counterpart in black has been worn in convents in Romania until the present. Other examples of white as mourning dress appear in numerous 19th and 20th century folk costumes. In some examples in Germany, the white veil completely covers the costume underneath. In other folkloric sources, the white veil is worn over a black garment. White mourning as funeral dress appears to have long been a trans-European fashion, with historical antecedents in the Byzantine court, and even in Roman mourning clothing.

A related costume known as "half-mourning," combining a white headveil with a black garment, became highly fashionable in 19th century European court dress. This style has lasted well into the 20th century in folk dress, examples having been found as far west as Great Britain. This combination of white veil and black dress was standard processional wear for almswomen in Europe in the 1600's.

The persistence of archaic headdress forms in village costume is the hallmark of funeral dress. Headdress styles which may have completely disappeared as a part of regular folk costume often remain unchanged when required as part of a ritual. The village of Cicmany in central Slovakia provides a fascinating example of a Gothic "horned" headdress. Mourning rituals in this highly decorated village make use of a "wailing wall" and white grave decorations.

Black as a preferred color for mourning costume has been well documented since the 15th century in European court funerals. It only became the norm in village dress during the 19th century in Hungary and Slovakia. In Transylvania and some parts of Slovakia, mourning costume conforms only to a more sombre, dark color scheme, with fewer floral ornaments. This toned-down version of the normally cheerful costume mirrors the wardrobe specified by the status of widowhood.

Textiles accompanying the funeral vigil or wake are specific for the occasion. Since the funeral vigil is usually held at home, extra precautions must be taken to assure its protection. Mirrors are cloth-covered, clocks are stopped, and windows are closed. In 1996 in Slovakia, I visited two different exhibition rooms showing funeral vigils. In Cicmany, the cloth covering the mirror was white; in the north, in Stara Lubovna, the cloth mirror-cover was black. In this room, the "deceased" was laid out on a striped red and white cloth. In Transylvania, the usual pall cover resembled a woven tablecloth, blue and white or black and white being preferred. One European medieval illumination shows an abbot laid out on a wooly sheepskin; however, it was probably the usual white or undyed linen which accounts for most funeral palls. Linen was generally considered to be a "pure" form of woven goods, and closely related to the earth due to its origin, unlike animal fibers.

The proper dress for the body appears, across Eastern Europe, to be age-related. Infants and children usually are dressed in white, either in baptismal or first communion clothes. White flowers and ribbons properly accompany the funeral procession. An older person who passes on will be dressed in his or her "best" clothes. These clothes may be purchased well ahead of the needed time and kept unworn for the occasion. A young married woman, even one who has died in childbirth, may be buried in her wedding dress, and a young married man in his "best," or wedding, suit. This practice was carried to the U.S. by Eastern European immigrants even in this century. I have been told of several family funerals of this type by Hungarian and Slovakian family members. In addition, unmarried women could be buried in wedding dresses, including some of rather advanced years. Curators of funeral photographs in the U.S. have often been puzzled by the large number of "deceased brides."

The funeral shroud is still used in regions where interment is the practice. It is, in the village, always white; although not always of linen.

Another category of death which must be solved satisfactorily in a ritual way is the death of a young man or woman who has not married. Such a premature death, whether natural or accidental, is considered a great tragedy, since the person has died unfulfilled or led an 'incomplete life'. In order to remedy this situation, a ritual wedding is performed. The funeral proceeds with the costumes, banners and burial procession exactly as if for a wedding. This tradition is well established in Transylvania, where it still takes place. In some places, a stand-in speaks for the deceased, and a representative is chosen for the marriage partner. In other places, the deceased is considered the "Bridegroom of Heaven" or the "Bride of Heaven." In every case where black would accompany the corpse, white or wedding clothing is substituted.

Grave decoration consistently follows the other elements of the funeral itself. A young person's grave is decorated piled high with flowers, and a young man's grave is decorated with a tree covered with ribbons and flowers. There is some documentation for graves in Romania decorated with the clothing of the deceased. This appears to be a rare custom.

A final type of funeral ritual should be mentioned here in this context. The "death goddess" or "morena" is a doll-like effigy, carried by the young girls of the village in procession; after which it is thrown into a stream. This spring ritual is still a part of the living folklore of Slovakia, and was practiced until recently in Hungary. The "morena" is made of straw, dressed like a young girl, festooned with paper ornaments and "disliked objects," all symbolizing the old year, celebrating the triumph of spring and renewal over winter and death. Due to their ephemeral character, few examples of these dolls survive, but those older ones in museums show the doll dressed in white. Recent photographic documents show the doll in a white apron, and more recently, with no white garments. This custom has become more of a children's festival in recent years, and its enactment far less serious; somewhat like the celebration of Halloween in the United States.

In conclusion, we can say that no clear geographic pattern emerges which accounts for the survival of certain textiles and costumes used in mourning rituals in Eastern Europe. The factors of geographic remoteness or the lack of urbanization and modernization, as well as the inherent traditionalism and conservatism of some village cultures, are the main contributing factors. These survivals should be viewed as more than mere geographic oddities and anachronisms. They are certainly the remnants of a much larger, pan-European tradition, which through continued use in a ritual setting remained viable and functional for many centuries.

Bibliography

Cunnington, Phillis and Lucas, Catherine. *Costume for Births, Marriages and Deaths.* London: Adam and Charles Black, 1972.

Dömötör, Tekla. *Hungarian Folk Customs.* Budapest: Corvina Press, 1972.

Ethnographic Institute of the Slovak Academy of Sciences. *Ethnographic Atlas of Slovakia.* Bratislava: VEDA, Publishing House of the Slovak Academy of Sciences, 1994.

Habenstein, Robert W. and Lamers, William M. *Funeral Customs the World Over.* Milwaukee: The National Funeral Directors Association of the USA, 1960.

Hofer, Tamás and Fél, Edit. *Hungarian Folk Art.* Oxford: Oxford University Press, 1979.

Hutchinson, Walter, ed. *Customs of the World.* Delhi: Neeraj Publishing House, 1984.

Kligman, Gail. *The Wedding of the Dead. Ritual, Poetics and Popular Culture in Transylvania.* Berkeley: University of California Press, 1988.

Korniss, Péter and Csöóri, Sándor. *The Bridegroom of Heaven.* Budapest: Corvina Press, 1975.

Kunt, Erno. *Folk Art in Hungarian Cemeteries.* Budapest: Corvina Press, 1975.

Markov, Jozef. *The Slovak National Dress Through the Centuries.* Prague: Artia, 1956.

Newton, Stella Mary. *Fashion in the Age of the Black Prince. A Study of the Years 1340-1365.* London: Boydell Press, Rowman and Littlefield, 1980.

Nicolescu, Corina. *Istoria Costumului de Curte in Țarile Romane.* Bucharest: Editura Stiintifica, 1973.

Slovak National Museum. *Karol Plicka 1894-1982.* Martin: Slovak National Museum, 1989.

Sotkova, Blazená and Smirous, Karel. *National Costumes of Czechoslovakia.* Prague: Artia, 1956.

Sroñkova, Olga. *Gothic Women's Fashion.* Prague: Artia, 1954.

Taylor, Lou. *Mourning Dress. A Costume and Social History.* London: George Allen and Unwin, 1983.

Václavik, Antonin and Jaroslav, Orel. *Textile Folk Art.* London: Spring Books, 1956.

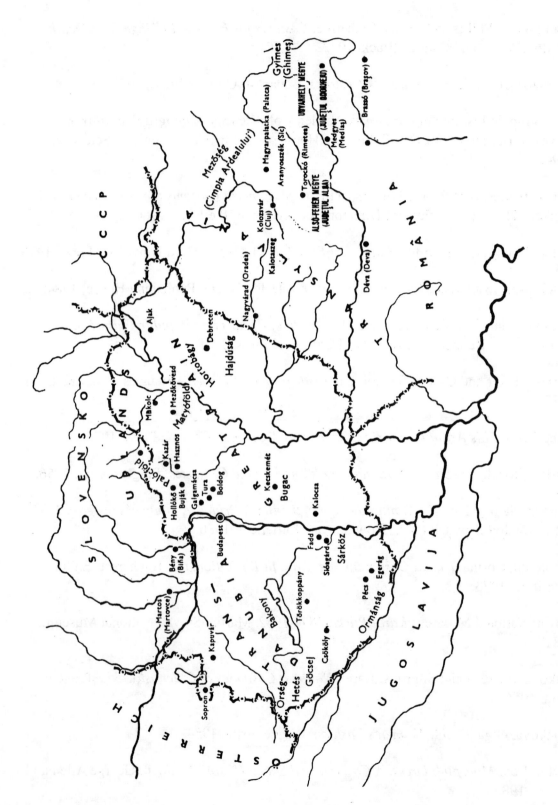

MAP OF TRANSYLVANIA, ROMANIA; HUNGARY; AND EASTERN SLOVAKIA.

White mourning. Csököly, Hungary, 1926.

Right: Praying women in white, Košeca Valley,
        Slovakia, ca. 1930.
        Photo: Karol Plicka

Left: Half mourning. Exhibit, the Slovak
        Ethnographic Museum, Martin, Slovakia.
        Photo: J. Corbett, 1996.

Right, above: Headaddress of an older woman, ca. 1364.
               (In Gothic Woman's Fashion, op. cit.)
Left, above: Headdress of an older woman, Čičmany,
               Slovakia, ca. 1930.

Left, below: Exhibit, Funeral vigil; Open Air
               Museum, Stará Lubovňa, Slovakia.
               Photo: J. Corbett, 1996.
Right, below: Exhibit, Funerary objects; Čičmany,
               Slovakia.
               Photo: J. Corbett, 1996.

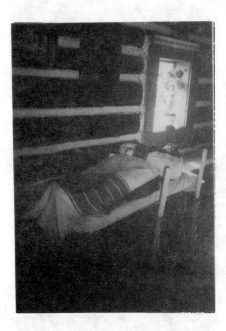

Above: Funeral procession for "Heaven's Bridegroom",
        Rimoc, (Bezirk Nograd), Romania, 1970.
        Photo: Peter Korniss.
Below: Death goddess spring festival, Vrbov, Slovakia.
        1934.
        Photo: Karol Plicka

BEAUTY ENHANCES RITUAL

by Jennifer Wearden

The Torah, that is the five books of Moses - Genesis, Exodus, Leviticus, Numbers and Deuteronomy - and the Law they contain, emanate from God. This is the Word of God revealed to the Israelites and recorded in the Scriptures. It is impossible to exaggerate the importance of the Torah for a Jewish congregation, so it is not surprising that the most dominant feature of a synagogue is the Ark of the Law in which the Torah scrolls are kept. This may be a large, elaborate structure or a simple cupboard or recess but there is always a decorative curtain hanging in front of it. Immediately in front of the Ark is the reading-desk on which the scrolls of the Torah are placed to be read; the reading-desk is also covered with a decorative cloth. In this paper I am going to consider the ritual and ceremonial significance of a *parochet* or curtain for the Ark of the Torah and an *almemor* or cover for the reading-desk - both are in the Victoria & Albert Museum in London[1] and were embroidered in Northern Italy in the late 17th century.

They were purchased in 1877 from a man called Caspar Clarke, who later became Sir Purdon Clarke and Director of the Museum; he had visited Italy eight years previously and may have acquired the textiles then. Although the Victoria & Albert Museum was among the first museums to collect Jewish ecclesiastical art, the ritual and cultural significance of these hangings was hardly considered by the Museum - it was far less important than their interest as textiles. They were acquired by a museum of decorative art primarily as examples of 17th century Italian needlework and have been regarded only as Italian needlework until recently. When any-one begins to study Jewish textiles they encounter a very big problem - because of persecutions and the deliberate destruction of synagogues and Jewish communities, few of the early pieces have survived and there is little related documentary evidence easily available for study, but the V&A hopes to explore the original significance of these embroideries and the author will be grateful for any comments provoked by this presentation.

The reading desk cover (illustration 1) has an embroidered panel is 27" long by 48" wide. Although the panel is not dated, the woven silk surrounding it is an attractive and expensive late 17th century one. The greater part of the

---

[1] The Museum Number of the *parochet* is 511-1877 and of the *almemor* 511A-1877. At the time of acquisition the Victoria & Albert Museum was known as the South Kensington Museum.

embroidery is worked with floss silk in brick stitch on a plain weave linen ground which had been extensively pieced together before being embroidered. The black inscriptions and and the outlines of the motifs are corroding. Technically the embroidery is relatively complex: there is metal thread in certain areas: in the Ten Commandments, the vases, the crown and the oval frame which encircles the central motifs. There is silk couched over white silk padding and there are french knots in the centre of flowers.

At first glance the Torah Ark curtain (illustration 2), which measures 76" long by 64" wide, looks very similar in style and technique to the reading desk cover, but there are small differences[2] which suggest that although the two textiles may have been used together in the same synagogue, they were not deliberately made as a pair. Like the reading desk cover, the plain weave linen ground had been extensively pieced - suggesting a domestic rather than professional origin. The metal thread is limited to the text of the Ten Commandments and to small amounts in the twelve scenes in the borders. Most of the black inscriptions in this piece have been reworked in satin stitch. The borders were worked separately and then the whole was assembled and the seams embroidered over with a decorative pattern. There are two dates included in the inscriptions: one in the upper part of the narrow border around the central panel states that all work was completed in *Ellul* 5436 (August-September 1676) and a later addition in the lower border gives the name of the donor and the date of the donation: Joseph bar Haim Segal Polacko, 5463 (1703). There is a difference of 27 years between the two dates and I suggest that the curtain was first made for private use within the home and was then donated to a synagogue.

The well-balanced design of the curtain and the reading desk cover suggest the hand of a professional artist. Most probably an artist who illuminated marriage certificates or *ketubahs*. Every bride received a written contract from the groom and these were usually beautifully decorated in whatever style prevailed at that time. Late 17th century marriage certificates from Northern Italy may be usefully compared with these embroidered synagogue hangings as all are decorated in an artistic style which included formal vases of flowers.[3] An

---

[2] The thread count per inch for the linen ground of the reading-desk cover is 21 x 17. The count for the Torah Ark curtain is 26 x 16. Both pieces are embroidered in brick stitch but it is worked over two threads across the lower thread count in the reading desk cover and over four threads over the higher thread count in the curtain.

[3] For example see a *ketubah* from Verona dated 5438 (1678) ilustrated in the <u>Catalogue of The Jewish Museum London</u> edited by R D Barnett, London, 1974, p.87.

embroidered reading desk cover from the Jewish Museum in New York, dated 1714 is also from Northern Italy and illustrates the popularity of large floral arrangements.[4] A careful examination of the Ark curtain reveals half of a formal vase arrangement in the lower part of the pillars which form the central arch. There are rather odd, thin-stemmed blossoms floating in the border on the outer side of these pillars. It might be thought that these are the amateur additions of the embroiderer but isolated flowers fill the same spaces in marriage contracts.

Vases of flowers had no intentional symbolic meaning, although some people might see them as representations of fertility and abundance. But other images on these synagogue hangings were deliberately chosen for their symbolism. The central features of the the reading desk cover are the tablets on which the first word of each of the Ten Commandments is written, representing God's revelation to the Israelites, small hillocks represent Mount Sinai on which there are tongues of fire and above everything is the cloud from which God spoke. Unleavened bread to the right is a symbol of the Passover and to the left are bitter herbs. The inscriptions are from the Book of Proverbs (chapter iii verses 16 and 18) and refer, in this context, to the importance of the Torah scroll: "Length of days is in her right hand and in her left hand riches and honour. She is a tree of life to them that lay hold upon her". The wooden rollers on which the scrolls were wound were called trees of life.

The design of the Torah Ark curtain is more complex: in the centre there is the cloud, the tablets with the Ten Commandments, the fire and what is probably the Mount of Olives, because the hillocks are decorated with small leafy sprigs. In the top right are symbols for the Passover - bread, herbs and a roasted lamb bone and in the top left are symbols for the feast of Succot - a palm branch, willow, myrtle and a lemon-like citrus called an etrog.

The main border contains 12 scenes of which some represent important festivals and some represent Sabbaths on which there are special readings or on which special events are commemorated. Each scene is surrounded with relevant quotations. From the top right these scenes represent: *Shabbat Shekalim, Shabbat Chol Hamo'ed Pesach, Shabbat Hagodol, Shabbat Chanucah, Shabbat Ha-Chodesh, Simchat Torah* (at the bottom), *Shabbat Parah, Shabbat Purim, Shabbat Nachamu, Shabbat Chol Hamo'ed Succot, Shabbat Zachor, and Yom Kippur* (at the top). *Chanucah*, for example, is represented by a *Menorah* (a candelabrum). Although a seven-branched one is used in synagogues, a nine-branched (like this) was used in the Temple in Jerusalem and at *Chanucah* because the feast

---

[4] Inventory Number F4172. For an illustration see catalogue entry 4 in <u>Fabric of Jewish Life</u>.

recalls the re-dedication of the altar in the Temple in the time of Judas Maccabeus. *Parah*, an important Sabbath on which ritual purification is the theme, is represented by a hand holding cedar wood, hyssop and scarlet (all these scenes should be read from right to left, like Hebrew). The inscription surrounding the scene is taken from the Book of Numbers (chapter xix verse 6): "and the priest shall take cedar wood and hyssop and scarlet and throw them into the fire".

The sequence in which the scenes have been placed is not chronological and readers should consult Treasures of the Jewish Museum (page 72) for one explanation of the complex iconography of this embroidery. The Ark curtain illustrated from their collection is very similar to the V&A curtain. It is dated 1698, is probably from Venice and was embroidered by a woman called Leah Ottolenghi. A third, similar curtain is in the Jewish Museum in Florence, Italy.[5]

One striking features of Jewish embroideries from North Italy is that most were embroidered by women. There are many known examples - one Ark curtain in the Jewish Museum in New York is dated 1680; it is from Venice and was embroidered by Simah, wife of Manahem Levi Meshullami, a member of a wealthy and prosperous family.[6] Another older curtain, dated 1630, was worked by the wife of the donor for a synagogue in Ancona[7] and a binder for the Torah scrolls, also from the Jewish Museum in New York,[8] was embroidered by Rikah Polacco in 1662. In all probability, Rikah was the mother of Joseph Polacko whose name appears on the V&A's curtain and it is probable that she made the curtain 13 years after she made this Torah binder.

There are two questions which I cannot answer:
(1) Does any evidence exist to show how designs for embroidery were comissioned and distributed?
(2) Were these hangings the donations of pious (and skilled) women or were some of them commissioned from professional embroiderers?

What was the ceremonial significance of these elaborately decorated hangings? Jews living under Christian rule were never secure enough to enable them to build large synagogues to rival cathedrals and churches. Their synagogues were

---

[5] The inventory number of the New York *parochet* is F3432.

[6] Treasures of the Jewish Museum pages 70-71 and Fabric of Jewish Life page 6.

[7] See Landsberger 'Old Time Torah Curtains' in Beauty in Holiness.

[8] Inventory Number 1988-21, illustrated in Judische Lebenswelten page 89 catalogue entry 4/37.

modest and unassuming, from the outside - although their location was discreet, the decoration of the inside of the building and its furnishings was often opulent, attesting to the prosperity of the worshippers. A reasonably prosperous synagogue would possess several curtains and reading-desk covers and the ones used would be chosen to compliment the season, or the feast or the occasion, for example, a marriage. As well as hanging in front of the Ark of the Torah, curtains might also be hung in front of the cupboards or recesses which are often found on either side of the Ark and in which sacred books and ritual objects are kept. These hangings were prominantly displayed.

This curtain and the similar ones which have survived from Northern Italy, probably came from the area around Venice. This was a relatively secure place for Jews in the 17th century. In the previous century all Jews had been expelled from Southern Italy; Rome and Ancona were the only places within the Papal States where they could live; in Tuscany Jews could live only in Pisa. But in Northern Italy they were able to live in a number of places - and except for occasional incidents, the Jewish communities there possessed enough stability and security to enable them to create beautiful works of art. Many faiths have a rich heritage of sacred music, art and architecture and they consciously use these media to transmit their doctrines, teachings or philosophies. For the Jews, God's teachings are freely available through the Scriptures which are read and interpreted in public worship and the predominance of The Word led to a high rate of literacy among Jews. The images used on these hangings were not for educational purposes .... religion of this type has little need for visual images. With their high level of literacy, it cannot be said that Jewish congregations required the equivalent of the visual 'Bible of the poor' often found in the decoration of many Christian churches.

These colourful embroideries fulfilled two distinct functions. On the more obvious level, they created a decorative background, much as painted and mosaic patterns did in churches and tilework did in mosques. They were used primarily for aesthetic purposes to create a beautiful environment and by doing so they gave pleasure and joy to the people who had gathered for worship - they enhanced the rituals. In a more subtle way, by using images which recalled specific instances where God had helped his people - guiding them, giving them victory, forgiving them - the worshippers could re-live positive spiritual experiences of personal and national redemption - in some way making these a continuing reality.

There is also a future dimension to Ark curtain. The scene from the centre of the left hand border shows the city of Jerusalem with the Temple in the centre and the words around it are taken from Isaiah (chapter xl verses 1 and 2): "Comfort ye, my people" and "Bid Jerusalem take heart". As a Christian, I have been taught to interpret this as a reference to the coming of the Messiah ... the Good Shepard who will forgive sins and take care of his flock. But there is great potential for mistakes when trying to read meaning into images and Messianic prophesies were probably not intended. The second scene from the top on the right hand border depicts the tombs of Adam and Eve, Abraham and Sarah, Isaac and Rebecca and Jacob and Leah with the words "Behold I will open your graves". This is from the passage in Ezekiel about dry bones (chapter xxxvii verse 12) and is closer to the truth - "I, the Sovereign Lord, am going to open their graves. I am going to take them out and bring them back to the land of Israel." The Jewish community in Venice identified itself closely with Israel and those images which seem to anticipate the Messiah are really expressions of their longing for their own return to the Promised Land and to Jerusalem. The images on these synagogue hangings are stimuli which evoke remembrance of the great events of the past and the anticipation of the end of their exile. They reinforced good feelings about themselves as Jews and as a community and they gave them hope. The congregation was reminded, in the words of St Paul, that "they were adopted as sons, they were given the glory and the covenants, the Law and the ritual were drawn up for them and the promises were made to them" (Letter to the Romans chapter ix verse 5). In a world of discrimination and active persecution, this positive feedback was necessary for their continued survival. And so these beautiful embroideries were more than decoration, they were a statement of identity ... to instil confidence and hope when it was most needed.

Specific references to these embroideries may be found in:

S Cohen 'A 17th Century Parochet' in Jewish Chronicle, London, 19 July 1953.

Fabric of Jewish Life, Textiles from the Jewish Museum Collection, (exhibition catalogue) The Jewish Museum, New York, 1977

Treasures of the Jewish Museum, New York, 1986

Kathryn Solomon Jewish Ceremonial Embroidery, Batsford, London, 1988

Michael E Keen Jewish Ritual Art in the Victoria & Albert Museum, HMSO, London, 1991

Judische Lebenswelten, (exhibition catalogue) Martin Gropius Bau, Berlin, 1991

Background Reading:

Josephine Bacon The Illustrated Atlas of Jewish Civilization, Andre Deutsch, London, 1990

Dalia Hardof Renberg The Complete Family Guide to Jewish Holidays, Robson Books, London, 1987

Franz Landsberger 'Old Time Torah Curtains' in Beauty in Holiness: Studies in Jewish Customs and Ceremonial Art ed. by Joseph Gutman, KTAV Publishing House Inc, USA, 1970

Franz Landsberger 'Illuminated Marriage Contracts with Special Reference to the Cincinnati Ketubahs' in Beauty in Holiness: Studies in Jewish Customs and Ceremonial Art op. cit

Albert C Moore Iconography of Religions: An Introduction, SCM Press Ltd, London, 1977

Cecil Roth 'Ritual Art' in Jewish Art: an Illustrated History ed. by Cecil Roth, W H Allen, London, 1961

Alfred Werner 'Modern Ritual Art' in Beauty in Holiness: Studies in Jewish Customs and Ceremonial Art ed. by Joseph Gutman, KTAV Publishing House Inc, USA, 1970

RITUAL CLOTH AS EMBLEM OF SOCIO-RELIGIOUS VALUES IN INDONESIA
Panel Introduction by Rens Heringa

Recent anthropological studies of Indonesian textiles have reported in detail on the important ritual role of locally-made heirloom cloths among a range of ethnic groups throughout the archipelago. Moreover, the few extant studies with a local comparative bias have shown how the function of one particular textile may vary between people living in different villages or belonging to different social groups. Geirnaert has pointed out that, obviously, this indicates that textiles may form part of a wider geographical or symbolical system (Geirnaert 1992:xxviii). It has also been shown that this type of comparative effort can be taken beyond the archipelago (see Gittinger 1992; Maxwell 1990). As yet, a concerted attempt at comparison of the meanings of ritual cloth among different ethnic groups within Indonesia has not been undertaken. Therefore, our panel will compare the manner in which one type of highlyvalued, locally-made ceremonial cloth functions among three ethnic groups in Indonesia: the Lio of central Flores, the Minangkabau of west Sumatra and villagers from Kerek, near Tuban on the northeast coast of Java.

The comparison concerns the most highly-valued type of textile and its ritual role among the highest-ranking social group in each of the three cultures: the *lawo butu,* the beaded sarong of the Lio, the *kain sandang gobo,* a heavily gold-decorated shoulder cloth of the Minangkabau and the *kain kembangan*, the flowered cloth of the villagers of Kerek. Certain differences in the symbolic meaning and function of the three cloth types will appear to be linked to the different forms of social organization and religious adherence of each of the three groups. Changes over time have influenced the cloths' function.

Weiner's distinction between alienable property - which may be owned by individuals or sections of the community, and is marketable or exchangable - and inalienable property - which is collectively and eternally owned by the whole group - in Oceania (Weiner 1992), has served as an additional analytical tool for the case of the Indonesian textiles.

Three aspects are of particular interest for the analytical attempt. First comes the question in how far "female" and "male" properties may be attributed to the textile by each of the three groups. Many scholars have described Indonesian textiles as female goods, primarily because textiles are made by women and also because they often function as gift from the side of the bride in exchange for "male" metal objects such as weapons, jewelry or money. It has however been suggested, that textiles from some areas in the archipelago may also be imbued with male qualities, depending upon the context (Gittinger 1979:107/108; Geirnaert 1992:93,101).

The second aspect of comparison to be considered are the differences in social organization among each of the three groups. The Lio have a double descent type, which means that a person inherits certain qualities or property from his or her mother and others from his or her father. For instance, membership in the ranked groups of nobles, commoners and slaves is inherited from the mother, while land and membership of a House are inherited from the father.

Minangkabau society is organized matrilineally, meaning that group membership and property are inherited from mother to daughter (or son). The Minangkabau adhere to a system in which descendants of the original population, who control *adat* titles and ancestral property, are ranked above newcomers.

The Javanese villagers of Kerek adhere to a bilineal system, which entails inheritance of membership in the group from both mother and father. Ownership of different categories of land divides the population into ranked groups. The highest category, agricultural land, is inherited from father to son.

The third aspect to be considered is the manner in which the three groups each combine a different foreign religion with their traditional customs (*adat*). All three still perform the rituals to honor their ancestors. The Lio converted to Catholicism in the beginning of this century. The Minangkabau, Muslim since the sixteenth century, have managed to forge a synthesis between matrilineal custom and patrilineally-biased Islam. The villagers of Kerek adopted the Muslim creed in the fifteenth century, and combine it with Hindu-Javanese custom.

In conclusion, the key to the comparative analysis can be summarized as follows. First, all three textiles will appear to incorporate male and female properties, be it differently stressed, in direct relationship to the male or female emphasis of each particular group's social organization. Secondly, all three textiles will be found to move from an alienable phase into an inalienable phase. The rituals indicate at which point this change occurs. The level of the Sumatran and the Javanese ritual differs from the one enacted in Flores. While the first two serve to increase the image of a single descent group, the latter functions to strengthen the whole village community. The first two rituals pinpoint the moment when the cloth changes into becoming inalienable. In the third, only an already inalienable cloth is appropriate.

Bibliography

Gittinger, Mattiebelle

1979 - Splendid Symbols. Textiles and Tradition in Indonesia. The Textile Museum: Washington

D.C. Gittinger, Mattiebelle and H. Leedom Lefferts, Jr.

1992 - Textiles and the Tai Experience in Southeast Asia. The Textile Museum: Washington, D.C.

Geirnaert-Martin, Danielle C.

1992 - The Woven Land of Laboya. Socio-cosmic ideas and values in West Sumba, eastern Indonesia. Ph.d Thesis Leiden, Centre of Non-Western Studies: Leiden.

Maxwell, Robyn

1990 - Textiles of Southeast Asia. Tradition. Trade and Transformation. Oxford University Press and Australian National Gallery: Singapore and Canberra

Weiner, Annette B.

1992 - Inalienable Possessions. The Paradox of Keeping While Giving. University of California Press: Berkeley

Heirloom and Hierarchy
The Sacred *Lawo butu* Cloth of the Lio of Central Flores

WILLEMIJN DE JONG
Department of Social Anthropology, University of Zurich, Freiensteinstr. 5, 8032 Zurich, Switzerland

INTRODUCTION

The most sacred ceremonial cloth of the Lio on the island of Flores in eastern Indonesia is an heirloom called *lawo butu*, a tubular skirt or sarong traditionally worn by high-ranking women at the most important fertility ceremony. This beaded sarong is only found in one of the main cultural centres of the Lio, the weaving village of Nggela on the south coast of Central Flores, a village of almost 1300 inhabitants. Until Indonesian independence in 1945 this village was more stratified by a rank system of nobles (*ata ria*), commoners (*ana fai walu*) and slaves (*ata ko'o*) than other Lio villages (Prior 1988: 62). Of the more than thirty types of the local cloth system only the *lawo butu* cloth belongs to the category of heirloom or inalienable possessions in the sense of the anthropologist Annette Weiner (1992)[1] – cloths that should be kept and cherished. The other cloth types belong to the category of alienable possessions. They may be given in ritual exchange or sold (see de Jong 1994, 1995, n.d.).

There exist a few other types of beaded cloths on Flores, all heirloom property (see Maxwell 1983: fig. 1, 2, Maxwell 1990: fig. 200–203, Khan Majlis 1991: fig. 163, Orinbao 1992: 129, 181–183, Hamilton 1994: fig. 2–16, 4–4, 5–14). The motifs of the Lio *lawo butu* have some resemblance to those on the beaded sarongs of the Sikka and the Ngada people, but the context of its production and its ceremonial function seem to have been different, at least as far as the Ngada *lawo butu* is concerned (see Hamilton 1994: 108-109). While the *lawo butu* of the Lio has figuratively been represented in publications on Indonesian and Southeast Asian textiles, there has been little information on the social significance and the ritual use of this cloth (see for example Khan Majlis 1991: 191).

To elaborate on the *lawo butu* is not easy, however, because it is no longer used in the original ceremonial context. Moreover, knowledge about it is almost lost, as I experienced during my anthropological fieldwork in Central Flores. Important sources of information for reconstructing the significance of the beaded sacred sarong were data from oral history by village elders and by old women who had continued to wear this cloth at former ceremonial occasions, a thesis by a local theologian (Ndate 1988) and my own observations of its use in the village at ceremonial events in 1987 and in 1988.

This paper examines the extent to which the *lawo butu* as an inalienable possession has strengthened the sociopolitical hierarchy of the rank system in the village society. To answer this question I will first describe the visual aspects of the *lawo butu* and explore its significance as a

---

Postdoctoral fieldwork in Central Flores in 1987–88 and 1990–91 was supported by the Canton of Zurich and conducted under the auspices of the Indonesian Academy of Sciences (LIPI), Universitas Indonesia in Jakarta and Universitas Nusa Cendana in Kupang.

[1] Weiner (1992: 33) defines an inalienable possession as follows: "What makes a possession inalienable is its exclusive and cumulative identity with a particular series of owners through time. Its history is authenticated by fictive or true genealogies, origin myths, sacred ancestors, and gods. In this way, inalienable possessions are trandscendent treasures to be guarded against all the exigencies that might force their loss."

collective and individual heirloom with regard to the social organization of the village. Then I will elaborate on the properties of this ceremonial cloth related to female and male aspects. Finally I will analyze the role of this sacred sarong in ceremonial contexts before independence and afterwards. I will suggest that the change in the ceremonial use of the *lawo butu* reflects a change in the sociopolitical system of the local society.

VISUAL ASPECTS OF THE *LAWO BUTU*

The beaded sarong is the only women's sarong type in the village without ikat design (Figure 1). This black indigo dyed and handspun cotton sarong has a centre panel with red morinda dyed and white undyed stripes and a panel at the lower border with six or seven motifs made of glass beads (see de Jong 1994: fig. 10–6). The technique of dyeing, weaving and sewing of the beaded sarong does not resemble the production of the warp ikat women's sarong, but of the warp striped men's sarong. The weave type, in particular, is plain weave and not warp-faced plain weave. However, no reed is used and, having a length of 85 cm and a width of 60 cm, it is much smaller than the men's sarong.

The bead motifs still found today are said to resemble octopuses and are designated accordingly (*maka kubi*). The diamond shaped inner part of the bead motif is called *mata bili*, which means 'round like a circle'. This motif design also appears on other cloth types (see de Jong 1994: fig. 10-8, 10–10).[2] It is sometimes associated with the female vulva and is said to symbolize fertility.[3] The yellow, white, red, green and blue beads are said to originate from the Portuguese, that is to say from the first wave of European colonization in the sixteenth century.

THE *LAWO BUTU* AS A COLLECTIVE AND INDIVIDUAL HEIRLOOM CLOTH

In the social organization of the Lio in Central Flores kin relations on both the female and the male side are important for the transfer of rights of group membership, of property and of ritual and political offices (see Sugishima 1994). In the research village, membership of rank in the sense of estate and rights of ritual and political tasks are transferred in the line of the mother. Membership of a 'House' as well as rights of land, however, are transferred in the line of the father (see de Jong 1996). The almost thirty Houses of the village are physically and symbolically represented in their ceremonial house (*sa'o*), where agricultural rituals (*nggua*) used to be celebrated and where the ancestors of the House are worshipped (see Howell 1995).[4] The high-ranking heads of the Houses with the title 'lord of the land' (*mosa laki*) formerly constituted the village council, and as village elders they organized ritual life.

There are two categories of property or possessions in the village: those collectively owned by the Houses which are inalienable and those owned by individual men and women which are mainly alienable. Collective possessions of the Houses are the ceremonial house and its treasures. Symbolically these heirlooms are closely related to the ancestors and therefore possess sacred properties (*du'a bapu*). Trade with these items is taboo (*piré*) and will be punished with illness by the ancestral spirits, people say. Besides heirloom items such as ivory tusks and ancient gold jewelry each House possessed three or more pieces of the beaded women's sarongs. The format of the sarong was presumably created by high-ranking weavers of the rich Houses whose ancestors have supposedly originated from Portugal, Malakka and from the islands of

---

[2] These motifs are probably borrowed from imported patola cloths. They also appear on Balinese ceremonial clothing (see Bühler et al. 1975).

[3] Ndate, personal communication.

[4] With the term 'House' I signify a socioreligious unit, with 'house' a physical building.

Figure 1. A young high-ranking woman wearing a *lawo butu* and a sarong called *lawo kéli mara* underneath.

Java and Sumba (Ndate 1988: 32). The collectively owned beaded cloths which still exist probably date from the last century, as none of the villagers ever saw them being produced.

Among the important individual possessions of women are all types of alienable cloths, which are passed down from mother to daughter. High-ranking women sometimes also possess a piece of beaded sarong as an heirloom cloth of their own. Individually owned *lawo butu*, as well as the beading, seem to have been made by high-ranking weavers until the beginning of this century. These sarongs look the same as the collectively owned ones. As they are not connected with ancestors of a large kin group, they are less sacred, but selling them may also be dangerous.

Before independence a total of more than a hundred pieces of this textile must have existed. Some of them wore out; others were sold. At present there may be at most approximately thirty pieces left in the village. Recently even new *lawo butu*, apparently with machinespun yarn and plastic beads, have been made by women from the village living in the neighbouring town. These are still ritual cloths, but as new individual possessions, produced and worn in new social contexts, they are again less sacred than the old ones. If we consider the three kinds of beaded sarongs, the old collective ones, the old individual ones and the new individual ones, we can scale them from more sacred to less sacred.

FEMALE AND MALE PROPERTIES OF THE *LAWO BUTU*

At first sight the inalienable possessions of the Houses seem to have properties either related to male or to female aspects. In the anthropological literature about Indonesian societies gold jewelry for example is often perceived as male, whereas cloth is perceived as female (see Niessen 1984). In the village where I conducted my research, however, the two ivory tusks that belong to the inalienable property of the most important Houses are conceptualized as male and as female.[5] In a similar vein the beaded sarong appears to embody both male and female properties (see also Geirnaert 1992: 93).

The properties of the *lawo butu* related to female aspects are most conspicuous. It is a female piece of clothing, traditionally made and worn by high-ranking young women who possess their rank membership through their mother and partly owned by individual elite women. Further, the sarong has female properties in the beaded motifs that resemble motifs on other types of women's ikat sarongs.

After a closer look, however, properties related to male aspects are also unmistakable. The sacred sarongs belong in the first place to the collective property of the Houses. These are kin groups who visibly acted as groups in agricultural ceremonies. Membership in these groups is accorded through the father. Moreover, male village elders used to determine the need to perform the fertility ceremony in which the beaded sarong was used. And since the 1960s, males have also sometimes stolen these sacred sarongs and sold them to finance school fees for their children, whereas women normally organize the use as well as the selling and giving of cloth. Finally, the fact that the sacred sarong is technically mainly produced as a men's sarong and is decorated with warp stripes and not with ikat motifs is also a significant male property.

---

[5] Interestingly, the bigger tusk is female and the smaller one is male. This corresponds with the pair of wooden ancestor statues in the local temple (*keda*) in former times in the Lio area, of which the female one also may have been larger than the male one (Howell 1990: 253).

THE *LAWO BUTU* IN TRADITIONAL AND MODERN CEREMONIAL CONTEXTS

Until the 1930s the *lawo butu* was worn as a prescribed ritual dress by young elite women in its original context, the ceremony of the rain dance (*muré*). As a preferred ceremonial dress the *lawo butu* was also worn at the meditation ceremony (*maru*) of the thatching of two of the most important ceremonial houses (*até sa'o nggua*) (see de Jong 1994: fig. 10–16). Here I will concentrate on the context in which the beaded sarong is prescribed, that is on the rain dance. This four-day ceremony was performed when, due to exceptional drought, starvation was imminent, or when after seven years of fallow new swidden fields were cleared for the cultivation of mainly cassava and corn. After periods of upheaval through World War II and the processes of decolonization the rain dance was revitalized in the beginning of the 1960s, but in a shorter version and additionally was now almost exclusively presented in state oriented ceremonial contexts (Figure 2–5).

According to village mythology the origin of agricultural rituals on the whole started with the rain dance ceremony. After an inundation and subsequent severe drought the village elders determined that young high-ranking maidens, because of their physical and spiritual capacities, were best suited to influence the spirits and finally the deities in these food crises. They had to bring about fertility and wealth to the village population.[6]

In pre-independence days numerous preparations had to take place, before the ceremony of the rain dance could be performed. The village elders fixed the timing of the ceremonial event through divination (*so au*). Despite scarcity, large quantities of food as well as clothing and gold jewelry in the shape of a crescent (*gebé rajo*)[7] had to be prepared. And about a hundred young women were to be chosen and had to be trained in dancing, singing and meditation (*maru*). In case there were too few dancers (*ata eo tau jo'i*), young elite women of the surrounding villages and, in exceptional cases, less respected non-elite young women of the village itself could also take part, but only after the elders had examined their strength of character and their physical and spiritual conditions. Many candidates may have applied, because women who had participated in the rain dance ceremony were higher valued than other women. Young women of the rank of slaves could only assist in cooking tasks and the like.

Because the performance of the ceremony lasted four days, the village population was put to high expense. Every day in the late afternoon and sometimes in the morning the dance was presented in the sacred village centre (*pusé nua*) near the public cult places (*kanga keda*) (see Arndt 1944). The movements expressed the content of the song text. This dealt with an invocation to the deities, the foundation of a ceremonial house and of a family, the actual request for rain (*rina ae*) or fecundation, and the expression of joy after the rain has come. The beginning and end of the dance were accompanied by rhythmic music of gongs and drums (*nggo lamba*). The dance movements were restrained and had a sacred and esthetic quality. This was emphasized by the clothing: the beaded sarong, within living memory worn over an ikat sarong (Figure 1).[8] Today a shoulder cloth (*luka sémba*), formerly the sacred cloth of the village elders, is additionally used as

---

[6] As in other parts of Indonesia (see Heringa 1993), in Nggela women as well as cloths are symbolically related to the fields. This also appears in the Lio myth of the rice maiden Ine Pare whose body was chopped up by her brothers and food plants such as rice grew out of it (see Yamaguchi 1989 and Howell 1990).

[7] Traditional vulva-shaped golden ear-drops (*wéa*), mainly used for bridewealth, are now worn as finery for the rain dance. The crescent-shaped gold jewelry has apparently mostly been sold.

[8] Today this sarong is of the type called *lawo kéli mara*, which was only created in the 1960s. Before, any type of ikat sarong is said to have been used. In earlier times the beaded sarong may have been worn without another sarong underneath.

Figure 2. The rain dance performed at the visit of the district governor in 1987.

Figure 3. The rain dance performed at the visit of provincial tourist authorities in 1988.

Fig. 4. The middle sequence of the rain dance. 1988.

Fig. 5. The last sequence of the rain dance. 1988.

a waist belt (Figure 2–5). The ceremony ended with a ritual rice meal (*aré kapo*) in the largest House of the village on the fourth night and with a purifying bath in the sea (*rio ae mesi*) the next day.

After independence the rain dance was performed as the embodiment of Lio culture in state oriented ceremonial contexts with a national character. Inside the village it was sporadically performed as a welcome ceremony for visiting high government officials and for special tourist groups. Outside the village it was shown at folk art exhibitions, inaugurations of electricity and the like at district level, at province level, and even once in the capital Jakarta. The people of Nggela tell with pride that in Jakarta it actually started to rain before the dance was finished. Recently the rain dance was also shown once at the occasion of a Catholic ceremony in the neighbouring town, supposedly with a strong religious intention.[9]

Formerly the beaded sarongs and the gold jewelry as inalienable possessions of the Houses were only allowed to be used in the sacred village centre. Initially, to perform the dance outside the village, blood sacrifices of pigs and even once of a water buffalo were made to avoid infuriating the ancestral spirits. Gradually the strict conditions related to the rain dance were given up. Government officials initiate the dance now instead of village elders. And it is the government indeed, that distributes rice, if rain fails and the villagers are starving. Participants are far fewer now and belong to all social groups, sometimes they are members of the local state-guided women's group (PKK), and they originate more often from other places.

CONCLUSIONS

The Lio cloth as an heirloom item or as an inalienable possession contains both female and male features in a non-hierarchical way, whereas as an exchange item or as an alienable possession it has female properties, I would suggest. Because Niessen (1984), as well as other anthropologists, mainly seems to focus on exchange cloth she may have come to the right conclusion, that cloth is predominantly female. If she had differentiated between heirloom and exchange cloth and studied the first in more detail, she also might have come up with qualities of these textiles related to both female and male aspects.

Weiner (1987, 1989, 1992) suggests that where the technologies for making cloth become more complex and where the cloth itself becomes an heirloom, certain cloths are regarded as treasures and they are endowed with sacred qualities. She further contends that societal transformations towards hierarchization according to rank most probably occurred as soon as "cloth is imbued with the inalienability of the social group and therefore, the authority attached to rank" (1989: 63). She exemplifies this thesis in case studies of precolonial Samoa and Hawaii in Polyesia. My case study of the *lawo butu* confirms Weiner's conclusions, in so far as this particular heirloom cloth is also perceived as sacred. As a garment merely worn by the young female elite in the most crucial village ceremony organized by the old male elite it also markedly supports the traditional sociopolitical hierarchy of the rank system in this local society. Unlike Weiner, I think that high-ranking women created this heirloom cloth only after, and not before the hierarchization of the village society had evolved. Apart from its important religious and esthetic meaning and function, the beaded sarong thus helped to legitimate and to reify the rank system of nobles, commoners and slaves. Heirloom and hierarchy were thus firmly linked.

---

[9] This ceremony concerned the inauguration of a new bishop. Ndate, personal communication.

With independence rank systems were formally abolished in Indonesia, and particularly the political autonomy of village communities. Moreover, the Indonesian government acknowledges Catholicism as one of the official religions, whereas the traditional belief system is not. In the process of nation building certain elements of the local cultures were absorbed in the national culture, expressed by the motto 'unity in diversity' (*bhinneka tunggal ika*). Singular religious expressions of regional ethnic groups thus have become particular forms of Indonesian performing arts. This has also happened with the ceremony of the rain dance. With the erosion of the traditional sociopolitical hierarchy and belief system the ceremony of the rain dance changed from a local ritual to a kind of national oriented state ritual. With it the beaded sarong as an heirloom generally has lost part of its former sacred character and has become more secular. Interestingly, its function of sustaining a sociopolitical order seems to continue, though in a wider frame.

REFERENCES

Arndt, P.P. S.V.D. 1944
> Der Kult der Lionesen (Mittel-Flores). In *Annali Lateranensi* 3: 155-182.

Bühler, Alfred, Urs Ramseyer, and Nicole Ramseyer-Gygi 1975
> *Patola und Geringsing.* Basel: Museum für Völkerkunde.

Geirnaert-Martin, Danielle C. 1992
> *The Woven Land of Laboya. Socio-Cosmic Ideas and Values in West Sumba, Eastern Indonesia.* Leiden: Centre of Non-Western Studies.

Hamilton, Roy W. (ed.) 1994
> *Gift of the Cotton Maiden. Textiles of Flores and the Solor Islands.* Los Angeles: UCLA Fowler Museum of Cultural History.

Heringa, Rens 1993
> Textiles, Land and Regeneration in an East-Javanese Area. In *Weaving Patterns of Life. Indonesian Textile Symposium 1991.* Ed. by Marie-Louise Nabholz-Kartaschoff, Ruth Barnes and David J. Stuart-Fox. Basel: Museum of Ethnography. Pp. 155–170.

Howell, Signe 1990
> Husband/Wife or Brother/Sister as the Key Relationship in Lio Kinship and Sociosymbolic Relations. In *Ethnos* 55: 248-259.

Howell, Signe 1995
> The Lio House: Building, Category, Idea, Value. In *About the House: Lévi-Strauss and Beyond.* Ed. by Stephan Hugh-Jones and Janet Carsten. Cambridge: Cambridge University Press. Pp. 149–169.

de Jong, Willemijn 1994
> Cloth Production and Change in a Lio Village. In *Gift of the Cotton Maiden: Textiles of Flores and the Solor Islands.* Ed. by Roy Hamilton. Los Angeles: UCLA Fowler Museum of Cultural History. Pp. 210-227.

de Jong, Willemijn 1995
> Cloth as Marriage Gifts. Change in Exchange Among the Lio of Flores. In *Contact, Crossover, Continuity. Proceedings of the Fourth Biennial Symposium of the Textile Society of America 1994.* Los Angeles: Textile Society of America, Inc. Pp. 169-180.

de Jong, Willemijn 1996
> Geschlechtersymmetrie in einer Brautpreisgesellschaft. Die Stoffproduzentinnen der Lio in Indonesien. Habilitationsschrift, Universität Zürich.

de Jong, Willemijn n.d.
> The Role of Women in Cloth Production and Exchange and the Impact on Household Relations and Social Networks (Flores). In *Indonesian Women in the Household and Beyond: Reconstructing the Boundaries.* Ed. by Juliette Koning, Marleen Nolten, Janet Rodenburg and Ratna Saptari. Leiden: KITLV Press. Forthcoming.

Kahn Majlis, Brigitte 1991
> *Gewebte Botschaften - Indonesische Traditionen im Wandel. Woven Messages - Indonesian Textile Traditions in Course of Time.* Hildesheim: Roemer-Museum.

Maxwell, Robyn J. 1983
> Ceremonial Textiles of the Ngada of Eastern Indonesia. *Connaissance des Arts Tribaux* 18. Geneva: Musée Barbier-Müller.

Maxwell, Robyn J. 1990
> *Textiles of Southeast Asia. Tradition, Trade and Transformation.* Melbourne: Oxford University Press.

Ndate, P. Aloysius 1988
> *Pentingnya Upacara Tarian Tradisional Mure Pada Masyarakat Nggela.* Skripsi, Sekolah Tinggi Filsafat Katolik Ledalero.

Niessen, Sandra 1984
> Textiles are Female ... but what is Femaleness? Toba Batak Textiles in the Indonesian Field of Ethnological Study. In *Unity in Diversity. Indonesia as a Field of Anthropological Study.* Ed. by P.E. de Josselin de Jong. Dordrecht: Foris Publications. Pp. 63-83.

Orinbao, P. Sareng 1992
> *Seni Tenun Suatu Segi Kebudayaan Orang Flores.* Nita, Flores: Seminari Tinggi St. Paulus Ledalero.

Prior, John Mansford 1988
> *Church and Marriage in an Indonesian Village. A Study of Customary and Church Marriage Among the Ata Lio of Central Flores, Indonesia, as a Paradigm of the Ecclesial Interrelationship between Village and Institutional Catholicism.* Frankfurt/M., Bern, New York, Paris: Lang Verlag.

Sugishima, Takashi 1994
> Double Descent, Alliance, and Botanical Metaphors Among the Lionese of Central Flores. In *Bijdragen tot de Taal-, Land- en Volkenkunde* 150: 146-170.

Weiner, Annette B. 1987
> Toward a Theory of Gender Power: An Evolutionary Perspective. In *The Gender of Power. A Symposium.* Ed. by Monique Leyenaar et al. Leiden: VENA. Pp. 41-77.

Weiner, Annette B. 1989
> Why Cloth? Wealth, Gender, and Power in Oceania. In *Cloth and Human Experience.* Ed. by Annette B. Weiner and Jane Schneider. Washington, London: Smithsonian Institution Press. Pp. 33-72.

Weiner, Annette B. 1992
> *Inalienable Possessions. The Paradox of Keeping-While-Giving.* Berkeley, Los Angeles, Oxford: University of California Press.

Yamaguchi, Masao 1990
> The Cosmological Position of Women in Two Societies: The Case of the Lio and the Jukun. In *Journal of Asian and African Studies* 39: 1–12.

HEIRLOOM AND MALE ANCESTORS
The flowered Kain Kembangan of Kerek, East Java

by Rens Heringa
Pieter de la Courtstraat 23 - 2313 BP Leiden - The Netherlands

Introduction

A range of handspun cotton textile types, in earlier times possibly made throughout Java, continue to be manufactured by the village women of Kerek, a subdistrict 30 kilometers southwest of the ancient north coast port of Tuban.[1] Cloth made in the Tuban area was mentioned by the first Dutch travellers as early as the late 16th century. Soon after Tuban harbor lost its importance to international trade and its hinterland became a backwater. The weaving enclave, enclosed by the mountains of the Northern Limestone Ridge, which offer access through a single entrance road, generated little economic interest from the outside world and could thus continue in its old ways. One of the culture's most striking features is its intricate textile system, in which the many types of locally-made cloths are combined with a few imported textiles to function as clothing and ritual objects (see ao. Heringa 1994).

During the past two decades, however, this system has undergone numerous changes, as the outside world has finally encroached upon the area. Men and both sexes of the younger generation now mostly wear shopbought clothing. Young girls, in particular those belonging to the elite families, follow secondary schooling, and will no more acquire the complicated skills of weaving and batiking the cloths with the highest social and ceremonial value which used to be the prerogative of their social group. Still, a large number of older married women continues to express through the colors, motifs and technique of their home-made hipwrapper their village of residence, their age, and the social rank acquired through marriage.

The *Kain Kembangan* : Visual and Symbolic Aspects

The highly valued and technically most complex of the textiles woven by the village women of Kerek, the *kain kembangan* - literally "flowered cloth" - will be the subject of this paper.[2] The handspun cotton cloth shows a tabby base in a variety of stripes or checks in blue-black, red and some white, sometimes enlivened with accents of a brighter shade of blue. The cloth's special feature, as indicated by its name, are the small floral motifs overlaid on this base. The textile is woven in two different sizes, the first intended for use as ankle-length hipwrapper for women and - originally - men. The second, a long narrow piece of material, is intended to be sewn into a men's jacket (*kelambi*).

First to be considered are the visual aspects of the *kain kembangan* as a symbolic expression of its relation to the main status group in the stratified social sytem of Kerek, the owners of inherited agricultural land. The production process of the cloth by the women of this elite group forms the second aspect of my paper, which will be concluded by the function of *kain kembangan* as heirloom property during the marriage ritual.

Kain kembangan and Land

The main and most immediate symbolic link is that between the *kain kembangan* and the *tegal,* non-irrigated agricultural land, as indicated by the terminology used by the villagers for the separate design sections of the hipwrapper. The center field is called *pelemahan,* cultivated land, a derivation from *lemah* (soil, land) [FIG 1]. The term for the selvages is *galengan,* also used to denote the low earthen banks edging the field. The dense overlay of flowers covering the central field is related to the flowering crop growing on the land. Near each end, in the so-called *tumpal* sections, the pattern changes into wider spaced floral bands. The weavers view these floral bands as a metaphor for the trees planted at each end of the field.

Male and Female

The second - though by non-weavers easily overlooked - aspect of *kain kembangan* are its two technically separate but symbolically related forms: in the first the floral decorations are generated by warp floats [FIG 2], in the second by a continuous suplementary weft . The women themselves express the distinction as follows: each row of the single type of flowers following the warp is compared to an unbroken line(age) of male landholders. These cloths are therefore intended for male wear. The pattern of the base is adjusted to the gender distinction as well: *bakal kelambi,* fabric made into jackets for men show contrasting warp stripes only. On hipwrappers patterned in the warp, the clearly contrasting warp stripes predominate over barely visible weft stripes in alternating picks of black and red.

In the second type, the rows of flowers generated by the extra weft are interrupted by the selvages, seemingly starting anew at each pick [FIG 3]. The weavers describe the weft stripes as "coming from the side, like women who marry in", which designates the cloth as female dress. Generally, hipwrappers of this type have a balanced checked base, with each check enclosing two alternating types of flowers. Is it too farfetched to suggest that the two flowers refer to the sons and daughters borne by the wearer of the cloth? The suggestion appears to be corroborated by the pattern names of the female cloths, as many of them are named for flowers of trees. Trees in general are conceptually related to men, while flowers are a metaphor for descendants. One example is *kembang jati,* flowers of the teak tree. It is one of the few forest trees which sheds its leaves in the dry season. With the first rains it blossoms on the bare branches, to the villagers a sign of abundant fertility. As the tree grows in most grave yards it is also linked to the ancestors. The pattern names for the male cloths all include the term *batur,* which means follower but also descendant, indicating another link to a direct line of descent from father to son.

Kain Kembangan, Statification and Age

The floral decoration which forms an extra layer on top of the tabby base inspires the link of the *kain kembangan* to the upper layer of the community, the landholding elite of the village. Originally only they, the affluent members of the community, could afford the shopbought yarn for the floral decoration. All other textile materials are products of the fields and easy available to any villager without financial expenditure. While the majority of *kain kembangan* combines handspun cotton yarn for the base cloth with finer quality shopbought cotton thread for the floral decorations, a few antique weft-patterned textiles were found to be adorned with silk. At present not used anymore, the precious material was only encountered on cloths carefully kept by the pinnacle of the village hierachy, those who not only trace descent from the settlers of the village, making them owners of land reclaimed from the wilderness, but who also have served in the elected village leadership for many generations. These village leaders are landholders twice over as, apart from their family land, they are entitled the right to cultivate a field of communal land *(tanah bengkok).* The choice between cotton or silk to delineate social gradations among the elite is even further refined by that between two shades of silk, yellow (or its recent replacements, mercerized yellow cotton or gold metallic thread) and white (or silver). A village head's wife was entitled to wear the golden yellow, his helpers' wives used the silvery white.

A distinction between age groups is in Indonesian textiles generally effected by the use of bright shades of red and indigo for the younger generation, and gradually darkening colors for the aged. The *kain kembangan,* with its contrasting bright and dark faces, offers a special possibility. It is customary for young people to wear the bright face of the cloth on the outside, while elderly persons prefer to show the darker side.

Residential Patterns

In recapitulation, the non-verbal messages enclosed in the *kain kembangan* link it to male-owned land, and to the different status levels and generations among the landholding elite. The cloth thus discloses a certain patrilineal bias which is corroborated by its female type, which visualizes women as in-married outsiders who bear sons and daughters for the husband's group. This image indeed conforms to the residential model of the village elite. A landholder lives in a large single-family house with his wife and unmarried children, at most giving shelter to his widowed mother or unmarried female blood relatives. All children marry out, except one of the sons who is chosen to succeed his father as owner of the house and most of the land. This is in marked contrast with the pattern adhered to by the rest of the village population. As a general rule, they live in large family compounds belonging to the eldest woman, whose husband has married-in. Her daughters also bring their husbands to live in or close to the main house of the compound.

Newly-made *Kain Kembangan* as Alienable Goods

In Kerek, no cloth is ever made by a single person from start to finish. A newly-made textile is considered the result of a regenerative group process and denoted as child or grandchild of an earlier cloth belonging to the group. Evidently therefore, textiles do not belong to individuals. It is noteworthy that the group of owners only consists of the blood kin members of a house or compound, excluding those who have married in. This distinction can be clarified by the local concepts regarding these two types of kin. Blood relations are referred to as *awaké déwé* (one's own body); those related by marriage as *wong liya*, (others, strangers). The relationship among the former is defined as *momong* (giving each other loving care), the term also used for a mother's care for her baby. Under all circumstances, never expecting anything in return, one should provide one's *awaké* with *sandang*, *pangan* and *papan* (clothing, food and shelter). In practice this entails that textiles are automatically and - as the women insist - without any ritual practice, provided for the blood kin of the group. The association with the *wong liya*, however, is referred to as *mung dolan* (literally: no more than play). This game among people related by marriage is subject to strict rules of exchange. One of the aspects regulated in this manner is the exchange of textiles. Thus, in-married husbands offer part of the proceeds of their inherited family land in return for clothing for personal use. How do the *kain kembangan* function in this system?

The matrilocal compound, in which mature women abound, provides the ideal situation for the joint production of textiles. The patrilocal residential pattern of the elite, however, has a scarcity of women, making it difficult to combine all textile tasks under one roof. Although raw cotton and plain handspun yarn can be obtained in the market, in exchange for products of the field or money, *kain kembangan* can only be woven by women of the elite. Only experienced weavers can master the complex and extremely labor intensive technique with its many variations. Traditionally, those wives of the elite who have gained expertise, spend much of their time filling the needs of their families. A live-in widowed or unmarried aunt often makes a welcome contribution. The *kain kembangan* needed as gifts from the husband's group may be ordered from less fortunate single women of elite backgrounds who make their living as professional weavers. Previously, the use of a house or part of the harvest was offered in return. Nowadays payment in cash has become the norm. While recently-made *kain kembangan,* that still accord with the traditional prescripts, have become rare and their money value has risen, all of these cloths can be used as gift or even sold for the benefit of the group. They can therefore be said to be alienable goods.

Heirloom *Kain Kembangan* as *Simpenan*

A special source of textiles are the heirlooms kept in the wooden treasure chest in the rice barn. These sacred textiles, related to the ancestors, are part of the *simpenan,* the "secret property" of the house. It consists of locally-made cloths, in particular *kain kembangan,* an occasional antique silk cloth imported from India, Chinese porcelains, and sacred weapons, all inherited from previous generations of the husband's family. These cloths can at most temporarily be given away which denotes them as inalienable property. Only important ritual occasions, a son's wedding or circumcision, merit the appearance of the precious heirlooms. Often too fragile to be worn, the textiles are present as a sign of the social status and the unbroken lineage of the group who owns them.

One particular ritual function specifically links the *kain kembangan* to Islam. During the Muslim fasting month, a silk-flowered version from the heirloom hoard is prescribed as covering for the huge ceremonial signal drum in the house of the village head. Thus the drum, symbol of the ancestors of the pre-Islamic period, is temporarily silenced, giving precedence to the foreign creed.

Kain Kembangan and the Marriage Ritual

The *kain kembangan*'s ultimate, and at present extremely rare role occurs about one week before the actual wedding of the son who will inherit the house, when the cloth forms an indispensable part of the *sasrahan,* the goods carried in procession to the bride's home to *ngrayuk* (entice) her into being taken away from her compound to take up the lonely and unstable position of the in-married daughter-in-law. The offering consists of kitchen utensils, furniture, gold jewelry and the *koper,* a large basket plaited from palm leaves, containing a maximum of 60 textiles. Some have been newly made by the groom's female blood kin, many have been ordered, but the most valued contribution has been taken from the heirloom hoard. Absolutely indispensable are the two types of *kain kembangan,* representing the groom's male and female ancestors.

In descriptions of Javanese wedding rituals, the *sasrahan* is generally referred to as a gift to the bride's parents, in return for their daughter and her descendants (ao. Mayer 1897 II:360; Bratawidjaja 1985:13). While the public procession to the bride's house may be suggestive of this conclusion, the villagers of Kerek denote the ritual as a show of force. In this case, a more appropriate translation of *sasrahan* appears "surrender [of the bride]", as the girl will soon be taken away to the groom's house. The wedding is moreover not organized by her parents, the usual procedure, but by his. Clearly in Tuban, the goods were never intended as a gift, as, in practice, only a few newly-made textiles are chosen for personal use by the bride or by her close female blood kin. The bulk will eventually be returned to its hiding place in the rice barn. Especially the *kain kembangan,* whether old or new, are the inalienable possessions to be inherited by the younger generation in the male line, like the land the cloths represent. Moreover, in case of a divorce, the wife shall lose her rights to any part of the *sasrahan.* Muslim law also denies her the right to take her children.

On the wedding day, untill a few decades ago, the bride first appeared in a *songket,* a red gold-flowered cloth from Bali. This "foreign" textile, though similar in technique to the female *kain kembangan,* is said to have marked her as a stranger or *wong liya.* After the actual wedding, a change of clothing presented the new pair in a coupled set of heirloom *kain kembangan.* The groom wore a jacket with the pattern running along the warp, while the bride was provided with a hip wrapper adorned with the same floral pattern in the weft, thus marking her incorporation into the house of her husband.

Conclusions

It can be concluded that the visual aspects of the *kain kembangan,* and its function as inalienable heirloom during rituals, epitomize the cloth as the metaphor for the landholding elite of Kerek. Although the cloth is encountered in a male and a female form, the latter appears subordinate to the first. The patterns on the male cloth have predominant male properties, whereas its female aspects have been toned down to the extent of being almost invisible. On the female cloth, however, next to female weft stripes, male warp stripes are consistently prominent. Moreover, the men wear *kain kembangan,* made into a jacket, on the conceptually higher upper part of the body and - formerly - as a hipwrapper, while women only use the hipwrapper.

All *kain kembangan* worn during rituals by the wives, are temporarily provided from the heirloom treasure owned by her husband's family. For personal use newly-made *kain kembangan* are made available to her from the husband's family store. This is at variance with the custom in most other areas in Indonesia, where textile gifts are provided by the side of the bride. The flowered cloths remain at the woman's disposal as long as she is available to her husband, in return for the flowers she brings forth, the children. The case of the *kain kembangan* eloquently expresses the Javanese bilineal social pattern, in a form modified by the elite group's male-biased views, which have been intensified by Muslim influences.

Notes

1. Fieldwork in Kerek (1978-1991) was supported in 1989-1990 by PRIS, Leyden University, and conducted under the auspices of the Indonesian Academy of Sciences).

2. See Heringa 1993 for the relation between the *kain kembangan* and batik cloth, and the agricultural cycle.

Bibliography

Bratawidjaja, Thomas Wiyasa

1985 - Upacara perkawinan Adat Tawa. Sinar Harapan: Jakarta

Heringa, Rens

1993 - "Tilling the Cloth and Weaving the Land. Textiles, Land and Regeneration in an East-Javanese Area", in Marie-Louise Nabholz-Kartaschoff et al. (eds.), Weaving Patterns of Life. Indonesian Textile Symposium 1991:155-176, Museum of Ethnography: Basel.

1994 - Spiegels van ruimte en tijd. Textiel uit Tuban. Museon: The Hague

Mayer, L.Th.

1897 - Een blik in het Javaansche Volksleven. 2 Vols. E.J. Brill: Leiden

HEIRLOOM CLOTH AND SOCIAL ORGANIZATION
The ceremonial *kain sandang gobo* of the Minangkabau, West Sumatra

LINDA HANSSEN
Department of Textiles, Museum of Ethnology Rotterdam,
Willemskade 25, 3016 DM Rotterdam, The Netherlands.

INTRODUCTION

The aim of this paper is to explore the role of the ceremonial shouldercloth —*kain sandang gobo*— as an inalienable possession in the social organization of the village society of Balai Cacang[1]. To this end I shall examine the *kain sandang gobo* for its several visual aspects and symbolic meaning, and as an heirloom cloth in the *harto pusako*[2]. The *kain sandang gobo* as a means of expressing rank and hierarchy will be explored by analyzing its role in the wedding-ceremony. The results will contribute to the aim of this panel, which is to come to a comparison of the meaning of highly valued locally made heirloom cloth among three ethnic groups in Indonesia.

THE *KAIN SANDANG GOBO* OF BALAI CACANG

The most important ceremonial cloth of women of the matrilineal Minangkabau society of Balai Cacang —a small hamlet located 6 km north of Payakumbuh in the centre of the Padang Highlands— is the *kain sandang gobo,* exclusively worn during wedding-ceremonies of the highest level. This red chequered cotton shouldercloth, densely decorated with gold thread, is only produced in this traditional weaving village for the use of its own inhabitants. It is combined with a head- and hipcloth and a blouse into a costume set called *pakaian sandang gobo*. It is completed with adjusting jewelry, shoes, make-up, hairstyle and accessories. Every item is carefully detailed and prescribed by the *adat*, which is the Minangkabau custom, tradition and rules for living. As such it is one of the fifteen costume sets that are worn by women during rites de passage as I experienced them during my fieldwork in Balai Cacang in 1993 (Hanssen, 1995).

---

[1] Weiner (1992:33) gives the following definition for an inalienable possession: *"What makes a possession inalienable is its exclusive and cumulative identity with a particular series of owners through time. Its history is authenticated by fictive or true genealogies, origin myths, sacred ancestors, and gods. In this way, inalienable possessions are transcendent treasures to be guarded against all the exigencies that might force their loss."*

[2] In the anthropological literature it is pointed out that heirloom cloth in South Pacific societies which is kept rather then given becomes "inalienable". As such, cloth can express rank and hierarchy in societies. It enlarges the integrity of the individual as well as of the group (Weiner 1989:35).

MINANGKABAU TEXTILES OF THE LIMO PULUH KOTO PROVINCE

Most textiles of the Minangkabau are characterized by abundant use of gold thread, so densely that the ground fabric is hardly to be seen. These cloths are called *kain songket* owing to the use of gold thread, but also to the supplementary weft technique. Like everywhere in Indonesia and South-east Asia the history of textiles follows the history of trade. Through its extremely strategic position on trade-routes in Southeast Asia and an abundance of natural sources —such as the enormous gold supplies which gave Sumatra the name of Golden Island— first the coastal region underwent the influences of migration and trade-contacts with China, India, Portugal, the Middle East and Holland. At a later stage the province of Limo Puluh Koto in the Padang Highlands got acquainted with new dye- and weaving techniques, colors, materials and designs. Silk, gold- and silver thread and the supplementary weft were incorporated in their weaving tradition. The locally made *kain songket* combined with imported cloths are part of an extensive textile system of the Minang people. The *songket*-cloths are considered to be of a higher status than imported cloths. As such they form a mirror of the people's worldview which is strongly imbued by *adat*.

PRESENT SITUATION

The traditional textiles have always been —and still are— dedicated to ceremonial use. The ceremonies are mostly *adat*-related, except for some Islamic ones. *Adat* prescribes the proper dress and although *adat* is flexible and adaptive to changes, the ceremonial cloths have not changed. This does not imply that modern developments did not find their way to the village people. Satellite-dishes and Western clothing are common in the Padang Highlands. As opposed to the changes in education, economy, and family life, the Minangkabau men and women —young and old— partake in ceremonial *adat*-life as often as their presence is required. However, the weaving of *songket* is liable to change. Young girls nowadays are not interested in weaving anymore, because education opens better perspectives for their future. In the village of Balai Cacang, weaving belongs to the female domain. At the time of my field research twelve female weavers still practiced weaving of ceremonial cloths.

THE *KAIN SANDANG GOBO*

The most valuable and technically most intricate cloth in the range of locally woven *songket*-cloths is *kain sandang gobo*. The word *gobo* derives from *gaba*, which means to string garlands, and refers to the row of *tanjung* —blue lotus-flowers or flowers of the coconut tree. In the wedding ceremony of the most affluent, it is worn by recently married women and women with young children. The complex designs are produced by the best qualified weavers, the eldest women. The *gobo*-cloth is characterised by a checked centrefield in red with black and white. The endpanels and borders along the selvage show motifs in gold thread. Out of a warplength of 550 cm the woven cloth is cut into two halves and sewn together.

THE VISUAL AND SYMBOLIC ASPECTS OF THE *GOBO*

Kain sandang gobo and Land

There is a clear twopartition —centerfield and borders— which is common throughout South-east Asia. The checked centerfield is seen as a mirror of the agricultural lands (Summerfield 1991:54 fig.50, Kartiwa 1979:59)[3]. The *sawah* belong to the ancestral properties which are of essential importance for the female descent group in providing food and surplus money. Men work the land of their mothers and sisters, but not the land of their wives' relatives. Only married women wear this type of cloth.

Kain sandang gobo and Age

The *gobo* is woven in a deep red color, with in the centre a combination of black and white warp and weft threads forming the checks. This red color combined with the large quantity of gold is the color for the young married women between twenty and thirty years of age with one or two young children. As such it marks the procreative stage of a woman, which is essential for the continuity of her descent group. When women grow older the intensity of red is fading by using more black, blue and white, and silver thread instead of gold. Comparable color symbolism in relation to age is found throughout the Indonesian archipelago.

The *gobo* is tied under the arm and across the shoulder, held together by a knot on top of the right shoulder, so that the decorated gold patterns are best visible. Wearing shouldercloths in this way is called *bengkak* (swollen) and meant only for married women[4]. Because of its big size and the placing so high on the body, the schouldercloth is the most significant part of a woman's *adat*-costume.

Kain sandang gobo and Stratification

In the *gobo* we can differentiate various layers; the ground fabric in plain weave shows a decoration in the centre with checks; the rich gold decoration of the motifs in supplementary weft and the finish of the edgings in a crocheted goldlace. The more layers and additional decorations, the higher the status of the wearer. Special attention deserve the endpanels, which are

---

[3] Kartiwa and Sanday state that this centerfield is accentuating the centre of power, which is embodied by borders with small motifs as protection. Village people are surrounded and tied down to *adat* (1984:21). Concerning the centerfield another explanation is given by Heringa: the chequered centerfield represents the *sawah* and the dry agricultural grounds. The dry land represents the woman, on which the man will seed the new plants (Heringa 1994:22).

[4] *buhul santak* (knot-untie); name for the way in which the knot is tied and easily untied. It symbolizes that a woman is tied to somebody or married and she is experienced in many things. For the Payakumbuh people this knot contains an extra meaning; it is the way one solves one's problems; although some decisions have already been made but are not acceptable, one can always change them (Kartiwa 1979:65).

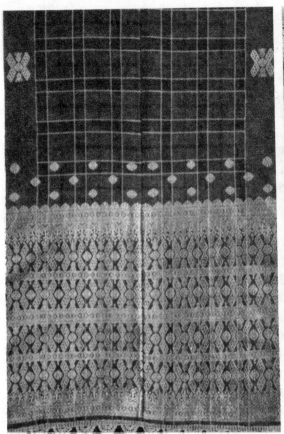

Kain sandang gobo

Detail of *kain sandang gobo*

Woman dressed in *pakaian sandang gobo* (second of the right),

Balai Cacang, 1993

densely filled with gold patterns with a continous warp, which usually gives a cloth a higher value then one with a discontinous warp.

Silk for the *gobo* was common in former days. These cloths still exist in the heirloom. Today there is a differentiation in quality, only in a small detail, but women do know it. Weavers use shop-bought cotton, *'katun'* for their clientele, but when weaving for their lineage members they choose a fine quality cotton called *'lenan'*. Silk is hardly used anymore, only on demand.

Not every descent group possesses a *kain sandang gobo*. Only the well-to-do own or are able to order a new *sandang gobo*. Otherwise it is borrowed from kin or weavers by paying in uncooked rice, raw eggs and cake. On account of the recent increase in nuclear families and a higher standard of living the demand of *kain sandang gobo* strongly increased: in 1993 it took three to five months to order a *gobo*-cloth.

The *kain sandang gobo* and the Male and Female Aspects

The *gobo* is woven by women for the use of women. As such it can be seen as female. However, it has male aspects as well. The loom and the weaving-comb are produced and carved by men. As such they form part of the heirloom and are inherited by the daughters. Mattiebelle Gittinger (1979:113) suggests that cloth decorated with gold thread possesses male properties. In relation to the 'consistent' pattern of exchange, she refers to the situation of bride-givers in Indonesia presenting textiles to family of the groom in order to accentuate the woman's position to the bride-takers. Bride-takers, though, return products of men's work, such as knives, cattle and jewelry (1979:107). In Gittinger's opinion *songket* textiles may have functioned more as male metal-ware rather than women's textiles.

In the matrilineal Minangkabau situation we must speak about bridegroom-givers and -takers, because the men are exchanged. Nowadays Balai Cacang no longer knows an exchange pattern as such, although Toorn reports in 1881 that there used to be a 'mixed' pattern of giving in Minang society (cited in Gittinger 1979:108). The groom and his female relatives presented textiles to the bride and her family; the bride and her family offered a set of symbolic *kain*, one of gold and silk, the other an imported cloth. Toorn states that in this matrilocal society the textiles symbolised the groom's welcome into the bride's house. If the marriage was due to end before there were children the set of *kain* were returned. The lack of further details on the type of *songket* cloth makes it impossible to look for any male details of the cloth.

The motifs on the *gobo* show rows of geometrical motifs. Among them stars filled with *tanjuang* flowers (*bintang bungo tanjuang*) and men-like figures with sticks in between them —*tirai*— which means "curtain". The weavers were not able to give an explanation. According to them it came from the ancestors —*turun menurun*. Flowers have indeed a female connotation in Sumatran symbolism (Heringa 1993:21). The row of men-like figures might symbolize the descendants of a the matrilineal descent group. The curtain is found on top of the nuptial bed, and might stand for fertility.

KAIN SANDANG GOBO AS AN HEIRLOOM

When discussing the function of the *sandang gobo* as an heirloom, it is essential to look at the social organization of the Minangkabau. The Minangkabau are organised matrilineally: group membership and property are inherited from mother to daughter. Women live with their families in the matrilineal longhouse —*rumah gadang*, while married sons live with their wives' relatives.

The collective properties of a matrilineal descent group are called the *harto pusako*, ancestral property which is inherited mainly by women. These properties are essential for a descent group, because they represent the property of the ancestors as well as the property for the future generation. To these properties belong the agricultural lands (*sawah* and gardens), livestock, ponds, houses, jewelry, ceremonial costumes, gold and money. Next to these material aspects, titles and *adat*-sayings are important. The latter category is inherited by the male kin, the former category mainly by women.

These goods are especially important to women, because they are greatly attached to them. Von Benda-Beckmann even speaks about it as *harto padoesi* "women's properties" (in Courtens & Thoonen 1990:18). A special category is formed by the *pusako gaib*, the ceremonial clothing for men and women, completed with jewelry and accessories.

Harto pusako is collective property which is not divisible and not to be sold. Women have usefruct over a part of it. The oldest woman of the lineage, *Bundo Kanduang,* controls the *harto pusako*; she keeps 'the key to the treasure-chest.' Land produce, such as rice, is first meant for the own sake of the lineage members; surplus proceeds flow back to the *harto pusako*.

The *sandang gobo* as such has a high esteem in the *harto pusako*, it is the most expensive cloth. Together with the other cloths it shows the cloth wealth as assets of a lineage. The old *gobo* is not actively worn anymore but kept in a treasure-box. On special occasions like a *penghulu*[5]-installation it is displayed. As such a *gobo* can have the status of an inalienable possession.'

A second group of properties belong to the *harto pencarian*. This is individual property gained by a husband and a wife separately. In a marriage these goods stay separate and will be inherited by the husband's and wife's lineage, respectively. Owing to pressure of the Islamic movement the gained properties of the father are inherited by his children. According to Von Benda-Beckmann, goods inherited by the daughters will flow back to the *harto pusako* of the mother's lineage (in Postel-Coster 1985:31). For cloth wealth including the *gobo* cloth it means that it starts its life as an alienable possession and once it is part of the *harto pusaka* it becomes inalienable.

A third group of heirloom is called *harto suarang* (common property). These goods are acquired by a couple and are not divisible. In case of death the goods are divided by the partner and the lineage of the deceased.

---

[5] *adat* title for the head of a lineage

The function of the *gobo* in the latter two groups is quite noticable as an 'alienable property.' Once it is adjusted to the *pusako gaib* of the lineage it becomes inalienable, normally after one generation.

THE *KAIN SANDANG GOBO* AND THE MARRIAGE RITUAL

Among *adat*-ceremonies marriage is one of the biggest events in village life. It offers the possibility to start new alliances or to enforce matrilinial kinship. The persons involved in a marriage-ceremony form part of large social networks. Such a ceremony gives the opportunity to display economical and social status of a descent group and to show how large the group is one can appeal to for the preparations. A marriage-ceremony is mainly a women's affair: they perform the role of organisers or guests. It is the mother of the bride and her kin (sisters, brothers, mother and aunts) and the *penghulu* who determine the level of the wedding.

In Minang-*adat* there are three levels, each prescribing the dress code and jewelry code, the length of the ceremony, and the food code[6]. Each level indicates a different amount of status and wealth. In the highest level the most important cloth is the *kain sandang gobo* in the costume set of the *pakaian sandang gobo*; the celebration lasts six to seven days and a waterbuffalo is slaughtered. The celebration takes place in the longhouse of the bride. The first time the *gobo* plays a role is when the bride's mother invites the guests personally by visiting each woman and offering them *sirih* which she carries in her pouch —*unciang*— under her shouldercloth. By decleering the wedding to be of highest level she indicates the use of costume sets of the highest level, including the highest proportion of *songket*-cloth, with the *gobo* as the most prominent one. She expresses the high status of her descent group. Furthermore the *gobo* expresses the level of the dress code, which consists of fifteen costume combinations for every ritual during the ceremony.

This dress code is based on two principles; the first and the most important on affinal ties and the second on individual aspects of the wearer. Groups related by marriage can be divided into the group that already provided a bridegroom to the same lineage in the past —called *bako*, the bridegroom-givers and the group that received a bridegroom from the descent group —called *sumandan*, the bridegroom-takers. Compared with the patrilineal situation when brides are exchanged and the bride-givers have a higher status, it is not the same with the actual group of the exchanged bridegroom. They are of a lower status. To show respect to group of the bride they will overdress. The female kin will wear the costume sets with the rich goldthreaded cloth. In the meantime the group of the bride pay respect by dressing lower than their high status entitles them. Their costume sets consist of few *songket*-cloth but more *batik* and *kain Bugis*. At a full-blown wedding

---

[6] These prescriptions are written down by the *penghulu* of each region. Clothing of women is called Bundu Kanduang, the name which refers also to the oldest women of a lineage and the ancestral mother. Costumes of Payakumbuh are called Bundu Kanduang Payakumbuah.

Wedding of the third level; sister of the bridegroom (on his left) dressed in *pakaian sandang gobo*, Tarok 1993

one may witness about fifteen costume sets, each telling the relationship of the wearer to the group of the bride or groom. Within this group affiliation also the individual status of a woman can be read: married/unmarried; age; number of children; married daughters; number of grandchildren.

Returning to the *sandang gobo*, one can see that it is worn by women of the lineage of the bridegroom on the day of the delivery of the bridegroom to his bride by his relatives —*batagak penghulu*/installing the *penghulu* rite. It is worn by his married sister or aunt in her twenties or thirties with young children. They stand beside him in front of the nuptial seat.

CONCLUSION

In considering the female or male properties of the *gobo* I have shown that this cloth is merely female-related. For it is woven by women, for women and worn and bought by women. Its most important function is that of dress, which symbolizes the status of a descent group and shows group affiliation of the wearer, but also her individual status. The symbolic meaning of the combination of gold thread and textile, which is quite obvious in other societies, cannot be explored. The men-like figures on the cloth might implicate male properties, however.

The role of the *gobo* in exchange does not exist anymore. The exchange pattern at present is merely to be found in the exchanging of food and paying the *mas kawin*, the bridegroom-price. The descent group of bridegroom presents raw food, such as fish, meat and uncooked rice, while the lineage of the bride offers cooked rice, meat and cakes. The most important issue of a marriage is that the continuity of their matrilineal group is being taken care of. The important role is played by the young woman in her reproductive period of life. Not by the man; he is the medium, brought in from the outside as producer for his wife's future lineage. The symbolic meaning of the exchange of food is that the raw food is turned into cooked food, which can be seen as a medium for affirming social relations for future reproduction. (Ng 1987:117)

Kain sandang gobo is therefore a visual representation of the continuity of a lineage by letting the kinwomen who are in their most procreative stage of life wear it. As such it shows the status of a descent group and will therefore continue its life as an inalienable possession.

REFERENCES

Courtens, I en L. Thoonen
1990   Bundo Kanduang; wijze vrouwen van West-Sumatra. (Bundo
                 Kanduang: wise women of West-Sumatra)
                 Nijmegen: Katholieke Universiteit

Gittinger, M.J
1979   Splendid Symbols: textiles and traditions in Indonesia.
                 New York: Oxford University Press.

Hanssen, L
1995   Ceremoniële doeken van de Minangkabau: metafoor van sociale
                 organisatie (Ceremonial cloth of the Minangkabau: methaphor for
                 social organization). Unpublished M.A.-thesis.
                 State University Leiden/Utrecht

Heringa, R
1993   Een schitterende geschiedenis. Weefsels en batiks van Palembang en
                 Djambi. (A splendid history. Cloths and batiks of Palembang and
                 Djambi) A.Boer (ed.)
                 Den Haag: Museon.
1994   Spiegels van ruimte en tijd. Textiel uit Tuban. (Mirrors of space and
                 time. Textile from Tuban) A. Boer (ed.)
                 Den Haag: Museon.

Kartiwa, S
1979   The social functions of the kain songket Minangkabau. In: Indonesian
                 Textiles; Irene Emery Roundtable on Museum Textiles.
                 Washington: The Textile Museum.

Ng, C.S.H
1987   The weaving of prestige. Village women's representations of the social
                 categories of Minangkabau society.
                 Unpublished Ph.D.-thesis. Australian National University.

Sanday, P en S. Kartiwa
1984   Cloth and custom in West-Sumatra; the codification of Minangkabau
                 worldview. In: Expedition, volume 26 number 4. The University
                 Museum Magazine of Archeology/Anthropology.
                 Philadelphia: University of Pennsylvania.

Summerfield, A & J
1991   Fabled Cloths of Minangkabau
                 Santa Barbara: Santa Barbara Museum of Art

Weiner, Annette, B
1989   Why cloth? Wealth Gender and Power in Oceania. In: Cloth and
                 Human Experience. Ed. by Annette B.Weiner and Jane Schneider.
                 Washington, London: Smithsonian Institution Press. Pp. 33-72.

Weiner, Annette, B
1992   Inalienable Possessions. The Paradox of Keeping-While-Giving.
                 Berkeley, Los Angeles, Oxford: University of California Press.

MAORI WEAVING: THE INTERTWINING OF SPIRIT, ACTION AND METAPHOR

SUZANNE MAC AULAY
Senior Lecturer, Fine Arts Department, Wanganui Polytechnic,
Wanganui, New Zealand.

KURA TE WARU-REWIRI
Lecturer, Maori Visual Arts Department, Massey University,
Palmerston North, New Zealand.

Ko koe ki tēnā, ko ahau ki tēne kīwai o te kete.[1]

Kura Te Waru-Rewiri and I stand positioned here like the two weaving sticks, *turuturu*, which are thrust into the ground to support Maori weaving as it emerges from repeated separations, twists, insertions, and alignments. Our words crisscross and overlap to form a rich verbal weaving embellished with our experience and expanded through our respective interpretations.

Our discussion examines Maori textiles in *Aotearoa*/New Zealand as elements in a continuum of sacred experience unbounded by the temporal and spatial limitations of a particular ceremony. The fusion of creative practice, ritual action and ceremonial presence in weaving Maori cloaks, *kakahu*, typifies a cultural attitude in which the sacred and the secular are inseparable.

Maori art is sacred, and by extension the artist, the weaver, is considered the medium. Thus, the weaver and the action of weaving incarnate the life force, *mauri*, the authority, *mana*, and the sacred, *tapu*. Maori weavers are also linked over time with the ancestors, *nga tupuna*, and with future generations.

THE *KAUPAPA*   A Maori weaver transmutes the tough and fibrous leaves of the flax plant of the species, *Phormium tenax*, or to Maori, *harakeke*, into a soft, pliable textile by a series of ritually prescribed actions. After gathering and preparation, the weaver works these fibres, *muka*, between her fingers moving horizontally from left to right, manipulating and intertwining the strands of *aho* and *whenu*, weft and warp. Each weaving session is initiated with a prayer to focus one's vision and engage one's talent, to acknowledge the skills inherited from the ancestors, *Nga Mahi Tuku Iho*, and for creative inspiration. The materiality of the weaving process is offset by ritual practice acknowledging the sacred, *tapu*, with its potency as well as its prohibitions.

---

[1]"You at that, and I at this handle of the basket."

The novice's first weaving is usually given away. Sometimes it is buried as a gift to *Papatuanuku*, the earth (who reclaims her "own"). But more often it is presented to a family elder - thus, releasing the weaver from the work so that more weaving can be created, and launching the woven piece into the public arena of family, friends and destiny. As it circulates, the object accrues value through its different associations and its travels over space and time. These dynamics underscore the concept of the transmission and embodiment of sacred power and add to the intrinsic value of Maori cloaks.

The spirit of the piece, the history of the weaving's source, its resultant lineage, and the apparent tracings of descent and ownership, contribute to the idea of the woven cloaks as reliquaries - not primarily objects of devotion but containers of the relics of time, cultural survivals, aesthetic decisions, past use and former contexts. This is the notion behind the cloaks as treasures, *taonga*, as sacred and collective history.

TYPOLOGY   The designation, *tatara* or rain cloak, suggests a possible utilitarian antecedent but belies the complexity of making such a garment. The amount of work and detail evident in its manufacture is one indicator of its status as a prestige item. The other indicator is the cape's associative power derived from its relationship to its owner, *Te Iho-o-te-rangi*, who is believed to have been a formidable Taranaki priest or *tohunga*, and from the fact that it was also worn during a decisive battle which successfully defended the Taranaki region in 1833.

Interestingly, the cloak's efficacy as a protection against rain is inversely proportional to the involved technical processes of scraping away epidermal layers, dyeing fibres and rhythmically inserting decorative strands of flax in order to achieve the subtle visual transitions of alternating areas of colour. The more work that went into this cape to increase its aesthetic value and status, the less rain-resistant it became. It was undoubtedly, more suitable for armour.

As part of the Taranaki Museum collection, this cloak is effectively "out of ceremonial circulation." However, its connection to a powerful *tohunga*, a wizard priest, elicits feelings ranging from awe to fear and discomfort in the reactions of different Maori viewers. These responses are compatible with the notion of *taonga* (treasures) embodying ancestral spirits, transmitting the forces of history or acting as immortal reminders of the owner's presence and life force. Appropriately, dust and loose fibres from this *tatara* are kept in an envelope in the storage drawer with the cloak because the same associative powers are also thought to extend to these virtually microscopic elements.

In New Zealand a number of Maori cloaks with specific tribal affiliations and family connections are held in trust by museums. According to various agreements made with families these can be borrowed for special occasions such as *tangis* (funerals), graduation ceremonies, etc. In addition, the Whanganui Museum lists loans for a language competition and, at another time, for a performance by a special Maori cultural group.

When pakeha or European descendants donate or sell Maori cloaks to museums, they are usually concerned with preservation and safe keeping. However, when these cloaks are acquired, if they have appropriate Maori family and tribal connections, they are regarded as lost "relatives" and allowed to circulate again subject to certain contractual conditions between the curatorial institution and the local tribes - conditions which monitor accessibility and use. For Maori it is the reality of accessibility and the consequent authorization of their interaction with objects that rejuvenate, replenish and sustain the *taonga*.

There have been other situations when a tribe aware of the history and reputation of a particular cloak believed it to be lost forever until it "surfaced" in a public exhibition like a relative who has long been out-of-touch. For instance, there was an early nineteenth century dog skin cloak created as a *kahu mamae* (a garment of pain and revenge) to mark the outcome of a tragic battle. This cloak passed through several powerful hands until at the end of the nineteenth century, it was given to a New Zealander who in turn sold it to the Auckland Museum. Years later in 1982 it was featured in a travelling exhibition at Rotorua, and groups of the original weaver's descendants came to greet and honour the *kahu mamae* of their ancestress (Pendergrast 1987:94).

The *kaitaka* is also an older form of the cloak probably contemporaneous with the rain capes. It is basically a finely worked *kaupapa* or foundation with little adornment except for the contrast provided by the decorated borders of geometric designs, *taniko* (Fig.1). Similar to the prestige rain capes, this cloak is a showcase of virtuosity and skill. Sparse designs of coloured wool from unravelled blankets are sometimes present along the outer margins of the design field. They repeat enlarged zigzag motifs from the *taniko* border below. Their presence and the frugal but elegant use of material, is not only an aesthetic measure of the preciousness of the cloak but an inspired response to the sacredness of this garment as well.

Other types of cloaks are the *korowai*, with its flax tags, *hukahuka* or corkscrew curls, *karure*, and the feather cape, the *kahu huruhuru*. The tags of the *korowai* add a kinetic dimension - enhancing or amplifying the slightest movement, suggesting breezes rippling over grass. Even when the cloak is still, the tags appear to vibrate and visually activate the space in front of it (Fig.2).

SACRED CONTINUUM   The feather cloak is especially valuable for its association with *Tane* the forest god, progenitor and protector of birds and plants. Photographs from 1922 show the young women of the Potaka family sharing the same feather cloak that was used to cover their father, Arapeta Tapui Potaka's, coffin in 1919. Nukutiaio, Utanga, and Wera Potaka pose literally enfolded in their father's *mana* and the *mauri*, the life force, of the cape, indicating the seamless extension of *tapu*, uniting the realms of the living and the dead (Figs. 4-6).

Similar oscillations between ritual behaviour and realism surround the numerous tasks associated with the conversion of flax into weaving. This duality also extends to specialized vocabulary with its shared pragmatic and spiritual meanings. Words derived from *kakahu or kahu*, cloak, generate a series of sacred analogues such as *kahu*, the membrane surrounding the fetus, *whare kahu* the birth house, *whakakahu* the person who cuts the umbilical cord, and *kahukahu* as the essence of a human being or the spirit of a deceased ancestor (Weiner 1985:215). *Takapau* is a woven floor mat. The term also appears in prayer, *karakia*, and oratory to convey separate facets of *tapu*. Additionally, during *tangis* the mat is placed under the coffin, but the expression "turning the floor mat" refers to *tapu*-lifting ceremonies.

Flax gathering is prohibited during menstruation and times of inclement weather. It is also considered an ill omen to leave a row of weaving unfinished. The secular obverse of these actions is grounded in practicality. Flax plants should not be harvested during storms because it adversely affects fibre quality, preparation, and ultimately, the construction of the garment. Weaving that has been abandoned in mid-row, creates frustration and a headache the next time it is resumed.

Sensibility, however, does not detract from the inherent sacred power of flax, *Tane's* plant. People speak of the tribes around Lake Taupo wearing blinders woven from flax when they travelled near the volcano, Ruapeho, so their eyes, and by extension themselves, would be shielded from its *tapu* and they would not be tempted to sneak a glance at the sacred mountain.

KURA TE WARU-REWIRI:

"In my paintings I try to weave without touching the paint....Like meditation, you have to visualize before you do it. You do it and then something better happens."

My collaborative contribution to this paper is to

discuss the customary basis of Maori weaving in my work as a Maori painter - especially with reference to the *kakahu* (cloak) of my people, specifically, the *korowai*. The *korowai* is symbolic of *mana*, status and power. The idea of the *korowai*, metaphorically, became for me the symbol of protection and shelter.

The making of the *korowai* is a long process. Today the *korowai* takes at least eight months to complete. Ceremonially, prayers are offered to the gods at the beginning and at various stages of the development of the *korowai*. Protocol is still adhered to and one is conscious of the psychological consideration given to the source of the material gathered, the maker and the wearer of the completed work. Embodied in this journey is the concept of spiritual "care." The sacred and ceremonial use of the *kakahu* is out of respect for the people and the land, and is incorporated into blessings and ritual openings of buildings and special occasions. At the *tangi* (funeral) to have a *korowai* draped over the deceased is the highest form of respect given.

It is the idea of fibre and the *kaupapa* (basis or foundation) of the *korowai* that has inspired a large part of my art giving the dimension required to strengthen the connections with our Maori customary base, traditional beliefs and the practice of those beliefs.

The connection of "fibre" and thought in my paintings occurs on three levels: the physical, the mental and the spiritual (Fig.7). Maori culture is undergoing reconstruction, remodification, and readaptation. Fibre in Maori society is engendered with meanings that refer to a sophisticated aesthetic base incorporating the ethereal and the intangible: one that requires no justification.

History provides us with a model of excellence that has been recognized and protected by time and space (Fig.3). We are aware of the presence of that level of excellence in our sacred and ceremonial cloaks as an aesthetic that has not been surpassed by modernity and civilization.

It is from this point that I have gravitated toward the expression of fibre, its spirit and the action of painting/weaving. The idea of fibre is metaphorically associated with the place of my people, where we come from, where we are now, and where do we go from here? (Fig.8).

With the advent of colonization and Christianity, Maori people have been assimilated at great expense. As an artist, I feel a responsibility to remind us of the strengths of our ancestors. The associations with the fibre of the *korowai* is with the land, the spiritual ownership of land and the people of the land. These are the elements that emanate from the *korowai* and that I attempt to embrace in my paintings (Fig.1).

CONCLUSION_____

In Maori art all boundaries demarcating creative action, ceremonial observance, and terminology apart from poetics, are permeable - pervaded by spirit and the accumulated power of association with people or events. What is the measure of sacredness against ceremony? Whatever its magnitude, it is always in excess of material and experiential limitations.

_____

We thank the following for their generous support which is woven into the *kaupapa* of this presentation: Michelle Horwood and Libby Sharp, Whanganui Regional Museum; Mary Donald, Taranaki Museum; Shirley Whata and Warren Warbrick, Manawatu Museum; Erenora Puketapu Hetet; and, Mina McKenzie.

REFERENCES

Awekotuku, Ngahuia, Roger Neich et al., eds. 1996. *Maori Art and Culture*. Auckland, N.Z.: David Bateman Ltd.

Pendergrast, Mick. 1994. *Te Aho Tapu: The Sacred Thread*. Auckland, N.Z.: Reed Publishing, Ltd.

Weiner, Annette B. 1985. "Inalienable Wealth." *American Ethnologist* 12:210-227.

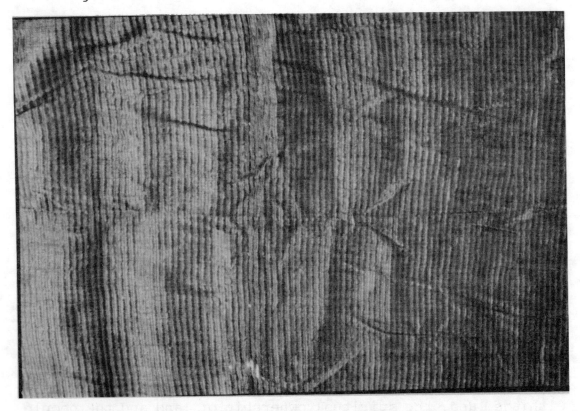

Fig. 1. *Kaitaka*, detail. Manawatu Museum, Palmerston North, New Zealand.

Fig.2. *Korowai* cloaks. Archives of Whanganui Regional Museum.

Fig.3.
"Whenua/whenua."
1996. Private
Collection. Image
is inspired by
hukahuka (tags) of
korowai.

Fig. 4. Nukutiaio Potaka, 1922. Wanganui, N.Z. Courtesy of
Mina McKenzie.

Fig.5. The Potaka Sisters, 1922. Courtesy of Mina McKenzie.

Fig. 6. A. Potaka's Coffin with Cloak, 1919. McKenzie Coll.

Fig.7. Kura Te Waru-Rewiri. *The Mantle*. 1994. Symbol of the colonization. Collection of University of Auckland.

Figure 8.
K. Te Waru-Rewiri.
Deliverance. 1996.
Collection of the
artist.

ENTRANCE GATES COMMISSION
MAUI ARTS AND CULTURAL CENTER
by Pat Hickman

When asked to design entrance gates for the MACC in
Hawaii, I drew on images of nets, from fishing nets used
around the world to the specific background structure of
ceremonial Hawaiian feather capes. As an artist, I'm intrigued
with more than the utilitarian function of nets. I'm drawn to
how nets filter light, air, visual ideas; I'm interested in
the shadows created.

I have explored specific Hawaiian beliefs and cultural
practices related to netting. My understanding of nets in the
Hawaiian context has grown out of "talking story" with
Hawaiian cultural specialists.

I learned of meanings and associations related to
suspended nets, "nets in the sky", of a visual connection with
the Pleiades or "Makali'i". The arrangement of stars in the
Pleiades are like knotted corners of a netted unit. When that
constellation, the Pleiades, arrives on the horizon, the rainy
season begins. (Oct.-Jan.) It is believed that the "maka" or
eyes (the openings) of the net in the sky need to be large
enough to invite the rain and other "good things" to come
through in abundance. This, the "makahiki" season is a time
of celebration and of rest and renewal, a time of dispersing
food--a time of that which sustains. It's a time for
appreciating the abundance of the season, a time for
receiving, a time for mending, a time of mending and patching
nets.

I heard stories of nets being hoisted up into coconut
trees, suspended for drying, sometimes stretched and under
tension. I thought of nets at rest, in a relaxed state. I
think of nets draping, and of the possible fluidity of nets
moving under water or blowing in the breeze. Sections of the
net gates suggest the weight of gravity and tautness.
Visually, this textile like structure, a broad, multi-paneled
expanse of netting, encourages passage from ordinary space to
space that may transcend the ordinary.

I was told of a special "hale", a house set aside for
storing nets, for protecting the net's "mana", a place for
caring for the nets. And before fishermen went out to sea,
there was a time to sleep and dream together, symbolically
taking responsibility for each other, for the safety of each
other--each individual part of a larger community.

In earlier Hawaiian history, the ritual of netmaking
consisted of the thoughtful way of approaching the forest
before taking natural plant materials and collecting fibers to
make a net. The gathering of mountain plants for dyeing
fishnets and for making the fibrous netting element seemed a

way of linking the mountains with the sea. In using the
structural imagery of netting as gates in this setting, this
specific site on the island of Maui, the "eyes of the net" in
the gate, speak of respect for both the mountains the gates
face and the sea, and of what they each give, being tied
together in this place.

In the gate design, I kept in mind these associations and
stories, the appropriateness of suspended nets as gates, and
my hopes for how this cultural center will function in the
community. The gates invite, symbolically welcome, and allow
people to pass through to a special, public space, to be
sustained and renewed by an experience of art in community, in
public performance and celebration. In translating fiber into
metal, I wanted to maintain the textile qualities of netting.
This commission was for me an opportunity to understand more
specifically the sacred and ceremonial context within which
nets and netting have been used in Hawaii.

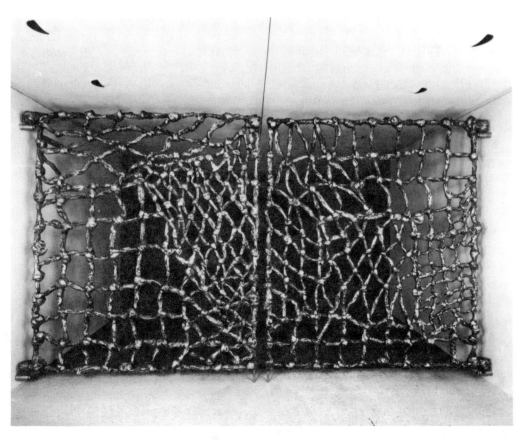

The Traditional Method of Masi Making
on the Island of Taveuni, Fiji

by
Daniel Roy Hildenbrandt

Masi or tapa is a traditional material which is made by the inhabitants of many of the islands in the Pacific region. This material is made from the bark of the young mulberry tree, which is soaked in water, beaten with mallets and formed into sheets. After drying, the Masi is decorated with traditional designs created by stencils, patterns and/or free-hand drawing. This documentary shows the process of Masi making as it is practiced on the "Garden Island" of Taveuni, Fiji. Each step is identified and explained in an English translation. The masi is made by the women of the Vanua of Bouma. (The Vanua is a group of landowners from 5 different villages within the region of Bouma.) Traditionally, masi was worn for ceremonial purposes by the Chiefs of the different villages. Masi is still used within the home as a blanket or mattress, and the accumulation of Masi is seen as a sign of wealth. Masi is also used for ceremonial purposes, and it is presented to dignitaries during special functions or celebrations. In the Kingdom of Tonga, the King often walks on masi carpets during official ceremonies. Masi is also used for funereal purposes.

As so often happens after contact with developed countries, this traditional "cloth" is being comoditized. Tapa is now being used for a variety of tourist souvenirs from postal cards to wall hangings. Some "entrepreneurs" are even applying traditional designs to stained cardboard creating quick, cheap, tapa imitations.

Daniel Hildenbrandt is a Professor in the Communication Department at the University of Guam. He has worked as a folklorist/documentary producer in many cultures primarily in the Pacific. This video tape on the making of masi was produced in 1990, when he was conducting documentary research as a Fulbright Scholar at the University of the South Pacific in Fiji. Professor Hildenbrandt holds a Masters Degree in Anthropology/Folklore from the University of Texas at Austin,
and a Masters in Public Visual Communication from Southern Illinois University at Carbondale. His documentary "Zydeco Gumbo" was produced in 1987 at the University of Southwest Louisiana in Lafayette. "Zydeco Gumbo" is available through Rhapsody Films of New York.

VIDEO
THREADS OF TIME
Handmade Textiles for Weddings in Fez, Morocco

Funded by the Barakat Foundation

Louise W. Mackie, Producer
Curator, Textiles & Costume Section, NEAC
Royal Ontario Museum, 100 Queen's Park, Toronto, ON M5S 2C6, Canada

Handmade textiles have been vitally important in many traditional societies where they achieved cultural, symbolic, and economic significance. Yet today, comparatively little urban production survives except in Fez, Morocco, where an astonishing variety of age-old handmade textile traditions exists, based on local demand especially for weddings.

This video documentary provides a rare opportunity to see the making and use of eight different types of fabrics and clothing, to meet artisans, merchants and consumers, and to attend a wedding where handmade fabrics symbolize regional pride. Among the woven, embroidered, and trimming fabrics is one loom of exceptional international significance. Elaborately patterned textiles are still woven on huge drawlooms, skillfully operated by two men, just as they were for more than one thousand years until replaced by jacquard looms. The ancient drawloom is actually an early computer wherein a weave structure (program) is tied on for continuous use and designs (files) are tied on any time and stored for retrieval when needed.

This 26 minute video is designed for educational institutions, individuals, and fiber artists. Anyone interested in textiles & costumes, anthropology, material culture, art history, and Middle Eastern & North African Studies will be impressed. The video was produced from fifty-five hours of video footage, twenty-one interviews, and three fieldwork trips by Louise W. Mackie, Project Director, Susan Schaeffer Davis, Anthropologist, Frieda Sorber & Lotus Stack, Textile Scholars, and Mark Stanley, Director of Photography.

Publications on Fez by the fieldwork team include: Louise W. Mackie, "The Threads of Time in Fez, Morocco," Rotunda, 24:3 (1991): 18-23; Louise W. Mackie, "New on Old, Handmade Textiles in Fez," Hali, 66 (1992): 88-93; Louise W. Mackie, "Pattern Books for Drawloom Weaving in Fes, Morocco," and Frieda Sorber & Lotus Stack, "A 20th Century Moroccan Drawloom Fabric," Bulletin du CIETA, 70 (1992): 169-185; Louise W. Mackie, Frieda Sorber, Lotus Stack, Susan S. Davis, "Textiles in the Everyday Life of Artisans, Merchants, and Consumers of Fez, Morocco," Textiles in Daily Life, Proceedings of the Third Biennial Symposium of the Textile Society of America, (1992): 9-49.

THE MEANING OF YORUBA *ASO OLONA* IS FAR FROM WATER TIGHT

LISA ARONSON
Department of Art and Art History
Skidmore College
Saratoga Springs, NY 12203

While researching the ritual meaning of cloth among the Eastern Ijo of the Niger Delta, I examined the contents of a number of family owned trunks in which were stored old and much valued cloths traded from elsewhere in Africa, Europe, and India. One type of cloth which I frequently found in these collections was this one (See Fig. 1) made up of three, or sometimes four, woven strips that are sewn along the salvage and decorated with supplemental weft-float design. The Eastern Ijo regard this cloth as a valuable heirloom for its trade value and for the fact that its designs evoke spiritual powers associated with the sea.. The Eastern Ijo refer to this particular cloth as *ikaki* or tortoise, a water spirit (*owu*) known in Ijo lore for his combination of trickery and wisdom. Not surprising, *ikaki* cloth is standard attire for kings in certain Eastern Ijo communities.

This textile, like all Ijo cloths, is not indigenous to the Ijo area. Rather, it comes from the Ijebu area of Yorubaland, a region separated from the Eastern Ijo by more than 100 miles of interconnecting rivers and streams (See Fig. 2). The history of its trade to the Eastern Ijo may very well stem from its ritual meaning to the Ijebu Yoruba who are the initial producers of it and in whose culture, the cloth is deeply rooted. This paper will examine the ritual use of this cloth among the Ijebu Yoruba in an effort to determine why it would have been traded outward as it was.

The Yoruba proverb "Eniyan l'aso mi" helps us to explain what cloth means to the Ijebu and other Yoruba peoples. Translated as "People are my cloth", the proverb explicitly equates cloth to the warmth, closeness, and concerns of things that are human. So it is with this weaving from the Ijebu Yoruba area of Nigeria. The Ijebu refer to it generically as *aso olona* meaning "cloth with patterns, a name derived from its characteristically rich array of weft-float designs. Bearing images of water spirits and other power-laden symbols, the cloth serves as emblems of chieftaincy, priesthood and membership in the ever-powerful Oshugbo society. Thus, it lies at the very core of Ijebu power and leadership as it eventually came to be, albeit on a lesser scale, among the Eastern Ijo.[1]

The delta environment in which the Ijebu Yoruba live is key to our understanding of the meaning of this cloth if not also its eventual spread outward. For the Ijebu Yoruba in particular, the riverine delta in an important source of their spiritual powers. In ceremony, it is not uncommon to see the Ijebu navigating boats in which masked dancers representing water spirits are being carried to shore. The delta is also the eventual avenue

---

[1] For more detailed information on *aso olona*, see Aronson, 1992.

through which Ijebu cloth was traded elsewhere. In his study of Ijebu masquerades, Henry Drewal writes:

> Ijebuland occupied the coastal plain between the Yoruba kingdoms of the interior and the lagoons, creeks, and rivers along the coast. Prior to the arrival of Europeans more than 500 years ago, these coastal waterways served as highways for the exchange of goods, ideas, and arts. With their strategic position, bountiful supply of fish, and trade with other Africans and later with Europeans, the Ijebu prospered (Drewal, 32, 1986)

One indicator of their prosperity is the power and extent of their kingdom. The Ijebu kingdom was said to have been founded in the late fourteenth century when, according to Ijebu myth, Obanta son of the God Oduduwa, was sent from Ile-Ife to reign as king of the Ijebu nation. Today the Ijebu are best described as a federation of states combining a divine king, known as the Awujale, with a more decentralized form of government. The Awujale, based in the central town of Ijebu-Ode, rules over a series of lesser crowned rulers located in a number of outlying towns such as Ijebu-Ife where I did my work. These lesser crowned rulers are expected to honor and serve the Awujale at the same time that they exercise some degree of autonomous rule over chiefs and others below them. In other words, similar to the Yoruba elsewhere, the Ijebu are essentially hierarchical in nature. A separate but not unrelated system of rule is known as Oshugbo (or Ogboni in other Yoruba areas) which functions, among other things, as a check and balance system on Ijebu royalty. Essentially a judiciary society, Oshugbo is made up of male and female elders who oversee court cases at various levels, decide the punishment of criminals who have been condemned to death, and tend to all affairs concerning the king from the time he is selected and installed to his burial. In contrast to Ijebu royalty, Oshugbo is more egalitarian but with the authority to oversee the power of the King and his lesser chiefs.

This paper will show that *aso olona*, through its symbolism and ritual use, serves to identify and mediate between these three ruling sectors of Ijebu society, the crowned rulers, the chiefs below them, and members of Oshugbo. Its ritual use may also suggest the relative history of these ruling bodies.

But, first, a detailed description of *aso olona* is in order. The category of cloth in question is woven by Ijebu women on an upright loom with a continuous warp (See Fig. 3). The loom is typical of the type women use throughout much of Nigeria. The upper cross beam is adjustable to allow the weaver to alter the length of the cloth. The width, however, never exceeds twenty inches; anything wider requires that more than one panel of cloth be sewn together along the selvage.

Using this technology, Ijebu women weave *aso olona* in two basic sizes. The larger one, intended as a wrapper, requires four individual panels sewn together along the selvage to create a cloth measuring approximately 1.8 by 2.5 meters (See Fig. 4). Referred to as *aso iborun-nla*, meaning "big covering cloth" it is worn toga style with one corner flung over the left shoulder. The Ijebu name for the smaller cloth is *itagbe*. It is constructed of only one panel of cloth approximately 1.2 meters in length (See Fig. 5). Depending on its use, the *itagbe* is worn either over the left shoulder, over the right, or on the head. This man wears it on his right shoulder because he is a chief rather than a member of Oshugbo, a point to which I will return later in this paper.

Whatever its dimension, *aso olona* is known for its rich array of weft-float patterns and shag textures, all created through the insertion of supplemental threads into design sheds as the weaver works. Much of the meaning of this cloth is conveyed through its surface treatment. An Ijebu priest interviewed by Henry Drewal said that the presence of weft-float patterns on the cloth symbolizes "long lives well lived" (Drewal, 1992), in sharp contrast to the plain white cloths the Ijebu Yoruba are said to wear when they first come into the world. Thus the patterns and colors represent the richness and diversity of an individual's experience in life, including acquired knowledge of the spirit realm.

Most of the specific designs woven into *aso olona* are associated with leadership or the spiritual powers by which it is exercised (See Fig. 6). Several represent water spirits -- the crocodile (*ooni*), frog (*opolo*), fishhead (*agbarieja*), and snake (*ejo*) -- all of them important components of the Ijebu cosmology. Furthermore, each is represented from a bird's eye perspective as though humans, or the divine, are viewing them from above as they typically float in or near water.

We can see this with the image of a crocodile (*ooni*), the backside of which is shown as a series concentric diamonds with four out-stretched legs and two heads, one at each end. Of all the designs on *aso olona*, the crocodile motif appears most frequently in accordance with its all-encompassing role as guardian of the spirits. Crocodiles typically float on the surface of the water as though to be hovering in a liminal space between the living world above and the spiritual one below. Given its all-encompassing nature, the crocodile image, whether represented through cloth or sculpture, is frequently placed in shrines for protection. Its omnipresent role might also explain why in woven form the crocodile is shown bearing two heads, one at each end, as if to suggest its all-seeing powers.

The fishhead or (*agbarieja*) is another common water-spirit motif appearing on *aso olona* (See Fig. 5 & 7). This image is best read as an abstract rendering of two interlocking mudfish. This curious sea creature, known for its flat head and multitude of whisker-like projections, may very well symbolize Olokun, goddess of the sea, on whose power royalty and Oshugbo greatly depend. In woven form, it is represented as a head with projections emanating out and downward. This image is also seen in a variety of Ijebu sculptural forms such as brass armlets, carved doors, and, as we see here, royal drums (*gbedu*) played to honor kings, lesser crowned rulers, and chiefs (See Fig. 8).

On the theme of projections, a curious design feature of some *aso olona* is the shag motif, referred to by the Ijebu as *shaki* (See Fig. 9). The weaver creates it by weaving supplemental threads through a small grouping of warp threads with their ends left hanging in front. Some of you may know the technique as *rya* knotting. Not unlike other patterns on *aso olona,* the shag is associated with power, prestige, and things that are good. The word *shaki* means tripe, or the inner lining of the cow's stomach. Those who are familiar with tripe know that, like the effect of the woven design it imitates, tripe has a series of projectiles extending from its surface, a quality that makes it less than desirable for many of us. For the Yoruba, however, tripe is regarded as one of the tastiest and most desired foods. It also has an deeper meaning in Oshugbo cosmology. Robert Thompson argues that within Oshugbo, *shaki* serves as a metaphor for one's inner vulnerability and transparency to what he calls the "minions of the earth" from whose gaze nothing can be concealed (Thompson, 1971: ch. 6/2).

It is not only the patterns or texture from which *aso olona* derives its meaning. Equally important is its ritual use. Worn by lesser crowned rules and chiefs as well as members of Oshugbo, the small shoulder cloth functions as a highly personalized symbol of one's status or identity. In this capacity, it is not uncommon for individuals to present their *itagbe* to their deities as an expression of their gratitude. The backs of Ijebu shrines are frequently adorned with *itagbe* that people have presented to their gods as a kind of visual equivalent of prayer (Se Fig. 10). I myself arrived at this conclusion by observing the recent Ijebu practice of weaving actual words (in Yoruba or English) on the cloth together with more traditional ideographic symbols. The words woven on one *itagbe* read *Jebemi Oluwa* meaning "God, answer my prayer".

Such cloth continues to mark its owner's status after death. Chiefs and other high-ranking individuals must be buried with their cloth to affirm their status within the spirit realm. Not surprising, the cloth may appear as an encasement for a deceased elder in *Egungun,* the Yoruba masquerade performance that brings the dead back to the living (See Fig. 11). As evidenced by the cloth he wears, this *Egungun* performer represents that of a deceased Oshugbo elder.

Note that the cloth he wears is replete with surface patterns, colors, and textures. The explosive visual display so typical of Oshugbo attire contrasts with the relative simplicity of chieftaincy garb (which I will discuss momentarily). It also stands in stark opposition to the garments of Oshugbo initiation. The Ijebu say that plain white cloth is what the Yoruba are believed to wear when coming into this world and when being initiated into secret societies such as Oshugbo. They also wear white when engaging in rituals within the secret chamber or "house" (*Iledi*) in which Oshugbo rituals are carried out. It is outside of this sacred domain – in the more public space – that the richly decorated dress (particularly the large wrapper) is displayed for public consumption and for the purposes of identity. This photograph of a photograph of an Oshugbo member shows him adorned with all of the visual opulence befitting an Oshugbo member (See Fig. 12). Note that he wears the *iborun-nla* on his body, an *itagbe* on his left shoulder and yet another *itagbe* on his head, that latter being a reliable indicator of Oshugbo membership. When important decisions are made at Oshugbo meetings, members drape the cloth over their heads so that the fringed ends rest on the chest. In public they wear the cloth turban-style, with the fringe falling toward the face. It creates an effect of fullness that alludes to spirituality, just as, according to Henry Drewal, the bulging eyes and forehead of the figures on Oshugbo staffs "evoke the moment of possession when…the head swells (*ori wu*) and divinity dwells within the devotee". In Yoruba art in general, projections from the head, such as we see with the fish head symbol discussed earlier, give visual form to spiritual power.

The cloth fringe, and in particular the way it is finished, also embodies the power of the office it represents. Often the *itagbe* fringe is divided into seven sections, each of them wrapped in an intricate way to create seven elaborate tassels (See Fig. 13). Or, the weaver may create six vertical slits at each end of the cloth to create seven woven sections (See Fig. 14). The number seven alluded to in each case suggests the delicate balance of power between Oshugbo and the ruling royalty. I was told by the Ajalorun, or crowned ruler, of Ijebu-Ife that six of the seven tassels refer to the six ruling figures (Iwarefa) of Oshugbo, and the seventh to the divine king (Awujale) over whom they officiate in certain matters.

This example illustrates that *aso olona* in its symbolism reflects the balance between Oshugbo and the divine king. Likewise, it illuminates the kings relationship to his lesser crowned rulers and chiefs during whose installment, the king ceremonially presents them with an *itagbe* as their sign of office. Thus, the *itagbe* serves as a symbol of their designated power at the same time that it reminds them of their subservience to the king. Chieftaincy attire is considerably less ostentatious than that of Oshugbo members. Chief Adesina Adeyemi of Ijebu-Ife, both a high-ranking chief (Orangun) and head (Apena) of Oshugbo, demonstrated this by modeling the modes of dress required for each of his roles. As the Apena of Oshugbo, he wore an *itagbe* on his left shoulder, another on his head and an *aso Iborun-nla* around his body, each richly embellished with the frog motif and shag in brilliant colors (See Fig. 15). As chief, he just wears just the itagbe component of *aso olona* (See Fig. 16).

Other differences are also noted. In principle, although not demonstrated by this photograph, those belonging to Oshugbo carry their *itagbe* on the left shoulder to distinguish themselves from chiefs who carry it on the right. The Ijebu associate the left side of the body with Oshugbo, as numerous practices substantiate. When society members assume the ritual gesture of clenched fists, it is always the left that rests on top of the right. They also shake with the left hand and dance in the direction of the left.

Some of the differences I have noted may suggest the history of *aso olona* and its related systems of rule. Morton-Williams (1960) and others assert that Oshugbo predates divine kingship and related chieftaincy. Marilyn Houlberg argues that the *itagbe* in its miniature size, may be a metaphor for the large *iborun-nla* implying among other things that the latter is historically older (Houlberg, 1992). Since chiefs only wear the *itagbe* and not the larger wrapper, might we conclude that chiefs appropriated Oshugbo's title cloths albeit in miniature form.

The question of the history and appropriation of *aso olona* becomes all the more complex when one realizes the extent to which it spread to groups living beyond the Ijebu Yoruba area. As early as the late eighteenth century, *aso olona* was being transported by canoe to the hands of the Eastern Ijo who then acculturated it and assigned meaning specific to their own beliefs (See Fig. 1). Identified as *ikaki* or tortoise, regardless of the configuation of its designs, it became and remains the official attire for political leaders and for spirits when manifested in masquerade. A late nineteenth century photograph of King Jaja of the Opobo shows him wearing *ikaki* cloth as his official royal attire (See Fig. 17). It is also shown being worn by an *Owu* masquerade, possibly that of a water-buffalo, illustrated in Talbot's 1926 ethnography of the Niger Delta (Talbot, 1969).

One has to question why a cloth so spiritually endowed and so deeply rooted in Ijebu's political history would have made its way to the Eastern Ijo some 100 miles to their east. Trade may not be the only answer. Igor Kopytoff, in his discussion of commoditization, argues that we must address the "cultural biography" of goods in order to understand their place in economic exchange (Kopytoff, 1986). Following this line of argument, it is reasonable to assume that the Ijebu brought *aso olona* into the delta for their own use and for reasons linked to its associations with power and authority. Could it be that they presented it to Ijo chiefs as gestures of good will or as mediums of exchange? We may never know the answer to this question. What we do learn from this is that the ritual meaning of cloth is forever in flux as it moves both within a culture and beyond it.

Works Cited

Aronson, Lisa. "Ijebu Yoruba *Aso Olona*: A Contextual and Historical Overview", <u>African Arts</u>, July 1992, Vol. XXV, 3, pp. 52-61:101.

Drewal, Henry. "Flaming Crowns, Cooling Waters: Masquerades of the Ijebu Yoruba", <u>African Arts</u>, November 1986, Vol. XX, 1, pp. 32-41; 99.

Drewal, Henry. Personal Communication, 1992.

Houlberg, Marilyn. Personal Communication, 1992.

Kopytoff, Igor. "The Cultural Biography of Things: Commoditization as Process", IN <u>The Social Life of Things: Commotidies in Cultural Perspective</u>, ed. Arjun Appadurai, Cambridge University Press, 1986, pp. 64-91.

Morton-Williams, P., "The Yoruba Ogboni Cult in Oyo", <u>Africa</u>, 4, 1960.

Talbot, Percy Amaury. <u>The Peoples of Southern Nigeria</u>, London: Frank Cass, 1969 (Reprint of 1932 Edition).

Thompson, Robert, <u>Black Gods and Kings</u>, Los Angeles, University of California, 1971.

Fig.1 - *Ikaki* (tortoise) cloth traded from the Ijebu Yoruba area and now in a Kalabari Ijo collection.

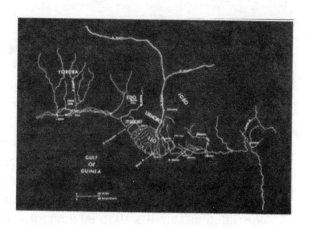

Fig.2 - Map of the Niger Delta region of Nigeria.

Fig.3 - The upright frame loom Ijebu Yoruba women typically use to weave *aso olona*.

Fig.4 - *Aso-iborun-nla* (big covering cloth) with its typical construction of four weft-float decorated panels sewn together along the selvage.

Fig.8 - *Gbedu* drum bearing the typical Ijebu motif of a figure with projections emanating from their head, much like the fish-head motif. University Museum, U. of Penn.

Fig.9 - Detail of the shag motif the Ijebu refer to as *shaki* (tripe).

Fig.10 - *Itagbe* are hanging at the back of this Oduduwa shrine in the town of Ijebu-Ife. Photo compliments of Marilyn Houlberg.

Fig.11 - Egungun masquerade of an Oshugbo member who has returned from the dead. Photo compliments of Marilyn Houlberg.

Fig.12 - Photograph of a photograph of an Ijebu man in his official Oshugbo attire. Photo compliments of Marilyn Houlberg.

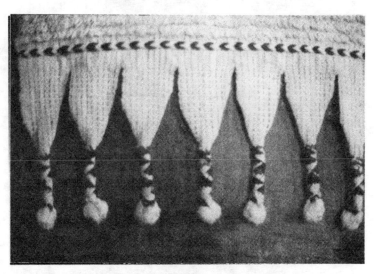

Fig.13 - Detail of seven-tasseled fringe on an *Itagbe*.

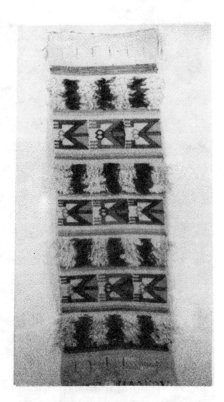

Fig.14 - *Itagbe* with six open slits to create the required seven sections.

Fig.15 - Man from Ijebu-Ife wearing his official attire as an Oshugbo member.

Fig.5 - A chief from Ijebu-Ife wearing an *itagbe* on his right shoulder.

Fig.7 - Detail of the *agbarieja* (fish-head) design.

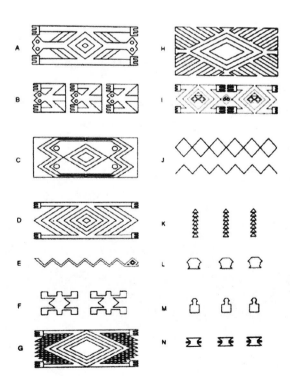

Fig.6 - Weft-float patterns used in Ijebu *aso olona*.

A. *Ooni* (Crocodile)
B. *Opolo* (Frog)
C. *Agbarieja* (Fishhead)
D. *Erin* (Elephant)
E. *Ejo* (Snake)
F. *Alangba* (Lizard)
G. *Gbedu* (Large single-membrane drum) and *Gangan* (Talking Drum)
H. Unidentified
I. *Fowoboju* ("Pass the Palm over the Face," a gesture that accompanies prayers or certain ritual ceremonies)
J. *Abalaye* (Hooked ceremonial staff)
K. *Eekono* (Fingernail)
L. *Atapo* (Stool)
M. *Waala* (Koran board)
N. *Omolobe* (Knife)

Fig.16 - Same man wearing his chieftaincy attire.

Fig.17 - Late nineteenth century photo of King Jaja of Opobo wearing *ikaki* (tortoise) cloth as his official royal attire.

MOURNING AND MEMORY: FACTORY-PRINTED TEXTILES AND THE BAULE OF COTE D'IVOIRE

Kathleen E. Bickford
Assistant Curator for African Art
The Art Institute of Chicago, 111 S. Michigan Avenue, Chicago, IL   60603-6110

The panel from which this paper stems united the theme of sacred or ceremonial textiles in Africa with that of the constitution of value. Here I address these issues as they relate to some uses of factory-printed textiles by the Baule of Côte d'Ivoire. The West African nation of Côte d'Ivoire, which is approximately the size of Arizona, lies at a crossroads of cultures, bringing together people of diverse ethnic backgrounds. Though not a numerical majority, those of Baule ethnicity are in many ways central within Côte d'Ivoire, tracing their heartland to the regional center of the country and dominating Ivoirian politics since independence in 1960. The wearing of factory prints at Baule funerals, and more broadly the association of particular motifs with Baule beliefs about death and mourning, is among the topics that is consistently identified as significant by Ivoirians of all ethnic origins in discussions concerning factory-printed textiles. However, before focussing on this topic it is important to first set the stage by briefly introducing the sorts of factory-printed textiles found in Côte d'Ivoire and the place they hold in contemporary Ivoirian society.[1]

There are two main types of factory-printed textiles in Côte d'Ivoire: factory-produced batik textiles, called 'wax,' and roller-printed textiles, called 'fancy.' Wax prints are made using a process that was developed by the Dutch in the mid-nineteenth century.[2] In it a thin resin resist is rolled by machine in a repeating pattern onto cotton yardage. The yardage is then immersed in dye, coloring the areas free of resin. Subsequent colors are either applied in an overall pattern by roller or to specific areas by hand using felt-padded wood blocks. Blocking, which results in a characteristic overlapping and misalignment of color areas, increases the price of wax because it is both time and labor intensive.

Quicker and less costly to make than wax, the production of roller-print or fancy textiles for sale in West and Central Africa burgeoned in the

---

[1] For a more extensive discussion of factory-printed textiles in Côte d'Ivoire see Bickford (1995).

[2] The wax technique was invented by the Belgium firm Prévinaire and Company which amalgamated into the Dutch N.V. Haarlemsche Katoen-Maartschappij in 1857 (Kroese 1976: 16-17). See also Bickford (1995) and Picton (1995).

second half of this century.[3] In the roller-print process a design is incised onto a series of brass rollers, one for each color to be used. The rollers are then attached to the printing machine in close succession. As fabric passes under the rollers, dye is applied on a single side in progression from the lightest to the darkest color. This technique results in less durable prints that fade more quickly than dye-saturated wax prints; however, because it does not use resin or blocking the technique allows for greater detail, more color variety, and the inclusion of photo silk-screen images. While fancy designs often imitate wax, the unique characteristics of the roller-print process have led to a blossoming of design possibilities that go far beyond the limitations of wax.

In Côte d'Ivoire factory-printed wax and fancy textiles are known mutually as "pagne," a French word literally meaning wrapper.[4] Worn in cities, towns, and villages by women and men of all ages and ethnic origins, pagne is intimately entwined in the daily lives of many people. Wax prints are relatively expensive—six yards can cost as much as one hundred dollars, a great deal more than the monthly income of most Ivoirians—hence, their purchase is considered an investment. In contrast, fancy prints are relatively affordable—costing only about eighteen dollars for six yards—and their purchase may lack many of the weighty considerations of quality and durability that can accompany the purchase of wax.

Despite these differences, in Côte d'Ivoire wax and fancy prints are both highly valued in ways that are unrelated to their market value. Like the Maori and Trobriand objects so succinctly discussed by Annette Weiner, pagne often has an inalienable and affective value for Ivoirians that is closely tied to its social or personal significance (1985, 1992). In such instances pagne is valued not for its resalability, but rather for its evocativeness, which is priceless. Igor Kopytoff contends that this kind of intangible value interacts with and influences the perceived worth of commodities like pagne and creates a complex relationship between the two (1986: 80). As Kopytoff demonstrates, things can move in and out of commodity status and can be viewed as commodities and non-commodities simultaneously; thus, even a single person might give multiple meanings to a thing, seeing it as valuable in diverse and perhaps conflicting ways (76). It is in just such a multifarious realm of meaning and value that pagne exists for Ivoirians.

The affective value of pagne in Côte d'Ivoire is rooted in the historic importance of textiles of many different kinds as symbols of wealth and a means of communication. Ivoirians invoke contemporary interpretations of this history to explain the importance of pagne today. Thus, while pagne manifests a modern sense of national identity, it is also perceived in distinct ways by Ivoirians of different ethnic origins and can signal the disparities

----

[3] For more on the history of roller prints for export to Africa see Bickford (1995), Faque and Wollenweber (1991), and Picton (1995).

[4] Renne discusses some origins of the word (1995: 208, n7).

among them. This is very much the case where the use of pagne at Baule funerals is concerned.

The fact that much of the pagne worn at Baule funerals has affective value was brought home to me one day as I was walking with a young Baule woman. Pointing to a passerby wearing a blue and white fancy print my companion said "that was my grandfather's pagne."[5] When I asked her what she meant by this comment, she explained that she and other members of her family had worn the same pagne as a uniform to her grandfather's funeral. The wearing of uniforms made from pagne by people who want to express solidarity is widespread in Côte d'Ivoire. However, I was struck by the highly personal tone of this woman's remark, which implied a sense of ownership of the pagne used for the uniform that seemed out of sync with its commodity standing. It was apparent that for her and others in her family this widely available and mass-produced textile was irrevocably tied to the memory of her grandfather.

This incident and others like it led me to take a closer look at pagne and Baule funerals. For the Baule an elaborate public funeral is an essential closing to a long life well-lived. Large amounts of time and money are invested in organizing and conducting the funeral of a Baule adult, and especially that of a Baule elder. Tremendous expense and effort are expended to create an event that will send the deceased into the otherworld with great fanfare. Funerals are also an opportunity for Baule people to demonstrate their own worth, whether in terms of success, influence, wealth, or respect for tradition. Describing funerals in his classic study of life among the Baule, Vincent Guerry states:

> "family and close friends bring their most valuable belongings, their finest robes, gold-topped canes and fly-chasers, gold jewels and head-bands, etc. They are exhibited near the corpse to honor the deceased while, at the same time, displaying personal wealth" (1970: 62).

Guerry also points out that:

> "funerals are the reimbursement of a debt. If the deceased was not generous at past funerals then he or she will receive little at his or her own funeral. Thus, people think of their own mortality at a funeral and try to lay the ground work for their own sumptuous burials..." (1970: 70).

Hence, Baule funerals become a forum for staging opulent individual and collective displays of wealth and well-being that are rewarding to all parties. The deceased and his or her family are honored by being shown to be deserving of such an outpouring, the sponsors are given the opportunity to show respect for the deceased as well as to demonstrate personal merit and increase social standing through their generosity, and those attending

---

[5]Fieldnotes, 1991-92.

find rewards in contributing to, witnessing, and being a part of the occasion.

Valuable textiles are used in several ways at funerals to create an atmosphere of abundance and wealth. In preparation for burial the deceased's body is wrapped in woven cloth once belonging to the deceased or given by relatives for this purpose. Woven cloth may also be used to drape over the coffin or the speaker's podium and cover the walls of the room where the deceased is laid out.

Likewise, the special textiles worn at funerals add richness to the scene. Such clothing may also communicate personal messages about the wearer's sense of identity and connection to the event. Pagne uniforms are an important means of delivering these messages. Uniforms made from a specially selected blue or red pagne are worn to signify the nature of the relationships that existed between guests and the deceased.[6] A blue print is selected to be worn by those directly related to the deceased, such as a spouse, sibling, or child. Slightly more distant relatives, such as an aunt, uncle, or cousin, might wear the same print or they might have a blue uniform of their own. A red print is often selected to be worn by the deceased's more tangential relatives, such as distant cousins, as well as by friends. At very extravagant funerals uniforms might differentiate the deceased's relatives by generation, with the children wearing one uniform and the spouse and siblings another. Also, if the funeral is held over several days the uniforms might vary from day to day.

Uniforms help funeral guests identify those who were related to or close to the deceased; however, careful attention must be paid to which print represents each group. Others attending a funeral may also wear blue or red pagnes, as these colors are considered appropriate funeral attire in general. Indeed, many of the prints worn to funerals may have been purchased as uniforms for previous funerals, giving them added significance. The commitment of money and time required to select, coordinate, and tailor uniforms also contributes to their meaningfulness. Hence, participating in a uniform is a way to publicly demonstrate esteem for the deceased and his or her family, as well as generosity and a sense of social obligation. When a person is seen in uniform others are reminded not only of his or her connection to the deceased but also of the sacrifice of money and time that he or she has made. The paying of such a tribute is not limited to those who attend a funeral. When I asked a friend about her new outfit, which was made from a red print, she explained that she chose the pagne because it had been selected as the uniform for the funeral of a parent of one of the local teachers.[7] While my friend was unable to attend the funeral, which was some distance away, she purchased and wore the cloth in a show of support and respect for the school teacher.

---

[6] Red and blue in this context refers to the predominant color in the print. "Red" cloth can range in hue from orange or brown to deep burgundy. "Blue" cloth includes a range of dark and light blues and blue-violets.

[7] Fieldnotes, 1991-92.

In December 1991 I attended the funeral of a Baule village chief, an important elder who had exercised influence locally and regionally. The man died in late August and his body was kept at the morgue during the five months it took for the planning of the funeral to be completed. Early in his adult life the deceased had served as a regional Secretary General for the Baule dominated Parti Démocratique de Côte d'Ivoire (PDCI), which was for many years the country's unique political party. Because of his PDCI affiliation the deceased's funeral was paid for by the state. These connections and his high standing regionally resulted in a funeral that was well beyond the means of most Baule, a fact attested to by the many regional dignitaries who attended, including representatives from the PDCI, the sub-prefecture, and numerous villages.

The clothing, including several uniforms, worn at this funeral interested me for the many different stories it told. Those in the deceased's immediate family wore clothes tailored from a specially selected blue-violet fancy print. These family members also sat together during the service, their proximity to each other further emphasizing the solidarity implied by their matching dress. More distant relatives and close friends of the deceased wore outfits made from a blue and white fancy print, also specially selected for the funeral.

Various other blue and white fancy prints were worn at the funeral, as were a variety of red prints. While not selected specifically for this funeral, the multiple number of guests wearing some of these pagnes had the effect, like uniforms, of drawing people together through visual repetition. Prominent among such improvised uniforms was a blue and white fancy print that had been worn as a uniform for the recent funeral of a former mayor of the region's main town. A green fancy print produced for the PDCI during the presidential election of December 1990 was also worn by several guests. Because the deceased had been an active and faithful member of the PDCI, those wearing the print declared their affiliation with and support of the party while simultaneously demonstrating an ideological link between themselves and the dead man.

Like pagne uniforms, other types of clothing that served to group and differentiate people were also worn to the funeral, reinforcing the valuable communicative role textiles can play in such an arena. Commemorative t-shirts featuring a photo silk-screened portrait of the deceased were made for the funeral and purchased to be worn by men and women alike.[8] Many of the male chiefs and dignitaries from neighboring villages attended wearing large wrappers. In Côte d'Ivoire men are rarely seen wearing wrappers outside of their home or village. When worn at a special event, such dress is associated with the conservatism of the village. In the context of this funeral, wrappers identified important men within the regional village hierarchy. While, unlike other uniforms, these wrappers did not match, their distinctive voluminousness drew the men together into a cohesive group.

In contrast, the men and women who came to the funeral as representatives of the Ivoirian government wore contemporary urban

---

[8] These were printed in blue on white t-shirts.

fashions such as suits and ties for men and stylishly tailored outfits for women. Such dress distinguished these people, whose official roles are associated with the urban milieu, from the villagers.

Pagne selected as a funeral uniform is purchased in conjunction with a specific event; however, the outfits usually continue to be worn long after the funeral is over. As I have discussed, uniforms made for one funeral are often worn to other funerals, where they may inspire memories of the person in whose honor they were made and the event where they were worn. Funeral uniforms are worn at other times as well, and it is in such instances that the affective value of pagne associated with a particular funeral is perhaps most evocative. In 1992 I attended a performance in a Baule town where a large funeral had recently been staged for the town's deceased chief. Though this performance was unrelated to celebrations held in the chief's honor, I saw several women wearing commemorative fancy prints that were produced as uniforms for the funeral. Dancing side-by-side the women demonstrated their continued respect for the deceased chief and once again honored him and the things he represented through a repetitive display of the print. Their dress also displayed solidarity and a sense of group identity that may have extended beyond an obvious association with the deceased chief to include their relationships to each other, to the town, and so on. Similarly when Côte d'Ivoire's long-time president, Félix Houphouët-Boigny, who was Baule, died in 1993, numerous textiles were printed in his honor. During a recent trip to Côte d'Ivoire I still found these textiles available in the market and worn on a daily basis, once again helping to keep him and all that he represented alive in people's memories.

The use of pagne at Baule funerals has led to the production and sale of pagne with this market in mind. Blue and red textiles with the potential for serving as funeral uniforms are printed in quantity by both wax and roller-print factories. Many of these prints feature popular designs that have no direct association with death, funerals, or mourning, and derive any significance related to them from context and personal association. Thus, when worn in other situations, for instance as the uniform of a church choir, they can have very different meanings. However, pagne that features funereal motifs is also produced. One such print, known as "Death Knows no Hour," is produced in both blue and red and includes a sickle, an hourglass, and a clock in its imagery. Another pagne, with a decidedly Christian slant, shows three crosses standing on a hill and flanked by slogans such as "Death is hard," "Death knows no pity," and the rhetorical question "What have I done?" Prints such as these, which illustrate popular sentiments about death, have broad resonance and are not considered to be uniquely for use at funerals. Indeed, one elderly Baule man I met in 1992 wore the cloth called "Death has Finished the Family" on a regular basis. Feeling little connection to the much younger, distant relations with which he lived, this man believed himself to be the last surviving member of his family. For him the pagne "Death has Finished the Family" seemed to be an apt representation of his own situation.

Like all objects, pagne has the potential to be valued in diverse ways. In Côte d'Ivoire the importance of pagne at Baule funerals and during mourning can stem both from its market value, for instance when the wearing of pagne is perceived as a demonstration of esteem or generosity through financial sacrifice, as well as its affective value, for instance when pagne worn at a funeral continues to have emotional associations and to inspire memories. As Igor Kopytoff points out, the division between market and affective value is not easily defined (1986). Baule funeral and mourning practices allow us to see how the value of mass-produced textiles may be constituted in complex ways.

BIBLIOGRAPHY

Bickford, Kathleen E. "Knowing the Value of Pagne: Factory Printed Textiles in Côte d'Ivoire". Ph.D. Dissertation, Indiana University, 1995.

_____. "What's in a Name: The Domestication of Factory Produced Textiles in Côte d'Ivoire." Proceedings of the Textiles Society of American Meeting, 1994.

_____. "The A,B,C's of Cloth and Politics in Côte d'Ivoire." Africa Today 41(2) 1994: 5-24.

Faque, Claude and Otto Wollenweber. Tissus d'Afrique. Paris: Editions Syros-Alternatives, 1991.

Guerry, Vincent. La Vie quotidienne dans un village baoulé. Abidjan, Côte d'Ivoire: INADES, 1970.

Kopytoff, Igor. "The Cultural Biography of Things: Commoditization as Process." The Social Life of Things. Arjun Appadurai, editor. Cambridge: Cambridge University Press, 1986 (64-91).

Kroese, Dr. W.T. The Origin of the Wax Block Prints on the Coast of West-Africa. Hengelo, Netherlands: NV Uitgeverij Smit, 1976.

Pedler, Frederick. The Lion and the Unicorn in Africa. London: Heinemann, 1974.

Picton, John, ed.. The Art of African Textiles: Technology, Tradition and Lurex. London: The Barbican Art Gallery, 1995.

Renne, Elisha P. Cloth that does not Die: The Meaning of Cloth in Bùnú Social Life. Seattle: University of Washington Press, 1995.

Weiner, Annette. "Inalienable Wealth." American Ethnologist 12 (2) 1985: 210-227.

_____. Inalienable Possessions: The Paradox of Keeping-While-Giving. Berkeley: The University of California Press, 1992.

WHITE ROBES FOR WORSHIP: THE *UMNAZARETHA* OF THE NAZARETH BAPTIST CHURCH IN SOUTH AFRICA

Karen H. Brown

South-eastern Africa was a major locus of Christian missionary activity during the 19th and early 20th century and some dozen or more denominations took to the mission field among the Zulus.[1] A Zulu man, Isaiah Shembe (c. 1879-1935) was one of many attracted to the Christian faith. His independent and questioning nature, however, did not allow him to fit into the structure of the white-led missions. Shembe founded his own church, the Nazareth Baptist Church (Ibandla lamaNazaretha), around 1910. Its beliefs and practices are based on a unique synthesis of Christian, largely Old Testament, dogma and Zulu traditional beliefs. In addition to its specific theology, the Church is well known for the charismatic family, the Shembes, who have led it for some 85 years and the characteristic uniforms for worship and dance worn by its followers. This paper is concerned with the white cotton textiles which have been shaped into gowns known as umnazaretha, after their followers, the amaNazaretha or Nazarites.[2]

From Isaiah Shembe's humble beginnings as an itinerant preacher and healer, the Church now has some 300,000 members who live throughout south-eastern Africa.[3] Church headquarters are in the black township of Inanda, near the port city of Durban, however, many Nazarites worship at regional branches through out south-eastern Africa. They are served by a network of ministers and other Church officials who work with Isaiah Shembe's descendants to maintain traditions. The majority of the members are Zulu-speakers and the predominant language used in services is Zulu. Despite the Church's seeming emphasis on Zulu identity, as seen in their dance uniforms, people from other ethnic groups (such as Swazi and Shangaan, both culturally and historically linked to the Zulus) do attend services and often wear their own "traditional dress".

The Church is best known to outsiders for its annual dance festivals which attract thousands of members and visitors. Dance groups are determined by gender, age and marital status and their uniforms are either based on traditional Zulu dress or on Highlands military apparel. Church members consider dance to be a form of prayer, and participation in a dance regiment is an important aspect of the religious experience (Mthethwa 1989). The majority of members, however, are merely spectators at the major festivals. It is possible that the focus on these dance uniforms in both the popular and scholarly literature tells us more about the interests and concerns of outsiders rather than the attitudes of Church members towards the emblems of their faith. The pervasiveness of the white gowns worn for worship services, funerals and other important gatherings indicate that these gowns are far more significant than the more spectacular dance apparel.

This paper will look at three aspects of these robes. First I will discuss their origins in the vestments of the white-led mission churches. Then I will turn to the ways in which a gown is acquired. Finally I will examine the spiritual significance of the robe and its place in the theology of the Church.

The origins of the <u>umnazaretha</u>

There is no evidence that Zulu-speakers in the pre-colonial era ever spun or wove cotton. Nor was woven cloth available to many before European traders arrived in the 1820s (Davison and Harries 1980). Popular dress in the early 19th century consisted of articles made from animal skins and plant fibers.[4] Thus the use of woven cloth and tailored clothing was part of the colonial and missionary penetration into the region (Etherington 1978). White communities required all African residents, Christian and traditionalist alike, to wear European clothing from the 1870s. An important step in converting to Christianity involved the casting-off of "heathen garments". African Christians who belonged to syncretic African churches like the Nazareth Baptist Church usually were initially converted through the mission churches and also retained their western apparel.[5]

Because Isaiah Shembe led an independent group of African Christians he came under the close scrutiny of various branches of the South African government. Many of the earliest reports of these encounters include a mention, sometimes a detailed description, of both his clothing and that of his followers. These long, white robes as described by police constables and native affairs officials set them apart from those African Christians who adhered to the missions and who would not have often worn vestments off the mission station.[6] Nazarites were (and still are) usually compared to (and conflated with) the Zionists who also wear white gowns somewhat different in style (see Kiernan 1991 and Sundkler 1961, 1976).

The earliest photographs I have seen of the <u>umnazaretha</u> were published in the 1930s (Dube 1936, Roberts 1936). They were taken during the last ten years of Isaiah Shembe's life and were clearly taken with his cooperation. In appearance, the gowns closely resemble those those worn today.[7] Shembe claimed that the inspiration for his own clothing and that of his followers was received in a series of visions.[8] His biographer, in 1936, described him as wearing clothing which "resembled that of the ancient priests of the Jews" (Dube 1936, 92). Shembe's robes, in their design, closely resemble both the ecclesiastical garb worn by missionaries as well as those worn by biblical figures in the illustrations found in Zulu language bibles, prayer books and bible stories that were published during the first third of the 20th century.[9] In turn, these prints were probably taken from a stock of Victorian-era bible illustrations popular in Europe and the United States at the end of the 19th century. The source of inspiration for these bible illustrations probably comes from two intertwined sources: liturgical dress and earlier religious painting.

Shembe, although illiterate until he was in his forties, was apparently able to repeat large sections of the Zulu-language bible from memory and had a vast knowledge of the Scriptures.[10] Most missionary societies throughout southern Africa by the turn of the century had published bibles and bible stories in the vernacular languages and these publications seem to have been widely available.[11] Additionally, mission schools, established by the middle of the nineteenth century included instruction in a variety of topics, including bible history (Etherington 1978, 128-131). The publications of two prominent societies with stations in the greater Durban area, the American Zulu Mission and the Trappist Mariannhill Monastery, share remarkably similar imagery, despite the ecclesiastical differences between the two societies.[12] Popular Old Testament scenes include Cain and Abel, the Judgement of Solomon, and Moses receiving the Law. New Testament illustrations predictably include the birth of Christ and other scenes from the life of Christ including the moneylenders being chased from the Temple, the miracle of the loaves and fishes, Christ washing the feet of his Apostles, praying in the Garden of Gethsemane, the Crucifixion and the Resurrection. Most of these images are easy to read and understand and readily convey their message to a largely illiterate readership. Although there is no evidence that Shembe saw these specific texts, they do share strong similarities both in content and the type of imagery with others published at the same time. Shembe's earliest known association with African Christians was in the Orange Free State around 1906 with the Methodist Church and later the African Native Baptist Church (Roberts 1936, 28-30) and it is likely that he was exposed to biblical literature in Zulu or Sotho at that time.[13] Many of his earliest followers in Natal had left the mission churches, including the American Board Church, and he is likely to have seen their publications.[14] Interesting comparisons can be made between the illustrations found in biblical literature published by missions close to Shembe's headquarters in Inanda and both the descriptions of Shembe's visions (recounted in Dube 1936 and Roberts 1936) and the photos taken in the 1930s, however, it is beyond the scope of this paper to examine this aspect of the dress of Shembe and his followers (see Brown 1995).

Contemporary reports noted that Shembe used a tailor in Durban to make up his designs and then sold them to his followers.[15] In the early photographs it is difficult to tell what types of material were used, but it appears to be heavy cotton sheeting. The umnazaretha worn today are made of light-weight white cotton sheeting and are fully cut with a yoke like that found on a choir robe. Although the male and female uniforms are similar, details clearly differentiate gender and social status. Men wear gowns which reach their knees while those worn by women are slightly longer and often have horizontal rows of stitching at knee-length. Married women cover their heads with a headscarf or an isicholo (the basket-like Zulu headdress).[16] They also wear a white shawl made of the same cotton material which is draped over their shoulders. A black fabric belt denoting their status as married women is tied around the waist.[17]

Group leaders and other individuals with authority wear extra garments to indicate their status - such as a detachable, black fabric yoke, known as an isiphika, worn by female group leaders.[18] Men who are preachers or evangelists wear a flowing gown which buttons down the front in either white, blue, green or turquoise modeled on those worn by Isaiah Shembe. Currently most wear dark green robes or cloaks.

Acquiring an umnazaretha

The majority of African Independent Churches regard baptism as an essential event in the life of every believer and this is also true for the Nazarites (Sundkler 1961, 1976; Oosthuizen 1985). Although children raised in the Church wear the umnazaretha when attending services, a person is not considered a full member until she or he reaches 18 years of age and elects to undergo baptism. Baptisms are usually scheduled for a weekend dedicated to the celebration of Church festivals and a large group will be baptized together. The Church observes Saturday as the Sabbath, so baptisms take place on Sunday morning. Those who are to be baptised gather with the ministers in the morning and they proceed together to the local water source. Men and women gather in separate groups on the river bank. Each person removes his or her street clothes and dons an old white gown, usually a cast off umnazaretha, often in poor shape. The two groups then rejoin in order to pray and sing hymns. After this the men and women form two lines down to the water. Each individual is given the opportunity to privately confess their sins to an elder and pray with him. Then he or she queues in order to enter the water where they undergo full immersion. Those who resurface spluttering and upset are said to have had demons expelled. Upon returning to land each person changes into dry clothes and a new umnazaretha. Once the group has reassembled on the shore, they pray and return singing to the temple grounds.[19]

Baptism, judging by the reactions of those who underwent it when I was in attendence, offers a fundamental spiritual experience for many followers. Many were clearly affected, some were weeping. All were in a solemn state preceding and following baptism. As they returned, singing hymns, the solemn mood slowly lifted and the singing became increasingly spirited. Interestingly, their return was not particularly acknowledged by the others who were busy preparing for the afternoon dancing. This experience thus is a personal one rather than one celebrated by the congregation of the faithful and is experienced internally rather than externally.

Although the design of the basic white gown has been clearly codified by years of Church tradition, I could find no evidence that there were strict controls placed over their manufacture today. This is different from the early reports where Isaiah Shembe is said to have had them made by a tailor and then sold them to his followers. Today, each new full member provides his or her own umnazaretha to be donned upon baptism rather than the elders providing such garb. These tend to cost nearly a full week's salary for a domestic worker or laborer, a large sum but considerably less than the dance uniforms. Most individuals order theirs from Church members who work as seamstresses.[20]

"Garments of Heaven"

Isaiah Shembe's son and successor, Johannes Galilee (1904-1976), called the umnazaretha "garments of Heaven" in a 1958 sermon. While speaking on the subject of faith, he told his congregation:

> You say this is the dress of Heaven. Don't think you will reach Heaven
> just because you have worshipped many years.... A white dress cannot

remove sin. We are evil and not worthy of being clothed in white. They are the garments of heaven. But Jesus lifts off the yoke. (Sundkler 1976, 185)

Here Johannes Galilee is reminding his followers that the white cotton gown alone will not absolve them from sin, and that each person must be vigilant against the many temptations of the world. This message was repeated quite vehemently in the 1990s to a Rockville, Soweto congregation I often visited. There Reverend Vilakazi and his fellow ministers called the umnazaretha a "reflection of heaven" when warming Nazarites of the very evident evils and temptations of the world around them.[21]

The choice of the color white for the umnazaretha must be deliberate given its origins in ecclesiastical garb. Additionally, cotton sheeting is inexpensive and easily available. But most significantly, the color white has ritual and symbolic significance in both Christian and traditional African cultures. White, for most Christians, is usually associated with notions of purity and innocence. For many Africans, Christian and traditionalist alike, white is an element of a triad of red, black and white which helps mediate many rituals (Jacobson-Widding 1979, Renne 1991, Turner 1967, Ngubane 1977). This can be seen in the uniforms, robes and vestments worn by members of many different independent churches (Kiernan 1991, Fogelqvist 1986, Sundkler 1961, 213) as well as in the garb of members attending mainstream Christian churches in southern Africa (Moss 1989). Within the Nazareth Baptist Church, these colors dominate the dance uniforms worn by women and girls. Additionally, much of the beadwork consists of Latin cross patterns in primary colors, outlined by a row of black beads. This is placed on a ground of white beads, and the overall effect emphasizes a balance between the colors. For Zulu traditionalists, white is associated with goodness, light and the "good things of life, good health and good fortune" (Ngubane 1977, 113). For African Christians, this is extended to an identification with purity, the angels or Christ and Sundkler writes that "white is an active and effective colour: it carries with it purity and purification and acts as a guarantee that....magic defilement has been washed away (1961, 213-4).

The umnazaretha, both a sign of baptism and membership in the Church, largely relate to notions of purity and strict rules determine the appropriate wearing of the gown. For example, they may not be worn following sexual intercourse when a Nazarite is considered ritually unclean. Acts of purification allow a return to normal behavior. This usually involves ritual bathing at a local water source, symbolically repeating the act of baptism. Members who break church laws have their gowns taken away for a period of time. This act, known excommunication, is done publicly and as is the reinstatement of the right to wear the umnazaretha (Roberts 1936, 79).

As the clergy of the Nazareth Baptist Church reminds us, a white umnazaretha is more than an outward sign of one's faith: it should reflect the thoughts and actions of its wearer. This inexpensive cotton sheeting, tailored into a simple, flowing gown, is transformed and given a sacred nature through the rite of baptism. It confers upon the

Church faithful both the rights and obligations of membership, giving them a solid structure of belief and practice in an increasingly unpredictable, dangerous and chaotic society.

NOTES

1.	These included Anglicans, the American Congregationalists and Presbyterians, Methodists, Swedish, Norwegian and German Lutherans, Scottish Presbyterians and German and French Catholics. See Etherington (1978, 1989) for the history of the missionary endeavor.

2.	This paper is based on research conducted from 1989-1993 in South Africa. I am grateful for the support of a Fulbright-Hays Doctoral Dissertation Fellowship (1989-91) and the assistance of the History of Art Department and the African Studies Program at Indiana University. The literature on Isaiah Shembe, his Church and his family is extensive and promises to continue to grow, see Brown (1995) for a recent bibliography.

3.	The figure of one million was provided by the late Bongani Mthethwa, an ethnomusicologist at the University of Natal, Durban and a Church member (interview, July 1 1988), while another academic, Prof. G.C. Oosthuizen of the University of Zululand, suggested that a more likely estimate was 300,000 (interview, 1990).

4.	See Conner and Pelrine (1983) and Kennedy (1978). Beadwork, which is usually identified as typical of Zulu dress, only became extensively used after Zululand was incorporated into the British Empire in 1879.

5.	Today many elders in the Nazareth Baptist Church claim that the majority of their members were traditionalists when they joined and that a major reason for joining was the Church's acceptance and even approval of traditional Zulu dress. Archival research, however, suggests that many of Shembe's earliest adherents were indeed Christians who had become disallusioned with the missions (Brown 1995).

6.	Papers of the Chief Native Commissioner (CNC) 349 562/1919, Letter from, F.J. Roach, Acting Supervisor of Locations and Mission Reserves, Block Area No. 3, Isipingo, to CNC, Natal, May 26, 1919 in the Natal Archives Depot, Pietermaritzburg. Papers of the Department of Justice (JUS) 334 4/567/21, W.E. Earle, Major for the Deputy Commissioner, South African Police, Natal Division, to the Secretary for the South African Police, Pretoria, 20 Sept. 1921 and papers of the Native Affairs Department (NTS) 1421 24/214, Statement of Dhlamvuza Dhlamini, Native Constable, South African Police, Ndwedwe, to Magistrate's Office, Ndwedwe, 31 Jan. 1923 in the Central Archives Depot, Pretoria.

7.	For good examples see Payne (1930), Roberts (1936), Dube (1936) as well as the Daily News, April 4, 1939 and the Natal Mercury, April 5, 1939.

8.   This is not unusual. Sundkler in writing more generally about African independent church leaders discusses the importance of dreams and visions for determining both the style and choice of color or uniforms (1961, 213-4; 1976, passim). Comaroff reports a similar situation among the Tswana Zionists (1985, 205) and Fogelqvist on the Swazi Zionists (1986, 65).

9.   This resemblance was also pointed out by Comaroff (1985, 204-206) in her study of Tswana independent churches and the clothing worn by their members in the late 1960s and 1970s.

10.   According to Sundkler, Shembe learned to read and write in order to record his hymns (1976, 186-187). Payne describes Shembe's prodigious memory (1930, 203), while his familiarity with the Scriptures, "which he quotes from memory", is described by Chas. McKenzie, Magistrate, Ndwedwe to the Chief Native Commissioner, Natal, Jan. 22, 1923, Papers of the Ndwedwe Magistrate, 1/NWE 3/3/2/17 file 2/26/22/2, Natal Archives, Pietermaritzburg.

11.   Etherington does not give any dates for the publications of vernacular language tracts but does note that "portions of the Bible...were translated and printed just as soon as missionaries acquired a reasonable amount of Zulu" (1978, 157).

12.   For examples, see the American Zulu Mission's Incwadi Yemibuzo Ngezindaba Zebaibeli (190?) and J.B. Sauter's Izindaba zas'eBaibeleni eliyiNgcwele published by Mariannhill (1933). The missionary Josiah Tyler who was responsible for printing some of the American Zulu Mission publications wrote that "the Zulu Bible, printed by the American Bible Society, answers not only for missionaries for the American Board of Commissioners for Foreign Missions, but for the Norwegian, German, and Swedish societies, as well as the London Missionary Society among the Matebele Zulus" (1891, 259).

13.   According to Tracey, Shembe attended a school at the Methodist Mission in the Orange Free State where he had reading and writing lessons and read the Old Testament "both in its Zulu and Sotho translations and was fired by the heroic stories, for they resembled the ones his father had told him concerning the great days of the Zulu chiefs" (1955, 401).

14.   Dube indicates that Shembe was familiar with certain aspects of the American Zulu Mission when he recounts one of the many successes Shembe had in healing the sick. Here Shembe requested that members of the Church sing a hymn entitled "Jesu Son of David, have mercy on me" which he identified as being from the American Board (1936, 66).

15.   The Star, June 15, 1924. This is also mentioned in LeMare (1935, 29).

16.   The built-up headdress, isicholo, typically worn by married female traditionalists is rarely seen in the early photos of Church members when they are wearing the umnazaretha. Most of these women are wearing large and bulky head-ties, which might cover an isicholo. Photos taken in 1939 at a secular event, also show the married women in the umnazaretha and head-ties. In these photos it is clear that the overwhelming majority of women are not wearing the izicholo. See the Daily News April 4 and April 8, 1939.

17.   This belt known as iforteen or isibamba, is modeled on one originally worn by Isaiah Shembe but was transferred to the woman's uniform because so many of his early followers were female. The name iforteen refers to the day of the month when the women hold their meetings. Isibamba is a more generic term for a belt worn by Zulu women, although it is usually was made of fiber (or less commonly of beads) when worn by traditionalists. These belts cen be seen in the photographs from the 1930s. Even if Isaiah Shembe did once wear a black belt and added this to the women's uniform, it only replaced an item which was once associated with the state of marriage by traditionalists.

18.   According to Doke et al., this is a cape for covering the shoulders (1990, 661). These women are known as the umkhokheli, a term which can mean "one who pays another's debts" and also means the leader in a woman's church society (Doke et al. 1990, 398). These women are also responsible for collecting church dues from other women (personal communication, Inah Shoba, Nov. 21, 1992).

19.   Information provided by Rev. M.D. Mpanza, Gibisila Temple, May 20, 1990. Baptisms only take place during important events during the Church calendar, in this instance being the isikhumbuzo of Isaiah Shembe. Here the baptism took place in a nearby river, rather than on Qubu Lake (the Temple is on its banks) as the lake is infested with crocodiles.

20.   For example, the Campbell Collections of the University of Natal, Durban, has several of these gowns which were made by Mrs. Thusi of Inanda who worked in this way. These were collected in 1984 and cost R25 each, then a substantial sum of money for a black laborer.

21.   Sermon, Rockville Temple, Soweto, Nov. 7, 1992.

WORKS CITED

American Zulu Mission. 190?. <u>Incwadi Yemibuzo Ngezindaba Zebaibeli</u>. Second Revised Edition. New York: American Tract Society.

Brown, Karen H. 1995. "The Function of Dress and Ritual in the Nazareth Baptist Church of Isaiah Shembe (South Africa)." Ph.D. Diss. Indiana University.

Comaroff, Jean. 1985. <u>Body of Power. Spirit of Resistance. The Culture and History of a South African People</u>. Chicago: University of Chicago Press.

Conner, Michael, and Diane M. Pelrine. 1983. <u>The Geometric Vision: Arts of the Zulu</u>. West Lafayette and Bloomington: Purdue University Galleries, Department of Creative Arts and the African Studies Program, Indiana University.

Davison, Patricia and Patrick Harries. 1980. "Cotton Weaving in South-east Africa: its History and Technology." <u>Textiles of Africa</u>, Dale Idiens and K.G. Ponting, eds. Bath: Pasold Research Fund Ltd.

Doke, C.M., D.McK. Malcolm, J.M.A. Sikakana, and B.W. Vilakazi, comps. 1990. <u>English-Zulu, Zulu-English Dictionary.</u> Johannesburg: University of the Witwatersrand Press.

Dube, John Langalibalele. 1936. <u>uShembe</u>. Pietermaritzburg: Shuter and Shooter.

Etherington, Norman. 1978. <u>Preachers, Peasants and Politics in Southeast Africa, 1835-1880</u>. London: Royal Historical Society.

_____. 1989. "Christianity and African Society in Nineteenth-Century Natal." In <u>Natal and Zululand: From Earliest Times to 1910. A New History</u>, edited by Andrew Duminy and Bill Guest, 275-301. Pietermaritzburg: Shuter and Shooter.

Fogelqvist, Anders. 1986. <u>The Red-Dressed Zionists. Symbols of Power in a Swazi Independent Church</u>. Uppsala: Uppsala Research Reports in Cultural Anthropology.

Jacobson-Widding, Anita. 1979. <u>Red-Black-White as a Mode of Thought</u>. Uppsala: Uppsala Research Reports in Cultural Anthropology.

Kennedy, Carolee. 1978. <u>The Art and Material Culture of the Zulu-speaking Peoples</u>. Los Angeles: UCLA Museum of Cultural History.

Kiernan, James P. 1991. "Wear'n' Tear and Repair: The Colour Coding of Mystical Mending in Zulu Zionist Churches." <u>Africa</u> 66(1): 26-39.

Le Mare, W.R. 1935. "Shembe: Strangest of all Native Preachers who have sprung up among the Bantu Peoples of South Africa." Sketches of Empire.

Moss, Barbara. 1989. "Clothed in Righteousness and Respect: The Use of Uniforms within Zimbabwean Women's Ruwadzano in the Methodist Church." Paper presented at the 32nd annual meeting of the African Studies Association, Atlanta, GA.

Mthethwa, Bongani N. 1989. "Music and Dance as Therapy in African Traditional Societies with Special Reference to the Ibandla lamaNazaretha ('the Church of the Nazarites')." In Afro-Christian Religion and Healing in Southern Africa, edited by G.C. Oosthuizen et al., 243-256. Lewiston, NY: Edwin Mellen Press.

Ngubane, Harriet. 1977. Body and Mind in Zulu Medicine. An Ethnography of health and disease in Nyuswa-Zulu thought and practice. London: Academic Press.

Oosthuizen, G.C. 1985. Baptism in the Context of the African Indigenous/Independent Churches (A.I.C.). KwaDlangezwa: University of Zululand.

Payne, A. 1930. "A Prophet among the Zulus: Shembe." Illustrated London News 176 (Feb. 8): 203.

Renne, Elisha P. 1991. "Water, spirits and plain white cloth: the ambiguity of things in Bunu social life." Man 26(4): 709.

Roberts, Esther L. 1936. "Shembe: The Man and His Work", Master's thesis, University of South Africa.

Sauter, J.B. 1933. Izindaba zas'eBaibeleni eliyiNgcwele. Translated into the Zulu by Th. Langa. Mariannhill.

Sundkler, Bengt G.M. 1961. Bantu Prophets in South Africa. 2d ed. London: Oxford University Press.

_____. 1976. Zulu Zion and Some Swazi Zionists. London: Oxford University Press.

Tracey, Hugh. 1955. "Zulus find the Middle Road." Natural History 64(8): 400-406.

Turner, Victor. 1967. The Forest of Symbols. Aspects of Ndembu Ritual. Ithaca: Cornell University Press.

Tyler, Josiah. [1891] 1971. Forty Years Among the Zulus. Boston and Chicago: Congregational Sunday-School and Publishing Society. Facsimile reprint. Cape Town: C. Struik, Ltd.

Divine Worth: Weaving and the Ancestors in Highland Madagascar

by

Rebecca L. Green

Textiles in Madagascar actively link the living and their ancestors and are therefore fundamental cultural components of the highland Merina and Betsileo peoples. The elaborate relationships between weaving, the ancestors, and reburial practices are issues that reflect a complex world of spiritual power, social significance, and potent symbolism. This paper is based upon my research in Madagascar's central highlands, where I lived and studied art, life, and culture among the Merina and Betsileo. In particular, I am interested in the powerful relationships between the living and the dead that are experienced and negotiated through periodic reburials and the manipulation of silk burial shrouds.

Malagasy culture is permeated by the ancestors, who are believed to originate all customs and traditions. They embody great power and are capable of influencing current events and manipulating the lives of their descendants, and as such, play a vital role in Malagasy life. The act of reburial, during which the living periodically re-enshroud and thus reclothe their ancestors, is called *famadihana*, and is an important event within the community (fig. 1). Depending on family, regional, and divinatory considerations, this recurring ceremony takes place every two to twenty years after the initial funeral. Reburials are essential in defining the deceased as "ancestor" by ensuring his or her final inclusion in the family tomb and envelopment in a proper shroud. Shrouds are offerings to, and integral parts of the ancestors. They are powerful tools that allow the living to tangibly care for and bestow honor upon their predecessors. Moreover, they are vehicles of communication through which the living request blessings of the ancestors, and the ancestors protect, bless, and care for their living descendants in return. Finally, shrouds identify the ancestors socially, politically, economically, and literally, that is, by marking specific placement within the tomb. Envelopment within the cloth distinguishes the ancestors as Malagasy and as fully civilized human beings. For ultimately, as the ancestors turn to dust, the "ancestors" become a mixture of their remains and that of the silk shroud, which becomes an indivisible element of those whom it was made to honor.

The burial shroud (fig. 2), called *lambamena*, is comprised of multiple panels that are woven on a horizontal, single heddle loom (fig. 3), and then sewn together lengthwise. The overall size varies depending on the dimensions of the individual panels and on the status and financial abilities of the deceased and the deceased's family. While other materials may be used, indigenous silk, called *landibe*, is considered the most prestigious and most traditional. Woven by men and women from weaving families, shroud decoration depends on personal preference and regional style. Embellishment generally consists of stripes and/or motifs made of warp floats and beadwork, the later frequently remaining along the borders.

The inclusion of color is potentially significant. Since divination and astrology play important roles in their lives, highland Malagasy consult diviners about important events or problems. Diviners consider a complex system that incorporates the cardinal points, calendric and numerical forecasts, and color symbolism in their prognoses. For example, each day of the week is associated with a particular destiny, set of characteristics, and colors. Thus, Monday is consecrated to remember the dead, is the preferred day to conduct purifications and inhumations, and is associated with the color red.[1]

The name of the burial shroud, *lambamena*, literally translates as "red cloth," but does not necessarily refer to the cloth's actual color. Malagasy say the name may have derived from the shroud's historic color, although currently red is often limited to decorative bands. Red may also relate to the significance, context, and function associated with its color. According to Mack, red is associated with authority, ruling classes, and all the characteristics accompanying a person of this position. A red umbrella signified a Merina sovereign, and red is incorporated in powerful charms, suggesting its "potent, ardent or forceful characteristics."[2] Such characteristics are appropriate for a textile that is intimately associated with the ancestors.

While shrouds frequently retain the color of natural silk (as in the illustrations), particularly when used by families in middle to lower economic situations, the traditional colors are remembered as various combinations of red, black, and yellow. Colors may be pre-selected by the deceased, chosen by his or her descendants, or determined by a diviner. More pragmatically, a shroud's color may depend on one's economic and social situation, the availability of pigments, or one's regional affiliation. Weavers who currently make dyed cloths often use imported chemical colors to do so, and reserve the vegetal and mineral dyes for specially commissioned shrouds. Using chemicals to supplant natural dyes began in the nineteenth century,[3] and continues to be a topic of contention for individuals who see the imports as inferior and "non-traditional."

For subtle color variation, a weaver may dye or stripe the weft thread, while more obvious color embellishment comes from dyeing the lengthwise warp. Still more intricate poly- or monochrome patterns are made through the addition of supplemental weft floats, or small glass, plastic, or metal beads woven into a shroud's weft (fig. 4). Floats and beads often create floral designs and geometric motifs, as well as words or phrases such as

---

[1] R.P. Callet, Histoire Des Rois (4v. Tananarive: Académie Malgache, 1953-58. Translation by G.S. Chapus and E. Ratsimba of Callet's original 1873 Tantaran'ny Andriana eto Madagascar), vol. 1:65.

[2] John Mack Malagasy Textiles (Shire Ethnography XIV. Bucks, United Kingdom: Shire Publications Ltd., 1989), pp.43-4. See also Mervyn Brown, Madagascar Rediscovered: A History From Early Times To Independence (London: Damien Tunnacliffe, 1978), pp. 194-5.

[3] According to Mack, "chemically produced aniline dyes have increasingly been used" in highland Madagascar since the 1820's (1989, p.33). Although, according to other sources, chemical dyes were first discovered in 18th century France, aniline dyes were not developed commercially until 1856 (Encyclopedia of Textiles 1980, p.435, Wingate 1970, p.21). It was the advent of aniline dyes, however, that finally made chemical dyes more readily available.

the deceased's name or a specific blessing.[4] White beads are currently used on highland shrouds, although in some regions, past royalty had the exclusive right to incorporate red and blue beads.

I was often told that decorative elements are included solely to render shrouds more beautiful. Yet, because of the shrouds' intimate ancestral associations, the significance of the cloth and its decorative elements may exceed simple ornamentation. Beads sold in the market by diviners and medicinal specialists are used as curative, protective, and cleansing devices. For example, the same white beads currently used on burial shrouds are also worn around children's wrists to ease the pain of teething. After a funeral, a person must wash away the pollution of death in a flowing river--one variation of this tradition involves bathing with small black beads that differ from those on burial shrouds only in color. A correlation may also exist between these beads and a black cloth worn in mourning, called *lambarano*,[5] a name meaning "water cloth." Both are black and both symbolically cleanse one of death. Moreover, beads removed from ancient shrouds are used as fertility enhancers, protective amulets, and vehicles of communication with the ancestral world. Thus, due to the relationships of beads, color symbolism, divination specialists, and the ancestors, beauty seems to be only one consideration.

The shrouds' material is also powerful. Indigenous silk is specifically identified as the quintessential ancestral material. It too is sought by individuals hoping to enhance their ancestral communication, increase their protection against misfortune, and augment their fertility and prosperity. Thus, burial shrouds are considered extremely powerful and must be handled carefully. They are associated with many prohibitions, particularly relating to their creation, handling, and storage. While the restrictions and their perceived force vary according to region and individual interpretation, the cloths are created for the dead, and direct contact with or storage too close to the living is often considered life threatening, especially for anyone in a weakened state, such as a child or someone in ill health.

Discrepancies in what is considered appropriate use of the burial shroud is currently a point of contention among highland Malagasy. Used in a socially accepted manner that Malagasy call "traditional," the shroud plays a primary role in both the initial funeral and subsequent reburials. The honor and reputation of the deceased and the deceased's family and town are based on the existence of the shroud, for it is seen as the element which separates humans from animals (fig. 5). To be buried without it is to be a person of no consequence, comparable to a dog. If the deceased's family is poor and unable to supply a shroud, Malagasy social mores stipulate that it must be contributed by the town. Thus, providing a shroud embodies a fundamental responsibility involved in being a civilized human. Even if the deceased was an enemy, one must do everything possible to ensure a shroud, for everyone is a human being first and an enemy second.

---

[4] In the past, it was taboo to utter the name of the deceased, implying that this may be a recent development. See Jørgen Ruud, Taboo: A Study of Malagasy Customs and Beliefs (Oslo: Oslo University Press, 1960), p.171.

[5] Anonymous, Monographie Sur Le Lamba En Imerina (Antananarivo: Musée d'Art et d'Archéologie, #TH726), no date.

This cultural responsibility includes respecting and caring for all ancestors, not only the recently dead. During reburials, many ancestors are taken out of the tomb to be honored and to receive new shrouds. It is considered inexcusable to allow ancestors to sit, unattended in the tomb for any appreciable length of time. If this occurs, they may feel cold and disrespected as a result of a deteriorating tomb or disintegrating shroud. Temperature, as described by the anthropologist Graeber,[6] is an important aspect in establishing the relationships between the two worlds. Heat keeps the living alive and the dead dead. When a living person becomes cold, he or she dies. Similarly, as long as the ancestors are kept warm, they will remain in the realm of the dead. If they become cold, they will communicate their displeasure to the living by causing misfortune, or by appearing in descendants' dreams.

Burial shrouds also act as a vehicles of communication. During reburial ceremonies, shrouds are used to request blessings of the ancestors. For example, on the walk to the tomb, a female descendant who wishes to become fertile may wear the cloth, draped across her breasts and stomach, or dance with it in her outstretched hands. During the process of re-enshrouding the ancestors, living descendants sit with the ancestors on their laps and talk to them of important family events or private matters and ask for blessings in return for hosting the ceremony--all the while touching and interacting with the ancestors and their shrouds. At this time, the living often take fragments of the ancient silk, beads, or mats used to carry the ancestors, items that will be used in the future to physically transmit requests of the ancestors and to transmit the ancestors' benedictions in return. Moreover, diviners also use silk as an ingredient in powerful protective amulets and medicinal cures.

Additionally, burial shrouds act as intermediaries between the living and the dead by allowing physical interaction. Because corpses are carried out of the tomb on mats, they are touched only minimally before a reburial's climax when they are wrapped in new shrouds. Once the ancestors are enshrouded, interaction with them is permissible and even encouraged (fig. 6). They are lifted onto the waiting shoulders of family members and danced around the tomb, sometimes traveling as far as the town or farm to view any developments since their last outing. As the primary means of atonement and appeasement, shrouds keep the ancestors happy and warm, and therefore receptive to granting their descendants' requests. Yet, the shroud is the only object that the ancestors touch or which touches them, making relevant the prohibitions concerning improper physical contact.

Thus, although silk shrouds are highly valued, they and the ancestral forces they embody, are not passive, but are powerful and potentially dangerous. If handled inappropriately, the ancestors may be angered and many people believe that the result could be fatal. Therefore, it is no surprise to find controversy over new materials, such as inexpensive cottons, replacing indigenous silk. Of greater significance for many Malagasy is that shrouds, which are imbued with the ancestors' tremendous spiritual power and which embody those aspects of the ancestors such as authority, power, legitimacy, and obligation, are now being sought by some Malagasy for use in non-ancestral contexts. Specifically, shrouds, whose greatest danger lies in their inappropriate proximity to and physical contact with the living, are being incorporated into the new cultural arena of highly

6 Graeber, personal communication 1990.

fashionable, tailored suits. To use a material associated with powerful ancestral forces in a way that contradicts socially prescribed use is indicative of an emerging cultural environment and an evolving sentiment of individuals within the society that challenge the ancestors, upon whom the living base their traditions, customs, and identities. Moreover, a person makes strong economic, political, religious, and social statements when choosing indigenous silk to create an expensive tailored suit and when wearing it in a cultural atmosphere that traditionally prohibits such use. It expresses the personal aesthetics and the moral and ethical positions of the creator and the wearer of the ensemble. This issue is highly controversial among many highland Malagasy due to a widespread belief in the potentially fatal consequences not only for the person who misuses a material reserved for the ancestors, but for anyone close to him or her.

Although it is generally expected that Malagasy youth will follow the latest fashions before returning in middle age to highland "Malagasy dress," whose primary element is a shoulder wrap, the current issue challenges traditionally accepted behavioral boundaries held by many Malagasy. While I have no illustrations of the silk being worn as a suit, this topic can trigger intense debate. One's sense of identity and cultural affiliation are integral to this issue, particularly if it is a Malagasy rather than a foreigner misusing the silk. Strangers may not be aware of the cloth's cultural connotations, or if aware, are not affected because they are not a product of the culture. Thus I found no adverse feelings towards foreigners using the shroud, even as furniture covers, table cloths, curtains, or bedspreads, but rather pride in the foreign interest and an attitude that outsiders using the cloth improperly do so out of cultural ignorance rather than malicious intent. Yet, if a Malagasy uses the shroud in an unorthodox manner, it can be interpreted as a clear violation of acceptable cultural norms.

This dilemma is exemplified by a young Merina woman I met in 1990 who closely followed current European styles and wanted to wear a fashionable suit of indigenous silk. Her mother, the matriarch of the family, was horrified at the suggestion and staunchly refused, declaring that silk is reserved solely for the dead and that no living person should wear it. In the elder woman's eyes, using the cloth in this manner would be disrespectful towards the ancestors and Malagasy culture, could prove a fatal mistake, and thus would not be tolerated in her family while she lived! Malagasy of all ages reacted to this story based upon each person's interpretation of tradition. For many people, the prohibition against wearing silk represents a faithful adherence to its historical use, and while many Malagasy agree with her, others feel that anyone who continues to believe that wearing a cloth meant for the dead will cause death is living in the past. Some people, however, feel that she is mistaken and that silk was in fact worn by important individuals, although interpretations of how it was worn vary. Consequently, various individuals hold firmly to distinct beliefs that the cloth was worn as a ceremonial wrap or as a tailored suit, was restricted to men or worn by men and women, or was reserved for elders or worn by fashion-conscious youths.

Literary sources support the contention that indigenous silk was worn in the past. The geographer Gade notes that formerly men's suits were made of the silk that "reflected a European fashion" until the influx of inexpensive cotton lowered the demand for clothing made in this costly material.[7] The historian Raherisoanjato further maintains that once imported cottons replaced silk, it subsequently became distinguished as ceremonial wear for such ritual events as births, marriages, and funerals.[8]

Wearing indigenous silk is a source of immense pride for some highland Malagasy. In choosing to wear silk, one is selecting a material of high quality, comparable to certain expensive and elegant imported textiles. When worn abroad, the silk reflects pride in one's own cloth and culture due to the silk's inextricable ties to its cultural and spiritual settings. Therefore, while to ignore the cloth's associated meanings is interpreted by some people as being disrespectful of the ancestors, for many Malagasy, once the material is taken out of its ancestral context, and more importantly, once it is altered, it is not seen as desecrating an essential ancestral element, but as taking pride in one of the primary features of Malagasy identity. According to individuals of this opinion, indigenous silk that has been decontextualized and tailored has left the realm of the ancestors.

Regardless of one's opinion on tailoring the silk, I found almost universal rejection of using the unaltered burial shroud as a blanket, or otherwise coming in direct physical contact with it outside of a funerary context (fig. 7). Interaction with the cloth by the living during a ceremony honoring the ancestors, as when women wrap themselves in shrouds during a reburial, is acceptable, whereas using the unaltered indigenous silk for non-ancestral purposes is not. Thus, I was frequently told that to sit next to someone wrapped in a blanket of indigenous silk would be like sitting next to a corpse. One reason given was that the shroud's color instills fear, and is therefore not as beautiful as a blanket. Yet, as noted above, shrouds are often embellished to enhance their appearance. It may well be that using a shroud as a blanket is visually and tactilely too similar to an enshrouded corpse.

Art and the world in which it is created and consumed are both sophisticated and complex. Therefore, art must be considered within its many social and cultural contexts. Art is an active element in the process of societal change, and artists and art consumers are conscious, vital agents in the negotiation of that change. As the art historian, Baxandall aptly states, individuals involved in the act of creation do not passively accept the "influences" of outside forces, but rather, make an "intentional selection from an array of resources."[9] This active role of artists and consumers of material culture invests the life experience with an essential dynamic quality. Thus, the choice to adapt indigenous silk into fashion based on international styles is a conscious and active manipulation of the

[7] Daniel W. Gade, "Savanna Woodland, Fire, Protein and Silk in Highland Madagascar," Journal of Ethnobiology vol. 5, no. 2 (1985), pp.109-122.

[8] Daniel Raherisoanjato, "Quelques Aspects des Problèmes Relatifs au Developpement de l'Industrie Textile à Madagascar: l'exemple des tissus de soie ou Lamba Landy," Symposium sur les 'Exigences Religieuses et Imperatifs de Developpement dans les Sociétes Malgaches. Académie Malgache - Tsimbazaza: 15-19 Décembre 1986. (Antananarivo: Musée d'Art et d'Archéologie Bibliotheque #TH.867, 1986).

[9] Michael Baxandall, Patterns of Intention: On the Historical Explanation of Pictures (New Haven; London: Yale University Press, 1988), p.59.

cultural environment by members of Malagasy society who are redefining their own life experiences, carefully selecting and incorporating those elements from different cultures which appeal to them most, and changing elements from within their own culture to fit their evolving needs and desires.

The desire to use indigenous silk outside of an ancestral context is a controversial subject challenging some of the fundamental principles currently associated with burial shrouds and related ideals held by highland Malagasy, just as they no doubt have in the past. Being challenged are Malagasy conceptions and interpretations of "tradition," and notions of what constitutes "Malagasiness," both of which form the basis for accepted and expected behavior. However, this process, which many interpret as a radical departure from the so-called "traditional" observances, is only one phase within the overall evolution of a vital and constantly changing culture. Moreover, even if "traditional" use is professed, it is functioning in a new environment and thus has changed, thereby revealing that the concept of a stagnant and unchanging "tradition" is unrealistic.

Fig. 1.   A newly re-enshrouded ancestor returning to the family tomb during a Merina reburial (1993).

Fig. 3. A Betsileo loom (1993).

Fig. 2. New burial shrouds transported to a Merina reburial ceremony in a new basket (1993).

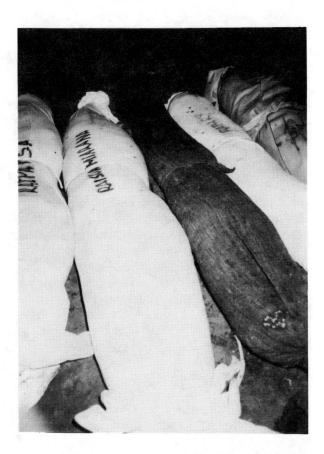

Fig. 4. Newly re-enshrouded Betsileo ancestors within the family tomb. Note the white beads on the dark shroud in the lower right corner (1993).

Fig. 5. Betsileo women wrapping a newly deceased elder woman in an indigenous silk burial shroud (1993).

Fig. 6. Family members gathered around a newly re-enshrouded ancestor before lifting it onto their shoulders to dance with it prior to re-entombment (1993).

Fig. 7. Two Betsileo women sit with a new burial shroud draped over their legs for warmth and to request blessings of the ancestors during a reburial ceremony (1993).

Cloth and the Corpse in Ebira

John Picton.

Abstract. Ebira-speaking people inhabit a region to the south-west of the confluence of the Niger and Benue rivers in Nigeria. The social environment is dominated by Islam, with a Christian minority. Nevertheless, in the late 1960s, when I began the research drawn upon in this paper, much of the pre-Islamic/pre-Christian ritual tradition remained intact; and all three religions presuppose a continuity of human existence beyond death. Yet the question of what persisted, and how, beyond the corpse and the grave remained unanswered in local metaphysics; and none of the Ebira words used of 'body' or 'person' were used of the deceased. Rather, the link between living and dead, enacted in rite and performance, was manifested by means of cloth; for the one index of that continuity was a textile woven by local women of hand-spun cotton with the indigo and white stripes, one pattern for the corpse of a man, and another for a deceased woman. This kind of cloth would be draped around the doorway of a house signifying the presence of the deceased, and later it would be taken down and used to wrap the corpse for burial. The lineage of the deceased's mother supplied the cloth, this constituting one of the means whereby relationships between lineages subsisted. The only other use for this kind of cloth, and then only if striped as for a man, was in the clothing of masked performers. It was as if people entered the world of the dead and returned, re-embodied in masquerade, wearing the same kind of cloth; and it was this, more than any other single aspect of social practice, that manifested the continuity between living and dead. Masked performers also enabled access to a healing energy determined by (male) ancestral precedent. Indeed, masquerade was an aesthetic, structuring, therapeutic and cognitive locus of much of Ebira social practice, a locus in which a form of textile was essential in the gathering together of ideas-and-practices wherein the relationship between living and dead was constru(ct)ed.

I

Um'okuku um'obooba - iruvo pit'aci : 'time past, time present - bottom tells the story of cloth': this is one of the best-known and most often quoted proverbs of the Ebira-speaking people of Nigeria. It summarises notions of time and tradition, making use of cloth as both artifact and metaphor in order to provide an understanding of ancestral precedent. The present is an inheritance. Current practice is legitimated by placing its inception in the past. It was established by others, and they have handed it on to us.[1] This is the point of juxtaposing the first two terms of the proverb: *ume* = time + *okuku* = old in the sense of having come into existence in the past; and *ume* + *obooba*, a word that in my experience was not in common use other than in this proverb where the sense is dependent upon its juxtaposition with *okuku*, thereby emphasising the status of modernity. In other words, the intention in placing these two words

---

[1] In the invocations that accompany any ritual activity, following the invocations of God, Earth, ancestors and so forth, there is characteristically the invocation of the person to whom the inception of the rite is attributed. If this is not known then the invocation is addressed to *onipaapa* , the generic term for the very first person to do whatever it is that is being done. The invocation would typically take the form: 'the very first person [to do this], and it was good for him, and he profitted thereby, and he had children as a result of doing it, this is your kola [or ram/palm wine/whatever is the sacrifice determined through prior consultation with a diviner]'.

together is to emphasise the dependence of the present on the past.[2] The juxtaposition is then explained in the second part of the proverb: *iruvo* = under, base, bottom, reason, buttocks, root (with literal, temporal and metaphorical implications); *pa + ita = pita* = to tell a story; *aci* = cloth. The durable quality of a piece of cloth is determined most effectively by means of that part of the human body that subjects it to the greatest amount of wear, by the bottom that sits on it.[3] So too the value of an element of practice ('cloth') will be tested in terms of its basis ('bottom') within a given tradition. '

II

Ebira-speaking people inhabit a region to the south-west of the confluence of the Niger and Benue rivers in Nigeria, with a "diaspora" throughout Nigeria at differing social and economic levels. On the one hand, there are the migrant labourers on Yoruba cocoa plantations, and the traders in textiles; while on the other are the participants in the public service institutions of post-colonial Nigeria. In the late 1960s, when I began the research drawn upon in this paper[4], the local social environment was dominated by Islam, but with a Christian minority. Nevertheless, the pre-Islamic/pre-Christian local ritual tradition remained substantially intact, if in an attenuated form, and masquerade was certainly its dominant public manifestation. The year was punctuated by the festivals of each of the three traditions, but whatever one's affiliation and level of participation therein, it was masquerade that provided the most distinctive vehicle for an Ebira [male] cultural identity within Nigeria; and this was manifest by the manner in which elite Ebira people would return home from other parts of Nigeria at these times, by the way in which surrounding non-Ebira peoples had taken up Ebira forms of masquerade, and in the weekly broadcasts on the Northern Nigerian public radio of recordings of the songs of the most popular performers.

III

Woven textiles provided the other domain of an Ebira identity in Nigeria. Okene was the administrative headquarters of the area with a market every other day. Cloth was on sale from the crack of dawn until about 7am when the sellers of foodstuffs and other commodities arrived. The cloth sellers were mostly the weavers themselves, arriving at the market with a headload of recently-woven cloth, while the buyers were either men from many parts of Nigeria (especially the regions to the north and south-west) or certain rich local women traders who worked all the local markets, Ebira and non-Ebira.

---

[2] In this view, modernity derives from antiquity. In reality, of course, this sense of tradition entails a social amnaesia wherein innovative practice, or innovative elements within accepted practice, have been incorporated into that tradition such that the memory thereof is erased.

[3] This was a material environment that until the present century did not include sleeved garments.

[4] I was an employee of the Nigerian government department of antiquities f rom 1961 to 1970 . I express my gratitude for the opportunities to live and work in that country. For support of various kinds I wish to thank Professor Ekpo Eyo, the late Alhaji Sanni Omolori, the Ohinoyi of Ebira, Dr Alexis Makozi, now Bishop of Port Harcourt, (but previously of Lokoja) , my field assistant, the late Andrew Ogembe, the British Museum, the School of Oriental and African Studies of London University and the British Academy. The research on which this paper is based was carried out at various times from 1965 to 1969 with subsequent visits. At my last, in 1990, I learned that masquerade had been abolished two years previously. I'm particularly grateful to Elisha Renne for sending me press cuttings since then with reports of illicit masked performance .

As a result they could be relied upon to have a wider range of textiles than those habitually woven by Ebira women. They also bought cloth from the weavers in the market as well as selling it to traders from elsewhere; and they would always have a supply of the distinctive shroud cloths that are the subject of this paper.

The region comprising the eastern and northeastern Yoruba-speaking peoples, the various northern Edo groups, and Ebira, was characterised for among other things, the active household production of hand-spun cotton textiles. In the 1960s women continued to spin and weave locally-grown cotton using an upright single-heddle loom. The cotton itself was mostly white, though a natural brown variety was also available, and some women were adept indigo dyers, producing cotton yarn in lighter and darker shades. Making use of these, weavers produced hand-spun cotton cloth in a range of patterns always with a wide variety of stripes in the warp. These cloths were largely intended for household consumption, but with a Nigeria-wide focus upon 'Okene cloth' much of this production found its way to the market. The generic term for these fabrics was *ikitipa* (clearly cognate with the Yoruba *kijipa*), though cloths only in white were known as *uba* . They too were a basic tough domestic fabric although they might also be employed with ritual implications. In particular, a woman afflicted by witchcraft might be told by a diviner to wear white cloth, white being a colour, in this context, associated with hardship. The afflicted woman would thereby be asking the witches to release her. (Without knowing the personal circumstances of each woman it was impossible to tell simply from her wearing white that that was her reason.) Industrial dyes as well as ready-dyed machine-spun cotton, and rayon and other lustrous yarns, were also available; and, of course, by the late 1970s, lurex, the laminated plastic fibre. Machine-spun cotton yarn seems to have been available in the area from the 1930s onwards; and also in the 1930s, a tradition of weaving in silk was established in one particular household of Alhaji Ibrahim, the Atta of Okene.[5]

This paper is concerned especially with a hand-spun cotton textile called *itokueta*, literally 'the cloth [*ita*] that gathers [*ku*] three' [*eta*], ie it is made of three pieces.[6] The distinguishing features were an indigo-dyed weft, and one or other of two distinctive sets of warp stripes, one for the corpses of men the other for women. I was given no explanation for this, and suspect there is none beyond a simple contextual assocation.[7]

---

[5]   Alhaji Ibrahim was established within British colonial rule as the 'Native Authority'. His reign lasted from 1917 until the late 1950s; and although ousted by a rival local oligarchy he was a major cultural innovator instituting the dominance of Islam, the importance of literate education, the building of a water resevoir, and so forth; and he also introduced silk yarn to the women of his household. Possibly under the influence of decorative techniques associated with women in Ilorin (but no longer extant there though it continues to be a flourishing centre of narrow-strip weaving on the horizontal double-heddle loom) the women of Ibrahim's household established supplementary-weft float-weave patterning quite distinct from the warp striping of hand-spun cotton, attracting publicity and establishing 'Okene cloth' as a distinctive, elite fashion textile among women in many parts of Nigeria. With the demise of Ibrahim's authority, these techniques spread throughout Ebira households and encouraged the cloth trade as already described.

[6]   Cloth of three pieces is an odd designation as almost all Ebira cloth was woven in three-piece sets for sale in the market. (Its name could also be said to be 'three-piece cloth for a corpse [*oku*]', but this was always denied.) *Itokueta* were not included in the category of *ikitipa* .

[7] By the 1980s, as handspun cotton was more difficult to obtain - the usal story: young girls did not want to learn how to spin! - women were now weaving *itokueta* in machine-spun yarn, though still keeping to the distinctive pattens of warp-striping, and, as important, the indigo weft.

A more expensive shroud cloth was known as *itogede*, literally 'banana cloth', and was distinguished by a simple indigo and white pattern of warp stripes together with bast fibres, also in the warp, giving the cloth a slightly shiny texture.

By the late 1960s most of the textiles woven by Ebira women used machine-spun yarns. This was hardly suprising given that it was this that had focussed attention on Okene and Ebira in the first place. In any case, the regular texture of machine-spun yarn made it easier and quicker to weave. Moreover, the greater part of the output of Ebira women was directed to the market place. These fabrics did not have any special name, however, other than the names of individual designs and the two generic terms for cloth, *aci* and *ita*.. [8] Other kinds of textile were available to Ebira people, as result of either trade or travel. These included the widesleeved embroidered gowns of Nupe, Hausa or Yoruba origin, and factory-printed textiles. Once upon a time, moreover, it had been the practice to purchase a particular form of funerary cloth from the Abinu (or Bunu) a northeastern Yoruba-speaking people near Kabba to the north of Ebira. Known as *ubanito* in Ebira, and *baleton* in the Kabba area, this fabric was woven of hand-spun cotton with geometric supplementary-weft patterns in red (said to be unravelled hospital blankets) and other colours. It was displayed on the roofs of houses where the corpse of an elite man was awaiting burial; and also used in masked costume. By the 1960s Ebira people no longer purchased them, but there were plenty in circulation.

IV

Life and death. In Ebira tradition there were two domains of human existence: *ehe*, life, the world of living people; and *eku* the world of the dead. Someone passed from the one to the other at death leaving behind a corpse. All the religions of Ebira people presupposed a continuity of human existence beyond death; but the *eku* of local tradition is not like the vision of God that constiutes the Christian heaven, or the paradise of Islam. It was evident that Muslims and Christians were using the term (sometimes qualified as *eku-oyiza*, the good *eku*) with considerable disadvantage, in my view, to an understanding of eschatological distinctiveness. Within local tradition *eku* was a place of shadow and uncertainty, very far from the sky that was a visible manifestation of God; yet there were means of coming back from it to revisit and reinhabit *ehe*, life, the world of living people.

Revisiting the world took the form of masquerade performance. The generic term for masquerade was *eku*., ie the same word as 'world of the dead'. The obvious implication is that masked performance was in some sense a manifestation of that other domain to which we pass at death. People often used the term *idaneku* to refer to the location rather than the performance; and this is made up of *idi*, place + *ani*, inhabitant of, + *eku*. Two masked types will figure in this discussion: the deceased elder and the usually unnamed servants of the world of the dead.[9] Masked performers were both entertainers and mediators of a healing energy that could be tapped through consultation. Indeed, the whole aparatus of divination, sacrifice and medicine was regarded as a mediation of

---

[8] I do not think that *aci* and *ita* had different particular semantic fields; and I had thought that *ita*, cloth, and *ita*, story, (two low tones in each case as with the possibly cognate Yoruba word *itan*) were homophones (until I began to think about that proverb).

[9] The *dramatis personae* of masquerade was more complex than merely elders and servants, but that is enough explanation for now.

energy in ways established and sanctioned by ancestral precedent; but although revisitation and mediation were overlapping, they were clearly not the same.

I use the term 'reinhabiting' to explain phenomena that were very different from masquerade in the sense that one was not now talking of a presence hidden by cloth, but the way in which a living person was in some overt manner the re-embodiment of someone who had died. Thus, a deceased person would come 'on the head' of a recently-born person; and the deceased in some sense live again. The titled man of a lineage embodied and represented the founding ancestor. When he died the title was said to enter the forest, to re-emerge only when a new man was installed. This distinction beween revisiting and reinhabitating will be considered a little further later in this paper.

In the meantime, while these aspects of ritual, performance and status presupposed a continuity between the two domains of human existence, an important question remained: if at death someone departs leaving behind a corpse, and some kind of continuity is taken for granted, what was it that constituted and manifested that bond of the continuity? what persisted? The Ebira language, however, provided no answer: there was a continuity and an identity, the proof was in the practices and assumptions as summarised, and that was (almost) that. The semantic fields of the Ebira words we translate as body, self, person, breath and life do not include the world of the dead. For them the one term *an'eku*, 'inhabitants of *eku*' sufficed. When speaking English, people might use the phrase 'dead people', and of course one can translate this literally into Ebira; but such was not the habitual usage of Ebira speakers. The question of what persisted beyond the corpse and the grave remained unanswered in local metaphysics.

V

What cannot be put into words can, nevertheless (sometimes), be suggested visually; and in Ebira the link between living and dead, presupposed and enacted in status, rite and performance, was made plain using cloth, For in the context of revisiting,the one index of that continuity was *itokueta*, the textile woven by local women of hand-spun cotton for use as a shroud. As already noted it had an indigo weft, and two standard sequences of warp stripes proceeding across all three pieces, in light and dark indigo, and white, one sequence for use with the corpse of a man, the other for that of a woman. The only variation in that I noted was that sometimes in place of the lighter indigo in the male sequence a commercial red or purple dye (purchased in the market) would be used.

It was the responsibility of the family of the deceased's mother to supply the *itokueta* to wrap the bodies of the deceased ready for burial; athough if the person had been a Muslim white cloth ought properly to be used.[10] For Christians, a wooden coffin might be used in place of the white cloth, though to some extent that would also depend on the economic and social standing of the family. If the death was premature, which in Ebira tradition would mean that the deceased had not achieved the status of grandparent, or if the deceased was otherwise a man or woman of no particular status, a grave would be

---

[10] Sometimes in that case, *itokueta* would be wrapped around the body first and then covered with white cloth. If the family of the deceased was predominantly Muslim the corpse would probably be so treated even though the deceased him/herself had not been a Muslim.

quickly dug, behind the house of the deceased elsewhere and the body buried the same day as the death itself.[11]

If, however, the deceased, whether man or woman, had achieved what was regarded in Ebira tradition as a good death, ie as a grandparent and dieing in birth order (it was socially difficult for a senior to mourn a junior, for example) the process of burial would be rather more elaborate. The body would be on view in the house preferably overnight laid out on a platform in the main passageway, or in a room, and the walls and doorways hung with *itokueta*. Anyone passing by would see immediately that someone of importance within that community was awaiting burial, and they would see whether it was a man or a woman. The family might also have invested in some *itogede*, indigo and white handspun cotton cloth and with undyed bast fibres. It was more costly, and thus prestigious, but not gender-specific in its patterning. The body itself would lie on *itokueta*, covered or dressed in the deceased's clothing, leaving the face and arms visible. Sometimes a cloth of machine-spun yarn, with float-weave patterns, would be placed over the clothing, but still leaving at least the face visible.

Within the house women relatives would sing all night long. Outside there would be musicians playing for people to dance, and if the deceased were a man masked figures might appear. Women and masquerades might even dance together. During the day that followed people would rest, though there might be some musical and masking activity, until late afternoon when people would reassemble for the burial procession. The body would be wrapped in the deceased's clothes, then in the *itokueta* and *itogede* that had been draped. around the walls and doorways. By the 1960s it was usual then to wrap the corpse in a more brightly coloured cloth, sometimes factory-printed, sometimes locally-woven of imported yarns. In the past it would have been expected that a senior man should be wrapped in the patterned red *ubanito* from the Kabba area, which had perhaps been displayed on the roof. Once wrapped, the corpse would be tied with strips of white cloth to a wooden door (ie the kind of broad plank placed unhinged across doorways to prevent animals entering). It would be paraded around the village (or in Okene to the graveyard) carried on a man's head and accompanied by the women and young men of the household and lineage, with drummers and, if the deceased were male, by masked performers.[12]

If the deceased and/or his/her household were Muslim, as already noted, little of this would be done as the body, wrapped in white cloth would have been buried as quickly as possible. If they were Christian, the adaptations and/or denials of these traditions were much less predictable. Masked performers might or might not appear, or perhaps only after the priest or minister had done his part and gone; and *itokueta* might or might not be used. The use of a coffin had become more commonplace, however, although the body was not placed in the coffin until the point of burial; and the procession with the corpse might well include a man carrying the empty coffin on his head following the man carrying the wrapped corpse. The grave for someone of importance would be dug during the morning of the burial. In the villages outside Okene, this would be in a

---

[11] At Okene, the deceased were buried in the graveyard just outside the town. If the deceased was Mulsim same-day burial was the requirement irrespective of status; and the tradition was in the process of other transformations during the 1960s and since, but the details go beyond the requirements of this paper.

[12] The masked performers at burials were always un-named servants in the world of the dead. Mask forms re-embodying a deceased elder would appear at post-burial commemorations.

prominent part of the house such as the front veranda, or the main passage, or its principal public room. What is most important to remember at this stage is that the corpse would enter the ground wearing, among other things, the appropriate form of *itokueta*. Whether visible or not under various layers, most people would have seen the corpse and its cloth during the night wake, and would know that *itokueta* was there, or at least would suppose it to be there.

VI

Dressing for death: *Itokueta* was the clothing within which a person's *oku*, corpse, was consigned to the earth at his or her departure to *eku*. The only other use for it, and then only if striped as for a man, was in the clothing of masked performers. Ebira people had [13] several differing categories of these, each with its particular formal characteristics, contexts of appearance, and relationships to and within *eku* (world of the dead/masked performer). Masked figures of the generic, servant type were known in Ebira as *ekuecici*, literally 'masquerades of rubbish'. They wore tunics and trousers typically of *itokueta*, as the basis of an otherwise often highly individualised costuming, together with a wooden or fabric mask. Current practice throughout the period of my research, however, was that this was one among many options, but that it was regarded as the basis of the tradition. Indeed, it had seemed a tradition so secure that people were free to to be creative within it in terms of the textures and colours of the fabrics and the nature of the mask actually employed. As a result, whether or not *itokueta* was used in any specific example, each masquerade costume was a referral to its use as the basis of the tradition.

However, in answer to the question 'where is the world of the dead?' (*eku, idaneku}* one was likely to be told 'all we know is that the corpse is buried in the earth'. Burial thus provided an image but not the literal truth of the matter. Indeed, one theory of masquerade, for the benefit of women and small children, is that they come out of the ground to inhabit the costumes we have got ready for them. Nevertheless, there was a rite, performed in relative secrecy, that was intended to re-establish once a year the link between *eku*, world of the dead, as if it were within the earth, and *eku*, masked performance.[14] The word *eku* clearly and literally determined the identity of masquerade with that other world. Yet it was the use of *itokueta* that determined the identity of what had once been a person living in this world and the manifestation of that other domain of existence in masked performance. Dressing in *itokueta* was the manner in which one entered *eku* and revisited this world as *eku*.. It was this particular form of textile whether directly as artifact, or indirectly as an idea about an artifact subsisting within an innovative tradition of practice, that manifested the continuity between living and dead, between *ehe* and *eku*.

---

[13] As previously noted, masquerade was proscribed some eight years ago for reasons of excessive violence.

[14] This rite took place at the *ireba*, a sacred place marked by a small heap of stones. and located just outside the community. This, in turn, marked a point of contact between the two domains of existence. The elders responsible for masking affairs would uncover whatever was hidden within the stones and listen; for it was only when they heard the voice of *eku* within the earth 'shout' that *eku* on the earth could 'shout'. This rite in fact opened the season and cycle of masked performances. (There is no doubt that these apparently differing senses of the term *eku* are not unrelated homophones.

Apart from *ekuecici*, the 'masquerades of rubbish', there was the *ekuoba*, the *eku* 'that stretches up'; and these two categories stood in relation to each other as servant to master, respectively. An *ekuoba* took the form of an animated shroud in that it consisted of a rather lengthy (something approaching three yards/metres) tube of cloth made up of *ubanito*, the red-patterned Abinu cloth from the Kabba area to the immediate north of Ebira, with a single panel of either *itokueta* or some other fabric to complete the tube. In preparation for its appearance, the tube would be pinned together at the top, this orientation determined by a stitching into the costume at one end of relics cut from the body of the deceased before burial. *Ubanito* is a very heavy cloth with a multiple cotton weft, and predominantly faced in red woollen (?unravelled blanket) supplementary weft floats, and the performer had to see by peering through the weave of the single panel of the other fabric. In contrast to the 'masks of rubbish' there was neither a face, nor arms and legs, but, and also in contrast to *ekuecici*, each *ekuoba* provided for the supposed re-embodiment of a particular named senior male elder in virtue of his relics sewn into the costume.[15]

VII

On colour and context. *Itokueta* were noticeably different from other Ebira textiles; and not just because they were indigo and white. In regard to their particular formal properties, as far as I could tell, **that** they were different was what mattered. First, they were not like everyday cloths (the indigo weft), and, second, gender was clearly marked out (the two sequences of warp stripes). There was a habitual contextual association which, in terms of form, was complete in itself without further referral to some hidden "symbolic" or metaphoric code.

As to some further implications of colour, the discussion runs in a different direction, however. Firstly, red and white were contrasted in the proverb *oz'o vu d'o vi*, 'a person is white before s/he is red'. The red/white contrast constitutes ideas of the relationship between success [red] and suffering [white], the latter term including both the affliction hopefully capable of healing, and the hard work needed in order to succeed. Secondly, black, a term that includes the colour of indigo dye, is a colour with varied associations: the prestige of owning an indigo-dyed gown; the disgusting sight of soot on the face of the smith in his smithy; the dangers of the night as a time of metaphysical activity, including masquerade and also witchcraft. 'Night' was indeed sometimes used as a euphemisim for witchcraft, and sometimes as a metaphor of death; and night is black.

The distinctive properties of *ubanito*, as the fabric once used for high prestige burials and ancestral re-embodiments, seem to fit in well here. Red, the colour of the fabric, marked the success in life of the deceased whose departure from life was celebrated in that way. On the other hand, the red of *ubanito* was a product of the colonial engagement (the hospital blankets), and such limited evidence as we have (bearing in mind that ancestral costumes were buried with a son of the deceased whose re-embodiment it had allowed) suggests that the use of *ubanito* was very probably a novel

---

15 By the time I began my research in the late 1960s, the invention of *ekuoba* had long since ceased (for reasons I am still not altogether clear about) but there were still many extant examples that appeared at the appropriate time in the annual cycle of masked events; and it will be evident that the relationship between living and dead, manifested by means of *itokueta*, would for the most prestigious of deceased men have also been manifested in the use of *ubanito*..

development of the early 20th century. Its qualities were apt; but so too was the the more recent use of any brightly coloured cloth to catch the eye of a bystander.

In contrast to the black and white of *itokueta*, titled men often wore, among other things, bunches of feathers in their [normally] red caps. These included red and white feathers as well as the breeding plumes of the Standard-winged Nightjar.[16] Titled men were not like other people. At their rites of their installation they were given charge of magical things prepared by the ancestor to represent and constitute the title. Title-taking was indeed a rite parallel to the post-burial celebrations of a deceased elder. The death of a titled man was not marked by the usual rites, for, as a titled man, he had not died: 'the title/chief [17] had entered the forest'. The titled man through his installation was the living presence of its founding ancestor. The ancestor responsible for founding the title reinhabited the world in virtue of the title he had established.

Then, in the other case of reinhabiting referred to earlier, someone would wear red and white feathers in their cap or hair if the deceased elder who had 'come on his head' was to appear re-embodied, though hidden, in masquerade. This 'coming on the head' was a relationship established in the infant child through the consultation with a diviner. It was not a transmigration of souls (the soul is a notoriously difficult concept to deal with cross-culturally) nor was it a reincarnation; yet it was a relationship considered to enable a deceased person to live again in the world. Both of these examples of the use of red and white feathers suggest a visual marking more subtle than a simple red/white/black contrast: rather a contrast between revisiting and reinhabiting, black and white contrasted with red and white, each with its differing implcations for the life and health of the household, the lineage and the wider community.

VIII

Returning to the *itokueta*, there were also its more immediate and overt social dimensions. The expectation that the lineage of the deceased's mother supplied the cloth constituted one of the means whereby relationships between lineages subsisted. Then, the display of *itokueta* when a corpse was awaiting burial placed the household in a very particular relationship to the rest of the community. In advertising the fact of a death, the cloth also marked out the transition within the composition and perhaps the status of the household, and it invited the wider community to participate in the grief of the household at least by visiting to greet the close relatives of the deceased.

The two forms or categories of masquerade brought into the discussion a little earlier each came into existence in the post-burial commemorations of senior deceased men, the elder now *in'eku* [in the world of the dead] revisiting his wives and children with his servant, the latter an entirely generic representation however.[18] Thereafter each had its time of appearance, the elder at the inception of the masking cycle, the servants especially at the final event of the cycle; and each had very different modes of behaviour. Each, however, quite apart from other aspects of performance, enabled access to a

---

[16] The standard-winged nightjar and its breeding plumes have markedly liminal implications.

[17] Another example in which one Ebira word covers concepts that are separated in English.

[18] It will be clear from my descriptions that the generic shroud-like costume re-embodied a specific person, whereas the servants had a merely generic identity in the world of the dead although with often highly individualised costuming.

healing energy determined by (male) ancestral precedent and located as its source in the world of the dead. Each masked performer could act, in other words, as an oracle speaking with ancestral authority in the diagnosis and healing of affliction; and this aspect of masquerade was at least as significant in the lives of people living within these traditions as the dramatic, temporal, and eschatological aspects of performance.

Itokueta was the basis for dressing a corpse **and** a masked performer. More than any other kind of artifact or, indeed, any other element of Ebira social practice, *itokueta* provided and constituted the marking out and summation of this complex of ideas-and-practices. *Eku*, as word, concept, category and practice, was a key institutional locus in the constitution of Ebira tradition. The actions, implications and presuppositions of masquerade could be listed as aesthetic, dramatic, structuring, social, ritual, therapeutic, cognitive, epistemological, etc. Yet here was a locus in which a form of textile was essential in that gathering together of ideas-and-practices wherein relationships between people and between living and dead were constru(ct)ed.

*   *   *

For illustrations of Ebira and related textiles and masked performances described see:
  Picton J & J Mack, 1989 [2nd ed], *African Textiles*, British Museum, London,
pp 14, 16, 20, 30, 45, 68 - 79

For futher accounts of Ebira masquerade and material culture see the follwing papers by John Picton:
  1988, Some Ebira reflexions on the energies of women,
African Languages and Cultures, 1,1, pp 61-76
  1989, On placing masquerades in Ebira,
African Languages and Cultures, 2,1, pp 73-92
  1990, Transformations of the artifact: John Wayne, plastic bags and the Eye-that-surpasses-all-other-eyes, in C Deliss [ed], *Lotte or the Transformation of the Object,* Graz, pp 36-65
  1991, What's in a mask, *African Languages and Cultures*, 3,2, pp 181-202
  1991, On artifact and identity at the Niger-Benue confluence,
African Arts, XXIV,3, pp 34-49,93-94

For a detailed account of Bunu/Abinu textiles immediately to the north of Ebira see:
  Renne E, 1995, *Cloth That Does Not Die*, University of Washington Press

SACRED TEXTILES FROM AN ANCIENT NUBIAN TEMPLE[1]

Nettie K. Adams, Associate Curator
William S. Webb Museum of Anthropology
University of Kentucky, Lexington KY 40506

Since so many of the temples of the Nile Valley were converted into churches after the coming of Christianity, most of the sacred objects of the temples were inevitably lost. The discovery of furnishings or ritual paraphernalia within the walls is extremely rare. As far as I know, our discovery of *textile* furnishings in the temple where they were once in use is quite simply unique.

INTRODUCTION

The discovery of a previously unsuspected temple at the archaeological site of Qasr Ibrim,[2] located in Egyptian Nubia, (Fig. 1) has provided us with a rich collection of sacred objects and temple furniture unknown from other early temples. It was built by the Kushites, an African people who, by 1500 BC, had developed a high civilization with its center at the city of Kerma, located on the middle Nile in what is now the Sudan. In 751 BC the Kushites were at the height of their power. They conquered Egypt, and remained there for over 100 years. Their dynasty was a period of extensive building, not only in Egypt, but even more in their homeland, known today as Nubia. Our temple was constructed during this period-around 750 BC.

Qasr Ibrim, for almost 3000 years, was the single most important settlement in Lower Nubia--that region immediately upriver from Egypt. During its long history Qasr Ibrim was a major religious center--the site of pagan temples and later of several Christian churches and a cathedral. Its dominating situation high on a bluff overlooking the Nile gave it a natural protection from enemies as well as protection from the flooding of the river. Because it has always remained completely dry, the temple and its contents were preserved.

Constructed of mudbrick, rather than stone, the Qasr Ibrim temple is small, especially when compared to grander buildings both to the north and to the south. But it must have been a very holy place, because it remained in use for almost 1300 years. In the period just before its destruction, it was a shrine for the worship of Isis, whose cult had swept the Mediterranean world. With the coming of Christianity to Nubia in 550 AD, the temple and its contents were destroyed in a single brief, violent episode. Altars

---

[1] This article has been adapted for the Textile Society of America 1996 Symposium, Sacred and Ceremonial Textiles, from an article in *Ars Textrina*. See Adams 1987: 85-124.

[2] Excavation at Qasr Ibrim has been carried out since 1961 by the Egypt Exploration Society of London under license granted by the Egyptian Antiquities Organization. All of the textiles mentioned in this article are the property of the Egyptian Antiquities Organization and are housed in the Cairo Museum.

were overturned and statues were smashed, actions consistent with Christianity's commandment against idols.[3]

In addition to statuary, offering tables, painted wooden plaques, and vessels of faience and glass, textile fragments of extraordinary quality were found within the Isis temple. Everything in the temple had been broken or damaged in some way; the fabrics were willfully torn into pieces and the fragments scattered throughout the several rooms of the temple. Ultimately, 115 textile fragments were identified as having been part of the temple furnishings; from these we recognized 20 separate specimens, of which eight were assembled or reassembled.

GENERAL CHARACTERISTICS OF THE TEXTILES

Considered as a group there are certain features which are worth noting. First, although the use these textiles served in the temple is unknown, it does not seem likely that they were garments. There are no signs of cutting or shaping, and the only sewing, except for the containers, is for the purpose of mending. Second, all but three were made of cotton. This is interesting in view of the flax and wool in general use in Egypt of the same period. The third remarkable feature of this collection is the limited color range. Again, with three exceptions which will be discussed later, the only colors found are dark blue, medium blue, and the natural color of the undyed cotton. Furthermore, the colors are so arranged that the two shades of blue are almost never in direct contact: they are separated by a narrow line of white.[4] This seems to be comparable to the law of medieval heraldry, which forbids contact between red and blue.

The temple textiles can be organized into six groups; curtains, containers, tassels, tapestry-woven fragments, three specimens which are like woven pictures, with borders and dark blue woven frames, and rolled cloths.

---

[3] For a fuller description of the temple and its contents see Driskell, Adams and French 1989: 11-54.

[4] Archaeological textiles connot be considered white by today's standards. Many factors affect the appearance of fabrics which have been buried. For these pieces, the conditions of use, rather than the actual age, seem to have determined their present appearance. The temple furnishings were darkened by smoke from lamps and incense. The oily residue left by the smoke tended to attract dust, which further darkened the colors. The appearance of dark blue was affected least by these factors; undyed yarns were changed the most. The pale blues and medium blues have taken on a greenish hue, a combination of the blue and the soiling elements, which by themselves leave a tannish or golden color.

By contrast, other textiles of the same age which were abandoned before they were finished were never put into use. Their blues are still quite bright, and some of the undyed areas are much closer to the original almost-white of the unspun cotton. (Raw cotton still in its calyx has been found from this period at Qasr Ibrim). In describing patterns with complex color relationships I will use the term white for the sake of simplicity; areas of plain weave will be called undyed.

CURTAINS

The first category, curtains, has been so designated because of their relatively large size, and the lack of any sewing or shaping. They are balanced plain weave, and all were dyed blue after weaving. As the first specimen (QI 86R660) has been assembled it measures 74 x 81 cm; it seems clear that only a small portion has been recovered. Just two sections of the right selvedge are present; all the other borders are missing and the original extent of the piece is impossible to know. The deliberate tearing is quite evident. A second curtain (QI 86R661) is similar to the first, but has a more open weave. Both of these are dark blue.

A pale blue curtain (QI 86R654) is 42 x 56 cm as reassembled. It has one selvedge and an end border of wrapped openwork. (Fig. 2) This decorative technique has been traced back to its probable place of origin at the city of Kerma, and seems to have been strictly African.[5] The maker used dark blue wrapping yarns as well as light blue to create an openwork pattern of diamond shapes. Like the other two curtains, the 32 fragments of this specimen are mute evidence of wanton vandalism.

CONTAINERS

In the second group are objects which can be identified as containers. The most structurally complex is a double-chambered case, (QI 86R70) which may originally have been fitted with glass vessels or other fragile objects Single chambered cases of this type have been found fitted with vessels of wood or ivory for the popular dark eye make-up, *kohl*. This case was constructed of a basketry framework covered by plain blue cloth. Each cylinder was originally provided with a circular bottom, and also with a lid attached to the case by a decorative plait, which acted as a hinge. The attachments can still be seen; the hinge is anchored to the case at the back with a stout knot, and on the front, a loop on the missing lid hooked over the knot. A lid which may very well be the missing member was found very near the temple. The case was decorated with an all-over pattern of couching, and decorative bands similar to the hinge strip.

The second container, a bag, (QI 86R643) may have served as a container for a pair of wooden arms. The arms were found nearby, and the bag was empty. The top is very deteriorated from long handling and possibly from being rolled or folded down. It is made from a single piece of cloth, folded along one side and the two edges stitched together along the side and across the bottom. The fabric is a complete piece--that is, having both starting and ending borders and both side borders. The dimensions are 91 x 60 cm. Decoration is provided by bands of blue and dark blue on an undyed ground.

The third member of the container group is part of a leather bag (86R71). The lining was composed of three layers of plain-weave linen cloth, attached to the leather by bold decorative stitching in flax thread. Elaborate patterns created by the decorative stitching mark it as a cover for a valued and important object. The lining is one of only three specimens from the temple furnishings containing flax.

---

[5] See Adams, in press.

TASSELS

The other two flax examples are tassels. The first is a row of connected flax tassels, sewn to a strip of plain linen cloth (QI.86R644). Ripped away from the rest of its fabric, this border was found in the same area as two large flax tassels, (QI 86R645a,b) which are obviously a pair. Analysis of the decorative wrapping revealed that the brownish yarns and the white yarn are cotton; the others are flax, the same as the tassel. The technique of wrapping is a clever one which conceals the unused yarns behind the visible ones until they are needed again. On examination, I discovered that the brown yarns, where they were protected from the light and air under the wrapping, were a bright red.

The red of these two tassels and red wrapping on a little cotton tassel (QI 86R651) are the only exceptions to the limited range of blues and natural color. The wrapping technique on the cotton tassel is the same as that of the flax tassels. An interesting feature of the cotton tassel is the finial, in which the cords have been worked into a pompom, with a bit of flax cloth inside to hold the circular shape.

TAPESTRY-WOVEN FRAGMENTS

Twenty-two cotton fragments, assembled into six specimens, comprise a group referred to as tapestry fragments because all are very fine examples of tapestry weave. The first specimen (QI 86R653), in two pieces, has a repeating pattern of closely-spaced *ankhs* . The weaving is very fine and close, having 36 weft yarns per cm. The dark blue ground forms a rich backdrop for the *ankhs*, which were originally almost white; their color has now aged to a tawny, light brown. The second specimen,(QI 86R652) represented by a single fragment, also has a small repeating motif on a dark blue ground. It is a dot with an attached hook, woven in the tiniest possible scale (8x3 mm) and probably represents a ladle. We see it from two perspectives: the bowl as seen from above and the handle from the side. Both the *ankh* and the ladle were important symbols in the Isis cult.

The next specimen (QI 86R650), reassembled from two fragments, is a tapestry-woven band (Fig. 3). It consists of a repeating linear pattern in two shades of blue, carefully separated from each other by narrow white lines. A tiny, white eight-pointed star is the central motif in each section. A narrow border of wrapped openwork, similar but much simpler than that on the pale blue curtain, has the addition of a row of very full, closely-spaced tassels. Above the tapestry band is a ground weave of undyed cotton in half-basket weave.

One small fragment (QI 86R657) has a tapestry band pattern similar to the above. A second piece (QI 86R648) is related, but has a vertical orientation, with just enough of the selvedge preserved to let us know that it formed part of one side of the fabric. The motif, instead of the eight pointed star, is a quatrefoil, suggesting a flower or a Greek cross. It is possible that each of these formed part of a border around a rectangular feature, but it is unlikely that they were part of the same fabric.

Fifteen fragments from three separate places in the temple were assembled for specimen QI 86R662. It is technically one of the most expert, and artistically one of the most striking of all the temple textiles. It consists of a row of figures variously termed the Knot of Isis or Meroitic *Sa* boldly rendered in white yarns, against a dark blue ground. (Fig. 4)   Where it is preserved, a solid bar bounds the row of knots along the top. The complete absence of borders gives us no hint of the size or configuration of the fabric.

This weaving is of such high quality that I was surprised to see both single and double wefts used with no discernible pattern. There is a narrow band of single wefts along the edges of two elements; all the other wefts are used in pairs, including the dark blue ground. A second area shows the weft yarns alternating quite randomly between singles and pairs, and here the ground is singles. It is difficult to understand the reasons for such changes; it may indicate that two weavers worked on this piece. In any case, despite the inconsistencies, this fabric remains an extraordinary example of weaving, and must have been greatly treasured in the temple before it was destroyed.

BORDERED CLOTHS

The most extraordinary group of temple textiles to be examined are three cotton bordered cloths which are like tapestry-woven pictures. These three cloths vary in size, but are structurally similar. All of them have a dark blue border which acts as a frame surrounding the pattern. This framing border is itself surrounded by an undyed ground weave with paired wefts. Instead of being square, the four corners of each framing border have a small triangular projection which protrudes into the ground weave. Two of the cloths were mended in antiquity.

Within the dark blue framing border of the smallest cloth (QI 86R649, Fig. 5) is a central field, and a second field which surrounds it. The pattern is woven in such a way that the central field appears to be superimposed over the outer field. Within the medium blue central field are seven horizontal dark blue rectangles, each outlined with a narrow white line. Their arrangement is staggered, with three in one row, four in the other. Inside each rectangle are two white horizontal *ankhs* lying side by side. The outer field has a diamond pattern made of dark blue stepped squares on a white ground. Within each diamond shape is a single horizontal *ankh* in white. Narrow lines of dark blue and white border the edges of the outer field. Along the inner edges of the dark blue framing border is a single row of alternately larger and smaller white dots.

The middle-sized bordered cloth, (QI 86R656) in addition to the ground weave and framing border found also in the small one, has two additional borders surrounding a single field. The field is similar to the one just described, except that the motif inside each dark blue rectangle is a quatrefoil suggesting a flower or Greek cross. The rectangles number thirty-eight, and are arranged horizontally in four staggered rows of alternately nine and ten easch. At the outer edge of the field is a narrow dark blue border with a single row of alternately larger and smaller white dots. Between the framing border and the inner border is a meander, which breaks into separate elements along the sides. There is no white line between the blues of the field and the border--one of the few cases where the practice of separating the blues is broken.

The largest and most complex of the three bordered cloths (QI 86R659) has the double field arrangement seen in the smallest cloth. (Figure 6) Both fields have the diamond pattern made of stepped squares, distinguished only by different use of the three colors. The outer field has the same color relationships as the outer field of the smallest cloth: dark blue on a white ground. The diamond pattern of the central field is made of sky blue stepped squares, completely edged with a narrow white line, against a dark blue ground. The motif inside each diamond shape of both fields is an eight-pointed star: white in the central field and dark blue in the outer field. A small dot in the center of each star is of the opposite color. Between the two fields are narrow lines of white and dark blue; the same occurs in reversed order between the outer field and an inner border. The inner border, one centimeter wide, has a dark blue ground through the center of which runs a row of sky blue dots joined side by side. Even these have been very carefully outlined in white to separate the two shades of blue.

The dark blue framing border is in four pieces, but, very fortunately, one of them still retains a corner of ground weave with part of a selvedge and a portion of end border having a few remaining stumps of wrapped openwork. Figure 7 reveals the extraordinary quality of the work. The even spinning of the yarn and the regularity of the weave make this piece the finest example of textile art yet recovered from this period.

ROLLED CLOTHS

The final group may have been the most sacred of all the textiles in the temple, although they are very plain compared to the preceding specimens. Eleven pieces were found placed together in one corner of the inner hall. All had been soaked in liquid and then wrapped in neat rolls before they dried. The bundles were quite hard and stiff, but not discolored as they would have been if they had been soaked in blood or wine. At first I thought that they contained something, but after unrolling three and finding nothing, I concluded that their importance lay in the liquid which caused their stiffness. An inorganic chemical analysis has revealed the presence of calcium, and organic analyses have indicated that certain amino acids found in proteins and fat are present.[6] These data suggest that milk may be the liquid which dried in these cloths. It is known that milk libations were an important part of the Isis ritual.[7]

Although it would seem that we have identified the liquid, we still need to know why milk was preserved by soaking it up in small rolls of cloth. Were these amulets for pilgrims to the Isis shrine to carry away back to their homes? Or were they perhaps a form of votive offering?

CONCLUSIONS

Despite the extraordinary circumstances of their discovery, the textiles themselves fit within the generally recognized parameters of textiles of late classical times in Nubia. These include the predominant use of cotton, all spinning in the "s" direction, weaves limited to plain weave, including half-basket and basket weaves, tapestry weave, and weft loop pile. The use of color was for decoration and was generally limited to shades of blue and very occasionally, red. One other feature, unique to the Kushites and their descendants, the Meroites and the Ballana people, is the technique of wrapped openwork.[8]

---

[6] I am very grateful to Textile Fibers, Research Division, of Petersburg, Virginia, and to Ms. Donna Harris, who kindly provided me with this information.

[7] Janice Yellin has discussed the use of milk in Isis ritual. See Yellin 1982: 151-155. For further information about the cult of Isis see Witt 1971.

[8] There are many examples from Qasr Ibrim of this technique reported by Crowfoot 1984: 10-17. Specimens have also been reported from Karanog by Randall-MacIver and Woolley 1910: Pl. 108, Fig. 5; from Gebel Adda by Crowfoot n.d.: number 5; from Qustul by Thurman 1979: 40-41; and from Aksha by Vila 1967: 176-77, Figs. 155b and 156a and b.

What then, has this discovery added to our knowledge of late classical Nubian textiles? The three blue curtains, all dyed in the piece, are a real departure from the prevailing practice. In analysing more than three thousand textile fragments of this period from elsewhere on the site, fewer than ten have been s-spun cotton, piece-dyed blue. It now seems possible that these few were also pieces of the destroyed curtains, since none of them was complete.

Although we have no idea where in the temple these curtains originally hung, it seems possible that they may have been a *parapetasma* which has been described as the "precious curtain which forms an essential part of the setting for a ritual sacrifice."[9] Such a curtain appears in the upper right corner of a carved ivory plaque of an Isis cult scene, now in Dumbarton Oaks.[10] The plain weave does not seem very special to our eyes, but to the ancients, a solid blue cloth most have been precious indeed, since most of their fabric was undyed.

A second contribution is the complex pattern of the cloths with woven frames. Nothing similar to these, with their framed, bordered, elaborate tapestry-woven rectangles, surrounded by an undyed plain ground weave has ever been reported. With the exception of the *ankhs* on the smallest cloth, the motifs are geometric, not iconographic. Yet, given their provenience, the religious nature of these fabrics must now be taken into account when temple furnishings are considered.

The outstanding quality of the tapestry-woven furnishings raises our estimation of weaving to higher levels of artistic achievement in this period. We had been aware that these people were competent spinners and weavers and were very skilled at sewing and embroidery. Fragments of tapestry weaving had been recovered previously, but nothing so complex or so finely woven as these.

The question arises, where were these textiles produced? We shall probably never be certain. Textiles are so easily transportable; these may have come long distances. A possible origin may have been the city of Meroe itself. Because of the climate, few textiles have been recovered from there. But, one small fragment of wrapped openwork has been reported[11] and it is far finer than any from Qasr Ibrim. Grace Crowfoot's descriptions of the several textiles she examined, and her thread counts, indicate that yarn and weaving were extremely fine at Meroe.

These are just some of the many issues raised by the discovery of this extraordinary temple and its contents. Although archaeological excavation provides us with many answers about the past, it also leaves us with questions we didn't even wonder about before the digging started.

---

[9] Weitzmann 1972: 6.

[10] ibid: 5-7, Plate 1.

[11] Griffith and Crowfoot 1934: 10, Fig. 1.

REFERENCES CITED

Adams, Nettie K. 1987. Textile remains from a late temple in Egyptian Nubia. *Ars Textrina,* Vol. 8.

------- in press. "Lace" of ancient Nubian and the Sudan: a unique decorative tradition. *Actes de la VIIIe Conférence Internationale des Études Nubiennes (Cahiers de Recherches de l'Institut de Papyrologie et d'Égyptologie de Lille).*

Crowfoot, Elisabeth, 1984. Openwork fringes from Qasr Ibrim. *Meroitic Newsletter* No. 23.

------- n.d. Notes on the Nubian Textiles from Gebel Adda. Manuscript on file in the Egyptian Department of the Royal Ontario Museum, Toronto.

Driskell, Boyce N., Nettie K. Adams, and Peter G. French. 1989. A Newly Discovered Temple at Qasr Ibrim. *Archéologie du Nil Moyen,* Vol. 3.

Griffith, F. Ll., and Mrs. G.M. Crowfoot. 1934. On the early use of cotton in the Nile Valley. *Journal of Egyptian Archaeology,* Vol. XX, Parts I and II, 5-12.

Randall-MacIver, D., and C.L. Woolley. 1910. *Karanog, the Romano-Nubian Cemetery (Eckley B. Coxe Junior Expedition to Nubia,* Vol. IV). Philadelphia: University of Pennsylvania, Egyptian Department of the University Museum.

Thurman, Christa C.M., and Bruce Williams. 1979. *Ancient Textiles From Nubia.* Chicago: The Art Institute of Chicago.

Vila, Andre. 1967. *Aksha II. Le Cimetière Meroitique d'Aksha .* Paris.

Weitzmann, Kurt. 1972. Byzantine and early medieval antiquities in the Dumbarton Oaks collection. *Ivories and Steatites,* Vol III, Washington, D.C. The Dumbarton Oaks Research Library and Collections.

Yellin, Janice W. 1982. Abaton-style milk libation at Meroe. *Meroitica* 6.

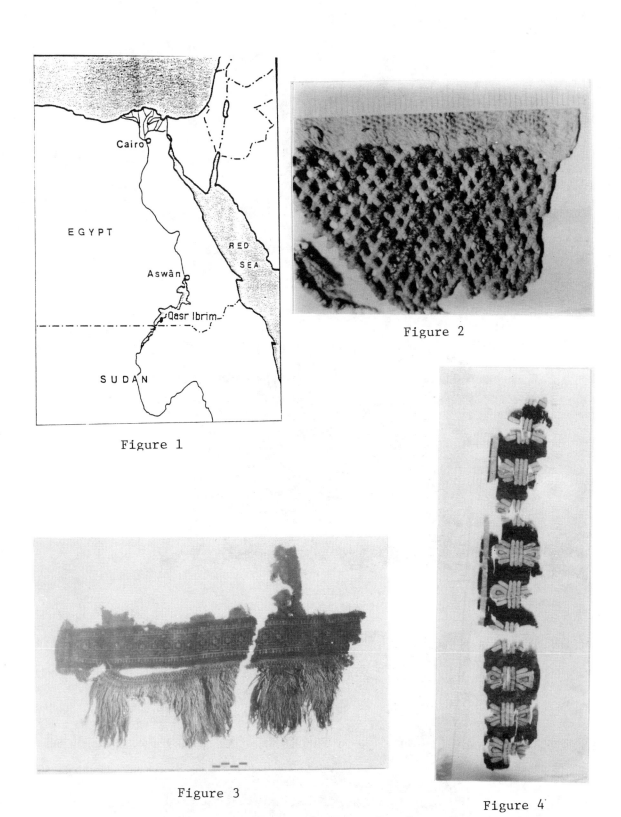

Figure 1

Figure 2

Figure 3

Figure 4

Figures 2-7 are shown with the direction of the warp oriented vertically.

Figure 5

Figure 6

Figure 7

CONTEMPORARY FASHIONS OF

TRADITIONAL TEXTILES AND CLOTHING IN THE GAMBIA

A Video Presentation

by

June Pearson Bland

The cultural and economic significance of textiles and clothing in Africa is still being documented. Most of this video profiling contemporary textiles and clothing in The Gambia, West Africa was taped in November and December 1995 as a part of a doctoral research study which examines the relationship of traditional textiles and clothing to the development of The Gambia. Historical and contemporary influences on dress in both urban and rural areas are shown in the context of the indigenous cultural setting. Brief scenes of weaving, tailoring, and cloth dyeing are included. The video is designed to be used as both an educational and marketing resource.

June Pearson Bland received her Ph.D. in African Studies from Howard University, Washington, D.C. As a result of studying and importing clothing and textiles from The Gambia, she has discussed various strategies with Gambians and U.S. Americans which would preserve the artistic traditions of handcrafted textiles and clothing that simultaneously provide via.ble options to craftpersons and contribute to the economic development of the country. She currently sells and markets African clothing and textiles through her company, *ORIGINALLY* AFRICA.

FOUR EIGHTEENTH-CENTURY MONUMENTAL ETHIOPIAN TABLET-WOVEN SILK CURTAINS*
by
Michael Gervers

In April 1868, a British expeditionary force led by Sir Robert Napier, laid siege to the Ethiopian King Tewodros in his highland fortress of Mäqdäla. Following a brief encounter, the king committed suicide on 13 April and the fortress fell into British hands. [1] Among the objects subsequently retrieved from Tewodros' treasury was a large tablet-woven curtain, and several panels from similar curtains, all made of heavy, thick, spun silk. One of the panels (BM1) was immediately acquired for the British Museum by Mr. Richard R. Holmes, of the Department of Manuscripts. [2]

The British Museum's Department of Ethnography acquired another panel (BM2) in 1973 from a descendent of Major-General Charles M. Griffiths who had also taken part in the expedition. [3] A third hanging, an entire curtain consisting of three panels, is presently in the Textile Department of the Royal Ontario Museum (ROM) in Toronto. It was loaned to the ROM before 1914 by Colonel George Augustus Sweny, and entered the institution's collections definitively in 1922. Sweny, too, had participated in the siege. He understood that this curtain had served as a screen separating the sanctuary in "the ancient cathedral at Gondar" from the body of the church. [4]

To date, only the ROM-piece (Fig. 1) has undergone a thorough physical analysis. [5] This shows that over 350 tablets incorporating more than 1,400 twisted silk threads were used to produce a single panel. [6] The monumental dimensions of the panels, measuring between 520 cms and 535 cms in length and 60 cms to 70 cms in width, make them the largest known tablet-woven fabrics in the world. [7] The colours are predominantly red, yellow and indigo blue, with blue-green and yellow-brown prominent in the left-hand panel. A largely deteriorated strip of bleached white warp threads provides a background for the middle third of the central panel. In terms of colour arrangement and iconography, that part is the most significant section of the entire curtain. The dominant fabric structure is a double-faced weave with three-span floats in alternate alignment.

Like the central panel of the ROM hanging, BM1 is divided into three vertical sections (Fig. 2). Designs are mostly rendered in red against a yellow background, while narrow blue stripes delineate the middle section and define the weft edges. Also like the ROM example, the middle section, which represents fully half the width of the panel, uses bleached white thread for the background warp. This white, probably the result of a milder bleaching agent, remains intact, leaving the woven pattern well preserved and distinct. Three silk cords are attached horizontally and one vertically. They still bear the occasional metal rings from which bells almost certainly once hung. The assumption that the panel was the central section of a tripartite hanging is confirmed by the short, broken threads discernible at the weft edges by which side panels were formerly attached.

The composition of BM2 (Fig. 3) is divided into five distinct vertical strips by four narrow turquoise bands, and further divided into nine unequal sections bearing woven ornamental motifs which can be compared with those in the ROM hanging, notably the vertical stripes, the small diamond network, the checker-board, zigzags and, in its centre, two bands with double rhombuses. The first four strips have alternating red and yellow and red and white threads, while the last is made of blue-green and yellow threads with some red. The over-bleached white threads have suffered the same fate as those in the ROM's central panel.

BM1 and the ROM "triptych" are decorated with figural scenes woven between a variety of ornamental patterns. The frontally arranged composition of BM1 is divided into six superimposed registers. In the centre of the uppermost register is an enthroned king wearing a rich vestment and a turban-like head-dress embellished with a cross and delineated by an applied blue silk cord. The absence of hands and feet suggests that he is seated cross-legged with his hands under the garment. The throne stands on a platform under a canopy and is covered with a fringed textile. On either side of the king stands an angel with stylised wings wearing a long robe ornamented with crosses.

A queen is positioned in an architectural frame directly beneath the king. She is clothed in a long, diamond-patterned, fringed tunic and court-style shoes with upturned toes. Around her neck hangs an applied blue cord, or mätäb.[8] Her ornamental cylindrical crown, the zäwd, surmounted by a cross and decorated with filigrees and pendants in the form of small bells, is of a type worn by Ethiopian rulers during the 17th and early 18th centuries.[9] The queen is accompanied by four female attendants holding whisks and cased manuscripts. Below her, a prince stands under a canopy or an architectural frame. He wears a long decorated robe, a mätäb, court slippers and a diadem. Three of the four flanking guards or courtiers wear three-quarter-length trousers and Ethiopian warriors' lion-skin head-dresses, and hold staff-crosses. The fourth bears neither staff nor head-dress.

Three subsequent registers group warriors wearing the same type of trousers, but differing in their attributes. Those in the first rank bear curved swords (the šotel) and present staff-crosses. The next four warriors hold shields on their left arms and a pair of spears with blades topped by a protective leather cover in their right hands. They also wear a lamd, or lion-skin cape. The last five figures are fusiliers armed with swords, cartridge-belts and matchlock guns.

Although technically and artistically somewhat less accomplished, the central panel of the ROM curtain is generally similar to BM1 and may be influenced by it. It consists of four figural registers. Uppermost stand three bearded ecclesiastics. They wear cone-shaped crowns, called aklil, and pectoral crosses, and hold hand-crosses with a pierced diamond-shaped design. In the centre of the second register is an orant queen whose stance, character and attributes are strikingly similar to those appearing in register 2 of BM1. She is flanked by two female orant attendants clothed in long garments. Below them, in the third register, an enthroned king sits, presumably cross-legged, under a canopy with his hands raised in praise. Although the fabric is badly deteriorated, he appears to wear a diadem, like the princely figure holding a similar position below the queen in BM1. Less successful than the throne in BM1, this one is also covered with a long, fringed textile. The king is flanked by two guards holding staff-crosses. In the lowest register are three sword-bearers closely resembling those in BM1. Each has his right hand raised and wears a head-dress combed upward in strands. A staff-cross stands before each warrior. The left and central figures are also associated with whisks, attributes of Ethiopian high-ranking officials.

It seems that this central panel is an abridged attempt to reproduce the figural registers of BM1 and also reflects a change in patronage and perhaps political succession. The king and angels of BM1 have been replaced by ecclesiastics. The queen retains an identical position in both panels, but the standing prince of BM1 has been replaced by an enthroned king. It would be unusual for a queen to appear hierarchically above her king, unless she were acting as a regent for a minor. As will be seen, there is a historical case in the Gondarene period which corresponds to this situation.

The upper of two figural scenes in the left-hand panel shows a person riding, or standing beside, a lion or lioness. The group is flanked by a pair of confronting open-bill storks. The lower scene represents processional crosses, hand-crosses and censers rendered in considerable detail. The composition is centred around a large diamond-shaped processional cross notable for its pattern of interwoven squares and the elaborate supporting arm at its base. The small, square cross attached to its top is flanked by two others. Immediately below and to the left and right of these are a green and a red square which find their counterparts in the crucifixion scene in the right-hand panel. Under the squares are two pairs of decorative hand-crosses and, below them, four processional crosses similar in form to the central cross, but smaller. These are followed by a row of seven censers, all but one of which are shown with bells attached along the supporting chains of the vessel. At the bottom are eight small crosses with slender handles and cube-shaped bases.

The figural scene in the upper part of the right-hand panel represents a religious ceremony. In the centre, a celebrant holds above his head a Gospel book marked with a cross. He wears typical liturgical vestments: a flat cap and a large cape, called the lanqa, with elongated flaps hanging down his sides. Two assistants accompany him; one, wearing a crown and a lanqa, holds a musical rattle known as the sistrum. The figures are separated from each other by two groups of censers and hand-crosses. The precisely rendered censers, each supported by three chains to which bells are attached, appear with their covers raised. Flanking hand-crosses inserted at the top are of the developed diamond-shaped type, while those at the bottom are of simple Roman form.

The lower scene on this panel represents the crucified Christ wearing a tunic which extends below his knees. Although the cross itself is absent, streamlets of blood can be seen flowing from his feet. The three crosses over him are a device for marking Golgotha, while the irregular outlines on either side could be identified as the hills Gareb and Agra. Christ is flanked by two soldiers wearing short tunics and pointed helmets, and carrying small, triangular shields. Conceived as evil persons, they are represented in profile according to Ethiopian pictorial tradition.[10] The blue rectangle above each of their heads may be interpreted as a symbol of the darkness which, according to the Gospel, immediately preceded Christ's death. Behind the soldiers stand two orant figures who wear long tunics and have hair hanging halfway down their necks. They bear some resemblance to the flanking female figures in the second register of the central panel, but may represent the two thieves between whom Christ was crucified. Above them can be seen a green and a red rectangle representing the Sun, which according to an apocryphal text became dark at the moment of Jesus' death, and the Moon, which turned into blood.[11]

The elaborate representation of crosses and censers which appear at the bottom of the left-hand panel may be seen as a symbolic representation of Christ and the apostles.

The largest cross would thus represent Christ, the two pairs of flanking processional crosses the four evangelists, and the eight hand crosses below, the rest of the apostles. Linking this scene with the Crucifixion scene opposite are the three small crosses which appear above the main cross in the left-hand panel and over the head of the crucified Christ in the right-hand panel. Equally important is the fact that in both scenes the Sun and the Moon are represented as green and red rectangles.

The last scene on the side panels of the ROM hanging, representing a man with a lion between a pair of confronting storks, remains somewhat enigmatic. The obviously religious programme points to a saintly figure. The legends of the saints contain numerous references to hermits and anchorites who kept tame lions which frequently assisted them in their arduous life in the desert. The Vita[12] of the 15th-century abba Samuel states that he cured animals, including lions, that came to his hermitage. Grateful beasts allowed him to ride on their backs - a story which inspired his most popular representation.[13]

The monumental dimensions of these hangings, the double-sided weaving technique used to produce them, and the obviously religious iconography, strongly suggest that they originally served as church furnishings, most probably curtains separating the sanctuary from the other parts of the interior. The iconographical programme and the precise identification of the utilitarian and ceremonial objects appearing on them indicate that the ROM and BM curtains, at least, may well have been manufactured during the so-called Gondarene epoch of Ethiopian history, i.e. between 1630 and 1730.[14]

The use of expensive, heavy silk further suggests royal patronage, most probably by the very individuals who are represented on BM1 and the ROM central panel. Although their identification is not certain, there is good reason to believe that they are King Bäkaffa, his wife Menteuab and their son Iyyassu II. Bäkaffa, son of the famous King Iyyassu the Great, reigned between 1721 and 1730. Like his father he supported the economical and cultural development of the country. His wife, Wälättä Giyorgis (Menteuab), was herself a great patron of literature and the arts. Her political influence came to the fore only after Bäkaffa's death when she was the regent during the minority of their son Iyyassu.[15] We know that Bäkaffa built the magnificent church of the Archangel Raphael in Gondar. Menteuab founded a convent and church at Qusquam near Gondar. It is quite conceivable that the hangings were commissioned for one or the other of them.

An indication that other such hangings were once current in Gondar is provided by Eduard Rüppell's description in the 1830s of the two-storey, circular oratory built a century earlier by Queen Menteuab beside her palace at Qusquam. He noted traces of the heavy silk door hangings and alcove curtains which once adorned its interior.[16] Despite the many references to silk hangings in the historical sources, this is the only one which describes the material as being "heavy". This quality is one of the striking characteristics of the BM and ROM panels. If the remnants cited by Rüppell were a product of the same workshop, there is reason to think that Menteuab at least, not to mention Bäkaffa and Iyyassu II, ordered similar materials to hang in other churches in Gondar.

Further evidence links the production of these silk hangings to a workshop active at the time of this royal family. There is in the British Library a lavishly illustrated ms. which was made either for King Bäkaffa, for his queen or for his son and heir. In order to turn to each miniature, a piece of silk yarn has been passed through a small hole in each folio and knotted, to serve as a tab and protect the manuscript itself. That silk yarn, in blue, green, red and yellow, is of remarkably similar quality and colours as the silk used in the hangings.[17]

Such temporal and material associations would suggest that the royal figures appearing on BM1 may be King Bäkaffa, Queen Menteuab and their son Iyyassu. Those in the second and third registers of the central ROM panel may be the queen and her son. Following Bäkaffa's death in 1730, Menteuab acted as regent during Iyyassu's long minority. According to the chronicle of his reign, it was Iyyassu who not only acknowledged her as the real ruler of the country, but who also declared that she should wear his crown: "Make my mother reign, crown her with my crown because without her my reign cannot go on ...."[18] Seen in this light, it may be postulated that BM1 was produced under King Bäkaffa's patronage somewhere between 1721 and 1730, and that the central panel of the ROM hanging was ordered by Queen Menteuab sometime before Iyyassu II reached his majority in about 1738. The evidence reflects the posture of the chronicle, which makes it quite clear that although Iyyassu was the legitimate successor to the throne, the reins of government were held by his mother, who wore the crown.

There is a postscript to this story. In 1995, Paul Henze discovered another of these curtains in the rural monastery of Abba Garima, near Adowa, in the province of Tigray in northern Ethiopia (Fig. 4). Like its ROM counterpart, it consists of three panels and dye analysis performed by the Canadian Conservation Institute in Ottawa has shown that the dyes compare favourably with those from the silk in BL OR ms 590 and with those in the BM2 panel. Evidence is insufficient at this stage to conclude that the silk for all these hangings was prepared in the same imperial workshop, but the existence of the Abba Garima piece leads us to suspect that field research will bring other examples to light and that as their numbers grow the circumstances surrounding their manufacture will become increasingly clear.

NOTES

* The author is indebted to Dr. Ewa Balicka-Witakowska of Uppsala University for her major collaboration in the preparation of this paper, to Mr. Anthony North of the Metalwork Department of the Victoria and Albert Museum for his generous assistance in identifying the probable origin and date of the guns appearing on BM1, to Mrs. Gillian Long of the DEEDS Project in Toronto for assisting in the research process, to Ms. Anu Liivandi and Ms. Shannon Elliot of the Textile Department and to Mr. Brian Boyle of the Photography Department of the Royal Ontario Museum, and to Ms. Julie Hudson and Mr. Christopher Spring of the Ethnography Department of the British Museum. For a more comprehensive discussion of these hangings, with color illustrations, see EWA BALICKA-WITAKOWSKA and MICHAEL GERVERS, "Monumental Ethiopian tablet-woven silk curtains: a case for royal patronage", Burlington Magazine, CXXXVIII [June, 1996], pp. 375-85.

[1] TREVENEN JAMES HOLLAND AND HENRY M. HOZIER: Record of the expedition to Abyssinia, London [1870], I, pp. 12-13, 15, 56, 229-31 and II, pp. 22, 56-8, 72; S. RUBENSON: King of Kings, Tewodros of Ethiopia, Oxford [1966], pp. 67-89.

[2] O.M. DALTON: Catalogue of Early Christian Antiquities and Objects from the Christian East in the Department of British and Mediaeval Antiquities and Ethnography of the British Museum, London [1901], pp. 181-82. There, the hanging is erroneously identified as an altar-cloth, a mistake deriving from the Museum's hand-written Register of Acquisitions for 1868 where, among the objects "obtained in Abyssinia by R.R. Holmes Esq.", it is described as an "altar cloth of woven silk in various colours with fringe at each end [and] six sets of figures (chiefly three) down the centre: borders on each side with six single frames. L. 16ft 2, W. 2ft." Holmes was given £1,000, apparently to purchase on behalf of the Realm whatever objects he deemed worthy of the Museum's collections.

[3] British Museum, Register of acquisitions.

[4] Sweny goes on to relate that his information "was obtained from both Abyssinians and Europeans". Of the former, he cites only Beru Goshee (Berru Gošhu), dädjadj of Godjam and father-in-law of Tewodros, whom the king had taken prisoner during his campaign against Gondar in 1854. Of the latter, he mentions the traveller and missionary DR JOHANN LUDWIG KRAPF, author of Travels, researches and missionary labours during an eighteen years residence in Eastern Africa, London [1860, rpt. 1968] (for Gondar, see pt. III, chs. II and III).

[5] This analysis was commissioned by the Canadian Conservation Institute in Ottawa, prior to the much-needed conservation of the item which took place in 1993 and 1994 (see the report of M. FRAME, The Gondar Hanging: Structure and Construction, The Canadian Conservation Institute, Ottawa [1993]).

[6] Some of the widest examples of tablet weaving to have survived derive from northern Europe and belong to the first millennium AD (P. COLLINGWOOD: The Techniques of Tablet Weaving, London [1982], pp. 12-18).

[7] ROM (reg. no. 926.26.1): 535 cm long, 212 cm wide (consists of three 70 cm wide panels sewn together); BM1 (reg. no. 1868.10-1.22): 520 cm long, 60 cm wide (central section of a textile originally similar in format to that of the ROM); BM2 (reg. no. 1973 Af 38.1): 536 cm long, 60 cm wide.

[8] In Ethiopia, the mätäb is worn only by Christians (TADDESSE TAMRAT: "The Matab", Bulletin of the Ethnological Society, University College of Addis Ababa, 9 [1959], pp. 38-43.

[9] R. BRUS: "Ethiopian Crowns", African Arts, 8:4 [1974], pp. 8-13, 84.

[10] W. STAUDE, "Profilregel in der christlichen Malerei Äthiopiens und die Furcht vor dem 'Bössen Blick'", Archiv für Völkerkunde, 9 [1954], pp. 116-61.

[11] On the Anaphora Pilati, see K. VON TISCHENDORF: Evangelia apocrypha, Leipzig [1967], pp. 248, 310.

[12] B. TURAYEV, ed.: Vita Samuelis Valdebani, in: Monumenta Aethiopiae Hagiologica, Zapiski Istoriko-filologičeskogo Fakulteta Imp. S.-Peterburgskago Universiteta, 65/2 [1902], pp. 21-22.

[13] Cf. also J. LEROY: Ethiopian Painting in the Late Middle Ages and under the Gondar Dynasty, London [1964], p. 33, fig. 11; STANISLAUS CHOJNACKI: Major Themes in Ethiopian Painting, Wiesbaden [1983], fig. 133; Mensch und Geschichte in Äthiopiens Volksmalerei, Innsbruck [1985], fig. 97.

[14] J. DORESSE: La vie quotidienne des Éthiopiens chrétiens aux XVIIe et XVIIIe siècles, Paris [1972].

[15] E.A.W. BUDGE: A History of Ethiopia, London [1928] pp. 443-59.

[16] "Hier und da gibt noch eine Spur von schweren seidenen Thürvorhängen und Alkoven-Gardinen" (EDUARD RÜPPELL: Reise in Abyssinien, Frankfurt am Main [1840], II, p. 116).

[17] ELIZABETH MOFFATT, "Analysis of the Dyes on Silk Fibres from Three Ethiopian Artifacts", unpublished Canadian Conservation Institute Analytical Report, ARL 3534, file no. 5105-2, Ottawa [2 August 1996], pp. 4-5.

[18] IGNAZIO GUIDI, ed.: Annales regum Iyyasu II et Iyo'as, Corpus Scriptorum Christianorum Orientalium, Scriptores aethiopici, series altera, VI, Rome [1912; rpt. Louvain, 1955], pp.41-3.

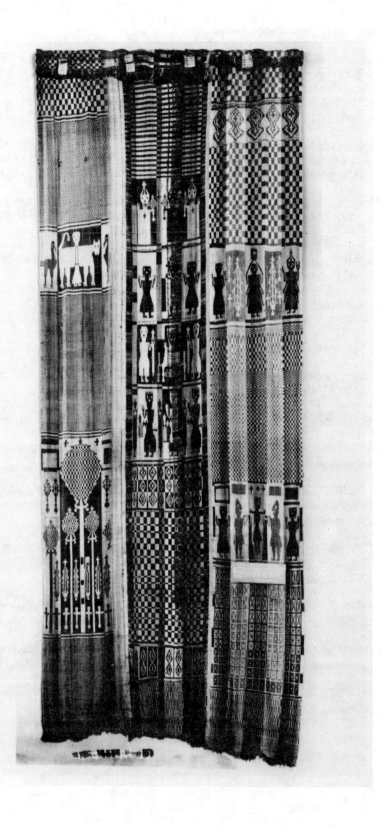

Fig. 1. Three-paneled, tablet-woven silk hanging from Ethiopia. Toronto, Royal Ontario
Museum: Textile Department, reg. no. 926.26.1 (photo: R.O.M.).

Fig. 2. Central panel of an Ethiopian silk hanging with six registers depicting a royal family
and armed attendants. London, British Museum: Ethnography Department, reg. no.
1868.10-1.22 (photo, 1995: Michael Gervers).

Fig. 3   Detail of a patterned silk hanging from Ethiopia showing deterioration of bleached
         white threads (second vertical strip from left) and tabs for supporting a rod so the piece
         could hang horizontally. London, British Museum: Ethnography Department, reg. no.
         1973 Af 38.1 (photo, 1995: Michael Gervers).

Fig. 4.   Three-paneled silk hanging from the monastery of Abba Garima, near Adowa, Tigray
Province, Ethiopia (photo, 1995: Paul Henze).

Naming and Meaning:
Ritual Textiles of the Iban of Sarawak

Traude Gavin
North Yorkshire YO17 0SH
U.K.

In conjunction with the exhibition of Iban ritual textiles I curated at the Fowler Museum of Cultural History in Los Angeles in 1996, I gave a number of lectures based on my field research. The present paper will address some of the questions that were raised by the audience in Los Angeles. All these question are characteristic of the manner in which members of a Western, literate society tend to approach Iban cloth patterns.

This paper is divided into several parts. I begin with a brief background on the Iban people and on the ritual and social function of Iban textiles. This is followed by a condensed account of the two main categories of pattern names used by Iban weavers. The last part is devoted to common Western preconceptions regarding Iban cloth patterns; why we have them, and why we are so reluctant to let them go.

The Iban

The Iban number about 500.000, the majority of whom live in the Malaysian state of Sarawak, in northwestern Borneo. While today many Iban live in Kuching, the capital, or in other urban centres, most continue to reside in longhouses, cultivating hill rice, the staple. Iban society is egalitarian without any form of hereditary leadership or rank. Status differentiation is based on personal achievement. Formerly, the main means of achievement for men was headhunting, and for women, the weaving of textiles.

Ceremonial textiles

Textiles are used only on ritual occasions. One basic function of cloth is to mark a ritual as such. The use of cloth indicates to humans that ritual action is under way and signals to the gods that their attention is being sought. Ritual functions vary. Shamans use cloth as a form of protection while performing healing rites. Cloths are hung in an enclosure around a corpse while it remains in the longhouse. Cloths are wrapped around a temporary shrine which is erected at major rites in order to create a sacred space.

On important occasions, cloths with powerful and high-ranking patterns are essential for the efficacy of the rite in question. The temporary shrine is one such occasion; others are the awning of cloth that is erected over sacrificial pigs, and the reception of the pig's liver on a plate which is formally received by a woman of high standing on a folded cloth. High-ranking patterns are distinguished by being a given a title to reflect their status. Titles thus indicate the rank of the pattern, the ritual occasion for which it is appropriate, but also the status of the weaver. Only acclaimed weavers dare to weave powerful patterns, aided by helping spirits and powerful charms.

Name categories

The most important textiles made by Iban weavers are blanket-size cloths called *pua*. Titles of high-ranking *pua* patterns generally refer to powerful concepts, such as the trophy head pattern (see Gavin 1996:46,81) with its associations to headhunting, and the creator deity pattern (fig.1), which refers to a powerful, beneficent personage in the Iban pantheon. It is important to note that in both examples there is no pictorial representation of either trophy heads or the deity. Iban weavers explain that pattern titles are like proper names. They say, "It is the same as you being called Traude and I, Bidah, she Rose, and so on". It follows that pattern titles cannot be deduced from the pattern itself, just as we cannot deduce a person's name from physical appearance or facial features. I tested this proposition again and again by taking cloths with titled patterns from one river area to another area where the pattern was not known. Invariably, I was told that the title can only be known by the people who made the pattern.

The second name category comprises what I refer to as labels. Labels simply indicate what a motif or pattern is called. Labels are a weaver's tools that are used to refer to practically each and every element in the Iban design repertoire. Vine-like patterns are usually filled with "rice grain" and "spirit's eye" motifs (fig. 2), to give just one example. The names of skirt patterns are also labels, rather than titles. Skirt patterns are not associated with ritual efficacy in the same way as are titled patterns of the larger *pua* cloths. The most well-known and oldest skirt patterns are named after animals, such as the deer, leech and hawk patterns, none of which are representational (for examples, see Gavin 1996:60-63,76,77).

Alfred C. Haddon

The subject of skirts brings us to Alfred C. Haddon whose study, first published in 1936, focused on skirt patterns. Haddon's study, reprinted in 1982, remains the standard reference today. Haddon visited Sarawak in 1898 at the invitation of Charles Hose, a colonial officer in the service of the Brooke Raj. Haddon later purchased a number of Iban cloths from Hose who had attached the names of motifs to the cloths. It is on the identifications provided by Hose that Haddon's study is based. While there is nothing wrong with Hose's original identification of motifs, Haddon's interpretation is rather problematic. Haddon is renowned for his pioneering work in anthropology as well as for his role in art history. In the latter discipline, he was instrumental in propagating the realist-degenerationist school of thought (Haddon 1895). Designs were thought to originate as realistic depictions of nature which eventually degenerated into simplified forms.

The problem of which Haddon was well aware is that, in the Iban case, no known realistic prototypes exist. More importantly, if Haddon had been able to interrogate Iban weavers himself, they would have told him, as they told me, that names of motifs do not tell us what is depicted or represented, but simply what the motif is called (and, in some cases, what it resembles). Examples from a Western cultural context are the checkerboard, the herringbone, and the houndstooth patterns. In these instances we do not assume that the original intention was to depict dogs' teeth or fish bones.

Figure 1:
Creator deity pattern (*buah Selempandai*); private collection (also featured in Gavin
1993:201; and Gavin 1996:87).

Persistent presuppositions

However, the question is, why do people who have never heard of Haddon and his theories expect depiction and representation when looking at Iban cloth patterns? This brings me to my first point, or what Ernst Gombrich (1979) refers to as the psychology of perception, or how we process visual information. When confronted with an unfamiliar image, our eyes scan the image in search for something recognizable so that we can "make sense" of it; or, to use a more appropriate term in this context, so that we can make "head or tail" of the image (Gombrich 1979:143). Iban patterns lend themselves to the process of "reading-in". It is often almost possible to make out some kind of shape or figure. Above all, we tend to seek human faces and figures in the welter of lines. In the literature it is quite common to find apparently abstract Iban patterns described as containing "stylized" human figures (for an example, see Bullough 1981:13, plate VIII; the design is commonly referred to as the whirlpool pattern by Iban weavers; see Gavin 1996:86).

Orality and literacy

The term "reading-in" brings me to my second point: literacy versus orality. In studying Iban textiles, we inadvertently apply the principles of a literate culture to objects that were produced by an oral culture. For literates, it is near impossible to imagine life without the written word and, more importantly, to imagine life without the mindset that comes with literacy (for details, see Ong 1982). As a thoroughly literate people, we also tend to see images linguistically. This is clear from the terminology that we commonly employ without much thought. We seek for "encoded" meaning (Morphy 1994) and want to "decipher" the "iconography" of patterns. In short, our dominant models are linguistic ones (cf. O'Hanlon 1995:469). Haddon assumed that designs devised by primitive man were "pictographs", or a primitive form of language (1895:217). In the case of Iban textiles, we expect named design motifs to add up to a story that can be "read", if only we can find the key. However, the notion of "reading" an image in this way is not part of orally based thought.

Orality differs fundamentally from literacy. Without written records, knowledge must be organized in a very specific way if it is to be accessible. As Ong writes, "You know what you can recall" (1982:33). If a cloth motif is to become part of a widely known design repertoire, its name has to be memorable and easy to recall. One of the cloths that were shown in the Fowler Museum exhibit may serve as an example from a Western context. The lenders of the cloth refer to the design as the "sock" pattern because the most prominent motif looks like a cartoon impression of a sock (see Gavin 1996:45). While organizing the exhibit, there was a succession of exhibition lists, involving the inevitable reshuffling of numbers. However, there never was a problem referring to this particular cloth, because once the connection is made between the design and the name "socks", it is a highly effective memory aid. Many Iban motif names are likely to have been conceived in a similar way. Nonetheless, as with the "sock" example, such names are almost always culture-bound and it is therefore often difficult to see why a particular name is so effective. To give an example, the name of a common border pattern is *bali mabok* (see both borders following the weft in figure 1); *bali* is a prefix commonly used in composite design names, and *mabok* is "drunk", or "intoxicated". The name is always given with a laugh, but no-one can explain the joke. What is clear, however, is that the name is effective since it is remembered by everyone.

Names of design motifs function as a mnemonic device. Often, names are chosen to reflect a formal characteristic of the design. Names that make use of some comical element are particularly effective. As with the sock example, part of the joke is that "socks" is not what the design "is" or represents, but what it looks like. Other properties that make names memorable are assonance, rhythm and rhyme. For example, a zigzag line often included in borders along the warp (see Gavin 1996:53) is called "crossing a river", which in Iban is *semerai sungai*, a rhyme that runs easily off the tongue.

A crucial distinction

To recapitulate, the distinction between titles and labels is critical if we want to understand the "meaning" of Iban cloth patterns in an Iban cultural context. In Iban oral art forms, powerful concepts must be referred to obliquely, using similes and metaphorical allusions (Masing 1981:205). The same applies to the titles of powerful patterns which are meant to invite the search through layers of meaning, hinted at in wordplay and double entendre. However, meanings should ultimately remain opaque and elusive. Keeping meaning opaque is a means of showing respect (cf. Barrett and Lucas 1993). To give an example, the title of the honeybear (*jugam*) pattern is a conundrum. Honeybears are ferocious animals and to kill a honeybear formerly could be counted as taking a human head. This meaning is appropriate in this context, for the *jugam* pattern is high in rank. *Jugam* also means "black", in reference to a honeybear's fur which is black. This meaning applies here as well. The distinctive characteristic of the *jugam* pattern is that it is dyed entirely with indigo (rather than the usual red), a colour which is also referred to as "black" in Iban (for an example, see Gavin 1996:84). The title thus combines both metaphorical and descriptive meaning and it is this combination that keeps its "real" meaning uncertain and hence elusive.

While the search for layers of symbolic meaning is appropriate in the case of titles, it is entirely inappropriate in the case of labels (for detailed field examples, see Gavin 1995:230-2). As Iban weavers say, these names are "just names". Labels are a weaver's reference system, or *aides-mèmoire*, which are used to recall and refer to a whole repertoire of designs and motifs. Iban labels function in a similar way as the names of our herringbone and houndstooth patterns: they denote a variety of cloth designs.

The problem with "original" meaning

The question that I am often asked by a Western audience is, "How about originally? Could these names not have had symbolic meaning when they were first conceived?" To begin with, there is no reason to assume that Iban weavers lack design names whose sole function is to denote. In asking this question, we deny the Iban the sort of two-dimensional thinking that we take for granted in our own culture. We do not presume that the names of the herringbone and houndstooth patterns were originally conceived with symbolic connotations in mind. However, in Indonesian textile studies it is common to assume that *all* motifs were originally endowed with symbolic meaning. When provided with named design motifs, it is accepted practice to search for the meaning of that term in a religious or ritual context and then to juxtapose or connect that meaning to the cloth motif.

For example, one common border pattern in Iban *pua* cloths is called the bamboo shoot motif (*pemucok tubu*; for an example, see the row of pointed triangles of the bottom border in Gavin 1996:54). In healing rites, the bamboo shoot is seen as the plant-counterpart of a person's physical vitality and vigour. It is this ritual significance of bamboo shoots that is applied by Western commentators to the cloth motif (see Sellato 1989:48 and Appel 1991). In our own culture we do not confuse different contexts so easily. Thus we would not connect the cross-stitch to the Cross as the most central symbol of the Christian world, nor would we draw a connection between the herringbone pattern and the fish as a symbol of Christ.

Crossing disciplines: art theory
The problems under discussion have been part of art historical and theoretical discourse for over a century. In his study in the psychology of decorative art (1979), Gombrich devotes an entire chapter to the issue, titled *Designs as Signs*. The discussion covers different art forms from all over the world, both from ancient and living cultures. Haddon's evolutionary theories are discussed in this section and placed into historical perspective. As indicated in the chapter's heading, the central issue is the distinction between designs and signs, between the merely decorative and the symbolic. As Gombrich points out, the problem is that, at least today, the assumption is that *all* motifs were originally conceived as symbols. What is called for then is a reassessment of our premises. Any study of decorative art forms should make allowance for both possibilities: designs as symbols, as well as designs as ornaments.

A change of paradigm
My research of Iban textiles challenges long-held views. However, my findings do not stand in isolation, but are part of a trend which, if it gains momentum, may lead to a paradigmatic change in how we approach the study of Indonesian textiles and other art forms.

Writing on New Guinea shield designs, O'Hanlon (1995:476) points out the defects of an iconographic approach and concludes that the names attached to designs are "little more than a set of fairly rough and ready mnemonics, used to recall and refer to design motifs". The existence of two name categories, the one descriptive, the other related to referential meaning, has been recognized in other Indonesian cultural traditions. Writing on Javanese dance, Hughes-Freeland (1991) discusses the content and meaning of a dance performance as being distinct from the sum total of its components. Javanese dance includes named hand gestures, which, as the author argues, tempt Western analysts to embark on a "quest for meaningfulness", searching for a "lexicon of gesture" (1991:347). Instead, these names serve as a memory aid and classificatory system.

In an even more striking analogy to the Iban case, writing on Javanese batik patterns, Boow (1988:154-5) distinguishes between proper names which are carefully chosen symbolic referents and names which are simply descriptive of design features, providing a kind of shorthand. These are just a handful of examples, which already may make it necessary to reassess part of the literature on these subjects. Batik filler designs are often interpreted as stylized representations of the objects after which they are named (see for example Fraser-Lu 1986:29).

The new paradigm may be viewed in some circles as being "less" than the old one with its insistence on symbolic meaning. However, in the search for a code of symbols, we tend to forget that the meaning of textiles and other material culture lies primarily in their ritual and social function (cf. Gombrich 1979:225-9). This applies most emphatically in the Iban case. The weaving of patterned cloth was, up until the middle of this century, the women's main means of gaining status and prestige. Most importantly, textiles are made to be used. On ritual occasions textiles are, and continue to be, essential. And this brings me, in a roundabout way, to the theme of this symposium: Sacred and Ceremonial Textiles.

Figure 2:
Design elements called "rice grain" (*igi beras*) and "spirit's eye" (*mata antu*); drawing by Julian Davison (also featured in Gavin 1993:202; and Gavin 1996:81).

REFERENCES

Appel, Michaela
  1991 Zur zeremoniellen Verwendung der Textilien. In *Borneo: Leben im Regenwald.* Illustrierte Texte zur Austellung. Staatliches Museum für Völkerkunde, München.
Barrett, R.J. and Lucas, R.H.
  1993 The skulls are cold, the house is hot: interpreting depths of meaning in Iban therapy. *Man* 28:573-96.
Boow, Justine
  1988 *Symbol and status in Javanese Batik*, Monograph series No.7, Asian Studies Centre, University of Western Australia.
Bullough, Nigel
  1981 *Woven treasures from Insular Southeast Asia.* Auckland Institute and Museum.
Fraser-Lu, Sylvia
  1986 *Indonesian batik: processes, patterns and places.* Singapore: Oxford University Press.
Gavin, Traude
  1993 The patterns of *pua kumbu* in an Iban cultural context. In M.L.Nabholz-Kartaschoff, R. Barnes, D.Stuart-Fox (eds) *Weaving patterns of life: Indonesian textile symposium* 1991, pp.191-202. Basel: Museum of Ethnography.
  1995 Iban ritual fabrics: their patterns and names. PhD thesis. Centre for Southeast Asian Studies, University of Hull.
  1996 *The women's warpath: Iban ritual fabrics from Borneo.* Los Angeles: UCLA Fowler Museum of Cultural History.
Gombrich, Ernst H.
  1979 *The sense of order: a study in the psychology of decorative art.* London: Phaidon Press.
Haddon, Alfred C.
  1895 *Evolution in art: as illustrated by the life-histories of designs.* London: Walter Scott Ltd.
Haddon, Alfred C. and Start, Laura
  1936 *Iban or Sea Dayak fabrics and their patterns.* Cambridge: Cambridge University Press (new edition 1982; Carlton: Ruth Bean Publishers).
Hughes-Freeland, Felicia
  1991 Classification and communication in Javanese palace performance. *Visual anthropology*, 4:345-366, Harwood Academic Publishers.
Masing, James J.
  1981 The coming of the gods: a study of an invocatory chant (timang gawai amat) of the Iban of Sarawak. PhD thesis, The Australian National University, Canberra.
Morphy, Howard
  1994 The anthropology of art. In Ingold, T. (ed.) *Companion encyclopedia of anthropology*, pp.648-85. London: Routledge.
O'Hanlon, Michael
  1995 Modernity and the "graphicalization" of meaning: New Guinea Highland shield designs in historical perspective. *Journal of the Royal Anthropological Institute* (n.s.) 1.
Ong, Walter J.
  1982 *Orality and literacy: the technologizing of the word.* London and New York: Routledge.
Sellato, Bernard
  1989 *Hornbill and dragon.* Jakarta: Elf Aquitaine Indonesie.

(RE)SITUATING CEREMONIAL TEXTILES IN IFUGAO, UPLAND PHILIPPINES

B. LYNNE MILGRAM
Department of Anthropology, York University, Toronto[1]

Introduction

Theories of macroeconomic development argue that as communities become integrated into a world-market economy, indigenous customs are increasingly threatened. This assumes that forces such as Western missionary activities and the commercialization of household production inevitably lead to a deterioration of local arts, religion and socio-economic practices. These theories, however, ignore the dynamics of local-level contexts and the agency of individual actors.

Since the early 1900s, the interaction of indigenous religious traditions with external religions like Christianity has created diverse ritual practices throughout the upland Philippines. An important part of the indigenous religion of the Ifugao of northern Luzon, for example, is the belief in and practice of ancestor worship. But the Ifugao are also Catholic and their woven ceremonial textiles figure prominently in both these religious practices. Since the 1950s, the Ifugao have also become increasingly dependent on a cash economy. To earn money they sell local household crafts such as woodcarvings and certain textiles produced for tourists and their labour. In this changing climate, local groups such as the Ifugao desire increased public recognition of their cultural identity and their role in society, yet they also possess national aspirations for material progress and development. These contradictory tendencies, raise many questions. For example, given the continuing challenges of social and economic integration, how can the principles of a market economy and those of Christianity, the religion of the dominant lowland majority, be reworked in ways that uphold unique local worldviews and practices?

This paper, based on my 1994-1995 fieldwork in the northern Philippines, examines the impact of changing economic and social conditions on the production and use of Ifugao ceremonial textiles in the village of Banaue, Ifugao Province. I suggest that the production and use of ritual textiles - women's skirts, men's loincloths and blankets - form a bridge between indigenous and external religious customs such as Catholicism. In fact, they are the medium through which this transformation is articulated. While the patterns in Ifugao ritual cloths continue to reproduce past designs, the contexts within which these textiles function are constantly in flux. In the face of change, Ifugao ceremonial textiles continue to provide a visual statement of an ongoing negotiation and an enduring ethnic identity. This focus on Ifugao ritual textiles adds to the related work on sacred textiles in Southeast Asia by documenting the survival, through redirection and reconfiguration, of this indigenous practice.

In this paper I use the term "ritual" or "ceremonial" textile to identify those cloths which are integral to the successful performance of Ifugao rituals such as rites of passage. Although they may, at times, participate in the secular sphere, textiles designated as "ritual" are primarily used in and associated with the sacred sphere. Secondly, the textiles I refer to as "ritual" cloths are identified as such because of their patterning. As I will outline later, only cloths designed with specific warp stripe arrangements may be used in ritual contexts. Although the category of "ritual" textiles is problematic, I argue for understanding this

[1] The author acknowledges the financial support of this research provided by the Social Sciences and Humanities Research Council of Canada, pre-doctoral fellowship.

designation, not as a static and bounded sphere, but as a category in which modernity is characterized through continuity.

The Setting: Banaue, Ifugao Province

The Ifugao are an ethnolinguistic group of people living on the western side of the Gran Cordillera Central mountain range which extends through the centre of northern Luzon. The term Ifugao identifies the ethnic group of people as well as their province and their language. The municipality of Banaue is comprised of seventeen villages or *barangays;* Amganad, the weaving village in which I conducted my fieldwork, has 260 households. The main economic activity in Banaue, as throughout Ifugao and the Cordillera, is subsistence wet-rice cultivation and raising pigs. With only one rice harvest per year and no agricultural surplus for sale, the production and sale of crafts is the most viable alternative for people to earn cash. While women concentrate on cloth production, men engage in woodcarving.

In Banaue, women of all ages weave, but not all women are weavers. For the most part, weaving is a part-time endeavour to be balanced with household responsibilities, childcare and work in the rice fields. Women learn to weave from their mothers and work individually in their homes on traditional backstrap looms. Weavers use factory-spun materials, mainly cotton, which they purchase from other local weavers who are also yarn sellers. The women who weave ritual textiles may or may not be involved in the larger, parallel production of ikat-patterned textiles targeted for commercial sale to tourists. The weavers producing ritual textiles most often respond to orders placed by their neighbours for specific ceremonial cloths since these textiles are always required for rites of passage such as births, weddings, funerals and curing rites.

Types of Ritual Textiles

This section identifies the types of ritual textiles woven in Banaue. I analyze the way they are designed and what this means to the women who make them and to those who use them. The main types of Ifugao ritual textiles include men's loincloths, women's skirts and blankets.

Men's loincloths in Ifugao are known generally as *wanoh.* Measuring approximately 250 centimetres long by 20 centimetres wide, they are worn wrapped around the waist and between the legs. The man's loincloth distinctive to Banaue is known as *binuhla'n.* The design displays two wide black stripes situated on either side of a central red stripe which is flanked by a series of thin yellow, white and red stripes.

Women's skirts or *tolge*, constructed from two or three rectangular pieces of cloth and measuring in total 140 centimetres long by 75 centimetres wide, are worn wrapped around the waist and secured with a cord or belt. The skirts are divided into three categories of first-, second- and third-class garments: the *pagawa baya'ong, baya'ong* and *binnalit* respectively. The *binnalit* or third-class *tolge* displays equal sized blue and white warp stripes with red and blue saw-toothed shaped embroidery stitching setting off the seams and selvedges. The design of the *baya'ong* or second-class *tolge* consists of alternating solid red and blue stripes of different widths, interspersed with selected stripes depicting geometric, human and animal motifs (rice mortars, snakes) in blue and white. The *pagawa baya'ong* similarly displays red and blue striped side panels, but adds a central white panel supporting two wide blue stripes. It is further distinguished by the striped end band or *langit* which is sewn to each selvedge.

The *gamong* or first-class blanket, 200 centimetres long by 150 centimetres wide, is constructed from four sections: two identical central panels display blue and white stripes overlain with blue supplementary weft patterning at either end; and two matching side panels display solid blue and red stripes alternating with warp-patterned blue and white stripes identical to those of the *baya'ong* blanket and skirt. The *baya'ong* or second-class blanket, approximately the same size as the *gamong* blanket, is also composed of four panels: the side panels are identical to those of the *gamong* blanket while the twin centre panels feature a different arrangement of the blue, red and white stripe elements. Both the *gamong* and *baya'ong* blankets support striped end bands or *langit* at each selvedge. The *hapé or* third-class blanket, slightly narrower than the *gamong* and *baya'ong* blankets, is constructed from three panels each displaying a simple central white stripe against a dark blue background.

The Striped Design Format

Throughout Ifugao, as in the other Cordillera provinces, warp stripes comprise the major patterning element of the region's warp-faced cloths. Each locality, such as Banaue, has developed its own distinctive arrangement and colouring of the fields of stripes for women's skirts and men's loincloths particularly, while continuing to share many of the features of the blankets.

What material aspect of these textiles identifies them as Ifugao and determines how they will be used in secular and sacred situations? In my M.A. thesis, *The Textiles of Highland Luzon, Philippines: A Case Study in Material Culture* (1991), I analyzed the striped design format of early twentieth-century textiles from the five Cordillera Provinces.[2] The examples I studied were drawn from a survey I had conducted of major U. S. and Canadian museum holdings of northern Luzon textiles. For my research in 1995, I took with me to Banaue a variety of photographs of the early Ifugao cloths to use in photo-elicitation. When I showed these photographs to weavers, they immediately recognized each textile type identifying them by name and explaining how the cloth would be used. In some instances, weavers identified a specific artisan in one of the weaving villages who was noted for her skill in weaving either loincloths, blankets or skirts.

In my conversations with weavers about these striped textiles, each repeatedly confirmed that the order and colour of the warp stripes, the primary design feature, must faithfully reproduce past arrangements in order to maintain its distinctive character as an Ifugao cloth from Banaue. Weavers may incorporate synthetic yarns into their weaving, where the colours may not be quite right, but the spatial layout remains constant. When I asked weavers, what would happen if this striped format was not followed, they responded that, "the textile would not be identified as being from this place [Banaue]..with a different design, the cloth could not be used in our *cañao* [rituals]; the weaving would not be suitable to offer as a gift." Juxtaposing examples of early twentieth-century textiles from my earlier research with the contemporary Ifugao ritual textiles I viewed during my recent fieldwork demonstrates a remarkable consistency in the organization of the stripes. These designs defy iconographic classification, but analyzing the patterns by the geometric symmetries

---

[2] For a more detailed analysis of Cordillera textile patterning, see B. L. Milgram, The Textiles of Highland Luzon, Philippines: A Case Study in Material Culture, Chapter Four, M.A. thesis, York University, 1991.

which repeat them, that is, by the way the parts or stripe fields are arranged in the whole design, suggests an underlying structure to which weavers still adhere.

In both the early twentieth-century and contemporary striped cloths, only horizontal and vertical mirror reflection occur as ordering principles. Mirror reflection divides the surface of the cloth across central horizontal and vertical axes, into a bottom half which is a mirror image of the top and into a right side, the mirror image of the left. All the ritual, striped cloths from Banaue, exhibit mirror reflection around two axes. Biaxial reflection is found in loincloths, skirts and in ceremonial blankets. In addition the centre sections of both types of ceremonial blankets restate this symmetry (Fig.1).

What then are the implications of biaxial mirror reflection in ritual textile design from Banaue? Exploring the cognitive significance of symmetry in cultural contexts, Washburn and Crowe (1988:19) examined the perceptual process to determine which features of a form are salient in how we process information. Studies established that bilateral symmetry is most important in shaping perception and in facilitating the correct identification of an object even without total analysis of the object (Washburn and Crowe 1988:22). Thus, the persistence of biaxial symmetry in these cloths from Banaue means that striped textiles emerge as a familiar and easily understood information code for the user and for the weaver. Weavers acknowledge, moreover, that the production of striped textiles remains today a process requiring specialized knowledge and that being particularly skilled in this type of weaving still brings prestige to the artisan.

Ritual Textiles as Cultural Performers

We are all architects fashioning from the materials of our lives...a framework that makes experience intelligible (Barnlund 1981:88).

Theoretical approaches in anthropology to the study of ritual objects generally revolve around two basic questions: what do things mean and what use are they (Augé 1982:6)? In Banaue, at the time of my research, no social or religious event was complete without textiles being bestowed, exchanged or buried. Banaue's striped textiles continue to be integral to all rites of passage such as marriages, special birthdays, mortuary and curing rites. As these cloths trace their origin to Ifugao creation myths and the spirit world, the same mythical font as the Ifugao people's sacred beliefs, they are an essential element in all ceremonial contexts. In their extensive interpretations of Ifugao mythology, early twentieth-century researchers such as Barton (1946, 1955) and Lambrecht (1939, 1958) repeatedly furnished links between cloth production and the cosmic world. Barton (1955:153-154), for example, outlined the myth of how weaving originated in the Ifugao Skyworld and translated chants which describe how the Ifugao picture their deities, not only in their own image, but "all wearing ritual loincloths, all wearing ritual skirts, all bedecked in blankets, beautiful all of them" (Barton 1946:135; cf. Lambrecht 1958:41, 1939:666) .

How then do these easily identified striped textiles manifest their meaning in contemporary Ifugao rituals and what are the implications for female producers? Sherry Ortner (1978:4-5) notes that ritual is a system of meanings conveyed by and for actors through the manipulation of symbolic objects and arrangements. As such, ritual is directed toward a transformation of the participants, either of individuals into new statuses or a group into a new or renewed sense of community. The use of ritual objects such as textiles manifest this transformation as they are the physical means through which this change is achieved.

In her discussion of ritual, Russell (1989:17) agues that we must examine not only the "preexisting set of conceptual understandings" that guide the interpretation and practice of ritual, but also the historical experience of changing political, economic and religious power relationships. Throughout the Spanish (1565-1898) and subsequent American (1898-1946) colonial periods, the ancestral cult in the Cordillera provinces proved to be remarkably resilient. During the early colonial period, celebration of the ancestral cult provided a visual statement proclaiming cultural resistance to Christian conversion and political domination. With the advent of a market economy and with increased political control and greater homogeneity among the general way of life of Cordillera peoples, the role of ritual and the use of ritual objects has emerged as a symbol of local, ethnic cultural identity (Russell 1989:19). The Ifugao, for example, continue to believe that the spirits of the dead dwell both in this world and in their sacred surrounding mountains. They believe that their ancestors must be respected and appeased with animal and material sacrifices in order to bring the community and family good luck and future prosperity. At the same time, the present-day boundaries of the Ifugao ancestral cult have proven to be porous enough to incorporate the external changes occurring in their increasingly commoditized and missionized society.

Rappaport (1979:125, quoted in Russell 1989:17, 19) maintains that it is the ability of ritual and of ritual objects to adapt to change by incorporating new "concrete" materials or ideas reflecting economic or political events, that allows the "higher-order" cosmological and symbolic meanings of religious ideology to persist. Ceremonial objects like textiles embody a transformative power in performance that structures meaning and encourages negotiation within a people's changing world. Striped textiles used in Ifugao ritual continue to chart the course of indigenous ceremony in a region which has undergone profound change. They co-exist in a setting where, from 1900, but increasingly since the 1950s, most Ifugao have been baptized as Roman Catholic and consider themselves active and observant Christians. Ifugao ritual and ritual objects also co-exist with a commercial market economy which began in the 1950s and, has accelerated since the 1970s with the growing tourist industry.

This juxtaposition has been facilitated by the Catholic Church's tolerance of animistic traditions throughout the Cordillera. For many years, the Church has viewed indigenous religions as "yet another religious route to God that is equally valid as long as Catholic doctrine is also maintained" (Russell 1989a:9; cf. Fry 1988:138-169). Indeed, the Ifugao, formerly headhunters like other Cordillera peoples, gave the Catholic Church little choice. What eventual success the Spanish friars achieved in attracting converts hinged on their strategy of tolerating the local ritual complex (Scott 1977:255). Conversion to Catholicism only increased during the American colonial period. Through their ongoing support of and participation in their ritual performances, the Ifugao have consciously maintained their distinctive system of social and resource exchange. The result is a complex pattern of ritual change and persistence that is "neither predetermined nor infinitely variable" (Russell 1989a:3).

At celebratory occasions such as rites of passage, the complex ethnic configurations, namely the use of traditional textiles and Catholic paraphernalia, reflect the integration of local attitudes toward accommodation. In many areas of the upland Philippines, religious conversion to Christianity is viewed as a civilizing mission intimately connected to national development and modernization. To be progressive is to follow Western religion. Thus the trappings of "progress" - elaborate coffins and formal Church services - join hands with Ifugao ritual textiles and animal sacrifices.

As illustration, I focus on the more elaborate and enduring rites, marriage, mortuary and curing rituals. Marriage ceremonies are divided between a Church service in which the formal vows are exchanged and the subsequent celebration or *cañao* which is always held at the house of the bride in her village. In both venues, the bride and groom often wear at least one piece of traditional Ifugao costume. Women wear an Ifugao *tolge* or skirt, while men, less eager to don the *binuhla'n* or loincloth, drape either a *baya'ong* or *gamong* ceremonial blanket over their shoulders. In addition, each couple nominates two other couples, friends or close relatives, to be their primary and secondary sponsors. As part of the formal wedding party, the sponsors may also wear traditional dress to signify their roles as supporters of the bride and groom and as witnesses to the ceremony. Those sponsoring the *cañao* also give public recognition to the men and women wearing Ifugao ritual dress. Special dances are mounted calling, for example, for all women wearing traditional *tolge* or for all men in *binuhla'n*. At one wedding I attended, the differentials in dress were noted at a dance announced for all unmarried men wearing blue jeans. Celebrations such as weddings provide an opportunity for people to wear their best quality Ifugao textiles and for weavers to demonstrate their skills in cloth production.

At death and in the subsequent mortuary rites, living descendants sacrifice their acquired wealth to enable the souls of their material belongings to escort the deceased to the land of the dead. *Gamong* and *baya'ong* blankets particularly, are integral to this process. For example, during the formal mourning period which often lasts three to four weeks, the deceased is placed in a coffin and displayed for family members and friends. The body is usually dressed in his or her best ceremonial textiles - skirt or loincloth and blanket. In addition, *baya'ong* and *gamong* blankets line the interior of the coffin and as ceremonial offerings they drape its exterior. It is customary for the oldest child, male or female, to give a *gamong* or first-class blanket and for the younger children and any close relative or friend to give *baya'ong* or second-class blankets. More blankets, especially *gamong*, are donated the higher the status and the greater the wealth of the deceased. A narrow, blue and red striped length of cloth, which is attached to the ends of blankets and which was formerly used as a ceremonial headband, is often wrapped around the outside of the coffin as a seal between the top and bottom halves. Before the introduction of coffins, the body was only wrapped in blankets. Although the funerals I attended used wood coffins, one of the artisans with whom I worked had decided not to use a coffin during the mortuary rites held for her father in 1993. Her photographs of the funeral proceedings show the body positioned on a sofa enveloped only in *baya'ong* blankets and surrounded by family members, some playing guitars and others playing cards.

Ritual striped textiles denote the position of each person involved in the ritual proceedings. The priest officiating the ceremony is cloaked in a *baya'ong* blanket as are those who will perform the ritual animal sacrifice, one to three pigs. To demonstrate their grief and their respect for the deceased, mourners may also wrap themselves in blankets. During mortuary rituals, the souls of the deceased are formally invited to join the family of living relatives where they actively participate and solicit offerings from their descendants in return for bestowing wealth and prosperity. This transformation is made visible by placing the striped textiles belonging to the deceased in a rice winnowing basket, a symbol of fertility, and enticing the spirit to again cloth him- or herself in the garments. If the deceased is male, a loincloth and blanket are placed in the basket, if female, a skirt and blanket are used.

Each family member wanting to demonstrate his or her respect for the deceased, hosts a day of mourning by sponsoring the appropriate feast and ceremonies. They arrange for a local Ifugao priest to officiate the rite and to make the requisite sacrifice of pigs and chickens and they subsequently sponsor a feast of cooked rice and meat for friends and relatives. Ifugao bronze gongs ring out with great fanfare to announce when the deceased is being moved to a different location. The coffin, bedecked with blankets, the deceased's personal effects and emblems of Christianity such as a cross, is lifted high and carried to another relative's home. At each venue, social relations are made visible and consolidated as relatives and friends donate additional blankets and gifts. While the bestowal of *gamong* or first-class blankets is expected if the deceased's family owns extensive rice land marking them as part of the landed elite, currently, anyone having enough cash to purchase *gamong* blankets, regardless of class, may offer them in such rites. At the conclusion of the mortuary ceremonies, all donated textiles are buried with the coffin.

Although the central tenets of the ancestral cult remain unchanged, the boundaries have been redrawn. The sacred sphere has been transformed through the appropriation of Catholic ritual objects and their integration into Ifugao indigenous rites. In this transformation, textiles may be best understood as actors playing a series of "bridging roles", not only between the mental and the physical world (Miller 1989:102-103), but also between Ifugao sacred custom and wider socio-economic forces. Textiles thus collapse the gaps between domains by crossing over oppositional spheres. When asked about this juxtaposition, the Ifugao with whom I spoke explained that the outward trappings of Catholicism demonstrate their modernity, but "without our traditions, there could be no funeral, no returning home for the spirits of our ancestors."

The ancestors are further placated through the performance of curing rites or *honga* and through the bone wrapping ceremony or *mamong'an*. Both rituals may be performed at any time that the living want to appease and demonstrate their respect to their ancestors, either to acknowledge good fortune or to dispel misfortune such as illness. In these rites, usually commencing one year after death, the bodies of one's parents or grandparents are exhumed. The bones are then cleaned and subsequently wrapped in newly woven ritual textiles. The fresh wrappings demonstrate the concern of those living on earth for the souls of the those in the Skyworld. Following the ceremony, the newly enveloped bones are stored in the rafters under the house to ensure the ancestors that the living will watch over them. Often called a secondary burial, I suggest we regard this process as one of many reburials. If illness recurs, or if one again wants to show his or her appreciation to the ancestors for new prosperity, the wrapped bundles are taken from their resting place and rewrapped, yet again, in new striped textiles. They are never reburied, but become part of an ongoing cycle of ceremony and sacrifice.

While the Ifugao have incorporated the use of Christian services and ritual objects into their ancestral cult, the Catholic Church in Banaue has started to use Ifugao ritual textiles to decorate the interior of the Church and to augment its vestments. These textiles are draped over tables, decorate the walls and pillars of the Church and combined with flowers, they decorate the niches containing religious statues. Where ritual textiles specifically are not used, the weaving techniques involved in their manufacture may be employed to decorate religious garments and hangings. One of the ties of the priest's vestment, for example, displays a design which is woven in the same "warp-pick-up" technique as that of the animal and geometric figures in the striped blankets. This juxtaposition of objects, both in Ifugao ritual and within the Catholic Church in Banaue reinforces that things and the contexts within which they function are not fixed and static entities. Rather, as Thomas (1991:30,13) argues for the exchange and use of Western and Oceanic goods, such circumstances must be understood as "conjunctures" - situations in which the meanings of things as "composite" and "mutable" are recursively recast and recontextualized in use through their historical "entanglement" with different systems.

Earlier, this paper asked what do ritual textiles mean and what use are they? The complexity of this question begins to emerge as one realizes that in Banaue, ritual textiles are not one thing or another, but a thing in a certain situation (Kopytoff 1986:65). The meaning of ritual cloths shifts according to the context within which they function. Today, ritual textiles commonly appear in the secular sphere when worn as everyday garments.

Older women in particular, often wear ceremonial skirts as their daily dress as a marker of status and ethnic identity. *Baya'ong* blankets, while essential to mortuary rites, also make excellent baby carriers. Both men and women use these blankets to wrap and secure younger children to their back as they continue their work.

Moreover, ongoing ritual activities and the need for ritual textiles provide an economic stimulus for producers. Since not all women weave, ceremonial textiles may be commodities at the time of private transmission from producer to buyer in the village, or when the textiles are offered for sale publicly in the Saturday morning market. As Appadurai (1986:13; cf. Kopytoff 1986:68-69) argues, this "commodity situation" is the point in the artifact's life history in which its exchangeability for some other thing of equivalent value is its most socially relevant feature at that particular moment. As no ritual textile in Banaue is "above [commodity] exchange," these cloths emerge as both alienable and inalienable possessions (Weiner 1992:6,17); they participate in both ceremonial gift-giving and in commodity transactions. As commodities, ritual textiles may, in turn, acquire consumer power. The number of cloths a person is able to purchase to offer at rituals functions as a form of conspicuous consumption enhancing the purchaser's status. As such, the production of ceremonial cloths brings both recognition and moderate economic gain to the weaver while simultaneously imparting prestige to the purchaser.

Conclusion

This case study has emphasized that a meaningful analysis of the significance of Ifugao ritual textiles cannot be made apart from the contemporary economic, social and political contexts to which they respond. The persistence of Ifugao ritual activity and the continued use of readily recognizable textiles as ethnic markers, may be understood as a form of group resistance to the acculturation and ethnic homogenization that those in Banaue perceive as threatening to their own cultural framework and political autonomy (Russell 1989:19-20). Ritual and ritual objects such as textiles, thus provide an essential commentary about the relationships between social change and cultural identity.

In Banaue, encounters between dominant and dominated groups have resulted in a blend of local and external customs, rather than leading to a unidirectional demise, marginalization of local religious traditions or simple accommodation. Banaue's ceremonial textiles and the rituals they serve must be understood as historically dynamic and still fluid phenomena. Their use and meaning continue to be transformed by the contexts in which they function.

References Cited

Appadurai, Arjun. 1986. "Introduction: commodities and the politics of value." In The Social Life of Things. ed. A. Appadurai. Cambridge: Cambridge University Press.

Augé, Marc. 1982. The Anthropological Circle: Symbol, Function, History. Cambridge: Cambridge University Press.

Barton, Roy F. 1946. The Religion of the Ifugaos. Menasha, Wisconsin: American Anthropological Association, Memoir Series 65.

---. 1955. The Mythology of the Ifugaos. Philadelphia: American Folklore Society Memoirs 46.

Fry, Howard T. 1983. A History of the Mountain Province. Quezon City: New Day Publishers.

Kopytoff, Igor. 1986. "The Cultural Biography of Things: commoditization as process." In The Social Life of Things: commodities in cultural perspective. ed. Arjun Appadurai. Cambridge: Cambridge University Press.

Lambrecht, Frances. 1939. "The Mayawyaw Ritual: Property and Property Ritual." Publications of the Catholic Anthropological Conference, Washington, D.C. 4 (4): 495-711.

---. 1958. "Ifugaw Weaving." Folklore Studies (Society of the Divine World, Tokyo) 17: 1-158.

Milgram, B. Lynne. 1991. "The Textiles of Highland Luzon, Philippines: A Case Study in Material Culture." M.A. Thesis, York University, Toronto, Canada.

Miller, Daniel. 1987. Material Culture and Mass Consumption. Oxford: Basil Blackwood.

Ortner, Sherry B. 1978. Sherpas Through their Rituals. Cambridge: Cambridge University Press.

Rappaport, Roy A. 1979. Ecology, Meaning and Religion. Richmond, CA: North Atlantic Books.

Russell, Susan D. 1989. "Ritual persistence and the Ancestral Cult Among the Ibaloi of the Luzon Highlands. In Changing Lives, Changing Rites: Ritual and Social Dynamics in Philippine and Indonesian Uplands. ed. Susan D. Russell and Clark E. Cunningham. Ann Arbor, Michigan: University of Michigan, Center for South and Southeast Asian Studies.

---. 1989a. "Introduction: Social Change, Cultural Identity and Ritual Response." In Changing Lives, Changing Rites: Ritual and Social Dynamics in Philippine and Indonesian Uplands. ed. Susan D. Russell and Clark E. Cunningham. Ann Arbor, Michigan: University of Michigan, Center for South and Southeast Asian Studies.

Scott, William Henry. 1977. The Discovery of the Igorots: Spanish Contacts with the Pagans of Northern Luzon. Quezon City, Philippines: New Day Publishers.

Thomas, Nicholas. 1991. Entangled Objects: Exchange, material culture and colonialism in the Pacific. Cambridge, MA: Harvard University Press.

Washburn, Dorothy and Donald Crowe. 1988. Symmetries of Culture: Theory and Practice of Plane Pattern Analysis. Seattle: University of Washington Press.

Weiner, Annette B. 1992. Inalienable Possessions: The Paradox of Keeping-While-Giving. Los Angles: University of California Press.

Figure 1: Biaxial reflection in Ifugao ritual textiles

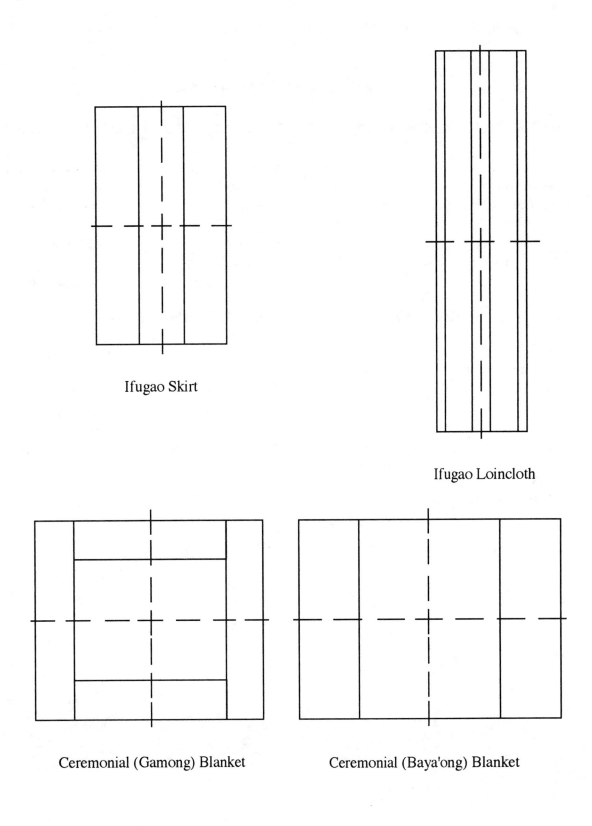

Ifugao Skirt

Ifugao Loincloth

Ceremonial (Gamong) Blanket

Ceremonial (Baya'ong) Blanket

TEXTILE SOCIETY OF AMERICA, INC.

1996 SYMPOSIUM CO-CHAIRS: Christa C. Mayer Thurman and Rita J. Adrosko

1997 GOVERNING BOARD

ADMINISTRATIVE OFFICERS

PRESIDENT*:	Louise Mackie
VICE-PRESIDENT*:	Beverly Gordon
MEMBERSHIP SECRETARY/ TREASURER*:	Blenda Femenias
RECORDING SECRETARY*	Diana Myers
FINANCIAL ADMINISTRATOR:	Marla Jean Huisman

SPECIAL INTEREST GROUP CHAIRS

ARCHAEOLOGICAL:	Amy Oakland Rodman
COMPUTERS:	Anu Liivandi
ETHNIC:	Patricia Anawalt
TECHNICAL	Jane Merritt
FIBER ARTS:	Pat Hickman and Barbara B. Goldberg

REGIONAL REPRESENTATIVES

EAST*:	Susan Anderson Hay and Julia Burke
MIDWEST*:	Mary Dusenbury
SOUTH*:	Ann Hedlund
WEST*:	Lynn Teague
CANADA*:	Lynne Milgram

TASK REPRESENTATIVES

NEWSLETTER:	Kathleen Moore
TEXTILE NETWORK:	Zoe Annis Perkins
1998 SYMPOSIUM:	Milton Sonday and Desiree Koslin
PUBLICATIONS COMMITTEE:	Kathleen Epstein

*These are elected positions